Lecture Notes in Computer Science   16201

Founding Editors

Gerhard Goos
Juris Hartmanis

Editorial Board Members

Elisa Bertino, *Purdue University, West Lafayette, IN, USA*
Wen Gao, *Peking University, Beijing, China*
Bernhard Steffen , *TU Dortmund University, Dortmund, Germany*
Moti Yung , *Columbia University, New York, NY, USA*

The series Lecture Notes in Computer Science (LNCS), including its subseries Lecture Notes in Artificial Intelligence (LNAI) and Lecture Notes in Bioinformatics (LNBI), has established itself as a medium for the publication of new developments in computer science and information technology research, teaching, and education.

LNCS enjoys close cooperation with the computer science R & D community, the series counts many renowned academics among its volume editors and paper authors, and collaborates with prestigious societies. Its mission is to serve this international community by providing an invaluable service, mainly focused on the publication of conference and workshop proceedings and postproceedings. LNCS commenced publication in 1973.

Alex Potanin
Editor

Programming Languages and Systems

23rd Asian Symposium, APLAS 2025
Bengaluru, India, October 27–30, 2025
Proceedings

Editor
Alex Potanin
Australian National University
Canberra, ACT, Australia

ISSN 0302-9743   ISSN 1611-3349 (electronic)
Lecture Notes in Computer Science
ISBN 978-981-95-3584-2   ISBN 978-981-95-3585-9 (eBook)
https://doi.org/10.1007/978-981-95-3585-9

© The Editor(s) (if applicable) and The Author(s), under exclusive license to Springer Nature Singapore Pte Ltd. 2026, corrected publication 2026

This work is subject to copyright. All rights are solely and exclusively licensed by the Publisher, whether the whole or part of the material is concerned, specifically the rights of translation, reprinting, reuse of illustrations, recitation, broadcasting, reproduction on microfilms or in any other physical way, and transmission or information storage and retrieval, electronic adaptation, computer software, or by similar or dissimilar methodology now known or hereafter developed.
The use of general descriptive names, registered names, trademarks, service marks, etc. in this publication does not imply, even in the absence of a specific statement, that such names are exempt from the relevant protective laws and regulations and therefore free for general use.
The publisher, the authors and the editors are safe to assume that the advice and information in this book are believed to be true and accurate at the date of publication. Neither the publisher nor the authors or the editors give a warranty, expressed or implied, with respect to the material contained herein or for any errors or omissions that may have been made. The publisher remains neutral with regard to jurisdictional claims in published maps and institutional affiliations.

This Springer imprint is published by the registered company Springer Nature Singapore Pte Ltd.
The registered company address is: 152 Beach Road, #21-01/04 Gateway East, Singapore 189721, Singapore

If disposing of this product, please recycle the paper.

Preface

This volume contains the proceedings of the Twenty-Third Asian Symposium on Programming Languages and Systems – APLAS 2025 – held during October 27-29, 2025 in Bengaluru, India.

APLAS brings together programming language researchers and practitioners and implementors *worldwide*, to present and discuss the latest results and exchange ideas in all areas of programming languages and systems. The list of topics includes, among others: programming paradigms and styles; methods and tools to specify and reason about programs and languages; programming language foundations; methods and tools for implementation; concurrency and distribution; applications and case studies.

APLAS is organised by the Asian Association for the Foundation of Software (AAFS), founded by Asian researchers in cooperation with many researchers from Europe and the USA. Past APLAS symposiums were held in Kyoto ('24), Taipei ('23), Auckland ('22), Chicago ('21), Fukuoka ('20), Bali ('19), Wellington ('18), Suzhou ('17), Hanoi ('16), Pohang ('15), Singapore ('14), Melbourne ('13), Kyoto ('12), Kenting ('11), Shanghai ('10), Seoul ('09), Bangalore ('08), Singapore ('07), Sydney ('06), Tsukuba ('05), Taipei ('04) and Beijing ('03) after three informal workshops.

The call for papers attracted 34 submissions, six of which were desk-rejected. The rest were reviewed double-blind: we aimed to keep the identities out of the picture during the whole review process. Each submission received three reviews. In addition, for some submissions, we sought opinions of external experts, whose prompt and very helpful comments were greatly appreciated.

At the end of the review period, the authors had 3 days to respond to the reviews. The PC considered the responses and decided on acceptance. In many cases, the reviews were augmented to account for the responses and to summarise the PC discussion. Quite a number of responses clarified the submission and resolved the reviewers' concerns. In some other cases, unfortunately, the responses did not address all the concerns and questions raised in the reviews.

No numerical targets were set for acceptance. The only criterion was a submission being understandable, interesting and instructive to the audience and publishable in the proceedings, after perhaps only *minor* revisions. After careful and thorough discussions, The Program Committee accepted 13 submissions.

The symposium program also included a plenary joint keynote with ATVA by Peter Müller (ETH Zurich, Switzerland).

Furthermore, APLAS 2025 included a student research competition and a associated poster session, as well as the APLAS-NIER pre-conference workshop (Oct. 27, 2025). This year, APLAS was co-located with the 23rd International Symposium on Automated Technology for Verification and Analysis (ATVA).

APLAS 2025 continued the tradition of recognising the best paper submitted to the symposium.

I am delighted to announce that the Best Paper award for APLAS'25 went to:

Beniamino Accattoli, Claudio Sacerdoti Coen, Jui-Hsuan Wu
Positive Sharing and Abstract Machines

Putting together APLAS 2025 was a team effort. First of all, I would like to thank the authors of the submitted papers and the presenters of the invited talks. Without the Program Committee, there would have been no program either, and I am very grateful to the PC members for their hard work. Complementing the PC were External Reviewers, whose contribution is gratefully acknowledged. I am indebted to the General Chair, Pritam Gharat (Microsoft Research India) for her support throughout the process. This year APLAS was held in co-operation with ATVA, whose organising committee – in particular, General Chair Deepak D'Souza, shared the burden. They have been invaluable in setting up the conference and making sure everything ran smoothly.

Finally, thanks are due to the Award Sponsor *Springer*.

September 2025   Alex Potanin

Organization

General Chair

Pritam Gharat — Microsoft Research, India

Program Chair

Alex Potanin — Australian National University, Australia

Program Committee

Alex Potanin	Australian National University, Australia
Alexander Bakst	Certora, USA
Andrea Costea	TU Delft, Netherlands
Atsushi Igarashi	Kyoto University, Japan
Ganesan Ramalingam	Microsoft, India
Ina Schaefer	Karlsruhe Institute of Technology, Germany
Jeff Foster	Tufts University, USA
Kartik Nagar	IIT Madras, India
K. C. Sivaramakrishnan	IIT Madras and Tarides, India
Kihong Heo	KAIST, South Korea
Liam O'Connor	Australian National University, Australia
Lionel Parreaux	Hong Kong University of Science and Technology, China
Liyi Li	Iowa State University, USA
Manas Thakur	IIT Bombay, India
Meenakshi D'Souza	International Institute of Information Technology Bangalore, India
Oleg Kiselyov	Tohoku University, Japan
Pascal Weisenburger	University of St Gallen, Switzerland
Sanjiva Prasad	IIT Delhi, India
Stephen Kell	King's College London, UK
Swarnendu Biswas	IIT Kanpur, India
Tachio Terauchi	Waseda University, Japan
Umang Mathur	National University of Singapore, Singapore
V. Krishna Nandivada	IIT Madras, India

Zhenjiang Hu   Peking University, China

External Reviewers

Andy Gordon, Daniele Varacca, Huan Zhao, Rujie Meng, Zihan Zhou

Contents

Type Systems, Safety, and Verification

Memory Safety: Uniqueness as Separation 3
   Pilar Selene Linares Arévalo, Arthur Azevedo de Amorim,
   Vincent Jackson, Liam O'Connor, Peter Schachte, and Christine Rizkallah

Fair Termination for Resource-Aware Active Objects 22
   Francesco Dagnino, Paola Giannini, Violet Ka I Pun, and Ulises Torrella

A Formal Foundation for Equational Reasoning on Probabilistic Programs 44
   Reynald Affeldt, Yoshihiro Ishiguro, and Zachary Stone

Control, Effects, and Decidability

Reachability is Decidable for ATM-Typable Finitary PCF with Effect
Handlers 67
   Ryunosuke Endo and Tachio Terauchi

Expressive Power of One-Shot Control Operators and Coroutines 88
   Kentaro Kobayashi and Yukiyoshi Kameyama

Positive Sharing and Abstract Machines 107
   Beniamino Accattoli, Claudio Sacerdoti Coen, and Jui-Hsuan Wu

Quantum Programming and Logic

IMALL with a Mixed-State Modality: A Logical Approach to Quantum
Computation 131
   Kinnari Dave, Alejandro Díaz-Caro, and Vladimir Zamdzhiev

A Quantum-Control Lambda-Calculus with Multiple Measurement Bases 151
   Alejandro Díaz-Caro and Nicolas A. Monzon

Program Analysis, Specifications, and Decision Procedures

Checking Consistency of Event-Driven Traces 173
   Parosh Aziz Abdulla, Mohamed Faouzi Atig, R. Govind, Samuel Grahn,
   and Ramanathan S. Thinniyam

Specification Inference Modulo Oracles for Database-Backed Web
Applications 195
  Nitesh Trivedi and Subhajit Roy

Decision Procedure for a Theory of String Sequences 217
  Denghang Hu, Taolue Chen, Philipp Rümmer, Fu Song, and Zhilin Wu

AI and Compiler Optimisation for Performance

ELTC: An End-to-End Large Language Model-Based Tensor Compilation
Optimization Framework 241
  WenBo Ma, QingZeng Song, Fei Qiao, YongJiang Xue, and MingZe Sun

Performance Optimization of HPC Workloads in Cloud Using AI-Driven
Algorithms 260
  Aman Iftekhar and Rahul Mishra

Correction to: Reachability is Decidable for ATM-Typable Finitary PCF
with Effect Handlers C1
  Ryunosuke Endo and Tachio Terauchi

Author Index 275

Type Systems, Safety, and Verification

Memory Safety: Uniqueness as Separation

Pilar Selene Linares Arévalo[1]([✉]) [iD], Arthur Azevedo de Amorim[2] [iD],
Vincent Jackson[1] [iD], Liam O'Connor[3] [iD], Peter Schachte[1] [iD],
and Christine Rizkallah[1] [iD]

[1] The University of Melbourne, Melbourne, VIC, Australia
{linaresareva,v.jackson,schachte,christine.rizkallah}@unimelb.edu.au
[2] Rochester Institute of Technology, Rochester, NY, USA
[3] Australian National University, Canberra, ACT, Australia
liam.oconnor@anu.edu.au

Abstract. Programming languages with uniqueness type systems prevent pointer aliasing, simplifying memory safety reasoning. However, code implemented in these languages often interoperates through foreign function interfaces with external components implemented in languages lacking the same level of static safety guarantees. To verify safe updates in a combined system, one must manually verify that the external components preserve the safety invariants of the uniqueness type system. In particular, recent work showed that one can manually discharge such obligations on C components from a cross-language Cogent-C system by directly reasoning about the C code in higher-order logic. However, even for simple examples, discharging the uniqueness safety obligations, known as *frame conditions*, within a logic not specifically designed for direct reasoning in terms of heaps and pointers was not ideal. Separation logic is an established logic that facilitates reasoning about imperative programs by localising reasoning to the parts of the heap that the program mutates. This raises a vital question. *Can we use separation logic to discharge the safety obligations imposed by uniqueness types?* The answer is yes. This paper demonstrates that the frame conditions can be inferred from particular separation logic triples and, hence, discharged by reasoning using separation logic. We identify and verify the soundness of specific separation logic triples that imply the frame conditions imposed by a uniqueness type system.

Keywords: Memory Safety · Uniqueness Types · Separation Logic

1 Introduction

Modern languages such as Clean [15], SAC [16], Mercury [18], and more recently, Cogent [9] leverage uniqueness type systems [17], a form of substructural type systems, to rule out the largest known class of common software vulnerabilities: *memory safety errors*. In particular, uniqueness types are typically used in these languages to prevent *pointer aliasing*: having multiple live references to the same memory location. As such, they support the development of code that is *safe* by design and remove the need for garbage collection, enabling efficient compilation.

However, the safety guarantees of uniqueness typing are limited to code that adheres to the type system constraints. While the uniqueness condition is a conceptually simple restriction, it sometimes imposes a considerable burden when writing code in such languages. For example, a simple uniqueness type system would prohibit passing both an array and a reference to one of its elements to a function because of the aliasing this introduces, even if we only read from them, and no mutation is involved.

Therefore, in practice, languages with uniqueness types often include an *opt-out mechanism*, to enable interoperation with external components written in *unsafe* fragments or unsafe languages, such as C, which do not enforce safety by design. This often involves using a foreign function interface (FFI) to enable interoperation with surrounding infrastructure, such as system calls, and with existing components such as external libraries.

For instance, SAC, a functional programming language with uniqueness types, provides an FFI to interoperate with external C libraries [5]. Similarly, the Cogent language [9] has an FFI to act as a bypass mechanism that enables interoperation with C components.

To verify the memory safety of a combined system, one must manually verify that the external components preserve the invariants of the uniqueness type system that result in safety. Leaving these unverified could invalidate the guarantees obtained from using uniqueness types, even for the safe components. Recent work demonstrated that one can manually discharge such uniqueness conditions on C code in the context of a cross-language Cogent-C system, by directly reasoning about the C code in higher-order logic. This shows that composing proofs in such a cross-language setting is possible and that it is possible to discharge the uniqueness conditions on foreign code. However, even for a simple example, discharging uniqueness *frame conditions* in a logic not designed to verify such safety obligations was quite tedious [4].

These proofs should ideally be developed in a framework that facilitates reasoning about memory. One such framework is separation logic [14], a logic for reasoning about heap-manipulating programs that enables *local* reasoning about separate parts of memory, through separating conjunction and the frame rule.

This paper presents an imperative language with specific features for reasoning about memory safety. In particular, we extend an existing imperative language [1] to distinguish memory safety errors from other type of errors and present a sound separation logic for this extension. Moreover, we present separation logic triples FC TRIPLE and prove that they imply the uniqueness type invariants imposed by Cogent on foreign C code, on the shared heap between Cogent and C, called through Cogent's FFI, which allows for verified interoperability of Cogent-C code [4]. We demonstrate that the FC TRIPLE we identified can be discharged for a number of language constructs, including memory-related constructs. While the formal proofs do not form a contribution of this paper, our core results have been formalised in ROCQ (formerly Coq) to gain higher confidence in our results.

2 Enforcing Uniqueness on Foreign Functions

For this paper, we consider the memory safety invariants from Cogent, which is a functional programming language intended for low-level software and designed to write code in a safe, verifiable way without a garbage collector or heavy runtime [10]. Cogent's uniqueness type system ensures exclusive ownership of mutable data, preventing aliasing and enabling direct updates without corrupting memory.

The uniqueness type system used in Cogent is quite sophisticated (see the Cogent paper [10] for a full description); here, we only focus on the precise conditions under which external C code imported into Cogent, maintains the memory safety guarantees that its uniqueness types provide.

Cogent's typing relation tracks a set of pointers w transitively accessible through a value v, called the *heap footprint*—note that w is a subset of the domain of the current heap. Written $v : \tau \langle w \rangle$, this judgement states that v has type τ and an associated footprint w. By annotating the relation in this way, the required non-aliasing requirements can be included in the typing rules.

For example, the rule for typing tuples is:

$$\frac{x : \tau_1 \langle w_x \rangle \quad y : \tau_2 \langle w_y \rangle \quad w_x \cap w_y = \emptyset}{(x, y) : \tau_1 \times \tau_2 \langle w_x \cup w_y \rangle}$$

The disjointness condition $w_x \cap w_y = \emptyset$ prevents internal aliasing in non-abstract structures, preserving the uniqueness guarantee. For abstract types implemented in C, however, internal aliasing may occur without breaking the uniqueness guarantee. This is permissible because the type system enforces uniqueness at the abstract interface level, not within the hidden implementation.

Let $f : \tau \to \rho$ be a function implemented in C and imported into Cogent. Let v be the input value such that $v : \tau \langle w_i \rangle$, h_i the initial heap (a partial map from pointers to values), and $f(v)$ the result such that $f(v) : \rho \langle w_o \rangle$ with final heap h_o. For f to respect the uniqueness invariants, the following *frame conditions* must hold:

Leak Freedom $\forall p.\ p \in w_i \land p \notin w_o \longrightarrow p \notin \mathrm{dom}(h_o)$, that is, any pointer in the input footprint that is not in the domain of the final heap must not appear in the initial heap. We use the equivalent yet more convenient formulation: $w_i \cap \mathrm{dom}(h_o) \subseteq w_o$.

Fresh Allocation $\forall p.\ p \notin w_i \land p \in w_o \longrightarrow p \notin \mathrm{dom}(h_i)$, that is, any pointer in the output footprint that is not in the input footprint must not alias with any pointer in the initial heap. We use the equivalent yet more convenient formulation: $w_o \cap \mathrm{dom}(h_i) \subseteq w_i$.

Inertia $\forall p.\ p \notin w_i \wedge p \notin w_o \longrightarrow h_i(p) = h_o(p)$, that is, any part of the heap not in the input or output footprint remains unchanged.

These conditions ensure that the function only relies on the memory it is permitted to access. Collectively, they are called the *frame conditions*, named after the frame problem in knowledge representation [8].

Manually discharging these proof obligations for external C code without the support of a suitable logic for reasoning about state is tedious [4]. The next sections will explain how these conditions can be verified using separation logic [14], which is specifically designed for reasoning about heap-manipulating programs.

3 Language Syntax and Operational Semantics

We introduce a simple imperative language $\mathcal{L}_{IMP}$ for which we will define our separation logic. We adopt an imperative language [1] that captures key features of low-level memory manipulation: heap allocation and deallocation as well as reads and writes from and into the heap. This language is mechanised in ROCQ, and it was used to define a formal notion of memory safety. As such, it provides a solid foundation for our work. We extend the language to distinguish memory-related errors from other errors.

$$
\begin{array}{ll}
\text{Block identifier} & id \in \mathcal{I} \\
\text{Variable} & x \in \text{Var} \\
\text{Naturals} & n \in \mathbb{N} \\
\text{Boolean} & b \in \mathbb{B} = \textbf{true} \mid \textbf{false} \\
\text{Pointer} & p \in \mathcal{P} = \mathcal{I} \times \mathbb{N} \\
\text{Value} & v \in \mathcal{V} = \mathbb{N} \cup \mathbb{B} \cup \mathcal{P} \cup \{\textbf{nil}\} \\
\text{Binary operator} & \oplus ::= + \mid - \mid \times \mid = \mid \leq \mid \wedge \mid \vee \\
\text{Expression} & e \in \mathcal{E} ::= x \mid n \mid b \mid \neg e \mid \textbf{offset}\, e \mid e \oplus e \\
\text{Command} & c \in \mathcal{C} ::= \textbf{skip} \mid x := e \mid \textbf{load}\, x\, e \mid \textbf{store}\, e_1\, e_2 \mid \textbf{alloc}\, x\, e \mid \\
& \quad \textbf{free}\, e \mid \textbf{seq}\, c_1\, c_2 \mid \textbf{if}\, e\, \textbf{then}\, c_1\, \textbf{else}\, c_2 \mid \textbf{while}\, e\, \textbf{do}\, c
\end{array}
$$

Fig. 1. Syntax

Figure 1 presents the syntax of the extended language and supporting components. It features values v that include booleans, naturals, and pointers. A pointer is a pair (id, n) where id is a block identifier drawn from a countably infinite set $\mathcal{I}$ of memory identifiers, and $n \in \mathbb{N}$ is an offset. The distinguished value **nil** represents the result of an ill-typed expression (e.g., $3 + \textbf{true}$) and is used to uniformly propagate errors. The language has standard expressions e that have no side effects on the state, including **offset** e, which returns the offset of a pointer value. It also features standard imperative commands c such as skip, local assignment, heap operations, and control flow constructs including loops. Figure 1 also presents the definition of states on which commands evaluate. States consist of a pair of components: a *local store* l, a finite partial map from variables to values, and a heap h, a finite partial map from pointers to values.

Local store $l \in \mathcal{L} = \text{Var} \rightharpoonup_{\text{fin}} \mathcal{V}$

$$\boxed{\text{Expression evaluation } [\![-]\!]^e :: \mathcal{E} \to \mathcal{L} \to \mathcal{V}}$$

$$[\![x]\!]^e\, l \;=\; \begin{cases} l(x) & \text{if } x \in \text{dom}\, l \\ \texttt{nil} & \text{otherwise} \end{cases} \quad (x \in \text{Var})$$

$$[\![v]\!]^e\, l \;=\; v \quad (x \in V)$$

$$[\![e_1 + e_2]\!]^e\, l \;=\; \begin{cases} n_1 + n_2 & \text{if } [\![e_1]\!]^e\, l = n_1 \text{ and } [\![e_2]\!]^e\, l = n_2 \\ p +_{\text{p}} n & \text{if } [\![e_1]\!]^e\, l = p \text{ and } [\![e_2]\!]^e\, l = n \\ & \text{or if } [\![e_1]\!]^e\, l = n \text{ and } [\![e_2]\!]^e\, l = p \\ \texttt{nil} & \text{otherwise} \end{cases}$$

$$[\![e_1 - e_2]\!]^e\, l \;=\; \begin{cases} n_1 - n_2 & \text{if } [\![e_1]\!]^e\, l = n_1 \text{ and } [\![e_2]\!]^e\, l = n_2 \\ (id, n_1 - n_2) & \text{if } [\![e_1]\!]^e\, l = (id, n_1),\, [\![e_2]\!]^e\, l = n_2, \text{ and } n_2 \le n_1 \\ \texttt{nil} & \text{otherwise} \end{cases}$$

Fig. 2. Evaluation of expressions (excerpt).

Now that we have presented the syntax, let's define an operational semantics for evaluating expressions and commands. Expression evaluation, $[\![e]\!]^e : \mathcal{S} \to \mathcal{V}$, depends only on the local store. Hence, pointers may not be dereferenced in an expression. Base values, such as booleans, naturals, and nil, evaluate to themselves. Arithmetic and boolean operations behave in the standard way. Addition and subtraction can additionally be used for performing pointer arithmetic on pointer offsets; we use the notation $(i, n_1) +_{\text{p}} n_2$ as shorthand for the pointer addition $(i, n_1 + n_2)$. Equality comparison is allowed on all values, with pointer equality comparing both the block identifier and offset. The $\le$ operator applies only to naturals. Any operation applied to ill-typed values returns nil. Expression evaluation is standard, and an excerpt of the expression evaluation function is presented in Fig. 2.

Heap $h \in \mathcal{H} = \mathcal{P} \rightharpoonup_{\text{fin}} \mathcal{V}$
State $s \in \mathcal{S} = \mathcal{L} \times \mathcal{H}$

Memory error $m \in \mathcal{M} ::= \texttt{invalidRead} \mid \texttt{invalidWrite} \mid \texttt{invalidFree}$
Error $err ::= m \mid \texttt{other}$
Result $rs \in \mathcal{R} ::= \textbf{done}\, s \mid \textbf{error}\, err \mid \textbf{notYet}$

$$\boxed{\text{Bind operation bind} :: (\mathcal{C} \to \mathcal{S} \to \mathcal{R},\, \mathcal{R}) \to \mathcal{R}}$$

$$\text{bind}(f, \textbf{error}\, err) = \textbf{error}\, err$$
$$\text{bind}(f, \textbf{notYet}) = \textbf{notYet}$$
$$\text{bind}(f, \textbf{done}\,(l,h)) = \begin{cases} \textbf{done}\,(l', h') & \text{if } f(l,h) = \textbf{done}\,(l', h') \\ \textbf{error}\, err & \text{if } f(l,h) = \textbf{error}\, err \end{cases}$$

$$\boxed{\text{Command evaluation } [\![-]\!] :: \mathcal{C} \to \mathbb{N} \to \mathcal{S} \to \mathcal{R}}$$

$[\![c]\!]_0\, s = \textbf{notYet}$
$[\![\texttt{skip}]\!]_{n+1}\, s = \textbf{done}\, s$
$[\![x := e]\!]_{n+1}\, (l,h) = \textbf{done}(l[x \mapsto [\![e]\!]^e\, l], h)$
$[\![\texttt{seq}\, c_1\, c_2]\!]_{n+1}\, s = \text{bind}([\![c_2]\!]_n, [\![c_1]\!]_n\, s)$
$[\![\texttt{if}\, e\, \texttt{then}\, c_1\, \texttt{else}\, c_2]\!]_{n+1}\, (l,h) = \text{if } [\![e]\!]^e\, l \text{ then } [\![c_1]\!]_n\, (l,h) \text{ else } [\![c_2]\!]_n\, (l,h)$

$[\![\texttt{while}\, e\, \texttt{do}\, c]\!]_{n+1}\, (l,h) = \begin{cases} [\![\texttt{seq}\, c\, (\texttt{while}\, e\, \texttt{do}\, c)]\!]_n\, (l,h) & \text{if } [\![e]\!]^e\, l = \texttt{true} \\ \textbf{done}(l,h) & \text{if } [\![e]\!]^e\, l = \texttt{false} \\ \textbf{error}\, \texttt{other} & \text{otherwise} \end{cases}$

$[\![\texttt{load}\, x\, e]\!]_{n+1}\, (l,h) = \begin{cases} \textbf{done}(l[x \mapsto v], h) & \text{if } [\![e]\!]^e\, l = p \text{ and } p \in \text{dom}\, h \\ \textbf{error}\, \texttt{invalidRead} & \text{if } [\![e]\!]^e\, l = p \text{ and } p \notin \text{dom}\, h \\ \textbf{error}\, \texttt{other} & \text{otherwise} \end{cases}$

$[\![\texttt{store}\, e_1\, e_2]\!]_{n+1}\, (l,h) = \begin{cases} \textbf{done}(l, h[p \mapsto [\![e_2]\!]^e\, l]) & \text{if } [\![e_1]\!]^e\, l = p \text{ and} \\ & \quad p \in \text{dom}\, h \\ \textbf{error}\, \texttt{invalidWrite} & \text{if } [\![e_1]\!]^e\, l = p \text{ and} \\ & \quad p \notin \text{dom}\, h \\ \textbf{error}\, \texttt{other} & \text{otherwise} \end{cases}$

$[\![\texttt{alloc}\, x\, e]\!]_{n+1}\, (l,h) = \begin{cases} \textbf{done}(l[x \mapsto (i,0)], & \text{if } [\![e]\!]^e\, l = k \text{ and} \\ \quad h[(i,j) \mapsto 0 \mid 0 \leq j < k]) & \quad i = \text{fresh}(\text{ids}(l,h)) \\ \textbf{error}\, \texttt{other} & \text{otherwise} \end{cases}$

$[\![\texttt{free}\, e]\!]_{n+1}\, (l,h) = \begin{cases} \textbf{done}(l, h[(i,k) \mapsto \bot \mid k \in \mathbb{N}]) & \text{if } [\![e]\!]^e\, l = (i,0) \text{ and} \\ & \quad \exists j.\, (i,j) \in \text{dom}\, h \\ \textbf{error}\, \texttt{invalidFree} & \text{if } [\![e]\!]^e\, l = (i,0) \text{ and} \\ & \quad \forall j.\, (i,j) \notin \text{dom}\, h \\ \textbf{error}\, \texttt{other} & \text{otherwise} \end{cases}$

Fig. 3. Evaluation of commands

The function $[\![-]\!] : \mathcal{C} \to \mathbb{N} \to \mathcal{S} \to \mathcal{R}$ defines big-step evaluation for commands. It evaluates a program c in a given state s, with a maximum of n execution steps, and produces a result. The result is either done s' with final state s', an error error err, which could be a memory-related error m or an other error, or a timeout result notYet if the execution limit n is reached before completion. Note that the number of steps n provided as fuel is a formalisation detail that is only necessary to conveniently formalise this semantics as a total function in ROCQ.

The language enforces safety by raising errors that immediately halt execution, preventing undefined or unpredictable behaviour due to memory misuse. The command evaluation function is presented in Fig. 3. Unlike the original language semantics [1], our semantics distinguishes memory safety errors from other runtime errors. This distinction is necessary to define a separation logic validity triple that is sensitive to memory safety violations. Specifically, we extend the semantics to support the following memory safety errors: invalidRead, reading from an invalid memory location, invalidWrite, writing outside the bounds of a block or to otherwise invalid memory, invalidFree, freeing an invalid pointer.

The evaluation follows the standard imperative semantics for skip, seq c_1 c_2, $x := e$, if e then c_1 else c_2, and while e do c. The load x e heap lookup command first evaluates e to a pointer and then attempts to read from that location in the heap. If e does not evaluate to a pointer, evaluation results in error other. If the pointer is invalid, either because the block identifier is not allocated or the offset is out of bounds, the result is an invalidRead error. Similarly, the heap mutation command, store e_1 e_2, requires e_1 to evaluate to a valid pointer. If not, evaluation results in an invalidWrite error. The allocation command, alloc x e, evaluates e to a natural k and then produces a fresh block identifier that is not currently in use. A new block of size k is added to the heap, with all cells initialised to 0. This initialisation is important for ensuring that allocation does not leak information present in blocks that have been previously freed. The resulting state binds x to a pointer that refers to the first cell in the new block. Block identifiers in this language are immutable once assigned, making it impossible to fabricate a pointer to an allocated block. The heap deallocation command, free e, evaluates e to a pointer. If the pointer is valid, the result is a heap where all cells associated with the corresponding block identifier are removed. If the pointer is invalid, evaluation results in an invalidFree error.

To summarise, our semantics extends an existing imperative language with manual memory management [1] that was formalised in ROCQ, by explicitly distinguishing memory safety violations from other errors. In the next section, we present a separation logic for reasoning about this language and prove its soundness with respect to the operational semantics described here.

4 Separation Logic

Now that we have defined the language and its operational semantics, we are ready to develop a separation logic for reasoning about programs in this language.

In standard separation logic [14], a triple (P, c, Q) is considered valid if whenever command c evaluates from a state satisfying precondition P, if evaluation terminates, it does so successfully in a state satisfying postcondition Q. In particular, this notion of *strong validity* $\{P\}\,c\,\{Q\}_\mathsf{S}$ holds exactly when $\forall s\,k.\,P\,s \to (\llbracket c \rrbracket_k\,s \neq \mathsf{error}\,err) \land (\forall s'.\,\llbracket c \rrbracket_k\,s = \mathsf{done}\,s' \to Q\,s')$. That is, for any state s satisfying P, the execution of the program c in s will not trigger an error and, if the execution terminates, it will do so in a state satisfying Q.

As previously observed in the literature [1], strong validity makes it difficult to distinguish reasoning about the validity of *heap-related behaviour*. For example, the triple $\{\mathsf{emp}\}\,\mathtt{free}\,\mathtt{true}\,\{\mathsf{emp}\}_\mathsf{S}$ (where emp denotes the predicate that holds on states with an empty heap) is invalid, even though it accurately describes the behaviour of the heap: when the program runs on an empty heap, we obtain an error. However, when the program stops, the heap remains empty.

To address this issue, a more permissive variant of separation logic allowing certain classes of errors was introduced [1], where *weak validity*, written $\{P\}\,c\,\{Q\}_\mathsf{W}$, holds if evaluating c from a state satisfying P either diverges, triggers an error, or terminates in a state satisfying Q. Formally, $\{P\}\,c\,\{Q\}_\mathsf{W}$ holds iff $\forall s\,k.\,P\,s \to (\forall s'.\,\llbracket c \rrbracket_k\,s = \mathsf{done}\,s' \to Q\,s')$. Note that, under weak validity, $\{\mathsf{emp}\}\,\mathtt{free}\,\mathtt{true}\,\{\mathsf{emp}\}_\mathsf{S}$ holds.

However, this relaxed notion of validity introduces two major drawbacks. First, it invalidates the soundness of the *frame rule*[1], which is an essential component of separation logic, enabling the extension of local reasoning to parts of the heap that the command has not modified. Second, it is insensitive to the particular error that has occurred. In this way, it undermines efforts to characterise memory-safe programs: for instance, $\{\mathsf{emp}\}\,\mathtt{load}\,\mathtt{x}\,\mathtt{e}\,\{\mathsf{emp}\}_\mathsf{W}$ is deemed valid, even though the command may raise a memory safety error.

To remedy this, we introduce a third notion of validity that explicitly *distinguishes memory safety violations* from other kinds of errors. A *memory-safe validity* triple, written $\{P\}\,c\,\{Q\}_\mathsf{M}$, holds if evaluating c from a state satisfying P does not result in a memory safety error and if it terminates successfully, the resulting state satisfies Q. In particular, memory-safe validity $\{P\}\,c\,\{Q\}_\mathsf{M}$ holds iff $\forall s\,k.\,P\,s \to (\llbracket c \rrbracket_k\,s \neq \mathsf{error}\,m) \land (\forall s'.\,\llbracket c \rrbracket_k\,s = \mathsf{done}\,s' \to Q\,s')$. All other behaviour, including divergence or non-memory-related errors, is permitted.

This definition achieves the desired balance: it rejects $\{\mathsf{emp}\}\,\mathtt{load}\,\mathtt{x}\,\mathtt{e}\,\{\mathsf{emp}\}_\mathsf{M}$ as invalid reads violate memory safety; on the other hand, since the evaluation results in a non-memory-related error, $\{\mathsf{emp}\}\,\mathtt{free}\,\mathtt{true}\,\{\mathsf{emp}\}_\mathsf{S}$ is a valid triple. An added benefit of this notion is that it turns out that it preserves the soundness of the frame rule, enabling modular reasoning about heap-manipulating programs using the standard frame rule. Since this separation logic triple is the one we focus on in this paper, we simply refer to it as $\{P\}\,c\,\{Q\}$ in the rest of the paper.

Before introducing the assertion logic used to describe program predicates, we first present the basic notation that underpins our logic (see Fig. 4). We write set disjointness as $\#$; this holds when two sets have no elements in common. Heap

---

[1] A detailed explanation of this issue can be found at the end of this section.

Map notation
$f_1 \cup f_2$ $\equiv \{(k,v) \mid (k,v) \in f_1 \wedge k \notin \mathrm{dom}(f_2)$ (map union)
 $\vee (k,v) \in f_2\}$
$f \upharpoonright S$ $\equiv \{(k,v) \in f \mid k \in S\}$ (map restriction)

Local store, heap, and state notation
$(l_1, h_1) \cup (l_2, h_2)$ $\equiv (l_1 \cup l_2, h_1 \cup h_2)$ (state union)
$h_1 \perp h_2$ $\equiv \mathrm{dom}(h_1) \cap \mathrm{dom}(h_2) = \emptyset$ (heap disjointness)
$\mathrm{blocks}(l, h)$ $\equiv \{i \in \mathcal{I} \mid \exists n, (i,n) \in \mathrm{dom}(h)\}$ (live block identifiers)
$\mathrm{ids}(l, h)$ $\equiv \mathrm{blocks}(l, h)$ (all identifiers)
 $\cup \{i \mid \exists x\, n.\ l(x) = (i,n)\}$
 $\cup \{i \mid \exists p\, n.\ h(p) = (i,n)\}$
$\mathrm{vars}(l, h)$ $\equiv \mathrm{dom}(l)$ (state vars)
$\mathrm{vars}(c)$ $\equiv$ local variables of program c (command vars)

Nominal notation
$\pi \cdot (b, k)$ $\equiv (\pi(b), k)$ (permute pointer)

Fig. 4. Basic notation

disjointness, written $\perp$, holds when the domains of two heaps, treated as partial maps from addresses to values, are disjoint. The union operator $\cup$ is overloaded in our setting: For sets, it denotes the usual set-theoretic union. Map union, also $\cup$, is the union of the key-value pairs from the two maps, choosing the first map's values for pairs with the same key. For states, which consist of both a local store and a heap, union is defined pointwise by applying the map-union operator to both components. We write map restriction as $f \upharpoonright S$, which denotes the restriction of a map f to a set S: this is a new map containing only the entries in f whose keys belong to S. With this notation in place, we can now define the predicates of our separation logic.

Preconditions and postconditions are logical predicates over states. Separation logic predicates extend usual logical predicates with operators that enable local reasoning about the heap. It has the following additional predicates.

Empty heap emp holds when the heap is empty, that is, when $\mathrm{dom}(h) = \emptyset$.
Singleton heap $(p \mapsto v)$ holds iff the heap contains exactly one binding $p \mapsto v$. That is, when $\mathrm{dom}(h) = \{p\} \wedge h(p) = v$.
Separating conjunction $P * Q$ holds iff the heap splits into disjoint parts satisfying P and Q respectively (with a shared store).
That is, when $\exists h_1\, h_2.\ h_1 \perp h_2 \wedge h = h_1 \cup h_2 \wedge P(l, h_1) \wedge Q(l, h_2)$. Separating conjunction is associative, commutative, and has emp as unit:
$P * (Q * R) \leftrightarrow (P * Q) * R, \quad P * Q \leftrightarrow Q * P, \quad P * \mathrm{emp} \leftrightarrow P.$

The separation logic rules are presented in Fig. 5. We define a separation logic rule for each command in our language. We also include the standard consequence rule and the central frame rule. We verified the soundness of these separation logic triples with respect to the operational semantics.

The rules for assignment, skip, if, seq, and while adhere to the standard Hoare logic conventions. More interesting are rules for primitive memory opera-

$$\boxed{\text{Separation Logic Memory-Safe Validity } \{P\}\,\mathtt{c}\,\{Q\}}$$

$$\{P\}\,\mathtt{skip}\,\{P\} \qquad\qquad \{P[e/x]\}\,\mathtt{x} := \mathtt{e}\,\{P\}$$

$$\{\lambda s.\ [\![e]\!]^e s = p \wedge (p \mapsto v)s\}\,\mathtt{load\,x\,e}\,\{\lambda s.\ (x = v)s \wedge (p \mapsto v)s\}$$

$$\{\lambda s.\ [\![e_1]\!]^e s = p \wedge (p \mapsto \_)s \wedge [\![e_2]\!]^e s = v\}\,\mathtt{store\,e_1\,e_2}\,\{p \mapsto v\}$$

$$\{\lambda s.\ [\![e]\!]^e s = k \wedge \mathtt{emp}\,s\}\,\mathtt{alloc\,x\,e}\,\{\lambda s.\ \exists i.\ [\![x]\!]^e s = (i,0) \wedge [((i,j) \mapsto 0) \mid 0 \le j < k](s)\}$$

$$\{\lambda s.\ [\![e]\!]^e s = (i,0) \wedge ((i,0) \mapsto \_)s\}\,\mathtt{free\,e}\,\{\mathtt{emp}\} \qquad \dfrac{\{P\}\,\mathtt{c_1}\,\{Q\} \quad \{Q\}\,\mathtt{c_2}\,\{R\}}{\{P\}\,\mathtt{seq\,c_1\,c_2}\,\{R\}}$$

$$\dfrac{\{\lambda s.\ [\![e]\!]^e s \wedge Ps\}\,\mathtt{c_1}\,\{Q1\} \quad \{\lambda s.\ \neg[\![e]\!]^e s \wedge Ps\}\,\mathtt{c_2}\,\{Q2\}}{\{P\}\,\mathtt{if\,e\,then\,c_1\,else\,c_2}\,\{\lambda s.\ Q1s \vee Q2s\}}$$

$$\dfrac{\{\lambda s.\ [\![e]\!]^e s \wedge Ps\}\,\mathtt{c}\,\{P\}}{\{P\}\,\mathtt{while\,e\,do\,c}\,\{\lambda s.\ \neg[\![e]\!]^e s \wedge Ps\}}$$

$$\dfrac{\forall s.\ P's \to Ps \quad \{P\}\,\mathtt{c}\,\{Q\} \quad \forall s.\ Qs \to Q's}{\{P'\}\,\mathtt{c}\,\{Q'\}} \qquad \dfrac{\{P\}\,\mathtt{c}\,\{Q\}}{\{P * R\}\,\mathtt{c}\,\{Q * R\}}\ \text{Frame}$$

Fig. 5. Separation logic inference rules. Note that Frame holds under the condition that the variables referred to in R are independent of the variables modified by c.

tions. We begin with the load rule. To load x e, since pointers cannot be dereferenced within an expression e, the expression e must evaluate to a pointer p referring to some value v. After loading from p, the variable x now stores v, and the heap at p remains unchanged. For the store rule, given a program store $e_1\ e_2$, the precondition requires that the expression e_1 evaluates to a pointer p and the heap consists solely of this pointer. The value v resulting from evaluating e_2 is then stored at the pointer location p in the output heap, and the postcondition reflects this update.

The allocation rule requires an empty heap. While the precondition for this rule is not necessary for the correctness of alloc x e; it helps strengthen the postcondition, having it refer to the size of the allocated memory block k. The postcondition ensures that x stores the new pointer and the heap holds k contiguous cells initialised to 0.

In the rule for free, the precondition states that the heap contains exactly one cell, the one to be freed. After execution, the heap is empty. Regarding structural rules, we include the rule of consequence, which allows strengthening the precondition and weakening the postcondition. This rule is justified purely by logical entailment and does not depend on the operational semantics of commands. Last but not least, we prove the soundness of separation logic's vital frame rule, which enables local reasoning. We will elaborate further on this rule below.

The Frame Rule. Separation logic features the *frame rule*, which offers a principled solution to the frame problem. It allows an independent assertion R to be appended to both the pre- and postconditions of a triple using a separating conjunction.

$$\frac{\{P\}\,c\,\{Q\}}{\{P*R\}\,c\,\{Q*R\}} \text{ (Frame)}$$

where variables modified by c are independent of the validity of R

The purpose of the frame rule is to facilitate *local reasoning*. If a program c safely executes on a minimal state described by P and results in a state satisfying Q, then it also safely executes in any larger state and does not invalidate any predicates R that are true of the independent parts of the larger state. Hence, the frame rule guarantees that the execution of c is unaffected by and does not interfere with these unrelated parts of the state.

As discussed in the definition of weak validity triples, however, allowing all types of errors undermines the soundness of the frame rule. For example, consider the triple $\{\texttt{emp}\}\,\texttt{load}\,\texttt{x}\,\texttt{e}\,\{x = 0\}_\texttt{W}$ where $\forall s.\llbracket e \rrbracket^e\, s = y$ noted in prior work [1]. This triple satisfies weak validity only because all types of errors (including memory errors) are allowed. Framing such a triple with $R = y \mapsto 1$ yields the triple $\{y \mapsto 1\}\,\texttt{load}\,\texttt{x}\,\texttt{e}\,\{x = 0 \land y \mapsto 1\}_\texttt{W}$, which is invalid. Since the load from an uninitialised address would now succeed due to the presence of $(y \mapsto 1)$ in the combined state, but the postcondition is false. Thus, the program's faulty behaviour is masked by the extended heap, and the faults are not propagated, violating the principle of local reasoning. Prior work [1] addressed this by introducing the *isolating conjunction* $P \triangleright Q$, defined as:

$$(P \triangleright Q)(l, h) \equiv \text{ids}(l, h_1) \mathrel{\#} \text{blocks}(l, h_2) \land h = h_1 \cup h_2 \land P(l, h_1) \land Q(l, h_2).$$

The isolating conjunction prevents repairing a dangling pointer through heap union, when appending an independent assertion R. In this way, it avoids turning an erroneous execution into a successful one when extending the state. In contrast, our approach avoids these restrictions. Since our memory-safe validity triple explicitly distinguishes memory safety violations from other errors, programs that suffer from such errors are excluded by design. This allows us to safely apply the standard frame rule without introducing the isolating conjunction.

This section provided an overview of the standard separation logic features. We showed how we adapted the definition of triple validity [1] to prevent memory errors. Additionally, to facilitate reasoning about program specifications, we presented suitable separation logic rules for our language and proved their soundness with respect to the operational semantics. The following section outlines how we express the frame conditions imposed by uniqueness types, as presented in Sect. 2, into our separation logic to verify that a safe program respects the uniqueness imposed safety invariants.

5 Uniqueness as Separation

As previously mentioned, we aim to formally verify whether an imperative program meets the memory safety invariants from a uniqueness type system. To reduce our formal verification effort, we express these invariants within a framework suitable for reasoning about programs that access and mutate memory.

In this section, we represent the frame conditions (Sect. 2) using separation logic through the triple FC TRIPLE. Additionally, we present Theorems 2, 3 and 4 showing that FC TRIPLE implies each of the frame conditions.

It has been shown that expressing and manually proving the frame conditions requires considerable effort [4]. To mitigate this challenge, we begin by representing the frame conditions as a single separation logic triple:

Definition 1 (FC TRIPLE). *Given a program c with an input set of pointers w_i and an output set of pointers w_o, we express the frame conditions as the single triple:*

$$\{ *_{\ell \in w_i} \exists v. \ell \mapsto v \} \ c \ \{ *_{\ell \in w_o} \exists v. \ell \mapsto v \}_{\mathsf{M}} \qquad \text{(FC TRIPLE)}$$

FC TRIPLE describes w_i and w_o as the input and output footprints of the command c. It requires that all locations in w_i are valid pointers in the initial state. Additionally, it asserts that all locations in the output footprint are valid pointers in the final state and guarantees the integrity of non-overlapping memory.

To better understand the theorems that assert that FC TRIPLE implies the frame conditions, it is useful to recall some basic notions of nominal set theory, which is a mathematical framework to formally reason about names, binding and alpha-equivalence.

Let $\pi : \mathcal{I} \to \mathcal{I}$ be a bijective function on the set of block identifiers $\mathcal{I}$. In nominal, the renaming operation $\pi \cdot (-)$ is a function on structures containing block identifiers, that renames every block identifier in that structure using the function π. For example, considering the state s, $\pi \cdot s$ has the effect of changing all block identifiers contained in the state using the function π.

The support of π is the set of names that π actually change, i.e., the smallest set of names such that outside of it, π behaves as the identity. Formally, this is represented as $\operatorname{supp} \pi = \{ x \in \mathcal{I} \mid \pi(x) \neq x \}$. Lastly, when we state that π fixes a set A, we mean that for all elements in A, π maps them to themselves.

The proofs of our theorems rely crucially on the following two results. The first lemma asserts that given a set of pointers w, if we can split the heap into $|w|$ different subheaps, where the domain of each subheap consists of a single element of w, we can conclude that the domain of the heap is precisely the heap footprint w, and vice versa.

Lemma 1 (Big-Sep as Domain Equation)

$$(*_{\ell \in w} \exists v. \ell \mapsto v)\ (ls, h) \longleftrightarrow \operatorname{dom}(h) = w$$

The Frame OK theorem, as introduced by Azevedo de Amorim et al. [1], states that if a program terminates successfully, then we can extend its initial state without affecting its execution, up to some permutation that accounts for different choices of fresh names to guarantee no clashes between identifiers.

Theorem 1 (Frame OK). *Let c be a command, and s_1, s'_1, and s_2 be states. Suppose that $[\![c]\!]_n\, s_1 = s'_1$, $\mathsf{vars}\,(c) \subseteq \mathsf{vars}\,(s_1)$, and $\mathsf{blocks}\,(s_1) \,\#\, \mathsf{blocks}\,(s_2)$. Then, there exists a permutation π such that $[\![c]\!]_n\,(s_1 \cup s_2) = \pi \cdot s'_1 \cup s_2$ and $\mathsf{blocks}\,(\pi \cdot s'_1) \,\#\, \mathsf{blocks}\,(s_2)$.*

Having reviewed some nominal set basic concepts and presented important previous results, let us now turn to the main theorems. The first theorem states that if FC TRIPLE holds for a program c with an input set of pointers w_i, and an output set of pointers w_o, then we know that any pointer initially available that is not returned in the final set, must have been freed – since freeing a pointer is the only way to remove pointers from the domain of the heap.

Theorem 2 (FC TRIPLE Implies Leak Freedom). *Let c be a program, w_i the set of input pointers, and w_o the set of output pointers. Let s be the input state, s' and s'_1 output states, and π a permutation.[2] Additionally, let $s = (ls, h)$, $s' = (ls', h')$, and $s'_1 = (ls'_1, h'_1)$.*
Then, we have the following theorem:

$$\begin{aligned}
&\text{assuming}\\
&\quad \mathsf{vars}\,c \subseteq \mathsf{vars}(s \upharpoonright w_i)\\
&\quad w_i \subseteq \mathsf{dom}(h)\\
&\quad [\![c]\!]_n\,(s \upharpoonright w_i) = \mathsf{done}\,(\pi_1 \cdot s'_1)\\
&\quad \mathsf{blocks}(h \upharpoonright w_i) \,\#\, \mathsf{blocks}(h \upharpoonright \overline{w_i})\\
&\quad [\![c]\!]_n\,s = \mathsf{done}\,(\pi \cdot s')\\
&\quad \{*_{\ell \in w_i} \exists v.\, \ell \mapsto v\}\ c\ \{*_{\ell \in w_o} \exists v.\, \ell \mapsto v\}_{\mathsf{M}}\\
&\text{then}\\
&\quad w_i \cap \mathsf{dom}(h') \subseteq w_o.
\end{aligned}$$

The first premise, $\mathsf{vars}\,c \subseteq \mathsf{vars}(s \upharpoonright w_i)$, guarantees that all the variables needed to run c are already defined in the state $s \upharpoonright w_i$. This implies that their values remain unchanged when we extend that initial state with $s \upharpoonright \overline{w_i}$. The second premise, $w_i \subseteq \mathsf{dom}(h)$, ensures that we can indeed split the heap h, and consequently the state s, into two distinct parts: $h \upharpoonright w_i$ and $h \upharpoonright \overline{w_i}$.

The fourth premise prevents the splitting of allocated memory blocks. The fifth premise assumes that the command c executes successfully on the state s, allowing us to refer to the final heap in the theorem's conclusion. Permutations are needed to facilitate expressing properties on states independently of the new

---

[2] Note that, instead of exposing the nominal monads used in the ROCQ proofs, we will just present proofs with permutations.

block identifiers potentially allocated by the command. Finally, the theorem's conclusion states that leak freedom (Sect. 2) holds on the final heap h'.

The proof of the Theorem 2 relies crucially on the fact that the result of $[\![c]\!]_n\,(s \restriction w_i)$ does not change when we extend the initial state with $h \restriction \overline{w_i}$, aside from some permutation that we pick to be π_1.

Additionally, the proof relies on the conditions $\mathrm{supp}(\pi_1) \,\#\, \mathrm{ids}(s \restriction \overline{w_i}) \cup w_o$ and $\mathrm{supp}(\pi) \,\#\, w_i$. This means that π_1 fixes $\mathrm{ids}(s \restriction \overline{w_i}) \cup w_o$ and π fixes w_i. Moreover, the proof uses the fact that $\mathrm{dom}(h \restriction w_i) = w_i$ (true by construction), and $\mathrm{dom}(\pi_1 \cdot h'_1) = w_o$ (deduced by Lemma 1).

The second theorem states that if FC TRIPLE holds for a program c with an input set of pointers w_i, and an output set of pointers w_o, then we know that any pointer in the final set of pointers that is not in the initial footprint, must have been allocated – which implies that the new pointer is fresh with respect to the initial state.

Theorem 3 (FC TRIPLE Implies Fresh Allocation).
Let c be a program, w_i the set of input pointers, and w_o the set of output pointers. Let s be the input state, s'_1 an output state, and π_1 a permutation. Additionally, let $s = (\mathit{ls}, h)$, and $s'_1 = (\mathit{ls}'_1, h'_1)$.

If

$$\mathrm{vars}\,c \subseteq \mathrm{vars}(s \restriction w_i)$$
$$w_i \subseteq \mathrm{dom}(h)$$
$$\mathrm{blocks}\,(h \restriction w_i) \,\#\, \mathrm{blocks}\,(h \restriction \overline{w_i})$$
$$[\![c]\!]_n\,(s \restriction w_i) = \mathsf{done}\,(\pi_1 \cdot s'_1)$$
$$\{\scalebox{1.2}{$\ast$}_{\ell \in w_i} \exists v.\, \ell \mapsto v\}\; c\; \{\scalebox{1.2}{$\ast$}_{\ell \in w_o} \exists v.\, \ell \mapsto v\}_{\mathsf{M}}$$

then

$$w_o \cap \mathrm{dom}(h) \subseteq w_i.$$

Note that, in this case, the Theorem 3 does not require the assumption $[\![c]\!]_n\,s = \mathsf{done}\,(\pi \cdot s')$. Instead, we derive this information throughout the proof from hypotheses three and four, along with the theorem Frame OK.

The proof of the theorem relies on the condition $\mathrm{supp}\,(\pi_1) \,\#\, \mathrm{ids}(s \restriction \overline{w_i}) \cup w_o$. This means that π_1 fixes $\mathrm{ids}(s \restriction \overline{w_i}) \cup w_o$. Additionally, the proof uses the fact that $\mathrm{dom}(h \restriction w_i) = w_i$ (which holds true by construction) and $\mathrm{dom}(\pi_1 \cdot h'_1) = w_o$ (deduced from Lemma 1). Moreover, the proof uses $\mathrm{dom}(\pi_1 \cdot h'_1) \perp \mathrm{dom}(h \restriction \overline{w_i})$ (inferred from Theorem 1) that leads to the fact that $w_o \,\#\, \mathrm{dom}(h \restriction \overline{w_i})$.

The third and final theorem, shows that if FC TRIPLE holds for a program c with an input set of pointers w_i, and an output set of pointers w_o, we can conclude that the program does not modify any pointer outside of the specified input and output footprints.

Theorem 4 (FC TRIPLE Implies Inertia).
Let c be a program, w_i the set of input pointers, and w_o the set of output pointers. Let s be the input state, s' and s'_1 output states, and π a permutation. Additionally, let $s = (\mathit{ls}, h)$, $s' = (\mathit{ls}', h')$, and $s'_1 = (\mathit{ls}'_1, h'_1)$.

Then, we have the following theorem:

assuming
$$\text{vars}\, c \subseteq \text{vars}(s \restriction w_i)$$
$$w_i \subseteq \text{dom}(h)$$
$$\text{blocks}\,(h \restriction w_i) \,\#\, \text{blocks}\,(h \restriction \overline{w_i})$$
$$[\![c]\!]_n\,(s \restriction w_i) = \text{done}\,(\pi_1 \cdot s'_1)$$
$$[\![c]\!]_n\, s = \text{done}\,(\pi \cdot s')$$
$$\{\ast_{\ell \in w_i} \exists v.\, \ell \mapsto v\}\, c\, \{\ast_{\ell \in w_o} \exists v.\, \ell \mapsto v\}_\mathsf{M}$$
then
$$\forall p.\, p \notin w_o \cup w_i \rightarrow h(p) = h'(p)$$

Similar to the proof for Theorem 2 and 3, this proof relies on π_1 fixing ids$(s \restriction \overline{w_i}) \cup w_o$. Additionally, it uses the fact that dom$(h \restriction w_i) = w_i$ (holds by construction) and dom$(\pi_1 \cdot h'_1) = w_o$ (deduced from Lemma 1).

Based on Theorems 2, 3, and 4 we can conclude that to prove that a safe program complies with the memory safety invariants from uniqueness types, specifically the frame conditions, it is enough to show that the program satisfies FC TRIPLE . We now have a framework suitable for reasoning about the safety invariants from uniqueness types, namely the separation logic presented in Sect. 4, and the exact triple we need to discharge for a program intended for integration into the uniquenessly typed program.

6 Examples: Discharging Frame Conditions

For convenience, we define a validity triple on expressions $\{P\}\,\mathsf{e}\,\{\lambda v.\, Q\,v\}_e$. Given an expression e, a precondition on states P and a postcondition predicate on values Q, $\{P\}\,\mathsf{e}\,\{\lambda v.\, Q\,v\}_e$ holds iff $\forall (l, h).\, P\,(l, h) \rightarrow (\forall e [\![e]\!]^e\, l = v \rightarrow Q\,v)$.

Figure 6 has some examples of derived separation logic rules for single commands, maintaining the frame conditions separation logic triple under specific constraints on the input and output pointer sets that represent the heap footprint. These demonstrate that one can discharge the frame condition separation logic triples, which in turn imply that the uniqueness type invariants are satisfied (as per the theorems in Sect. 5). We verified these examples in ROCQ. These derived rules can be directly used to verify larger programs when each command within the larger program respects the uniqueness constraints. In complex cases, when the entire program respects the separation logic frame conditions triple, but single commands within the program do not respect these conditions, such programs can still be verified manually. Even then, one can rely on the general separation logic rules to aid with the manual proofs.

$$\frac{w_i = w_o}{\{*_{\ell \in w_i} \exists v.\, \ell \mapsto v\}\, \texttt{skip}\, \{*_{\ell \in w_o} \exists v.\, \ell \mapsto v\}}$$

$$\frac{w_i = w_o}{\{*_{\ell \in w_i} \exists v.\, \ell \mapsto v\}\, \texttt{x} := \texttt{e}\, \{*_{\ell \in w_o} \exists v.\, \ell \mapsto v\}}$$

$$\frac{w_i = w_o \quad \{*_{\ell \in w_i} \exists v.\, \ell \mapsto v\}\, \texttt{e}\, \{\lambda v.\, v \in \mathcal{P} \to \mathit{fst}\, v \in w_i\}_e}{\{*_{\ell \in w_i} \exists v.\, \ell \mapsto v\}\, \texttt{load x e}\, \{*_{\ell \in w_o} \exists v.\, \ell \mapsto v\}}$$

$$\frac{w_i = w_o \quad \{*_{\ell \in w_i} \exists v.\, \ell \mapsto v\}\, \texttt{e}_1\, \{\lambda v.\, v \in \mathcal{P} \to \mathit{fst}\, v \in w_i\}_e}{\{*_{\ell \in w_i} \exists v.\, \ell \mapsto v\}\, \texttt{store}\, \texttt{e}_1\, \texttt{e}_2\, \{*_{\ell \in w_o} \exists v.\, \ell \mapsto v\}}$$

$$\frac{\{*_{\ell \in w_i} \exists v.\, \ell \mapsto v\}\, \texttt{e}\, \{\lambda(p,n).\, (p,n) \in \mathcal{P} \to (p \in w_i \wedge w_o = w_i \setminus \{p\} \wedge p \notin \mathit{fst}\,{}^{\backprime} w_o\}_e}{\{*_{\ell \in w_i} \exists v.\, \ell \mapsto v\}\, \texttt{free e}\, \{*_{\ell \in w_o} \exists v.\, \ell \mapsto v\}}$$

$$\frac{\{*_{\ell \in w_i} \exists v.\, \ell \mapsto v\}\, \texttt{e}\, \{\lambda v.\, v \notin \mathcal{P} \to w_o = w_i\}_e}{\{*_{\ell \in w_i} \exists v.\, \ell \mapsto v\}\, \texttt{free e}\, \{*_{\ell \in w_o} \exists v.\, \ell \mapsto v\}}$$

$$\frac{\{*_{\ell \in w_i} \exists v.\, \ell \mapsto v\}\, \texttt{c}_1\, \{*_{\ell \in w'} \exists v.\, \ell \mapsto v\} \quad \{*_{\ell \in w'} \exists v.\, \ell \mapsto v\}\, \texttt{c}_2\, \{*_{\ell \in w_o} \exists v.\, \ell \mapsto v\}}{\{*_{\ell \in w_i} \exists v.\, \ell \mapsto v\}\, \texttt{seq}\, \texttt{c}_1\, \texttt{c}_2\, \{*_{\ell \in w_o} \exists v.\, \ell \mapsto v\}}$$

$$\frac{\{*_{\ell \in w_i} \exists v.\, \ell \mapsto v\}\, \texttt{e}\, \{\lambda v.\, v \in \mathbb{B}\}_e \quad \{*_{\ell \in w_i} \exists v.\, \ell \mapsto v\}\, \texttt{c}\, \{*_{\ell \in w_o} \exists v.\, \ell \mapsto v\} \quad \{*_{\ell \in w_i} \exists v.\, \ell \mapsto v\}\, \texttt{c}'\, \{*_{\ell \in w_{o'}} \exists v.\, \ell \mapsto v\}}{\{*_{\ell \in w_i} \exists v.\, \ell \mapsto v\}\, \texttt{if e then c else c}'\, \{\lambda s.\, (*_{\ell \in w_o} \exists v.\, \ell \mapsto v)s \vee (*_{\ell \in w_{o'}} \exists v.\, \ell \mapsto v)s\}}$$

Fig. 6. Derived uniqueness separation logic triples. Note that $f\,{}^{\backprime} S$ is used to denote the image of a function f on a set S, and $S_1 \setminus S_2$ is used to denote set difference.

7 Related Work

The foundations of this work rest on three separate areas: separation logic, uniqueness and ownership types, and verified interoperability through foreign function interfaces.

Separation Logic. Separation logic [11,12,14] extends Hoare logic to enable local reasoning about heaps and pointers. Its key feature, the frame rule, ensures that the mutation of one part of the heap does not invalidate assertions about unmutated parts of the heap. Particularly relevant to the present work is the use of separation logic to formally define memory safety [1] as well as the RustBelt project [6,7].

Azevedo de Amorim et al. extend separation logic with a memory-safe variant of the frame rule accommodating errors [1]. While this work accounts for a weak form of validity that holds for programs that potentially return an error, it requires a stronger separation between the states resulting in a non-standard definition of separating conjunction. In contrast, we introduce a notion of validity that precludes memory errors while still allowing other types of errors and prove the soundness of the frame rule using the traditional notion of separating conjunction. Moreover, we verify the soundness of an entire inference system, facilitating more extensive reasoning.

The RustBelt project aims to ensure that Rust's core safety properties are preserved even for programs incorporating *unsafe* code, which can bypass Rust memory safety features. RustBelt provides a formal semantic model for a significant subset of Rust. This model provides the verification conditions necessary to guarantee that a program with unsafe code preserves Rust's type system invariants. RustBelt uses Iris, an advanced separation logic, to prove that specific unsafe code is sound, by associating it with logical invariants that mimic Rust's safety guarantees. Unlike RustBelt, the present research focuses on expressing the safety invariants within separation logic, rather than embedding a semantic interpretation of the type system into separation logic.

Uniqueness Types. Uniqueness types [17] track exclusive access to data, ensuring that unaliased data remains unaliased. We focus on the memory safety guarantees induced by uniqueness types, especially the frame invariants they establish. Clean [2], Idris [3], and Cogent [10] are some of the languages incorporating uniqueness systems. In particular, our research builds on Cogent's type system and its approach to memory safety.

FFI Verification. Significant research on FFIs aims to ensure that external code adheres to the safety requirements of the host language.

For example, Patterson et al. [13] present a framework for reasoning about cross-language correctness at the compiled level. The framework uses logical relations to model the semantics of the source language type system. This allows for identifying type equivalences across languages, facilitating safe data exchange between them and reasoning about the program's behaviour after compilation.

VeriFFI is a project that establishes a verified FFI between ROCQ and C. It ensures that C functions comply with ROCQ programs specifications. This is achieved by translating ROCQ types and models into specifications compatible with the Verified Software Toolchain (VST). Then, developers can prove that the corresponding C implementations satisfy these specifications, guaranteeing type safety.

Cheung et al. manually verified that certain C components align with Cogent's type system invariants, including the frame conditions. They abstracted a monadic C embedding in Isabelle/HOL into a functional Cogent embedding within the same assistant. While their work successfully verified safety invariants of C code, it also showed the significant effort required, especially when using a framework not designed to facilitate pointer reasoning.

While these approaches to FFI verification are more general and often require comprehensive models of both the host and the guest languages, our approach focuses on expressing the invariants of a uniqueness type system within a version of separation logic suitable for reasoning on safe imperative languages.

8 Conclusion and Future Work

This paper describes the obligations that a programming language with uniqueness types, specifically Cogent, imposes on references and heaps to fully verify a program written in Cogent incorporating C code. We show how these frame obligations can be expressed in separation logic. Furthermore, we formally prove, using ROCQ, that the proposed formulation in separation logic implies the frame obligations of the uniqueness-type system.

In the process of formally verifying programs with uniqueness types that feature a bypass mechanism, it is typical to assume the memory safety obligations on the external code. This practice leads to a verification that, while potentially encompassing safety, remains incomplete. Our formulation of the frame obligations derived from Cogent's uniqueness-type system into separation logic FC TRIPLE, marks progress toward fully discharging these conditions.

We also aim to explore proof composition: given two programs c_1 and c_2 that satisfy the frame conditions expressed in separation logic, does it follow that the program $c_1; c_2$ also satisfy the frame conditions? We suspect that proof composition requires a weaker version of our FC TRIPLE proposed.

Finally, we believe that this formulation of the frame conditions helps solidify the connection between uniqueness types and separation logic. Type systems and program logics are both tools for formal reasoning, and we run the risk of reinvention if we do not realise the connections between them.

References

1. Azevedo de Amorim, A., Hriţcu, C., Pierce, B.C.: The meaning of memory safety. In: Bauer, L., Küsters, R. (eds.) POST 2018. LNCS, vol. 10804, pp. 79–105. Springer, Cham (2018). https://doi.org/10.1007/978-3-319-89722-6_4
2. Barendsen, E., Smetsers, S.: Conventional and uniqueness typing in graph rewrite systems. In: Shyamasundar, R.K. (ed.) FSTTCS 1993. LNCS, vol. 761, pp. 41–51. Springer, Heidelberg (1993). https://doi.org/10.1007/3-540-57529-4_42
3. Brady, E.C.: Type-driven development of concurrent communicating systems. Comput. Sci. **18**(3) (2017). https://doi.org/10.7494/CSCI.2017.18.3.1413
4. Cheung, L., O'Connor, L., Rizkallah, C.: Overcoming restraint: composing verification of foreign functions with cogent. In: Proceedings of the 11th ACM SIGPLAN International Conference on Certified Programs and Proofs, CPP 2022, pp. 13–26. Association for Computing Machinery, New York, NY, USA (2022). https://doi.org/10.1145/3497775.3503686
5. Herhut, S.B.S.S., Penczek, F., Grelck, C., Shinkarov, A., Viessmann, H.N.: Single assignment C tutorial (2025)
6. Jung, R.: Understanding and evolving the Rust programming language. Ph.D. thesis, Universität des Saarlandes (2020). https://doi.org/10.22028/D291-31946
7. Jung, R., Jourdan, J.H., Krebbers, R., Dreyer, D.: RustBelt: securing the foundations of the rust programming language. Proc. ACM Program. Lang. **2**(POPL) (2017). https://doi.org/10.1145/3158154
8. McCarthy, J., Hayes, P.: Some philosophical problems from the standpoint of artificial intelligence. In: Meltzer, B., Michie, D. (eds.) Machine Intelligence, vol. 4, pp. 463–502. Edinburgh University Press (1969)

9. O'Connor, L., et al.: Refinement through restraint: bringing down the cost of verification (2016)
10. O'Connor, L., et al.: Cogent: uniqueness types and certifying compilation. J. Funct. Program. **31**, e25 (2021). https://doi.org/10.1017/S095679682100023X
11. O'Hearn, P., Reynolds, J., Yang, H.: Local reasoning about programs that alter data structures. In: Fribourg, L. (ed.) CSL 2001. LNCS, vol. 2142, pp. 1–19. Springer, Heidelberg (2001). https://doi.org/10.1007/3-540-44802-0_1
12. O'Hearn, P.W.: Resources, concurrency, and local reasoning. Theore. Comput. Sci. **375**(1), 271–307 (2007). https://doi.org/10.1016/j.tcs.2006.12.035. https://www.sciencedirect.com/science/article/pii/S030439750600925X. festschrift for John C. Reynolds's 70th birthday
13. Patterson, D., Mushtak, N., Wagner, A., Ahmed, A.: Semantic soundness for language interoperability. In: Proceedings of the 43rd ACM SIGPLAN International Conference on Programming Language Design and Implementation, PLDI 2022, pp. 609–624. Association for Computing Machinery, New York, NY, USA (2022). https://doi.org/10.1145/3519939.3523703
14. Reynolds, J.: Separation logic: a logic for shared mutable data structures. In: Proceedings 17th Annual IEEE Symposium on Logic in Computer Science, pp. 55–74. IEEE (2002). https://doi.org/10.1109/LICS.2002.1029817
15. Rinus Plasmeijer, van Eekelen, M.: Clean version 2.2 language report. Language report (2011)
16. Scholz, S.B.: Single assignment C: efficient support for high-level array operations in a functional setting. J. Funct. Program. **13**(6), 1005–1059 (2003)
17. Smetsers, S., Barendsen, E., van Eekelen, M., Plasmeijer, R.: Guaranteeing safe destructive updates through a type system with uniqueness information for graphs. In: Schneider, H.J., Ehrig, H. (eds.) Graph Transformations in Computer Science. LNCS, vol. 776, pp. 358–379. Springer, Heidelberg (1994). https://doi.org/10.1007/3-540-57787-4_23
18. Somogyi, Z., Henderson, F., Conway, T.C.: The execution algorithm of mercury, an efficient purely declarative logic programming language. J. Log. Program. **29**(1-3), 17–64 (1996). https://doi.org/10.1016/S0743-1066(96)00068-4

Fair Termination for Resource-Aware Active Objects

Francesco Dagnino[1], Paola Giannini[2], Violet Ka I Pun[3],
and Ulises Torrella[3]

[1] DIBRIS, Università di Genova, Genova, Italy
francesco.dagnino@dibris.unige.it
[2] DiSSTE, Università del Piemonte Orientale, Vercelli, Italy
paola.giannini@uniupo.it
[3] Western Norway University of Applied Sciences, Bergen, Norway
{violet.ka.i.pun,unto}@hvl.no

Abstract. Active object systems are a model of distributed computation that has been adopted for modelling distributed systems and business process workflows. This field of modelling is, in essence, concurrent and resource-aware, motivating the development of resource-aware formalisations on the active object model. The contributions of this work are the development of a core calculus for resource-aware active objects together with a type system ensuring that well-typed programs are fairly terminating, i.e., they can always eventually terminate. To achieve this, we combine techniques from graded semantics and type systems, which are quite well understood for sequential programs, with those for fair termination, which have been developed for synchronous sessions.

Keywords: graded types · active-objects · resource-aware · fair termination · workflows

1 Introduction

Active object systems [12] are the object-oriented instantiation of the *actor model* [4,9]. They provide a useful abstraction of distributed systems with asynchronous communications, which are represented as collections of active objects (actors)[1] interacting through asynchronous method calls and futures. Active object languages, such as those presented in [13,28,39], capture this form of concurrency model by means of distributed multithreaded computational entities with cooperative scheduling, where each actor can handle multiple messages at a time, by explicitly yielding control when awaiting on certain conditions to be fulfilled, for instance, a resolved future.

Active objects have been adopted for formalising and analysing workflow models [5,6] by capturing the behaviour of the internal (resource-sensitive) processes of organisations. Workflow processes handle business cases (a customer

---
[1] We use actors and active objects interchangeably when it is clear from the context.

order, a service ticket, etc.) by executing a sequence of tasks, and are primarily demanded to reach case resolution, hence termination [1,2]. Active objects directly capture the workflow management notion of active resources (employees, machines, etc.), representing the operational power a system possesses to carry out its tasks. As such, these are available in a fixed number and cannot be dynamically instantiated. However, workflow models often need to take into account also *passive/informational resources* [34],[2] which, while performing a workflow, move through processes, undergo transformations, can be created or destroyed, and crucially, have a *limited availability* according to the specification domain. The interplay of asynchronous message passing, cooperative multithreading and resource management makes it challenging to ensure that a system can complete its tasks and consequently be terminating. For instance, if a thread tries to access a resource that is not available, it remains stuck as it cannot yield control, thus preventing the whole system from successfully terminating.

To model such systems, we propose a core calculus for resource aware active objects. This calculus models systems with a fixed number of active objects which manipulate dynamic (passive) resources. These are represented as values with a limited availability, described by a *grade* annotation constraining their usage. For instance, a resource can be indicated for a quantitative use with a numerical grade, or for a mode of use with a *public/private* grade, ensuring that private resources are not made public. Resources are local to each object and can only be shared by message passing. Moreover, all threads of an actor can hold and release the resources it owns, where getting hold of resources is *blocking* if the requested amount is not available.

It is important to note that the introduction of graded resources has an impact on the synchronisation mechanism. Indeed, typically futures can be accessed an arbitrary number of times [28,35,40]. However, this is not the case in our setting because futures may contain graded resources and so, by copying the future, we would copy its content as well, leading to a violation of the constraint on the resource usage expressed by the grade. To overcome this issue, we treat futures *linearly*, allowing them to be read only once.

We endow our calculus with a type system ensuring that well-typed programs are *fairly terminating* [16]. This result does not forbid non-termination, but rather it guarantees that termination is always possible. Hence, well-typed programs, unless they systematically avoid going towards termination, which is considered an unfair behaviour, are guaranteed to terminate. This result guarantees several desirable properties of concurrent systems, such as *livelock freedom* and *orphan message freedom*, in addition to the main goal of this work, which is that resources are handled correctly, i.e., actors do not run out of resources they need for executing their tasks. In this context livelock freedom means that an object waiting for a future, the result of an asynchronous method call, will eventually get it and orphan message freedom means that a message requiring the execution of a method will eventually be read and the method executed. To achieve this, we combine techniques from graded semantics and type

---

[2] In this paper, "resources" always refer to passive/informational resources.

systems [3,11,14,15,21,41], which are quite well understood for sequential programs, with those for fair termination [16–18,20] that have been developed for synchronous sessions.

The rest of the paper is structured as follows: Section 2 introduces the algebraic preliminaries that are used in the paper and Sect. 3 defines our core calculus. The type system guaranteeing fair termination as well as its soundness are presented in Sect. 4. Finally, we discuss some related work and conclude the paper with future work in Sect. 5. Omitted rules, results and full proofs of the theorems in Sect. 4 can be found in the extended version of the paper [19].

2 Algebraic Preliminaries: Grade Monoids and Subtraction

Resource-aware semantics and type systems are often parameterised over an algebraic structure whose elements, usually dubbed *grades*, model the "modes" of availability of resources, e.g., their number of copies, their privacy level or the degree of imprecision affecting them. This structure is typically a variant of ordered semirings [3,7,11,14,15,21,27,33,41] with addition and multiplication operations for combining grades and a compatible order relation enabling their approximation.

In this section, we introduce the algebraic structure of grades we use in this work, which is different from the previously mentioned algebras. In particular, multiplication is not needed while *subtraction* is required. The latter is a novelty of this paper in the current context, thus we describe it in more detail. We start by introducing the notion of grade monoid.

Definition 1. *A* grade monoid *is an ordered commutative monoid* $G = \langle |G|, \leq, +, \mathbf{0} \rangle$ *such that, for all* $g \in |G|$, $g \leq \mathbf{0}$ *implies* $g = \mathbf{0}$.

This means that, in a grade monoid $G = \langle |G|, \leq, +, \mathbf{0} \rangle$, $+$ is an associative and commutative binary operation on $|G|$ with $\mathbf{0}$ as a neutral element and $\leq$ is a partial order on $|G|$ making $+$ monotone in both arguments. The last requirement ensures that there is no grade below $\mathbf{0}$. This is reasonable since $\mathbf{0}$ intuitively models the absence of a resource.

Example 1. We show some standard examples adapted from the literature, e.g., [11].

1. The ordered monoids $\mathsf{Nat}_\infty^= = \langle \mathbb{N} + \{\infty\}, =, +, 0 \rangle$ and $\mathsf{Nat}_\infty^\leq = \langle \mathbb{N} + \{\infty\}, \leq, +, 0 \rangle$ of extended natural numbers, ordered either by equality or by the standard ordering on them, with addition and zero, are grade monoids. The former tracks *exact usage* of resources, while the latter tracks *bounded usage* of resources.
2. The ordered monoid $\mathsf{Lin} = \langle |\mathsf{Lin}|, \leq, +, 0 \rangle$ where $|\mathsf{Lin}| = \{0, 1, \infty\}$, with $0 \leq \infty$ and $1 \leq \infty$, and the addition is given by
$$0 + x = x + 0 = x \qquad 1 + 1 = \infty \qquad \infty + x = x + \infty = \infty$$

for all $x \in |\mathsf{Lin}|$, is a grade monoid. It tracks resources that are either not used (0), or used exactly once (1) or in an unrestricted way (∞). Adding $0 \leq 1$ we get the affinity grade.
3. Let $\mathsf{Lev} = \langle |\mathsf{Lev}|, \leq, \vee, 0 \rangle$ be a join-semilattice. Then, Lev is a grade monoid. Intuitively, elements of $|\mathsf{Lev}|$ represent the (maximum) mode in which a resource can be used. For instance, if $|\mathsf{Lev}| = \{0, \mathsf{priv}, \mathsf{pub}\}$ is a set of privacy levels with $0 \leq \mathsf{priv} \leq \mathsf{pub}$, a resource with grade priv can only be used in a private mode.

Recall that grades $g \in |G|$ such that $\mathbf{0} \leq g$ play a special role: they represent usages that can be *discarded*, as they can be reduced to $\mathbf{0}$ through the approximation relation. For instance, in the linearity grade monoid Example 1(2), the grade ∞ is discardable, while 1 is not, modelling the fact that 1 represents resources which must be used exactly once. In the affinity grade 1 also is discardable as it means usage at most once.

As mentioned, we extend the algebraic structure of grades with a subtraction operation. This will be used in the operational semantics to model resource consumption in a deterministic way. Hence, we define it to be a partial binary operation, which we expect to be undefined when the current grade is not enough to cover the required consumption. More precisely, we have the following definition.

Definition 2. *Let $G = \langle |G|, \leq, +, \mathbf{0} \rangle$ be a grade monoid. A subtraction is a partial binary function $- : |G| \times |G| \rightharpoonup |G|$ such that, for all $g, h, h' \in |G|$, if $h - g$ is defined and $h \leq h'$ then $h' - g$ is defined and $h - g \leq h' - g$.*

A subtraction operation is a partial binary function, which is monotonic in the first argument. Note that here monotonicity also requires that subtraction is defined on the larger argument.

Definition 3. *A subtractive grade monoid is a structure $G = \langle |G|, \leq, +, \mathbf{0}, - \rangle$, where $\langle |G|, \leq, +, \mathbf{0} \rangle$ is a grade monoid and $-$ is a subtraction operation on it such that, for all $g, h, h' \in |G|$, $g + h' \leq h$ if and only if $h - g$ is defined and $h' \leq h - g$.*

Intuitively, in a subtractive grade monoid the subtraction $h - g$ is defined whenever there is a residual grade h' such that $g + h' \leq h$. When $h - g$ is defined, we have $g + (h - g) \leq h$. This means that, when it is defined, $h - g$ is the largest grade that added to g stays below h. As a consequence, the partial function $(\cdot) - g : |G| \rightharpoonup |G|$, when it is defined, behaves as a right adjoint of the function $g + (\cdot) : |G| \to |G|$. Finally, notice that, from Definition 3, we get that, if $g \leq h$, then $h - g$ is defined and it is discardable. Indeed, we have $g + \mathbf{0} = g \leq h$ and this implies $\mathbf{0} \leq h - g$.

Example 2. We show how to define subtraction operations on grade monoids of Example 1.

1. In both grade monoids $\mathsf{Nat}_\infty^=$ and $\mathsf{Nat}_\infty^\leq$ of Example 1(1) the subtraction $y-x$ is defined only when $x \leq y$ and in this case is given by

$$y - x = \sup\{z \in \mathbb{N} + \{\infty\} \mid x + z \leq y\}$$

Note that when $x \leq y$ the set of which we take the supremum is not empty as 0 belongs to it. Furthermore, this definition implies that $\infty - x = \infty$ for all $x \in \mathbb{N} + \{\infty\}$.
2. In the grade monoid Lin of Example 1(2), the subtraction is defined by the following table $x - 0 = x$ and $\infty - x = \infty$, for all $x \in |\mathsf{Lin}|$, and $1 - 1 = 0$. Similarly for the affine grade. Note that, even if $1 + 1 = \infty$, we have that $1 \neq (1+1) - 1 = \infty - 1 = \infty$, that is, even if we have a subtraction, the monoid does not need to have inverses.
3. In the grade monoid Lev of Example 1(3), observe that, if $x \leq y$, we have $x \vee y = y$ and so $y - x$ must be defined and should be equal to y. On the other hand, if $y - x$ is defined, then $x \vee (y - x) \leq y$, which implies that $x \leq y$. Therefore, we have that $y - x$ is defined if and only if $x \leq y$ and in this case we have $y - x = y$.

Other useful properties of subtractive grade monoids can be found in [19].

3 A Calculus of Resource-Aware Active Objects

In this section we introduce the syntax and operational semantics of our core calculus, which are based on active object languages [12]. It models systems with a fixed number of objects communicating through asynchronous method calls and synchronising over futures. Active objects are multithreaded, thus, they can handle multiple messages at a time, but with a cooperative scheduling, i.e., only one active thread is allowed and it has to explicitly yield control to the others.

The distinctive feature of our calculus is that it models *resources* needed by objects for carrying out their tasks. Resources are located within objects and have a *limited availability*. Each thread of an object can hold and release a certain amount of a resource, and crucially, is not allowed to hold a resource that is not available in the object. Therefore, we abstractly represent resources as constants decorated by a *grade*, which specifies their availability. In the following we fix a subtractive grade monoid $G = \langle |G|, \leq, +, \mathbf{0}, - \rangle$. The syntax of the language is

$$
\begin{array}{ll}
e ::= a!m(\overline{ve}) \mid ve? & \lambda ::= \overline{x \mapsto v} \\
\quad \mid \mathsf{hold}\ g\ r \mid \mathsf{release}\ g\ ve & P, Q ::= a^\bullet[\lambda \mid e]^f \mid \mathsf{idle}^a \mid a^\circ[\lambda \mid e]^f \\
\quad \mid \mathsf{op}(\overline{ve}) \mid e_1 \oplus e_2 & \quad \mid f \leftarrow a!m(\overline{v}) \mid f \leftarrow v \mid P \parallel Q \mid \mathsf{done} \\
\quad \mid \mathsf{ret}\ ve \mid \mathsf{let}\ x = e_1\ \mathsf{in}\ e_2 & \rho ::= \overline{r^g} \\
ve ::= x^g \mid x \mid v & \Phi, \Psi, \Theta ::= \overline{a : \rho} \\
v ::= r^g \mid f \mid \mathsf{unit} & \sigma ::= \Phi \parallel P
\end{array}
$$

Fig. 1. Syntax where g and r are grades and resource identifiers, respectively

shown in Fig. 1. With a and m we denote actor and method names, with x, y variable names, and r and g are respectively resource names and grades. Overbar denotes a list of elements, e.g., $\overline{ve}$ stands for $ve_1, \ldots ve_n$ for $n \geq 0$. Actors have associated methods and resources. The methods are abstractly modelled by the function

$$\mathsf{mbody}(a, m) = (\overline{x}, e)$$

which gives the parameters and body of method m of actor a. Similarly, resources owned by each actor are specified by a mapping, dubbed *actor context*, denoted as Φ, Ψ and Θ, associating with each actor a its resource environment ρ, which is a sequence of graded resources with unique names, i.e., it is a finite partial function from resources to their grades.

The syntax of *expressions* is fine-grained [30] and it is parameterised over a signature $\mathcal{S}_{\mathsf{op}}$ of primitive operations, ranged over by op, for creating, transforming and destroying resources. *Value expressions* ve are either (graded) variables or values, which can be graded resources, futures or $\mathtt{unit}$. Expression $a!m(\overline{ve})$ is the request of the asynchronous execution of the method m of actor a on parameters $\overline{ve}$. This expression will return a (new) future, that can be used to wait for the result of the call through the expression $ve?$. Resources can be added to or taken from the resource environment of the actor running the method by $\mathtt{release}$ and $\mathtt{hold}$ expressions, specifying the resource name and the amount (the grade) to be transferred. The expression $\mathsf{op}(\overline{ve})$ denotes a call to the primitive operation op of $\mathcal{S}_{\mathsf{op}}$. The construct $e_1 \oplus e_2$ models a non-deterministic choice between the execution of e_1 and e_2. Expression $\mathtt{ret}\ ve$ ends the execution and returns the value of ve, and finally the $\mathtt{let}$ construct binds the variable x to the value of the expression e_1 in the evaluation of e_2.

```
1  makeCoffee(x: Order¹, y: CleanCup¹)
2             : Coffee¹
3  washCup(x: DirtyCup¹): CleanCup¹
4  drink(x: Coffee¹): DirtyCup¹
5
6  Customer {
7    main(): Unit {
8      let f1 = Barista!takeOrder(order)in
9      let x = f1? in
10     let f2 = Counter!pickup() in
11     let x1 = f2? in
12     let x2 = drink(x1¹) in
13     let f3 = Barista!clean(x2¹) in f3?;
14     (return unit
15     ⊕
16     y=Customer!main();y?;return unit }
17 }
```

```
18 Counter {
19   place(c : Coffee): Unit {
20     release 1 c¹;return unit }
21   pickup(): Coffee¹ {
22     let x=hold 1 Coffee in return x¹ }
23 }
24
25 Barista {
26   takeOrder (o : Order¹): Unit {
27     let cc = hold 1 CleanCup in
28     let c = makeCoffee(o¹,cc¹) in
29     let f4 = Counter!place(c¹) in
30     f4?; return unit }
31   clean(dc : DirtyCup¹): Unit {
32     let cc = washCup(dc¹) in
33     release 1 cc;return unit }
34 }
```

Fig. 2. A workflow example of a cafe

Example 3. Figure 2 shows a simple workflow of a cafe modelled in our calculus, involving three active objects `Customer`, `Barista` and `Counter`, and three types of resources, namely, clean cups, dirty cups and coffee. For simplicity, we use ";" instead of let-constructs for sequential composition wherever it is obvious. The customer starts the workflow by (asynchronously) ordering a coffee from the barista (Line 8) and then waits. The latter, upon receiving the order, grabs a clean cup (Line 27) to make a coffee (Line 28). After that, the barista places it on the counter (Line 29), and notifies the customer (Line 30). The awaiting customer now picks up the coffee from the counter and drinks it (Lines 10–12), which subsequently produces a dirty cup, which s/he then asks the barista to clean (Line 13). Upon request, the barista washes the dirty cup and produces a clean cup which is now available for the next coffee (Line 33). When the cup is cleaned, the customer can non-deterministically choose to leave the cafe or order another coffee by repeating the workflow (Lines 14–16).

The manipulation of resources is captured by the operations `makeCoffee`, `drink` and `washCup` (whose signatures are given in Lines 1–4 and used in Lines 12, 28 and 32) as well as the `hold` and `release` statements on Lines 20, 22, 27, and 33. The barista uses `makeCoffee`, which takes an order and a clean cup, to produce a coffee, and adopts `washCup` to convert a dirty cup into a clean one. Getting hold of resources, *one* coffee and *one* clean cup, is modelled by Lines 22 and 27, respectively, while the release of these two resources is captured by Lines 20 and 33. Note that the resource quantity to be held or released is explicitly specified, and the action of holding resources is only possible if the number of available resources can fulfil the requested amount. Observe that the program is *resource safe* only if the barista starts with at least one clean cup. With the non-deterministic choice in Lines 14–16, non-termination is possible in this workflow model, and it is fairly terminating if it is resource safe.

System configurations σ consist of the association between actors and their resources Φ, and a process P, which is a parallel composition of threads and messages. A *running* actor comprises precisely one *active thread* $a^\bullet[\lambda \mid e]^f$ and any number of *suspended threads* $a^\circ[\lambda \mid e]^f$, where λ is a local environment mapping variables to values, e an expression to be executed and f a future that hold the final result. An actor can also be *idle*, signaled by the presence of idle^a.

There are two kinds of messages: $f \leftarrow a!m(\overline{v})$ denotes a call to method m of actor a with parameters $\overline{v}$ and expects the final result on future f; conversely, $f \leftarrow v$ represents a completed computation whose value v is stored in future f. Threads and messages are composed by the operator $\|$ which is assumed to be associative and to have done as neutral element. However, $\|$ is *not* commutative as futures impose a dependency between thread and messages, preventing us from freely swapping them, which will be clarified in the definition of the structural precongruence (see Fig. 4).

In the following we assume that configurations are well formed, meaning that for any actor appearing in a configuration, it either has exactly one active thread or it is idle. This assumption ensures that each multithreaded actors, i.e., active objects, can only execute one task at a time. Our operational semantics

$$\text{(E-CL)} \quad \frac{\lambda_i \mid ve_i \Rightarrow \lambda_{i+1} \mid v_i \quad \forall i \in 1..n}{\lambda_1 \mid a!m(\overline{ve}) \xrightarrow{f \leftarrow a!m(\overline{v})} \lambda_{n+1} \mid \texttt{ret } f} \text{fresh}(f) \quad \text{(E-AWT)} \quad \frac{\lambda \mid ve \Rightarrow \lambda' \mid f}{\lambda \mid ve? \xrightarrow{f \leftarrow v} \lambda' \mid \texttt{ret } v}$$

$$\text{(E-RLS)} \quad \frac{\lambda \mid ve \Rightarrow \lambda' \mid r^h}{\lambda \mid \texttt{release } g \texttt{ ve} \xrightarrow{\texttt{rls } r^g} \lambda' \mid \texttt{ret unit}} g \leq h \quad \text{(E-HLD)} \quad \frac{}{\lambda \mid \texttt{hold } g \ r \xrightarrow{\texttt{hold } r^g} \lambda \mid \texttt{ret } r^g}$$

$$\text{(E-LET)} \quad \frac{\lambda \mid ve \Rightarrow \lambda' \mid v}{\lambda \mid \texttt{let } x = \texttt{ret } ve \texttt{ in } e_2 \xrightarrow{\tau} \lambda', y \mapsto v \mid e_2[y/x]} \text{fresh}(y)$$

Fig. 3. Evaluation of expressions

presented below enforces that one thread can pass control to another only in specific situations. See Example 4 for examples of configurations.

We now introduce the *operational semantics* of our active object based calculus by presenting the most significant rules. We first define the semantics of (value) expressions. This is a resource-aware semantics in the style of [10,11,15,41]. Notably, the evaluation takes place within a local environment and, instead of performing substitutions, variables are replaced one at a time when needed, consuming their corresponding value in the local environment. This behaviour is realised by the relation $\lambda \mid ve \Rightarrow \lambda' \mid v$, which reduces a value expression to a value, possibly modifying the local environment. The main rule is

$$\text{(VR-RS)} \quad \frac{}{\lambda, x \mapsto r^h \mid x^g \Rightarrow \lambda, x \mapsto r^{h-g} \mid r^g}$$

which reduces a graded variable, with grade g, to a graded resource r^g, provided that the variable is associated with r^h in the local environment and the subtraction $h - g$ is defined; the local environment is then updated, mapping the variable to the resource r^{h-g}. In this way we model resource consumption: the reduction is *stuck* if the current amount h of the resource is not enough to satisfy the required amount g (i.e., $h - g$ is undefined); otherwise, the amount g is consumed, leaving only the difference. Compared to the literature, here resource consumption is *deterministic* thanks to the use of the subtraction operation. This allows us to prove a standard subject reduction theorem which in general does not hold for resource-aware semantics.

Evaluation of Expressions. The semantics of expressions is described by a labelled reduction relation $\lambda \mid e \xrightarrow[l_i]{l_o} \lambda' \mid e'$, whose most representative rules are given in Fig. 3. Labels record how an expression interacts with the external environment, and are defined as follows:

$$l ::= \texttt{hold } r^g \mid \texttt{rls } r^g \mid f \leftarrow a!m(\overline{v}) \mid f \leftarrow v \mid \tau$$

The first two labels state how the resources are taken from or released to the current actor context: by $\texttt{hold } r^g$ the expression requests from the environment the resource r with grade g, while by $\texttt{rls } r^g$ it moves to the environment the

(▷-SWAP) $P \parallel Q \bowtie Q \parallel P$ if $\mathit{fp}(P) \cap \mathit{fr}(Q) = \emptyset$ and $\mathit{fp}(Q) \cap \mathit{fr}(P) = \emptyset$
(▷-ACT) $\mathtt{idle}^a \parallel a^\circ[\lambda \mid e]^f \triangleright a^\bullet[\lambda \mid e]^f$
(▷-YLD) $a^\bullet[\lambda \mid e]^f \triangleright \mathtt{idle}^a \parallel a^\circ[\lambda \mid e]^f$ if $\lambda \mid e \xrightarrow[f' \leftarrow v]{}$

$$\text{(CALL)} \quad \frac{\lambda \mid e \xrightarrow{f \leftarrow a!m(\overline{v})} \lambda' \mid e'}{\Phi \parallel b^\bullet[\lambda \mid e]^{f'} \longrightarrow \Phi \parallel f \leftarrow a!m(\overline{v}) \parallel b^\bullet[\lambda' \mid e']^{f'}}$$

$$\text{(SPAWN)} \quad \frac{}{\Phi \parallel f \leftarrow a!m(\overline{v}) \parallel \mathtt{idle}^a \longrightarrow \Phi \parallel a^\bullet[\overline{x} \mapsto \overline{v} \mid e]^f} \quad \mathsf{mbody}(a, m) = (\overline{x}, e)$$

$$\text{(GET)} \quad \frac{\lambda \mid e \xrightarrow{f \leftarrow v} \lambda' \mid e'}{\Phi \parallel f \leftarrow v \parallel a^\bullet[\lambda \mid e]^{f'} \longrightarrow \Phi \parallel a^\bullet[\lambda' \mid e']^{f'}}$$

$$\text{(RLS)} \quad \frac{\lambda \mid e \xrightarrow{\mathtt{rls}\ r^g} \lambda' \mid e'}{\Phi, a : \rho, r^h \parallel a^\bullet[\lambda \mid e]^f \longrightarrow \Phi, a : \rho, r^{h+g} \parallel a^\bullet[\lambda' \mid e']^f}$$

$$\text{(HOLD)} \quad \frac{\lambda \mid e \xrightarrow{\mathtt{hold}\ r^g} \lambda' \mid e'}{\Phi, a : \rho, r^h \parallel a^\bullet[\lambda \mid e]^f \longrightarrow \Phi, a : \rho, r^{h-g} \parallel a^\bullet[\lambda' \mid e']^f}$$

Fig. 4. The precongruence on processes and the reduction on configurations.

resource r with grade g. Communications between actors are enabled by the two following labels, $f \leftarrow a!m(\overline{v})$ and $f \leftarrow v$, which are interpreted as the two kinds of messages of the same shape in the configurations described above. Finally, the label τ denotes the absence of interaction.

Labels are divided into two classes: $\mathtt{rls}\ r^g$ and $f \leftarrow a!m(\overline{v})$ refer to outputs that the expression produces towards the environment, while $\mathtt{hold}\ r^g$ and $f \leftarrow v$ represent inputs that the expression reads from it. To highlight this semantic difference, we write labels of the former class above the arrow denoting the reduction relation, while those of the latter class will appear below it. The label τ can appear in both places, but we will often omit it for clarity.

Rule (E-CL) evaluates the parameters, produces the corresponding label and returns a fresh future. Note that here we do not use the mbody function, i.e., we do not access the method table. In this way, this expression is never stuck modelling the fact that calling a method corresponds to sending a message which will be asynchronously read. Rule (E-AWT) evaluates the value expression to a future and returns the corresponding value reported in the label. Rule (E-RLS) evaluates the value expression to a graded resource with grade h, and checks if h suffices to cover the amount to be released and, in this case, it produces the corresponding label and returns $\mathtt{unit}$. Rule (E-HLD) returns the graded resource reported in the label. Rule (E-LET) adds the local variable x to the environment, modulo renaming with a fresh variable to avoid clashes. No interaction with the external environment is involved.

Precongruence and Reduction on Configurations. The main semantic relation is a reduction $\sigma \longrightarrow \sigma'$ on configurations, whose rules are given in the bottom section of Fig. 4. As it is customary in process calculi, the definition of the reduction relies on a precongruence relation on processes $P \triangleright Q$, generated by the clauses in the top section of Fig. 4. We write $P \bowtie Q$ when both $P \triangleright Q$ and $Q \triangleright P$ hold. This relation accounts for bureaucratic rearrangements of threads and messages within a process. As mentioned, the $\|$ operator is assumed to be associative, but it is not commutative. The precongruence relation specifies in which case we can swap two processes in a parallel composition. To this end, we consider, for every process P, the sets $fp(P)$ and $fr(P)$ of futures *produced* and *consumed*, respectively, which, intuitively, represent the input and output "channels" through which P can be connected to other processes. For a thread $fp(P)$ is the future specified as superscript and for a message is the target of the arrow. For a thread $fr(P)$ is the set of futures occurring in the expression in its body plus the ones in the values of the local environment and for a message is the set of futures occurring in values which are parameters or result of the message. For parallel composition we take the union of the set of the futures consumed by the process on the left and the ones of the process on the right from which we first remove the future produced by the process on the left, which are not consumed by the parallel composition. The formal definition can be found in [19].

Let us now consider the rules for $\triangleright$. Clause ($\triangleright$-SWAP) states that we can swap two processes only if they are disconnected, i.e., they do not depend on each other. The other two clauses instead regulate the (de)activation of threads of a certain actor: ($\triangleright$-ACT) enables the activation of any thread of an actor, provided that the actor is idle, while ($\triangleright$-YLD) states that an actor can suspend the execution of the current thread to become idle only if it is awaiting on a future. This last rule makes the relation $\triangleright$ only a precongruence and not a congruence: the clause ($\triangleright$-ACT) can be inverted only if the thread is awaiting on a future (by ($\triangleright$-YLD)), in all other cases the execution of a thread cannot be suspended.

Rules (CALL), (SPAWN) and (GET) realize the asynchronous communication mechanism of our calculus. When an active thread calls a method, Rule (CALL) adds the call to the parallel composition on the *left* of the active thread. If an idle actor has a pending call to itself, it can start a new thread executing the method body by Rule (SPAWN). Note that if the actor does not have the called method, i.e., mbody(a, m) is undefined, this rule is not applicable and the call will never be executed. If an active thread is awaiting on a fulfilled future, it can retrieve the value from the future and remove the latter from the parallel composition (Rule (GET)). Observe that both the new pending call in Rule (CALL) and the fulfilled future in Rule (GET) are on the *left* of the active thread, so that the structure of produced and consumed futures is respected. Resource management is modelled by Rules (RLS) and (HOLD). The former allows an active thread to add to the actor's resource environment resources at a certain grade, while the latter allows an active thread to move resources from the actor's resource environment to its local environment at a certain grade. Note that Rule (HOLD) is applicable only if the actor resource environment has enough resources to satisfy the request, i.e., the subtraction $h - g$ is defined. The precongruence on processes and the reduction are propagated to parallel composition in the obvious way.

Example 4. In Fig. 5 we show a *possible* reduction for Example 3 starting from an initial configuration, σ, containing a message for the Customer asking to execute method main, when all the actors are idle. Moreover, the Barista has a CleanCup, i.e.,

$$\sigma = \Phi \,\|\, \mathtt{f} \leftarrow \mathtt{Cs!main()} \,\|\, \mathtt{idle}^\mathtt{B} \,\|\, \mathtt{idle}^\mathtt{Cs} \,\|\, \mathtt{idle}^\mathtt{Cn} \quad \text{where} \quad \Phi = \mathtt{B} : \mathtt{CC}^1$$

where names are shortened taking their initials, among other natural abbreviations. In the reductions we underline the processes that are reduced modulo precongruence.

In Line 1, the Barista, who is idle, answers to the pending request of the execution of takeOrder by starting an active thread containing the body of takeOrder. The configuration in Line 2 is produced by the evaluation of expression hold of a CleanCup by the running thread of the Barista, which subtract a CleanCup from his resources and returns it to the expression, whose evaluation, in the next step, places it in the local environment of the thread. The reduction in Line 3 shows how the evaluation of a method call consumes the resources on λ_1 required for its arguments, creates a new future ff4 and adds a message with the call to the configuration, and finally reduces the call expression to ff4. The message is added to the left of the thread, so the future ff4, once fulfilled, can be consumed by the thread. The configuration in Line 4 is produced by the evaluation of expression release of a Coffee by the Counter, which puts it in its resource environment removing it from its local environment, so the actor context becomes Φ_1. In this example all the actors were either idle with no queued threads or running a thread. However, we could apply Rule (▷-YLD) of the pre-congruence to the active thread of Custumer with any reduction starting from Line 2 to produce $\mathtt{Cs}^\circ [\mathtt{y1} \mapsto \mathtt{ff1} \mid \mathtt{let\ x = y1?}...]^\mathtt{f} \,\|\, \mathtt{idle}^\mathtt{Cs}$ since $\mathtt{y1} \mapsto \mathtt{ff1} \mid \mathtt{let\ x = y1?}... \xrightarrow[\mathtt{ff1} \leftarrow v]{} \mid \mathtt{let\ x = ret\ ff1}....$

4 The Type System

In this section we introduce a type system ensuring that well-typed configurations can always successfully complete their execution. To this end, besides the standard concurrency-related errors such as deadlocks, we also have to prevent incorrect usages of resources, i.e., whenever a thread tries to access a resource, it must be available with the requested amount in the resource environment of the actor running the thread. To achieve this, we adapt techniques from graded type systems to track resource requirements in typing judgments of processes and expressions. The key challenge here is that the availability of resources crucially depends on when threads are executed because, for instance, one may rely on a resource released by another one. Thus, the tracking of resource requirements and the future-based synchronisation mechanism should properly interact to ensure a correct resource usage.

$\sigma \longrightarrow \Phi \parallel \mathtt{Cs}^\bullet[\,\mid\,\mathtt{let\ f1=B!tkOr(order)}...]^f \parallel \underline{\mathtt{idle}^B} \parallel \mathtt{idle}^{Cn}$
$\longrightarrow \Phi \parallel \underline{\mathtt{ff1} \leftarrow \mathtt{B!tkOr(order)}} \parallel \mathtt{Cs}^\bullet[\,\mid\,\mathtt{let\ f1=ret\ ff1}...]^f \parallel \underline{\mathtt{idle}^B} \parallel \mathtt{idle}^{Cn}$
1. $\longrightarrow \Phi \parallel \mathtt{B}^\bullet[\mathtt{o} \mapsto \mathtt{order} \mid \mathtt{let\ cc = hold\ 1\ Cf}...]^{ff1} \parallel \underline{\mathtt{Cs}^\bullet[\,\mid\,\mathtt{let\ f1=ret\ ff1}...]^f} \parallel \mathtt{idle}^{Cn}$
$\longrightarrow \Phi \parallel \mathtt{B}^\bullet[\mathtt{o} \mapsto \mathtt{order} \mid \mathtt{let\ cc = hold\ 1\ CC}...]^{ff1} \parallel \mathtt{Cs}^\bullet[\lambda \mid \mathtt{let\ x=y1?}...]^f \parallel \mathtt{idle}^{Cn}$
2. $\longrightarrow \Phi_0 \parallel \mathtt{B}^\bullet[\mathtt{o} \mapsto \mathtt{order} \mid \mathtt{let\ cc = ret\ CC}^1...]^{ff1} \parallel \mathtt{Cs}^\bullet[\lambda \mid ...]^f \parallel \mathtt{idle}^{Cn}$
$\longrightarrow \Phi_0 \parallel \mathtt{B}^\bullet[\lambda_0 \mid \mathtt{let\ c=mkCf(o,y2)}...]^{ff1} \parallel \mathtt{Cs}^\bullet[\lambda \mid ...]^f \parallel \mathtt{idle}^{Cn}$
$\longrightarrow \Phi_0 \parallel \mathtt{B}^\bullet[\lambda_0 \mid \mathtt{let\ c=ret\ Cf}^1...]^{ff1} \parallel \mathtt{Cs}^\bullet[\lambda \mid ...]^f \parallel \mathtt{idle}^{Cn}$
$\longrightarrow \Phi_0 \parallel \mathtt{B}^\bullet[\lambda_1 \mid \mathtt{let\ f4=Cn!plc(y3)}...]^{ff1} \parallel \mathtt{Cs}^\bullet[\lambda \mid ...]^f \parallel \mathtt{idle}^{Cn}$
3. $\longrightarrow \Phi_0 \parallel \underline{\mathtt{ff4} \leftarrow \mathtt{Cn!plc(Cf}^1)} \parallel \mathtt{B}^\bullet[\lambda_2 \mid \mathtt{let\ f4=ret\ ff4}...]^{ff1} \parallel \mathtt{Cs}^\bullet[\lambda \mid ...]^f \parallel \underline{\mathtt{idle}^{Cn}}$
$\longrightarrow \Phi_0 \parallel \underline{\mathtt{Cn}^\bullet[\mathtt{c} \mapsto \mathtt{Cf}^1 \mid \mathtt{rls\ 1\ c}^1;..]^{ff4}} \parallel \mathtt{B}^\bullet[\lambda_2 \mid \mathtt{let\ f4=ret\ ff4}...]^{ff1} \parallel \mathtt{Cs}^\bullet[\lambda \mid ...]^f$
4. $\longrightarrow \Phi_1 \parallel \mathtt{Cn}^\bullet[\mathtt{c} \mapsto \mathtt{Cf}^0 \mid \mathtt{ret\ u}]^{ff4} \parallel \mathtt{B}^\bullet[\lambda_2 \mid \mathtt{let\ f4=ret\ ff4}...]^{ff1} \parallel \mathtt{Cs}^\bullet[\lambda \mid ...]^f$
$\longrightarrow \Phi_1 \parallel \underline{\mathtt{ff4} \leftarrow \mathtt{u}} \parallel \mathtt{idle}^{Cn} \parallel \mathtt{B}^\bullet[\lambda_2 \mid \mathtt{let\ f4=ret\ ff4}...]^{ff1} \parallel \mathtt{Cs}^\bullet[\lambda \mid ...]^f$
$\longrightarrow \Phi_1 \parallel \underline{\mathtt{ff4} \leftarrow \mathtt{u}} \parallel \mathtt{idle}^{Cn} \parallel \mathtt{B}^\bullet[\lambda_3 \mid \mathtt{y4?};..]^{ff1} \parallel \mathtt{Cs}^\bullet[\lambda \mid ...]^f$
$\longrightarrow \Phi_1 \parallel \mathtt{idle}^{Cn} \parallel \mathtt{B}^\bullet[\lambda_3 \mid \mathtt{ret\ u}]^{ff1} \parallel \mathtt{Cs}^\bullet[\lambda \mid ...]^f \longrightarrow \quad ...$

$\Phi_0 = \mathtt{B} : \mathtt{CC}^0 \quad \Phi_1 = \mathtt{B} : \mathtt{CC}^0, \mathtt{Cn} : \mathtt{Cf}^1 \quad\quad \lambda = \mathtt{y1} \mapsto \mathtt{ff1} \quad \lambda_0 = \mathtt{o} \mapsto \mathtt{order}, \mathtt{y2} \mapsto \mathtt{CC}^1$
$\lambda_1 = \lambda_0, \mathtt{y3} \mapsto \mathtt{Cf}^1 \quad \lambda_2 = \lambda_0, \mathtt{y3} \mapsto \mathtt{Cf}^0 \quad \lambda_3 = \lambda_2, \mathtt{y4} \mapsto \mathtt{ff4}$

Fig. 5. A reduction sequence for Example 3

Types and type contexts. Types are then defined by the grammar:

$$T ::= \mathtt{Unit} \mid r^g \mid \mathtt{Fut}\langle T, \Phi \rangle$$

where Unit is the type of unit, r^g is the type of a resource with name r that has to be used according to the grade g, and $\mathtt{Fut}\langle T, \Phi \rangle$ is the type of a future. This specifies, beside the type T of the held value, an actor context Φ saying which resources will be available after synchronising on a future of this type. Note that for simplicity resource types are just resource names, i.e., they are singleton types.

Typing judgments rely, in addition to the actor contexts introduced in Sect. 3, on standard variable contexts $\Gamma, \Delta ::= \overline{x : T}$, which are finite partial maps from variables to types, and on future contexts $\Sigma, \Omega ::= \overline{f :_\mu \mathtt{Fut}\langle T, \Phi \rangle}$, which are also finite partial maps from future names to their types and marking μ that is either empty or χ. The use of the marking will be clarified later in this section.

As it is customary in graded type systems, we need operations for combining contexts. In particular, we consider the following operations and relations.

- We define addition and partial order on actor contexts $\Phi + \Psi$ and $\Phi \leq \Phi$, by extending pointwise the addition and the partial order of the grade monoid G first to resource environments ρ and then to actor contexts, assuming that resources and actors not appearing in the contexts associated with $\mathbf{0}$ and an empty resource environment, respectively.
- The sum of typing contexts $\Gamma = \Gamma_1 + \Gamma_2$ is defined by constructing the union of the variables defined in one context and not in the other and

$$\text{(T-CALL)} \quad \frac{\Sigma_i;\ \Gamma_i \vdash ve_i : T_i \quad i \in 1\ldots n \qquad \Sigma = \Sigma_1,\ldots,\Sigma_n \qquad \Gamma = \Gamma_1 + \cdots + \Gamma_n}{\Phi + \Theta;\ \Sigma;\ \Gamma \vdash_a^{k+3} b!m(\overline{ve}) : \mathtt{Fut}\langle T,\Psi\rangle;\ \Theta \qquad \mathtt{mtype}(b,m) = (\Phi, \overline{T} \to T, k, \Psi)}$$

$$\text{(T-AWT)} \quad \frac{\Sigma;\ \Gamma \vdash ve : \mathtt{Fut}\langle T,\Psi\rangle}{\Phi;\ \Sigma;\ \Gamma \vdash_a^1 ve? : T;\ \Phi + \Psi} \qquad \text{(T-RLS)} \quad \frac{\Sigma;\ \Gamma \vdash ve : r^h}{\Phi;\ \Sigma;\ \Gamma \vdash_a^1 \mathtt{release}\ g\ ve{:}\mathtt{Unit};\ a{:}r^g + \Phi}\ g \le h$$

$$\text{(T-HOLD)} \quad a : r^h + \Phi;\ \emptyset;\ \emptyset \vdash_a^1 \mathtt{hold}\ g\ r{:}r^g;\ \Phi \qquad g \le h$$

$$\text{(T-LET)} \quad \frac{\Phi_1;\ \Sigma_1;\ \Gamma_1 \vdash_a^m e_1 : T';\ \Phi_1' + \Phi_2' \qquad \Phi_2 + \Phi_1';\ \Sigma_2;\ \Gamma_2, x : T' \vdash_a^n e_2 : T;\ \Psi_2}{\Phi_1 + \Phi_2;\ \Sigma_1, \Sigma_2;\ \Gamma_1 + \Gamma_2 \vdash_a^{1+n+m} \mathtt{let}\ x = e_1\ \mathtt{in}\ e_2 : T;\ \Phi_2' + \Psi_2}$$

Fig. 6. Typing rules for expressions

$$\Gamma_1(x) = T_1 \ \wedge\ \Gamma_2(x) = T_2 \implies$$
$$(T_1 = T_2 = \mathtt{Unit}\ \wedge\ \Gamma(x) = \mathtt{Unit})\ \vee$$
$$(T_1 = r^{g_1}\ \wedge\ T_2 = r^{g_2}\ \wedge\ \Gamma(x) = r^{g_1+g_2})$$

As we can see a variable with a future type can be defined either in Γ_1 or Γ_2 but not in both, i.e., futures are typed linearly.

- for all contexts we will use a comma to denote their disjoint union. For instance, Σ, Ω is the union of Σ and Ω, which is defined only if they have disjoint domains.

Finally, we say that the typing context Γ *is discardable*, dubbed $dis(\Gamma)$, if no variable has a future type and for variables having a resource type, r^g, the grade g must be "discardable", i.e., $0 \le g$. This reflects the fact that futures are treated linearly and that our grade monoid is not necessarily affine.

Typing Rules for Expressions. The typing of value expressions is given by the judgement, $\Sigma;\ \Gamma \vdash ve : T$ where Γ and Σ contains variables and futures used by the value expression. The most significant rule is

$$\text{(T-VAR-R)} \quad \frac{}{\emptyset;\ x : r^h, \Gamma \vdash x^g : r^g} \qquad g \le h\ \wedge\ dis(\Gamma)$$

that types a graded variable x^g provided that x appears in the context with a grade h larger than or equal to g. Note that in this rule the future context is empty and additional (not used) variables are allowed only provided that they are discardable.

Expressions are typed through the judgement $\Phi;\ \Sigma;\ \Gamma \vdash_a^n e : T;\ \Psi$, partially defined in Fig. 6. Besides the type of the expression and the typing and future contexts containing variables and futures used in it, the judgements reports an actor name a, a natural number n and two actor contexts Φ and Ψ. The actor name a records the *actor running this expression*. The context Φ, dubbed *required actor context*, keeps track of the resources the expression requires from each actor for being executed, while Ψ, dubbed *produced actor context*, those it releases to the system, which could be used by subsequent expressions or by other threads having access to the future which this expression writes its result to. Finally, the number n provides a *measure* in number of steps of the effort required to terminate the execution of the expression.

To type method and primitive operation calls, we assume some additional typing information. For methods, apart from the information about parameters and body, given by mbody(a, m), we assume to have their typing information

$$\mathsf{mtype}(a, m) = (\varPhi, \overline{T} \to T, n, \varPsi)$$

Furthermore, we assume that when this is defined, then

$$\mathsf{mbody}(a, m) = (\overline{x}, e) \text{ and } \varPhi; \emptyset; \overline{x : T} \vdash_a^n e : T; \varPsi$$

that is, mtype(a, m) and mbody(a, m) are consistent.

Rule (T-CALL) checks that the arguments of a method call have the types specified by mtype, and assigns to the call a future type containing the return type of the method and the actor context it promises to make available when its execution terminates. The resources required by the method are added to the actor context required by the call, while the produced one is not affected. The measure is obtained by adding 3 to the measure of the method. These 3 additional units account for the three steps needed: one for sending the message, one for starting the thread handling the call, and one for terminating it.

Rule (T-AWT) checks that the value expression has a future type, assigns to the await expression the type of the value held by the future and adds to the actor environment produced by the await the actor context reported in the future type. In this way, we allow resources promised by the future to be used. The required actor context instead is not affected. Rules (T-HOLD) and (T-RLS) govern the holding and releasing of resources. A `hold` expression has a graded resource type with the same name and grade of the requested resource and adds it to the required actor context for the actor running the expression, but with a larger grade. Conversely, the argument of a `release` expression must have a graded resource type with a grade larger than the one that should be released. The resource is added with the released grade to the produced actor context for the actor running the expression. Rule (T-LET) is pretty standard except for the handling of actor contexts. The required and produced actor contexts of the `let` expression are obtained by summing up those of the two subexpressions, but removing from both the context $\varPhi'_1$. Indeed, this context provides resources which are used *internally* by the `let` expression: they are produced by e_1 and consumed by e_2. Therefore, we do not have to track them in the final typing. The measure of the `let` is just 1 plus the measure of the two subexpressions, so that we account for the step needed for passing the result of e_1 to e_2.

The variable and the future contexts in the conclusion of these rules are obtained by combining those in the premises: variable contexts are summed up with +, while future contexts are combined using the comma, ensuring that variables of graded resource types have a grade covering the needs of all premises and those with a future types and futures themselves are used only in one of the premises. Finally, all rules except (T-LET) have an actor context added to both the required and the produced ones in the conclusion, thus allowing an expression to promise additional resources provided that it requires them to the environment. This makes the rules more flexible, simplifying the proof of subject reduction.

$$\text{(T-THRD)} \frac{\Phi;\ \Sigma;\ \Gamma \vdash_a^n \lambda \mid e : T;\ \Phi'}{\Phi;\ \Sigma \vdash^{n+1} a^\alpha[\lambda \mid e]^f :: f{:}\mathsf{Fut}\langle T, \Phi'\rangle} \alpha \in \{\bullet, \circ\} \quad \text{(T-RES)} \frac{\Sigma;\ \emptyset \vdash v : T}{\Phi;\ \Sigma \vdash^0 f \leftarrow v :: f{:}\mathsf{Fut}\langle T, \Phi\rangle}$$

$$\text{(T-MSG)} \frac{\Sigma_i;\ \emptyset \vdash v : T_i \quad i \in 1 \ldots n}{\Phi;\ \Sigma_1, \ldots, \Sigma_n \vdash^{n+2} f \leftarrow a!m(\overline{v})::f{:}\mathsf{Fut}\langle T, \Phi'\rangle} \mathsf{mtype}(a,m) = (\Phi, \overline{T} \to T, n, \Phi')$$

$$\text{(T-PAR)} \frac{\Phi_1;\ \Sigma_1 \vdash^n P :: \Sigma_1', \Sigma_1'' \quad \Phi_2;\ \Sigma_2, \Sigma_1' \vdash^m Q :: \Sigma_2' \quad \mathsf{dom}(\Sigma_1'') \cap \mathsf{dom}(\Sigma_2) = \emptyset}{\Phi_1 + \Phi_2;\ \Sigma_1, \Sigma_2 \vdash^{n+m} P \parallel Q :: \Sigma_2', \mathsf{mark}(\Sigma_1'), \Sigma_1''}$$

$$\text{(T-CONF)} \frac{\Phi;\ \Sigma \vdash^n P :: \Sigma'}{\Phi_\Theta;\ \Sigma \vdash^n_\Theta \Psi \parallel P :: \Sigma'} \Phi + \Theta \le \Psi$$

Fig. 7. Rules for processes

Typing Rules for Processes and Configurations. Processes are typed by the judgement $\Phi;\ \Sigma \vdash^n P :: \Omega$, defined in Fig. 7. The actor context Φ tracks the resources required by the process. The future contexts Σ and Ω records the futures consumed and produced by the process, respectively, with their types. That is, one can prove that $fp(P) = \mathsf{dom}(\Sigma)$ and $fr(P) = \mathsf{dom}(\Omega)$. Note that there is no actor context on the right hand side, because resources can be made available to other thread only through futures. Rule (T-THRD) states that a thread (active or suspended) is well-typed with the actor context required by the running expression. The required futures are those of the expression in the local environment, while it produces only the future f assigned to it. Note that the type of the future f states that it will hold a value of the same type as the running expression and that it will provide resources of the produced actor context of the running expression. The measure is 1 plus the measure of the expression, where 1 accounts for the step needed for terminating the thread. This rule relies on an auxiliary typing judgment for expressions in a local environment $\Phi;\ \Sigma;\ \Gamma \vdash_a^n \lambda \mid e : T;\ \Omega$, which extracts a variable context from the local environment λ through the judgment $\Sigma \vdash \lambda :: \Gamma$ and uses it to typecheck the expression e. The resulting actor contexts are those of e, while the future context is the union of those typing λ and e. The formal definition can be found in [19]. Rules (T-RES) and (T-MSG) are similar except that they have to check a value and a method call, respectively, instead of an expression in a local environment. They only differ for the measure: the former has measure 0 as it is terminated, while the latter 2 plus the measure of the method, where the 2 accounts for the steps for starting and terminating the execution of this method.

The parallel composition of two threads is handled by Rule (T-PAR), which has to enforce the correct usage of futures, that is, they are consumed from left to right and used linearly. The key fact is that the rule allows the right process Q to consume futures produced by the left process P, recorded in the context Σ_1'. The other futures used by the two processes, which must be distinct, are propagated in the required future context of the parallel composition. The produced future context instead is the union of all the futures produced by the two processes, which again must be distinct. Note that the futures in Σ_1', i.e., those produced by P and consumed by Q, are not erased from the final context of produced futures, but rather they are marked by χ. This is needed for remembering that these futures have already been used in the process, and so they cannot appear elsewhere as they must be used linearly. Indeed, it is easy to see that marked futures cannot appear on the left-hand side of a typing judgment, hence they cannot be consumed by other processes. Last but not least, the side condition ensures that Σ_1' contains all futures consumed by Q matching a future produced by P. Also, the actor context and the measure are the sum of those of P and Q.

Lastly, configurations are type-checked by the judgement $\Phi; \Sigma \vdash_\Theta^a \sigma :: \Omega$ and defined by the Rule (T-CONF). This typechecks the process and requires that the actor context of the configuration suffices to cover the one required by the process plus a residual that annotates the judgement. The latter takes into account that the process may be part of a larger parallel composition and so the actor context in the configuration must provide resources also for the rest of the composition, modelled by the residual context.

Soundness. The main property of the type system is that well-typed configurations are *fairly terminating* [16]. This property does not forbid infinite computations, but guarantees that termination is always possible. Moreover, it entails several good properties of concurrent systems with asynchronous communication, such as livelock and orphan message freedom.

In our context, a configuration is *terminated* if it consists only of threads of the form $\mathtt{idle}^a$ or $f \leftarrow v$. Furthermore, a configuration σ is said to be *weakly terminating* if it can reach a terminated configuration. Then, a configuration σ is *fairly terminating* if, whenever $\sigma \longrightarrow \sigma'$, σ' is weakly terminating, i.e., σ can only reach weakly terminating configurations.

Following the proof strategy of [16], fair termination is an immediate consequence of two key properties of a type system: subject reduction and weak termination. In our resource-aware setting, the former is stated as follows:

Theorem 1 (Subject reduction). *If $\Phi; \Sigma \vdash_\Theta^n \sigma :: \Sigma'$ and $\sigma \longrightarrow \sigma'$, then it exists Ψ, m, Ω' such that $\Psi; \Sigma \vdash_\Theta^m \sigma' :: \Omega'$, where $\Omega' = \Sigma', \mathsf{mark}(\Omega'')$ with Ω'' fresh.*

This guarantees that, for a well-typed configuration, reduction steps do not affect its "interface", i.e., the futures consumed and produced by the configuration remains essentially the same, except that the latter ones can grow, but only by fresh and marked ones. Furthermore, the residual actor context is also preserved, ensuring that resources required by other processes, that will be composed with the current configuration, are not affected.

On the other hand, the weak termination result states that well-typed and closed configurations are weakly terminating.

Theorem 2 (Weak termination). *If $\Phi;\ \emptyset \vdash^n \sigma :: \Sigma'$ then there exists a reduction $\sigma \longrightarrow^* \sigma'$ such that σ' is terminated.*

This result relies on a key lemma, dubbed "helpful direction", showing that for a well-typed and closed configuration with a positive measure, it is always possible to find a reduction step making the measure decrease. Moreover, we have that well-typed and closed configurations with measure 0 are terminated. Notice that this auxiliary result encapsulates deadlock freedom.

Then, since well-typed and closed configurations are weakly terminating and, by subject reduction, they can only reduce to other well-typed and closed configurations, we have that these are fairly terminating.

Finally, we observe that fair termination implies that well-typed and closed configurations enjoy the following properties:

- *input-lock freedom*: every future is eventually fulfilled,
- *orphan message freedom*: every method call is eventually executed,
- *resource safety*: the execution of hold expressions is never blocked.

These hold because a well-typed configuration can always eventually terminate, i.e., reach a configuration with no pending threads and no pending messages, hence all futures have been fulfilled, all method calls have been executed and all hold expressions have succeeded. We refer the readers to [19] for the complete proof of fair termination.

5 Related Work and Conclusions

We introduced a core calculus for resource-aware active objects, which is parametric over a subtractive grade monoid, representing the availability of resources. On top of the calculus, we defined a (graded) type system ensuring that well-typed configurations are fairly terminating. This property does not forbid non-termination, but ensures that termination is always possible. In this way, we can model processes with a potentially infinite execution, e.g., a barista taking an arbitrary amount of orders, but still retaining good properties such as deadlock, livelock and orphan message freedom. In addition, fair termination entails that well-typed configurations are resource-safe, i.e., threads always succeed in getting hold of resources.

Related Work. Our work is inspired by the modelling of workflow systems with active objects proposed in [5], for the looking at workflows in the active object environment; to the resource-aware calculus of [11], for the association of resources to variables; and to [16] for the use of indexed type system to ensure fair termination. Resource sensitive active objects have been adopted to model distributed systems and concurrent business process workflows [5,29], by extension of core ABS [28] with explicit notion of time advancement and resources to capture resource consumption. In contrast to our core calculus, resources in these two languages are directly accessible by (groups of) active objects, and cannot be transformed. In addition, resources in [29] are recovered for each interval when time advances, i.e., they are unlimited. Graded type systems, also dubbed coeffect systems, were introduced in [14,37,38] as a tool for statically controlling how programs use their context, i.e., their free variables, which abstractly represent external resources needed by programs. In order to properly state a resource-aware variant of type soundness for graded type systems, graded operational semantics were also considered [10,11,15,41], where variables are annotated by grades and, whenever a variable is used, its grade is consumed. This mechanism is usually non-deterministic, while our calculus supports a deterministic resource consumption thanks to the use of a subtraction operation.

Finally, in [31,32] graded types were introduced into the concurrent scenario for a channel based communication language with in a session-type system. They use grades to (re)introduce a safe non-linear usage of channels, which are the resources considered in these works. Instead, we focus on future based communication of multithreaded active objects, where resources are values with a limited availability.

Type systems ensuring fair termination have been studied in the context of synchronous session types [16,17,20]. The key idea to enforce this property, which is the same we have used in our context, is to assign a measure to each process quantifying the effort, i.e., the number of steps, needed to reach termination. Indeed, this approach resembles techniques used in the complexity analysis of concurrent systems. Notably, *resource-aware session types*[3] [22,23,25], augment standard session types with measure annotation designed to perform amortized cost analysis of concurrent system, where the cost is determined by the number of exchanged messages. This approach is closely related to fair termination and a more precise comparison can be found in [20]. Finally, we mention that in the literature there are other techniques to guarantee termination of concurrent system. For instance, Deng and Sangiorgi [26] annotate types with numbers representing priority levels used to constrain the order in which channels can be used. Note that this technique is designed to enforce strong normalization, i.e., no infinite execution is allowed, which is a much more restrictive property than fair termination, which is the target of our type system.

Future Work. This work lays a theoretical foundation for the formalisation of complex workflow systems with passive resources. To test the effectiveness of the proposed approach, it will be important to develop case studies comparing

---

[3] Note that these types are resource aware in a different sense with respect to our system: in a sense the resource they control is time while we focus on values with a limited availability.

our system with other solutions and identifying the different subtractive grade monoids required by the concrete application domains.

On the technical side, we are working on improving some limitations of the system. First, the linear treatment of futures is a sound but quite restrictive solution as, for instance, it forces to await on futures even if their value is discardable. A natural possibility to make the system more flexible is to grade futures as well. This poses non-trivial challenges for both the semantics and the type system, and it may require to further extend the algebraic structure of grades. Another limitation of the current type system is the way it guarantees fair termination. Essentially, it allows programs where termination only depends on the exchanged messages (method calls) and not on the exchanged values (parameters). Taking values into account as well would require the adoption of rather sophisticated techniques such as dependent types or sized types with arithmetic refinements [8,24,25,40]. Finally, another interesting extension of this work is to consider the full object-oriented power of active objects, by considering also object instantiation, thus enabling the modelling of systems with a variable and dynamically adjusted number of actors. As for the implementation of the type checking algorithm, a promising direction is along the lines of the one in [36].

Acknowledgement. We would like to thank the anonymous reviewers for their valuable feedback and constructive suggestions. This work is part of the CROFLOW project: Enabling Highly Automated Cross-Organisational Workflow Planning, funded by the Research Council of Norway (grant no. 326249); and is partially funded by the MUR project: T-LADIES (PRIN 2020TL3X8X); the COST action: EUROPROOFNET (CA20111); and has the financial support of the Università del Piemonte Orientale. The first author has been funded by the European Union - NextGenerationEU and by the Ministry of University and Research (MUR), National Recovery and Resilience Plan (NRRP), Mission 4, Component 2, Investment 1.5, project "RAISE - Robotics and AI for Socio-economic Empowerment" (ECS00000035).

References

1. Aalst, W.M.P.: Verification of workflow nets. In: Azéma, P., Balbo, G. (eds.) ICATPN 1997. LNCS, vol. 1248, pp. 407–426. Springer, Heidelberg (1997). https://doi.org/10.1007/3-540-63139-9_48
2. van der Aalst, W.M.P.: The application of petri nets to workflow management. J. Circuits Syst. Comput. **8**(1), 21–66 (1998). https://doi.org/10.1142/S0218126698000043
3. Abel, A., Bernardy, J.: A unified view of modalities in type systems. Proc. ACM Program. Lang. **4**(ICFP), 90:1–90:28 (2020). https://doi.org/10.1145/3408972
4. Agha, G.A.: Actors: a model of concurrent computation in distributed systems (parallel processing, semantics, open, programming languages, artificial intelligence). Ph.D. thesis, University of Michigan, USA (1985). http://hdl.handle.net/2027.42/160629
5. Ali, M.R., Lamo, Y., Pun, V.K.I.: Cost analysis for a resource sensitive workflow modelling language. Sci. Comput. Program. **225**, 102896 (2023). https://doi.org/10.1016/J.SCICO.2022.102896

6. Ali, M.R., Pun, V.K.I., Román-Díez, G.: EasyRpl: a web-based tool for modelling and analysis of cross-organisational workflows. CoRR abs/2502.20972 (2025). https://doi.org/10.48550/ARXIV.2502.20972
7. Atkey, R.: Syntax and semantics of quantitative type theory. In: Dawar, A., Grädel, E. (eds.) Proceedings of the 33rd Annual ACM/IEEE Symposium on Logic in Computer Science, LICS 2018, Oxford, UK, 09–12 July 2018, pp. 56–65. ACM (2018). https://doi.org/10.1145/3209108.3209189
8. Baillot, P., Ghyselen, A.: Types for complexity of parallel computation in pi-calculus. ACM Trans. Program. Lang. Syst. **44**(3), 15:1–15:50 (2022). https://doi.org/10.1145/3495529
9. Baker, H.G., Hewitt, C.: The incremental garbage collection of processes. In: Low, J. (ed.) Proceedings of the 1977 Symposium on Artificial Intelligence and Programming Languages, USA, 15–17 August 1977, pp. 55–59. ACM (1977). https://doi.org/10.1145/800228.806932
10. Bianchini, R., Dagnino, F., Giannini, P., Zucca, E.: Multi-graded featherweight java. In: Ali, K., Salvaneschi, G. (eds.) 37th European Conference on Object-Oriented Programming, ECOOP 2023, 17–21 July 2023, Seattle, Washington, United States. LIPIcs, vol. 263, pp. 3:1–3:27. Schloss Dagstuhl - Leibniz-Zentrum für Informatik (2023). https://doi.org/10.4230/LIPICS.ECOOP.2023.3
11. Bianchini, R., Dagnino, F., Giannini, P., Zucca, E.: Resource-aware soundness for big-step semantics. Proc. ACM Program. Lang. **7**(OOPSLA2), 1281–1309 (2023). https://doi.org/10.1145/3622843
12. de Boer, F.S., et al.: A survey of active object languages. ACM Comput. Surv. **50**(5), 76:1–76:39 (2017). https://doi.org/10.1145/3122848
13. Brandauer, S., et al.: Parallel objects for multicores: a Glimpse at the parallel language ENCORE. In: Bernardo, M., Johnsen, E.B. (eds.) SFM 2015. LNCS, vol. 9104, pp. 1–56. Springer, Cham (2015). https://doi.org/10.1007/978-3-319-18941-3_1
14. Brunel, A., Gaboardi, M., Mazza, D., Zdancewic, S.: A core quantitative coeffect calculus. In: Shao, Z. (ed.) ESOP 2014. LNCS, vol. 8410, pp. 351–370. Springer, Heidelberg (2014). https://doi.org/10.1007/978-3-642-54833-8_19
15. Choudhury, P., Eades III, H., Eisenberg, R.A., Weirich, S.: A graded dependent type system with a usage-aware semantics. Proc. ACM Program. Lang. **5**(POPL), 1–32 (2021). https://doi.org/10.1145/3434331
16. Ciccone, L., Dagnino, F., Padovani, L.: Fair termination of multiparty sessions. J. Log. Algebraic Methods Program. **139**, 100964 (2024). https://doi.org/10.1016/J.JLAMP.2024.100964
17. Ciccone, L., Padovani, L.: Fair termination of binary sessions. Proc. ACM Program. Lang. **6**(POPL), 1–30 (2022). https://doi.org/10.1145/3498666
18. Ciccone, L., Padovani, L.: An infinitary proof theory of linear logic ensuring fair termination in the linear π-calculus. In: Klin, B., Lasota, S., Muscholl, A. (eds.) 33rd International Conference on Concurrency Theory, CONCUR 2022, 12–16 September 2022, Warsaw, Poland. LIPIcs, vol. 243, pp. 36:1–36:18. Schloss Dagstuhl - Leibniz-Zentrum für Informatik (2022). https://doi.org/10.4230/LIPICS.CONCUR.2022.36
19. Dagnino, F., Giannini, P., Pun, V.K.I., Torrella, U.: Fair termination for resource-aware active objects (2025). https://arxiv.org/abs/2508.15333
20. Dagnino, F., Padovani, L.: sMALL CaPS: an infinitary linear logic for a calculus of pure sessions. In: Bruni, A., Momigliano, A., Pradella, M., Rossi, M., Cheney, J. (eds.) Proceedings of the 26th International Symposium on Principles and Practice

of Declarative Programming, PPDP 2024, Milano, Italy, 9–11 September 2024, pp. 4:1–4:13. ACM (2024). https://doi.org/10.1145/3678232.3678234
21. Dal Lago, U., Gavazzo, F.: A relational theory of effects and coeffects. Proc. ACM Program. Lang. **6**(POPL), 1–28 (2022). https://doi.org/10.1145/3498692
22. Das, A., Balzer, S., Hoffmann, J., Pfenning, F., Santurkar, I.: Resource-aware session types for digital contracts. In: 34th IEEE Computer Security Foundations Symposium, CSF 2021, Dubrovnik, Croatia, 21–25 June 2021, pp. 1–16. IEEE (2021). https://doi.org/10.1109/CSF51468.2021.00004
23. Das, A., Hoffmann, J., Pfenning, F.: Work analysis with resource-aware session types. In: Dawar, A., Grädel, E. (eds.) Proceedings of the 33rd Annual ACM/IEEE Symposium on Logic in Computer Science, LICS 2018, Oxford, UK, 09–12 2018, pp. 305–314. ACM (2018). https://doi.org/10.1145/3209108.3209146
24. Das, A., Pfenning, F.: Session types with arithmetic refinements. In: Konnov, I., Kovács, L. (eds.) 31st International Conference on Concurrency Theory, CONCUR 2020, 1–4 September 2020, Vienna, Austria (Virtual Conference). LIPIcs, vol. 171, pp. 13:1–13:18. Schloss Dagstuhl - Leibniz-Zentrum für Informatik (2020). https://doi.org/10.4230/LIPICS.CONCUR.2020.13
25. Das, A., Pfenning, F.: Rast: a language for resource-aware session types. Log. Methods Comput. Sci. **18**(1) (2022). https://doi.org/10.46298/LMCS-18(1:9)2022
26. Deng, Y., Sangiorgi, D.: Ensuring termination by typability. In: Levy, J.-J., Mayr, E.W., Mitchell, J.C. (eds.) TCS 2004. IIFIP, vol. 155, pp. 619–632. Springer, Boston, MA (2004). https://doi.org/10.1007/1-4020-8141-3_47
27. Gaboardi, M., Katsumata, S., Orchard, D.A., Breuvart, F., Uustalu, T.: Combining effects and coeffects via grading. In: Garrigue, J., Keller, G., Sumii, E. (eds.) Proceedings of the 21st ACM SIGPLAN International Conference on Functional Programming, ICFP 2016, Nara, Japan, 18–22 September 2016, pp. 476–489. ACM (2016). https://doi.org/10.1145/2951913.2951939
28. Johnsen, E.B., Hähnle, R., Schäfer, J., Schlatte, R., Steffen, M.: ABS: a core language for abstract behavioral specification. In: Aichernig, B.K., de Boer, F.S., Bonsangue, M.M. (eds.) FMCO 2010. LNCS, vol. 6957, pp. 142–164. Springer, Heidelberg (2011). https://doi.org/10.1007/978-3-642-25271-6_8
29. Johnsen, E.B., Schlatte, R., Tarifa, S.L.T.: Integrating deployment architectures and resource consumption in timed object-oriented models. J. Log. Algebraic Methods Program. **84**(1), 67–91 (2015). https://doi.org/10.1016/J.JLAMP.2014.07.001
30. Levy, P.B., Power, J., Thielecke, H.: Modelling environments in call-by-value programming languages. Inf. Comput. **185**(2), 182–210 (2003). https://doi.org/10.1016/S0890-5401(03)00088-9
31. Marshall, D., Orchard, D.: Replicate, reuse, repeat: capturing non-linear communication via session types and graded modal types. In: Carbone, M., Neykova, R. (eds.) Proceedings of the 13th International Workshop on Programming Language Approaches to Concurrency and Communication-cEntric Software, PLACES@ETAPS 2022, Munich, Germany, 3 April 2022. EPTCS, vol. 356, pp. 1–11 (2022). https://doi.org/10.4204/EPTCS.356.1
32. Marshall, D., Orchard, D.: Non-linear communication via graded modal session types. Inf. Comput. **301**, 105234 (2024). https://doi.org/10.1016/J.IC.2024.105234
33. McBride, C.: I got plenty o' Nuttin'. In: Lindley, S., McBride, C., Trinder, P., Sannella, D. (eds.) A List of Successes That Can Change the World. LNCS, vol. 9600, pp. 207–233. Springer, Cham (2016). https://doi.org/10.1007/978-3-319-30936-1_12

34. zur Muehlen, M.: Organizational management in workflow applications - issues and perspectives. Inf. Technol. Manag. **5**(3-4), 271–291 (2004). https://doi.org/10.1023/B:ITEM.0000031582.55219.2B
35. Niehren, J., Schwinghammer, J., Smolka, G.: A concurrent lambda calculus with futures. Theor. Comput. Sci. **364**(3), 338–356 (2006). https://doi.org/10.1016/J.TCS.2006.08.016
36. Orchard, D., Liepelt, V.B., Eades III, H.: Quantitative program reasoning with graded modal types **3**(ICFP), 110:1–110:30 (2019). https://doi.org/10.1145/3341714
37. Petricek, T., Orchard, D., Mycroft, A.: Coeffects: unified static analysis of context-dependence. In: Fomin, F.V., Freivalds, R., Kwiatkowska, M., Peleg, D. (eds.) ICALP 2013. LNCS, vol. 7966, pp. 385–397. Springer, Heidelberg (2013). https://doi.org/10.1007/978-3-642-39212-2_35
38. Petricek, T., Orchard, D.A., Mycroft, A.: Coeffects: a calculus of context-dependent computation. In: Jeuring, J., Chakravarty, M.M.T. (eds.) Proceedings of the 19th ACM SIGPLAN International Conference on Functional Programming, Gothenburg, Sweden, 1–3 September 2014, pp. 123–135. ACM (2014). https://doi.org/10.1145/2628136.2628160
39. Schäfer, J., Poetzsch-Heffter, A.: JCoBox: generalizing active objects to concurrent components. In: D'Hondt, T. (ed.) ECOOP 2010. LNCS, vol. 6183, pp. 275–299. Springer, Heidelberg (2010). https://doi.org/10.1007/978-3-642-14107-2_13
40. Somayyajula, S., Pfenning, F.: Type-based termination for futures. In: Felty, A.P. (ed.) 7th International Conference on Formal Structures for Computation and Deduction, FSCD 2022, 2–5 August 2022, Haifa, Israel. LIPIcs, vol. 228, pp. 12:1–12:21. Schloss Dagstuhl - Leibniz-Zentrum für Informatik (2022). https://doi.org/10.4230/LIPICS.FSCD.2022.12
41. Torczon, C., Acevedo, E.S., Agrawal, S., Velez-Ginorio, J., Weirich, S.: Effects and coeffects in call-by-push-value. Proc. ACM Program. Lang. **8**(OOPSLA2), 1108–1134 (2024). https://doi.org/10.1145/3689750

A Formal Foundation for Equational Reasoning on Probabilistic Programs

Reynald Affeldt[1(✉)] [iD], Yoshihiro Ishiguro[1,2], and Zachary Stone[3]

[1] National Institute of Advanced Industrial Science and Technology (AIST), Tokyo, Japan
reynald.affeldt@aist.go.jp, jb.15r.1213@s.thers.ac.jp
[2] Nagoya University, Nagoya, Japan
[3] The MathComp-Analysis Development Team, Boston, MA, USA

Abstract. Probabilistic programs with sampling and scoring are used to write probabilistic models to make probabilistic inferences. Despite their effectful nature, such programs can actually be verified by means of equational reasoning. We propose a formal foundation in the Rocq prover to mechanize such verifications. For that purpose, we extend an existing library for Lebesgue integration and formalize standard probability distributions. Using the resulting library, we extend the intrinsically-typed syntax and the kernel-based semantics of an encoding of a probabilistic programming language. Thanks to these extensions, we mechanize the main running examples of Shan's tutorial on equational reasoning for probabilistic programming at POPL 2018's TutorialFest.

Keywords: Probabilistic programming · equational reasoning · real analysis

1 Introduction

Probabilistic programming languages have many applications. They can be used to write probabilistic models to make probabilistic inferences. There exist several implementations of such probabilistic programming languages: Anglican [41], Hakaru [26], Pyro [10], Stan [39], etc. Probabilistic programming languages can also be used to write security proofs (as in, e.g., [14]) and of course to write randomized algorithms.

The many applications of probabilistic programming languages have raised the question of their formal verification. In particular, Shan has advocated for an approach using equational reasoning [32]. This idea has however not yet materialized as a tool. Heimerdinger and Shan did experiment with the formalization of equational reasoning for measures in the Rocq proof assistant but it was partly axiomatized [15]. Affeldt et al. have formalized monadic equational reasoning in Rocq [4,5]; this includes reasoning about probabilistic programs but only with sampling. Though not specifically about equational reasoning, there also exist formalizations of probabilistic programming languages in proof assistants. Zhang and Amin studied nested queries and recursion using a partially axiomatized formalization of measure theory in ROCQ [42]. Saito and Affeldt have formalized a syntax and a denotational semantics for a first-order probabilistic programming language called sfPPL in ROCQ [29]. It is based on a formalization of kernels [3] which itself relies on a formalization of measure theory and Lebesgue integration [1] available as part of the MATHCOMP-ANALYSIS library [23]. Hirata et al. provide in Isabelle/HOL a formalization of the semantics of higher-order probabilistic programs [17,18] using quasi-Borel spaces [16].

In this paper, we propose a formal foundation in the ROCQ prover and demonstrate it can be used to mechanize equational reasoning for probabilistic programs as advocated by Shan [32]. For that purpose, we extend the formalization of sfPPL [29] which originally featured only a handful a probability distributions to sample from or to score with. Yet, it turns out that the formalization of more probability distributions requires a substantial extension of MATHCOMP-ANALYSIS [23], the underlying library for real analysis used by sfPPL. In particular, when new probability measures to sample from are added, one must prove that the sampling expression as a function to the σ-algebra of probability measures is indeed measurable. Therefore, we start by extending MATHCOMP-ANALYSIS with a toolbox of lemmas to compute Lebesgue integrals such as the second fundamental theorem of calculus and its consequences (integration by parts and by substitution), for bounded and unbounded intervals, as well as continuity and differentiation under integral (Sect. 3). To the best of our knowledge, this is the first time that all these standard lemmas are formalized as an integrated library in ROCQ. We use this toolbox to develop the theory of probability distributions, including the beta and the normal distribution (Sect. 4). Using these new theories, we extend sfPPL with new probability distributions (Sect. 5) and use this extended language to mechanize the running examples from Shan's tutorial on equational reasoning for probabilistic programming [32]: Eddy's table game [12] (Sect. 6) and observation of a noisy draw (Sect. 7).

This paper starts with a reminder of the relevant mathematical notions (Sect. 2) and comes with a ROCQ development [6].

2 Mathematical Background

General Mathematical Notations. We use $f|_A$ to denote the restriction of the function f to the set A. We use $f(x) \xrightarrow[x \to a]{} l$ to denote the fact that the function $f(x)$ tends towards l when x tends towards a. We denote by $f(x) \xrightarrow[x \to a^+]{} l$ (resp. $f(x) \xrightarrow[x \to a^-]{} l$) the fact that the function $f(x)$ tends towards l when x tends towards a with condition $a < x$ (resp. $x < a$).

Measure Theory. A σ-algebra on a set X is a collection of subsets of X that contains the empty set $\emptyset$ and that is closed under complement and countable union. We denote such a σ-algebra by Σ_X, call *measurable sets* the sets in Σ_X and *measurable type* a type T equipped with a σ-algebra.

If Σ_X and Σ_Y are two σ-algebras, a *measurable function* $f : X \to Y$ is such that, for all measurable subsets $B \in \Sigma_Y$, the inverse image is a measurable subset $f^{-1}(B) \in \Sigma_X$.

A (non-negative) *measure* is a function $\mu : \Sigma_X \to [0, \infty]$ such that $\mu(\emptyset) = 0$ and μ is σ-additive, i.e., $\sum_i \mu(A_i) = \mu(\bigcup_i A_i)$ (where the sum is countable) for pairwise-disjoint measurable sets A_i. We write $k \cdot \mu$ for a measure μ scaled by a non-negative real number k.

A *probability measure* on Σ_X is a measure μ such that $\mu(X) = 1$. The Dirac probability measure is denoted by $\delta_a A$; it is 1 when $a \in A$ and 0 otherwise. We will display the probability measure pm as $\underline{pm}$ to distinguish probability measures from other measures.

We denote by $\int_{x \in A} f \mathbf{d}\mu(x)$ the integral of the function f over the set A w.r.t. the measure μ.

A *kernel* $X \rightsquigarrow Y$ is a function $k : X \to \Sigma_Y \to [0, \infty]$ such that (i) for all x, $k\,x$ is a measure and (ii) for all measurable set U, $x \mapsto k\,x\,U$ is a measurable function. We can see k as a family of measures indexed by X. A kernel $k : X \rightsquigarrow Y$ is a *finite kernel* when there is a finite bound r such that for all x, $k\,x\,Y < r$. Let us denote the type of finite kernels by $X \xrightsquigarrow{\text{fin}} Y$. A kernel $k : X \rightsquigarrow Y$ is an *s-finite kernel* when there is a sequence s of finite kernels such that $k = \sum_{i=0}^{\infty} s_i$. Let us denote by $X \xrightsquigarrow{\text{s-fin}} Y$ the type of s-finite kernels. We also denote by $X \xrightsquigarrow{\text{prob}} Y$ the type of *probability kernels*, i.e., the type of finite kernels k such that $\forall x, k\,x\,X = 1$.

3 A Toolbox to Compute Lebesgue Integrals in ROCQ

Our first step is to provide in ROCQ enough theory about the Lebesgue integral to formalize the probability distributions used in Shan's tutorial. This requires to develop a toolbox of lemmas of general interest such as the second fundamental theorem of calculus for continuous functions, differentiation under integral, etc.

3.1 Continuity and Derivability at the Borders of Intervals

We start by stressing one aspect of our formalization: the formalization of continuity and differentiation conditions at the borders of intervals, since the design of these conditions is important in practice.

The default notation for continuity of a function `f` over a set `A` in MATHCOMP-ANALYSIS is `{in A, continuous f}`. It means continuity at all points in `A`, i.e., $\forall a \in A, f(x) \xrightarrow[x \to a]{} f(a)$. This is often too strong a requirement because in particular continuity in a closed interval $[a, b]$ depends on values of `f` to the left of a and to the right of b, which usually is not what is intended. To deal with such situations, MATHCOMP-ANALYSIS has been extended with the notation `{within A, continuous f}` to mean that the function f is continuous for the subspace topology of `A` [7, § 5.1]. In particular, for a closed interval ``[a, b]``, `{within `[a, b], continuous f}` is equivalent to: f is continuous in $]a, b[$, $f(x) \xrightarrow[x \to a^+]{} f(a)$, and $f(x) \xrightarrow[x \to b^-]{} f(b)$. Put formally:

```
Lemma continuous_within_itvP {R : realType} a b (f : R -> R) : a < b ->
  {within `[a, b], continuous f} <->
  {in `]a, b[, continuous f} /\ f @ a^'+ --> f a /\ f @ b^'- --> f b.
```

Similarly to continuity, derivability in a closed interval $[a,b]$ is in general too strong a requirement. To deal with such situations, we introduce a predicate `derivable_oo_continuous_bnd f a b` defined as the conjunction of the following three propositions: f is differentiable in $]a,b[$, $f(x) \xrightarrow[x \to a^+]{} f(a)$, and $f(x) \xrightarrow[x \to b^-]{} f(b)$. Here is the corresponding formal definition [6, `realfun.v`]:

```
Context {R : numFieldType} {V : normedModType R}.
Definition derivable_oo_continuous_bnd (f : R -> V) x y := {in `]x, y[,
  forall x, derivable f x 1} /\ f @ x^'+ --> f x /\ f @ y^'- --> f y.
```

The `derivable` predicate formalizes the eponymous notion [23, `derive.v`].

3.2 Second Fundamental Theorem of Calculus for Continuous Functions

The first important lemma to compute integrals is the second fundamental theorem of calculus (FTC) for continuous functions[1]. Ignoring the precise hypotheses for the time being, it says that for a continuous function f with an antiderivative F, we have $\int_{x \in [a,b]} f(x) \mathrm{d}\mu = F(b) - F(a)$. Put formally[2]:

```
1  Corollary Rintegral_continuous_FTC2 f F a b : a <= b ->
2    {within `[a, b], continuous f} ->
3    derivable_oo_continuous_bnd F a b ->
4    {in `]a, b[, F^`() =1 f} ->
5    \int[mu]_(x in `[a, b]) f x = F b - F a.
```

Line 2 states the continuity of `f` within $[a,b]$ and line 3 states the derivability of `F`, as defined in the previous section. Line 4 states that `F` is an antiderivative of `f` in the open interval $]a,b[$; the ASCII notation `^`() is for derivatives.

One can see lines 2–4 as a formalization of what one could mean when stating that `f` belongs to the class C^1 of differentiable functions whose derivative is continuous, *except* that here we make the conditions at the borders precise. Indeed, informal presentations can indeed be sloppy about the conditions at the borders of the interval of integration. This is for example the case of standard textbooks (e.g., [28, p. 324]) where F is derivable in $[a,b]$ or the Wikipedia page on the FTC [40] where f is moreover continuous in $[a,b]$: these are too strong and formalizing them as such might hamper the application of the resulting lemma in practice. Our interpretation is that in pencil-and-paper proofs, when dealing with a closed interval, one sometimes implicitly thinks about any open interval larger than the closed one or implicitly restricts the function to the subspace

---

[1] This is not exactly the second FTC whose general version is stated for an absolutely continuous function.
[2] For a bounded interval. See, e.g., variants `{ge0,le0}_continuous_FTC2y` [6] for an unbounded interval.

topology of the closed interval. Our use of continuity-within is a formalization of the latter. This makes our formal statement of the second FTC easier to apply, as illustrated by the following example.

We use the second FTC to compute the integral of the indicator function of the interval $[0,1]$. The latter is defined as follows: $1|_{[0,1]}(x) \stackrel{\text{def}}{=} \begin{cases} 1 \ (0 \le x \le 1) \\ 0 \ (\text{otherwise}) \end{cases}$. The function $1|_{[0,1]}$ is continuous in $]0,1[$ but not continuous at 0 and 1, since

$$1|_{[0,1]}(x) \xrightarrow[x \to 0^+]{} 1|_{[0,1]}(0) = 1 \quad \text{and} \quad 1|_{[0,1]}(x) \xrightarrow[x \to 0^-]{} 0, \text{ and}$$

$$1|_{[0,1]}(x) \xrightarrow[x \to 1^-]{} 1|_{[0,1]}(1) = 1 \quad \text{and} \quad 1|_{[0,1]}(x) \xrightarrow[x \to 1^+]{} 0.$$

In other words, we only have continuity of $1|_{[0,1]}$ within $]0,1[$ and therefore we can use our formalization of the second FTC which has a weak-enough hypothesis about continuity: $\int_{t \in [0,1]} 1|_{[0,1]}(t) \mathrm{d}\mu = \mathbf{id}(1) - \mathbf{id}(0) = 1 - 0 = 1$. Note that we used the fact that the identity function $\mathbf{id}$ is an antiderivative of $1|_{[0,1]}$ for $x \in [0,1]$. A formalization of second FTC requiring continuity in the closed interval would not have been directly usable.

In fact, the conditions at the borders also play an important role in the proof of the second FTC (see [6]).

3.3 Integration by Parts and by Substitution

Integration by parts is a well-known equation to find the integral of the product of functions F and g (with G an antiderivative of g and f the derivative of F):

$$\int_{x \in [a,b]} F(x)g(x) \mathrm{d}\mu = F(b)G(b) - F(a)G(a) - \int_{x \in [a,b]} f(x)G(x) \mathrm{d}\mu.$$

See `Rintegration_by_parts` [6, ftc.v] for a formal statement. The proof is a consequence of the second FTC (Sect. 3.2) and of the product rule for derivation [2].

Integration by substitution (a.k.a. change of variables) is another important lemma to compute integrals. Let us consider the integration of a function G over the interval $[F(a), F(b)]$ where F is an increasing function F. Then we have:

$$\int_{x \in [F(a), F(b)]} G(x) \mathrm{d}\mu = \int_{x \in [a,b]} G(F(x)) \cdot F'(x) \mathrm{d}\mu.$$

We have formally proved this formula:

```
1  Lemma increasing_change F G a b : a < b ->
2    {in `[a, b] &, {homo F : x y / x < y}} ->
3    {within `[a, b], continuous F^`()} ->
4    derivable_oo_continuous_bnd F a b ->
5    {within `[F a, F b], continuous G} ->
6    \int[mu]_(x in `[F a, F b]) (G x)%:E =
7    \int[mu]_(x in `[a, b]) (((G \o F) * F^`()) x)%:E.
```

The fact that f is increasing is stated at line 2. Regarding the function F, we need the continuity within $[a,b]$ of its derivative (line 3) and its derivability (line 4). As for the function G, we only need its continuity within $[F(a), F(b)]$ (line 5). This can be proved as a consequence of the first FTC [7, § 10.1] and of the second FTC (Sect. 3.2). Note that contrary to the second FTC (Sect. 3.2) and integration by parts, we display a statement for the integral of extended real numbers-valued functions instead of real functions; this explains the presence of the notation %:E in the conclusion of the lemma to inject real numbers into extended real numbers.

See [6, ftc.v] for the formal proofs for increasing and decreasing functions as well as extensions to unbounded intervals.

3.4 Differentiation and Continuity Under Integral

We mention two more facts about integration that are useful to prove the properties of the normal distribution. The first one is differentiation under the integral sign. Precisely: suppose that B is a measurable set and that $a \in I = \,]u,v[$ is a real number. We consider a function $f(x,y)$ such that for all $x \in I$, $f(x,\cdot)$ is integrable and such that for all $x \in I$ and $y \in B$, $f(\cdot, y)$ is derivable at x. If we are also given a non-negative function $G(y)$ integrable in B such that for all $x \in I$ and $y \in B$, $\left|\frac{\partial f}{\partial x}(x,y)\right| \leq G(y)$, we have:

$$\frac{\int_{y \in B} f(a+h, y)\mathrm{d}\mu - \int_{y \in B} f(a, y)\mathrm{d}\mu}{h} \xrightarrow[h \to 0, h \neq 0]{} \int_{y \in B} \frac{\partial f}{\partial x}(a, y)\mathrm{d}\mu.$$

Intuitively, this lemma lets us commute differentiation and integration. It is a consequence of the dominated convergence theorem available in MATHCOMP-ANALYSIS [1, § 6.7] and is used to compute the Gauss integral. For the formalization, see the lemma cvg_differentiation_under_integral in the accompanying development [6, lebesgue_integral_under.v].

The lemma of continuity under the integral sign is a similar-looking lemma that we use in Sect. 4.4 to show that the normal probability measure as a function from real numbers (intended to represent the mean of the normal probability distribution) to the σ-algebra of probability measures is measurable.

4 Probability Distributions in MATHCOMP-ANALYSIS

We use the lemmas from the previous section to formalize the probability distributions required to extend sfPPL, which originally [29] only provided the Bernoulli distribution (_bernoulli_(p)) and the Poisson and exponential probability density functions. To formalize a probability distribution, we first define a probability mass function (hereafter, pmf) (resp. a probability density function, hereafter, pdf) $f: X \to \mathbb{R}$ for a discrete distribution (resp. for a continuous distribution) that we use to define a probability measure that to a set A associates $\sum_{x \in A} f(x)$ where the sum is potentially countable (resp. $\int_{x \in A} f(x)\mathrm{d}\mu$).

4.1 The Binomial Probability Distribution

The pmf of the binomial distribution (parameters n, p) is $k \mapsto \binom{n}{k} p^k (1-p)^{n-k}$:

```
Definition binomial_pmf k := p ^+ k * (1 - p) ^+ (n - k) *+ 'C(n, k).
```

The notation ^+ is for the iterated multiplication while the notation *+ amounts to multiplication here; these are standard notations from MATHCOMP [36].

The pmf is used to write the probability measure $\underline{binomial}(n,p)$ which is the function $U \mapsto \sum_{k \in U} \binom{n}{k} p^k (1-p)^{n-k}$ assuming $0 \le p \le 1$:

```
Definition binomial_prob {R : realType} n p : set nat -> \bar R := fun U
  => if 0 <= p <= 1 then \esum_(k in U) (binomial_pmf n p k)%:E else \d_0 U.
```

The MATHCOMP-ANALYSIS notation \esum_(k in U) ... is for sums of non-negative extended real numbers over sets that potentially have a countable cardinality. We handle the condition $0 \le p \le 1$ using an if-then-else; it defaults to \d_0 U, which is an ASCII notation for $\delta_0 U$ (Sect. 2). To complete the definition of the probability measure it remains to show that (1) binomial_prob is 0 for $\emptyset$, (2) its output is non-negative, (3) it is σ-additive (thus it is a measure), and (4) the measure of the whole set if 1 (thus it is a probability measure, see Sect. 2).

4.2 The Uniform Probability Distribution

Contrary to the Bernoulli and binomial distributions, the uniform probability distribution is defined over real numbers: it is continuous. The pdf of the uniform distribution over the interval $[a,b]$ ($a < b$) returns $\frac{1}{b-a}$ over $[a,b]$ and 0 otherwise:

```
Definition uniform_pdf x := if a <= x <= b then (b - a)^-1 else 0.
```

The corresponding probability measure is defined by the integral of the pdf:

```
Definition uniform_prob (ab : a < b) : set _ -> \bar R :=
  fun U => \int[mu]_(x in U) (uniform_pdf x)%:E.
```

Showing that uniform_prob is a probability measure relies on properties of the Lebesgue integral which were already available in MATHCOMP-ANALYSIS. In particular, σ-additivity is a consequence of the fact that $\int_{x \in (\bigcup_i F_i)} f(x) \mathrm{d}\mu = \sum_i \int_{x \in F_i} f(x) \mathrm{d}\mu$ for a sequence of pairwise-disjoint sets F_i. See [6] for details.

4.3 The Beta Probability Distribution

The pdf of the beta probability distribution is $t \mapsto \frac{t^{a-1}(1-t)^{b-1}}{\beta(a,b)}$ with $t \in [0,1]$, $a,b \in \mathbb{N}\setminus\{0\}$, and $\beta(a,b) \stackrel{\text{def}}{=} \int_{u \in [0,1]} u^{a-1}(1-u)^{b-1} \mathrm{d}\mu$ (the so-called β function). To formalize this probability distribution, we first define in ROCQ a function XMonemX $a\,b$ for the polynomial $X^a(1-X)^b$. The β function (beta_fun) is $\int_x$ XMonemX $(a-1)(b-1)|_{[0,1]}\, x \mathrm{d}\mu$ and the beta pdf is:

```
Definition beta_pdf a b t := XMonemX a.-1 b.-1 \_`[0,1] t / beta_fun a b.
```

The restriction to the interval $[0,1]$ (notation _ in ROCQ) is how we handle the requirement $t \in [0,1]$. Finally, the beta probability measure $\underline{beta}\,(a,b)$ is

$$U \mapsto \frac{1}{\beta(a,b)} \int_{x \in U} \texttt{XMonemX}\,(a-1)\,(b-1)|_{[0,1]}\,x \mathrm{d}\mu.$$

Properties of the Beta Probability Distribution. For an integrable function f, the beta probability measure and the beta pdf are related as follows (μ is the Lebesgue measure, lemma `integral_beta_prob` in [6]):

$$\int_{x \in U} f(x) \mathrm{d}\underline{beta}\,(\mathtt{a},\mathtt{b}) = \int_{x \in U} f(x)(\texttt{beta\_pdf a b }x)\mathrm{d}\mu.$$

This is a consequence of the change of variables for the Radon-Nikodým derivative, already used in MATHCOMP-ANALYSIS to prove the "chain rule" [20, § 4.4].

The β function is symmetric, i.e., $\beta(a,b) = \beta(b,a)$:

```
Lemma beta_fun_sym (a b : nat) : beta_fun a b = beta_fun b a.
```

The crux of the proof is the following integration by substitution: $\int_{x \in [0,r]} f(x)\mathrm{d}\mu = \int_{x \in [1-r,1]} f(1-x)\mathrm{d}\mu$ with $r \in]0,1]$, which is a consequence of the more general lemmas explained in Sect. 3.3.

The β function and the factorial are related as follows ($a, b > 0$): $\beta(a,b) = \frac{(a-1)!(b-1)!}{((a+b)-1)!}$. See lemma `beta_funE` [6, probability.v]. The proof is by induction, relying on the symmetry of the β function and integration by parts (Sect. 3.3).

4.4 The Normal Probability Distribution

The pdf of the normal distribution with mean m and standard deviation $\sigma \neq 0$ is $x \mapsto \frac{1}{\sqrt{2\sigma^2 \pi}} \exp\left(-\frac{(x-m)^2}{2\sigma^2}\right)$. It is formalized as follows:

```
Definition normal_peak s := (sqrtr (s ^+ 2 * pi *+ 2))^-1.
Definition normal_fun m s x := expR (- (x - m) ^+ 2 / (s ^+ 2 *+ 2)).
Definition normal_pdf0 m s x := normal_peak s * normal_fun m s x.
Definition normal_pdf m s x :=
  if s == 0 then \1_`[0, 1] x else normal_pdf0 m s x.
```

The normal probability measure $\underline{\mathcal{N}}\,(m,s)$ is $U \mapsto \int_{x \in U} \texttt{normal\_pdf}\,m\,s\,x\mathrm{d}\mu$. The proof that this is a probability measure follows from the Gauss integral.

Properties of the Normal Probability Distribution. The normal probability measure and the normal pdf are related similarly to the beta probability measure:

$$\int_{x \in U} f(x) \mathrm{d}\underline{\mathcal{N}}\,(\mathtt{m},\mathtt{s}) = \int_{x \in U} f(x)(\texttt{normal\_pdf m s }x)\mathrm{d}\mu.$$

This corresponds to Lemma `integral_normal_prob` in [6] and it is used several times in the example of Sect. 7.

Two normal probability measures can be composed to form a new one according to the following relation:

$$\int_x \mathcal{N}(m_2 + x, s_2) \, U \mathrm{d}\mathcal{N}(m_1, s_1) = \mathcal{N}\left(m_1 + m_2, \sqrt{s_1^2 + s_2^2}\right) U$$

where U is a measurable set of real numbers [6, lemma `normal_probD`].

In order to use the normal distribution in sfPPL, we must show that it is a kernel, i.e., that $m \mapsto \mathtt{normal\_prob}\,m\,s$ is measurable as a function from $\mathbb{R}$ to the σ-algebra formed by probability measures. For that purpose, it is sufficient to show that the function

$$m \mapsto \mathcal{N}(m, s) \, U = \int_{x \in U} \mathtt{normal\_pdf}\,m\,s\,x \mathrm{d}\mu$$

is continuous for any measurable set U. This is a consequence of continuity under the integral sign (Sect. 3.4) and results in the lemma `measurable_normal_prob2` that we will be instrumental in Sect. 5.3.

5 Extension of the sfPPL Language

We now use the probability distributions formalized in the previous section to extend the sfPPL language with new probability measures to do sampling, new pmfs/pdfs to do scoring, new comparison operators, etc. sfPPL is a first-order probabilistic programming language with a ROCQ encoding [29] which is an instance of an archetypal language proposed by Staton [33]. First, we recall background information about sfPPL and its formalization in Sect. 5.1–5.2. Then, we explain in Sect. 5.3 how we extend sfPPL to later mechanize Shan's examples.

5.1 Background: Informal Syntax and Typing Rules of sfPPL

The types of sfPPL are the unit type, the type of booleans, natural numbers, real numbers (respective syntax: **U**, **B**, **N**, **R**), a type for probability distributions (notation $P(\cdot)$) and the cartesian product:
$\mathbf{A} ::= \mathbf{U} \mid \mathbf{B} \mid \mathbf{N} \mid \mathbf{R} \mid P(\mathbf{A}) \mid \mathbf{A}_1 \times \mathbf{A}_2$.

The expressions of sfPPL are formed by the sole element of type unit (**tt**), boolean/natural/real numbers (resp. ranged over by b, n, and r), the application of measurable functions (denoted by $f(\ldots)$), pairs, their first and second projections, conditional branching, variables, the return expression and let-bindings, as well as the three instructions specific to probabilistic programming languages:

$$e ::= \mathbf{tt} \mid b \mid n \mid r \mid f(e_1, \ldots, e_n) \mid (e_1, e_2) \mid \pi_1(e) \mid \pi_2(e) \mid \text{if } e \text{ then } e_1 \text{ else } e_2 \mid x$$
$$\mid \text{return}\,(e) \mid \text{let } x := e_1 \text{ in } e_2 \mid \text{sample}\,(e) \mid \text{score}\,(e) \mid \text{normalize}\,(e)$$

Among the functions f, we find probability measures used for sampling, pmfs/pdfs used for scoring, and comparison operators. The main difficulty when

Table 1. Syntax of sfPPL as provided by previous work [29]

Informal syntax	Rocq syntax
tt, $b(\in \mathbb{B})$, $n(\in \mathbb{N})$, $r(\in \mathbb{R})$, x (variables)	TT, b:B, n:N, r:R, #{"x"}
let $x := a$ in b, return (e)	let "x" := a in b, return e
if e_1 then e_2 else e_3	if e1 then e2 else e3
sample (e), score (e), normalize (e)	Sample e, Score e, Normalize e
bernoulli (p)	Bernoulli p

adding such functions is to prove that they are indeed measurable; this is not always trivial as we explained for example in Sect. 4.4.

Typing judgments for sfPPL distinguish between *deterministic* and *probabilistic* expressions. Contexts (or typing environments) are tuples (x_1 : $\mathbf{A}_1; \ldots; x_n$: $\mathbf{A}_n$) ranged over by Γ. The typing judgment is $\Gamma \vdash_\mathsf{D} e : \mathbf{A}$ for deterministic expressions and $\Gamma \vdash_\mathsf{P} e : \mathbf{A}$ for probabilistic ones. For illustration, here are three typing rules for expressions (see [29, § 4] for the other typing rules):

$$\frac{\Gamma \vdash_\mathsf{P} e_1 : \mathbf{A}_1 \quad \Gamma, x : \mathbf{A}_1 \vdash_\mathsf{P} e_2 : \mathbf{A}_2}{\Gamma \vdash_\mathsf{P} \text{let } x := e_1 \text{ in } e_2 : \mathbf{A}_2} \qquad \frac{\Gamma \vdash_\mathsf{D} e : P(\mathbf{A})}{\Gamma \vdash_\mathsf{P} \text{sample}(e) : \mathbf{A}} \qquad \frac{\Gamma \vdash_\mathsf{D} e : \mathbf{R}}{\Gamma \vdash_\mathsf{P} \text{score}(e) : \mathbf{U}}$$

5.2 Background: Formal Syntax and Semantics for sfPPL

Syntax. In Rocq, the types of sfPPL are represented by an inductive type:

```
Inductive typ :=
Unit | Bool | Nat | Real | Pair : typ -> typ -> typ | Prob : typ -> typ.
```

The expressions are represented by an inductive type `exp DP g t` where `DP` is a flag (`D` or `P` marking whether the expression is deterministic of probabilistic), `g` is a context (a list of pairs of a variable name and the corresponding type), and `t` is the type of the expression being represented:

```
Inductive exp : flag -> ctx -> typ -> Type := (* [6, lang_syntax.v] *)
```

The expressions of sfPPL are intrinsically-typed: only well-typed programs can be represented [29, § 6.1]. Furthermore, there is a formal syntax for the above language of expressions that is summarized in Table 1. In Rocq, we can use this syntax inside square brackets [...], inside of which we can use curly brackets {...} to escape and use the syntax of Rocq. This is achieved using Rocq's "custom entries" [37]; see [29, § 5.3] for more details.

Semantics. The semantics of sfPPL types are σ-algebras. For example, the measurable type corresponding to $\mathbf{R}$ is the set $\mathbb{R}$ of real numbers with its Borel sets. The semantics of $P(A)$ is `pprobability A` which represents the σ-algebra of probability measures over A.

To give a semantics to sfPPL expressions, one interprets deterministic values as measurable functions and probabilistic values as s-finite kernels [33]. This is encoded by a mutually inductive relation `evalD`/`evalP` [29, § 7.2]:

```
Inductive evalD : forall g t, exp D g t ->
  forall f : dval R g t, measurable_fun setT f -> Prop := ...
with evalP : forall g t, exp P g t -> pval R g t -> Prop := ...
```

The definition dval stands for "deterministic value" and is essentially a function from (the measurable type corresponding to) the context g to (the measurable type corresponding to) the type t. The definition pval stands for "probabilistic value" and is an s-finite kernel from the context g to the type t (or more precisely their interpretation as measurable types). The conversion from a context (which is a list) and a measurable type is performed by nesting pairs and appealing to a standard construction of measurable types for the cartesian product.

From this relation, one derives two functions execD and execP to "execute" the syntax to the semantics. The function execD turns a deterministic expression into a deterministic value, while the function execP turns a probabilistic expression into a probabilistic value [29, § 7.3]. The interest of having these two functions is that one can produce one rewriting lemma for each kind of expression so that the semantics of a program can be obtained by syntax-directed rewritings.

For example, consider the semantics of let · := · in ·. Given a kernel $l : X \rightsquigarrow Y$ and a kernel $k : X \times Y \rightsquigarrow Z$, the composition of l and of k is $x, U \mapsto \int_y k(x, y) \, U \mathbf{d}(l\,x)$. It happens that the composition of s-finite kernels is an s-finite kernel [33]. Let letin' be the ROCQ formalization of the composition operation. Since let · := · in · is a probabilistic expression with probabilistic subexpressions, its semantics is given by:

```
Lemma execP_letin g x t1 t2
    (e1 : exp P g t1) (e2 : exp P ((x, t1) :: g) t2) :
  execP [let x := e1 in e2] = letin' (execP e1) (execP e2).
```

Note that while e1 is interpreted in a context g, e2 is interpreted in a context where the variable x has been bound to the type t1 of e1, hence the different types of each subexpression. The next section provides another example of such a rewriting rule.

5.3 Extending sfPPL with New Constructs

We now extended sfPPL in particular with the new probability distributions formalized in Sect. 4. The only potential difficulty when adding new constructs to sfPPL is to establish their measurability. For illustration, let us walk through the addition of the normal probability measure.

First, we add a constructor to the language of expressions:

```
Inductive exp : flag -> ctx -> typ -> Type := ...
| exp_normal g : exp D g Real -> forall s, s != 0 -> exp D g (Prob Real).
```

We only consider normal probability distributions with a non-zero standard deviation, hence the parameter proof s != 0. The return type of exp_normal is Prob Real, which corresponds to a continuous distribution over the real numbers.

Table 2. Extensions of sfPPL provided by this paper

Informal syntax	Rocq syntax
binomial (n, k)	`Binomial n k`
uniform (a, b)	`Uniform a b ab` (where `ab` is a proof that `a < b`)
beta(a, b)	`Beta a b`
normal (m, s)	`Normal m s s0` (where `s0` is a proof that `s` $\neq 0$)
$e_1 = e_2$, $e_1 \leq e_2$, $e_1 \,\&\&\, e_2$, $e_1 \,\|\|\, e_2$	`e1 == e2, e1 <= e2, e1 && e2, e1 || e2`
$e_1 + e_2$, $e_1 - e_2$, $e_1 \cdot e_2$	`e1 + e2, e1 - e2, e1 * e2`
e^n ($n \in \mathbb{N}$), e^r ($r \in \mathbb{R}$)	`e ^+ n, e `^ r`

We also add an entry to the autonomous grammar defined by custom entries so that we can write `Normal m s s0` instead of `exp_normal m s s0`.

Next, we add a constructor to the semantics that establishes that when `e` evaluates to a measurable function `r` (line 4 below), then `[Normal e s s0]` evaluates to a measurable function $x \mapsto$ `normal_prob` $(r\ x)$ `s` with a fixed, non-zero standard deviation but a variable mean (line 5):

```
1  Inductive evalD : forall g t, exp D g t ->
2    forall f : dval R g t, measurable_fun setT f -> Prop := ...
3  | eval_normal g s (s0 : s != 0) (e : exp D g _) r mr :
4    evalD e r mr ->
5    evalD [Normal e s s0] (fun x => normal_prob (r x) s)
6      (measurableT_comp (measurable_normal_prob2 s0) mr) ...
```

The proof, at line 5, that the result of the evaluation is indeed measurable is obtained by composing the proof `mr` that `r` is measurable with the proof `measurable_normal_prob2` that the normal probability measure is measurable, which requires advanced lemmas about Lebesgue integration as we have seen in Sect. 4.4.

Finally, we produce a lemma so that the execution of the normal probability distribution `[Normal e s s0]` can be performed by rewriting:

```
1  Lemma execD_normal g s s0 e :
2    let f := projT1 (execD e) in let mf := projT2 (execD e) in
3    @execD g _ [Normal e s s0] =
4    existT _ (fun x => @normal_prob _ (f x) s)
5      (measurableT_comp (measurable_normal_prob2 s0) mf).
```

This lemma is a direct consequence of the evaluation relation: the execution of `[Normal e s s0]` appears at line 3, the function resulting from execution appears at line 4, and the measurability proof at line 2 is similar to the evaluation relation.

Table 2 summarizes the constructs that we have similarly added to sfPPL and that we will use in the next section. Note that one difference between the informal and the formal syntax is that some probability distributions take a proof as a parameter, otherwise the correspondence is obvious.

6 Eddy's Table Game Using Equational Reasoning

The table game is described by Eddy [12]. This is a two player-game, the first player to get six points wins. First, the casino rolls a ball on a table and when the ball comes to rest, the casino marks the portion of the table to the left and to the right of the rest position. Each point is decided by the casino rolling the ball again. If it comes to the left of the initial mark, A wins, otherwise B wins. The casino reveals nothing except who wins the point. The problem posed by Eddy is the following one. Imagine that A leads 5 points to 3 and bets that he/she is going to win. *What is the expected probability that A wins?* Since A is leading, it seems to indicate that p is favorable to A. Thus A is likely to win, but the number of points is so small that it is not obvious what the chances are exactly.

We formalize the table game as the program 0 [32, § 2.1] in Fig. 1. The initial ball roll is modeled by sampling from a uniform distribution (line 2), the probability p corresponds to the left portion of the table, i.e., the probability that A wins a point. The eight first plays are modeled by sampling from a binomial distribution with parameter p (line 3). The observation that A has won 5 points is modeled (at line 4) by a "guard" command: $\mathrm{guard}(x = n) \stackrel{\mathrm{def}}{=}$ if $x = n$ then tt else score (0). To win, A needs at least one point among the next three plays which are modeled by sampling again from the binomial distribution (line 5). The program returns the result of comparing the output of this last sampling with 1 (line 6). Finally, the resulting measure is normalized (at line 1).

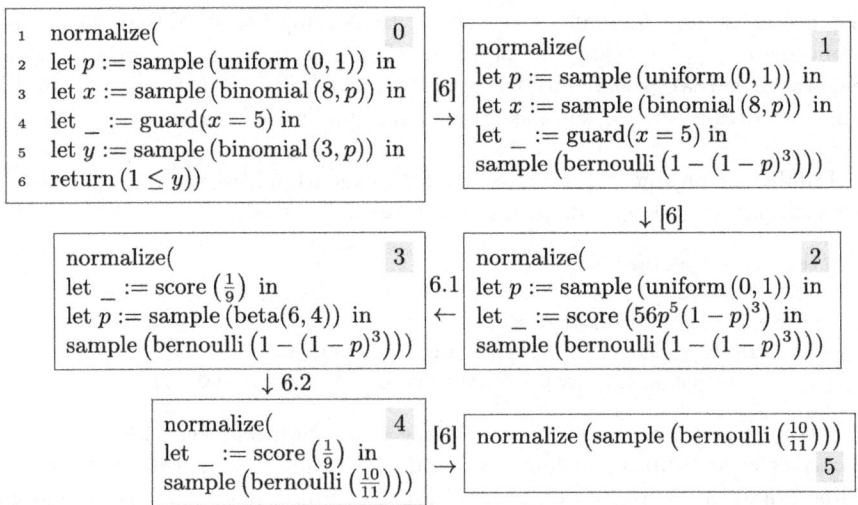

Fig. 1. Proof of the table game by equational reasoning (the labels of arrows indicate the sections where the transformations are explained in details)

The complete Fig. 1 displays the proof by equational reasoning of the table game that one can recover from the handouts of Shan's tutorial [32, § 2.1, § 3.2,

A Formal Foundation for Equational Reasoning on Probabilistic Programs   57

§ 3.4–3.5]. It consists of programs that are obtained by semantics-preserving program transformations. It shows that the probability of A to win is very high.

Using Table 1, we produce the following ROCQ encoding of program 0 :

```
Definition table0 : @exp R _ [::] _ := [Normalize
  let "p" := Sample Uniform {0} {1} {ltr01} in
  let "x" := Sample Binomial {8} #{"p"} in
  let "_" := {guard "x" 5} in
  let "y" := Sample Binomial {3} #{"p"} in
  return {1}:N <= #{"y"}].
```

where guard "x" 5 is `[if #{"x"} == {5}:N then return TT else Score {0}:R]`. The lemma ltr01 is from MATHCOMP that represents the proof that $0 < 1$. The resulting expression type-checks in the empty context (`[::]` is the empty list).

We now explain the transformations 2 → 3 and 3 → 4 by providing a ROCQ encoding of each program and explaining the key lemma that validates it. For the other transformations, see [6, lang_syntax_table_game.v] where the lemmas for each transformation are called table01, table12, etc.

6.1 Transformation 2 → 3

The transformation from program 2 to program 3 amounts to swap a sampling expression and a scoring expression as follows:

| let $p :=$ sample (uniform $(0, 1)$) in | let _ := score $\left(\frac{1}{9}\right)$ in |
| let _ := score $\left(56 p^5 (1-p)^3\right)$ in | → | let $p :=$ sample (beta$(6, 4)$) in |

Let us first provide an encoding for program 2 , whose continuation we represent as tail2:

```
Definition tail2 : @exp R _ [:: ("_", Unit); ("p", Real)] _ :=
  [Sample Bernoulli {1}:R - {[{1}:R - #{"p"}]} ^+ {3}].
Definition table2 : @exp R _ [::] _ := [Normalize
  let "p" := Sample Uniform {0} {1} {ltr01} in
  let "_" := Score {[{56}:R * #{"p"} ^+ {5} * {[{1}:R - #{"p"}]} ^+ {3}]} in
  {tail2}].
```

We encode program 3 similarly, again introducing an intermediate definition tail3 (note that the syntax in tail3 is the same as tail2 but the context is different):

```
Definition tail3 : @exp R _ [:: ("p", Real); ("_", Unit)] _ :=
  [Sample Bernoulli {1}:R - {[{1}:R - #{"p"}]} ^+ {3}].
Definition table3 : @exp R _ [::] _ := [Normalize
  let "_" := Score {1 / 9}:R in
  let "p" := Sample Beta {6} {4} in {tail3}].
```

To prove the program transformation, the first thing to show is that uniform$(0, 1)$ and beta$(1, 1)$ are the same distribution, this is by definition of the beta probability distribution (Sect. 4.3). We then execute both programs (in the sense of Sect. 5.2) to obtain the following equation between their semantics (U is a set of booleans):

$$\int_y \left(\underline{bernoulli}\left(1-(1-y)^3\right)U\right)|56y^5(1-y)^3|\mathrm{d}\underline{beta}\,(1,1) =$$

$$\int\left(\int_y \left(\underline{bernoulli}\left(1-(1-y)^3\right)U\right)\mathrm{d}\underline{beta}\,(6,4)\right)\mathrm{d}\left(\frac{1}{9}\cdot\delta_{\mathrm{tt}}\right).$$

The left-hand side can be rewritten into

$$\int\left(\underline{bernoulli}\left(1-(1-y)^3\right)U\right)|56(y^5(1-y)^3)|\,(\mathtt{beta\_pdf}\,1\,1\,y)\,\mathrm{d}\mu,$$

using the relation between the pdf and the probability measure (Sect. 4.3). Using the same lemma, the right-hand side can be rewritten into

$$\frac{1}{9}\int_y \left(\underline{bernoulli}\left(1-(1-y)^3\right)U\right)(\mathtt{beta\_pdf}\,6\,4\,y)\,\mathrm{d}\mu.$$

It therefore suffices to compare the integrands, which amounts to check that $56\frac{1}{\beta(1,1)} = \frac{1}{9}\frac{1}{\beta(6,4)}$, which can be proved using the relation between the β function and the factorial (Sect. 4.3) and by appealing to the lra [30] tactic to conclude.

6.2 Transformation 3 → 4

The transformation from program 3 to program 4 amounts to transform two successive samplings (the latter depending on the former) into one:

let p := sample (beta(6, 4)) in sample (bernoulli $\left(1-(1-p)^3\right)$)	→	sample $\left(\mathrm{bernoulli}\left(\frac{10}{11}\right)\right)$

We already defined program 3 in Sect. 6.1. Here follows program 4:

```
Definition table4 : @exp R _ [::] _ := [Normalize
    let "_" := Score {1 / 9}:R in Sample Bernoulli {10 / 11}:R].
```

If we state the equality between the semantics of the two programs and execute, we arrive at the following equality (for a set of booleans U):

$$\int_z \underline{bernoulli}\left(1-(1-z)^3\right)U\mathrm{d}\underline{beta}\,(6,4) = \underline{bernoulli}\left(\frac{10}{11}\right)U.$$

This can be proved by using the following generic lemma [32, Equation (32)]:

$$\int_{x\in[0,1]}\underline{bernoulli}\left(x^c(1-x)^d\right)U\mathrm{d}\underline{beta}\,(a,b) = \underline{bernoulli}\left(\frac{\beta(a+c,b+d)}{\beta(a,b)}\right)U.$$

In ROCQ, we name this lemma beta_prob_bernoulli_probE and prove it using integral_beta_prob (Sect. 4.3) and the relation between β and factorial (Sect. 4.3).

7 Observing a Noisy Draw from a Normal Distribution

The observation of a noisy draw from a normal distribution is considered a standard example of probabilistic programming [25, § 3.2.1] [32, § 2.3]. We assume that the position x of some particle is distributed according to the normal distribution (with mean 0 and standard deviation 1). The measurement for the position itself is noisy, i.e., normally distributed around the measured value (with standard deviation 1). Let us assume that we measure the value y_0. *What is the distribution of the next measurement?*

This distribution is represented by the program A of Fig. 2. Given the above informal description, it should be self-explanatory, except for line 3 where we update the prior distribution (resulting from the sampling at line 2) using scoring to take into account the observation of y_0 [31, § 6].

```
1  normalize(                                               A
2    let x := sample (normal (0, 1)) in
3    let _ := score (exp(-(y_0-x)^2/2) / √(2π)) in
4    let z := sample (normal (x, 1)) in
5    return (z))
```

$\downarrow$ [6]

```
1  normalize(                                               B
2    let _ := score (exp(-y_0^2/4) / √(4π)) in
3    let x := sample (normal (y_0/2, 1/√2)) in
4    let z := sample (normal (x, 1)) in
5    return (z))
```

$\overset{7}{\rightarrow}$

```
normalize(                                                  C
  let _ := score (exp(-y_0^2/4) / √(4π)) in
  sample (normal (y_0/2, √(3/2))))
```

Fig. 2. Proof of observing noisy draw from a normal distribution

We only explain the transformation B → C. (See [6, `lang_syntax_noisy.v`] for the other transformation.) It suffices to look at the tails of the two programs:

```
let x := sample (normal (y_0/2, 1/√2)) in
let z := sample (normal (x, 1)) in
return (z)
```
$\rightarrow$
```
sample (normal (y_0/2, √(3/2)))
```

First, we encode the tail of program B:

```
Definition tailB : @exp R _ [:: ("_", Unit); ("y0", Real)] Real :=
  [let "x" := Sample {exp_normal_Vsqrt2 [#{"y0"} * {2^-1}:R ]} in
   let "z" := Sample {exp_normal1 [#{"x"}]} in
   return #{"z"}].
```

The identifiers `exp_normal1` and `exp_normal_Vsqrt2` are intermediate definitions for resp. the normal probability measure with standard deviation 1 and $1/\sqrt{2}$.

We also encode the tail of program C :

```
Definition tailC : @exp R _ [:: ("_", Unit); ("y0", Real)] Real :=
  [Sample {exp_normal_sqrt32 [#{"y0"} * {2^-1}:R]}].
```

Again, the identifier `exp_normal_sqrt32` is for the normal probability measure with standard deviation $\sqrt{3/2}$.

We state the transformation from the tail of program B to the tail of the program C as the equality between the semantics of the two programs. We execute the semantics of the tail of program B and calculate (U is a measurable set of real numbers):

$$\int_x \left(\int_z \delta_z\, U \mathrm{d}\underline{\mathcal{N}}\,(x,1)\right) \mathrm{d}\underline{\mathcal{N}}\left(\frac{y_0}{2}, \frac{1}{\sqrt{2}}\right) = \int_x \underline{\mathcal{N}}\,(x,1)\, U \mathrm{d}\underline{\mathcal{N}}\left(\frac{y_0}{2}, \frac{1}{\sqrt{2}}\right)$$

$$= \underline{\mathcal{N}}\left(\frac{y_0}{2}, \sqrt{\frac{3}{2}}\right) U$$

The first step is a matter of integrating the Dirac function along the normal probability measure [6, lemma `integral_normal_prob_dirac`]. The last step is obtained as an instance of the composition lemma of Sect. 4.4. See [6, lemma `tailBC`].

8 Related Work

The formal verification of probabilistic programs in proof assistants is a long-standing topic. Hurd verified the Miller-Rabin probabilistic primality test in seminal work in HOL [19]. Audebaud and Paulin-Mohring used RocQ to verify randomized algorithms [8] but the measure theory they rely on has some limitations (discrete distributions only, etc.). More recent formalizations of probabilistic programs have been targeting artificial intelligence. For example, Tassarotti et al. represent stochastic procedures using the Giry monad to formalize PAC learnability for decision stumps in Lean [35]. These pieces of work do not feature the combined use of sampling and scoring. Regarding the formal verification of probabilistic programming languages include scoring, we already mentioned in Sect. 1 work in RocQ partly relying on axiomatization [15]. In Isabelle/HOL, Hirata et al. handle sampling, scoring, and higher-order features thanks to quasi-Borel spaces [17,18]; the measure theory they rely on is therefore not the standard one and the language encoding is different from sfPPL since it is shallow and of course does not rely on dependent types (that sfPPL uses to be intrinsically-typed). The formalization of probabilistic programming languages using proof assistants also serves as a mean to study their semantics [42] or their compilation [34].

Our work improves on existing formalization of measure theory and integration in RocQ by providing a rich set of practical lemmas using the Lebesgue integral in a single library (Sect. 3). Some of these lemmas can be found in RocQ for the Riemann integral, e.g., integration by parts [11, `Rint_analysis.v`], integration by substitution [22, § 4.3], but our formalization requires much more (dominated convergence (see Sect. 3.4), Radon-Nikodým (see Sect. 4.3), etc.), which justifies working on top of MATHCOMP-ANALYSIS. Yet, one can find lemmas similar to ours in Isabelle/HOL and Lean. For example, Avigad et al. formalized the second FTC for continuous functions and integration by substitution in Isabelle/HOL [9, § 3.7]. We have not found a formalization of the beta distribution in the library of Isabelle/HOL though. The formalization of integration by substitution in mathlib [13] is more general than ours, we did not need such generality so far but it nevertheless indicates desirable improvements.

9 Conclusions

We demonstrated the use of ROCQ to mechanize equational reasoning for a probabilistic programming language. To that aim, we extended an existing encoding of a probabilistic programming language with new probability distributions (Sect. 5). Beforehand, we needed to develop practical lemmas to compute Lebesgue integrals (Sect. 3). We used these lemmas to formalize the binomial, uniform, beta, and normal distributions[3] and their properties in Sect. 4. This is the first such comprehensive library in ROCQ and it made it possible to mechanize in detail non-trivial examples of probabilistic programs: Eddy's table game in Sect. 6 and observation of a noisy draw in Sect. 7. The resulting framework relies on foundational aspects of ROCQ, such as dependent types for intrinsic typing, and practical aspects of ROCQ, such as the availability of enough measure theory in MATHCOMP-ANALYSIS and automation to discharge arithmetic goals.

Future Work. Our experiment indicates a number of technical improvements of general interest. For example, we recently formalized the Γ function so as to generalize the relation between the β function and the factorial (Sect. 4.3). Now that several examples of probabilistic programs have been mechanized using sfPPL, we plan to investigate a more principled approach to equational reasoning in ROCQ by organizing the laws proposed by Shan [32, § 6] as interfaces like it is done in monadic equational reasoning [5,24].

Acknowledgments. The formalization of Eddy's table game started as a collaboration with Ayumu Saito. This work was supported by JSPS KAKENHI Grant Number 22H00520.

Disclosure of Interests. The authors have no competing interests to declare that are relevant to the content of this article.

References

1. Affeldt, R., Cohen, C.: Measure construction by extension in dependent type theory with application to integration. J. Autom. Reason. **67**(3), 28 (2023). https://doi.org/10.1007/S10817-023-09671-5

---

[3] We also formalized the exponential and Poisson distributions; they are not used in this paper but are needed for future work.

2. Affeldt, R., Cohen, C., Rouhling, D.: Formalization techniques for asymptotic reasoning in classical analysis. J. Formaliz. Reason. **11**(1), 43–76 (2018). https://doi.org/10.6092/issn.1972-5787/8124
3. Affeldt, R., Cohen, C., Saito, A.: Semantics of probabilistic programs using s-finite kernels in dependent type theory. ACM Trans. Probab. Mach. Learn. **1**(3) (2025). https://doi.org/10.1145/3732291
4. Affeldt, R., Garrigue, J., Nowak, D., Saikawa, T.: A trustful monad for axiomatic reasoning with probability and nondeterminism. J. Funct. Program. **31**, e17 (2021). https://doi.org/10.1017/S0956796821000137
5. Affeldt, R., Garrigue, J., Saikawa, T.: A practical formalization of monadic equational reasoning in dependent-type theory. J. Funct. Program. **35** (2025). https://doi.org/10.1017/S0956796824000157
6. Affeldt, R., Ishiguro, Y., Stone, Z.: Equational reasoning for probabilistic programming in Rocq—accompanying development. MathComp-Analysis Pull Request. https://github.com/math-comp/analysis/pull/1712
7. Affeldt, R., Stone, Z.: A comprehensive overview of the Lebesgue differentiation theorem in Coq. In: 15th International Conference on Interactive Theorem Proving (ITP 2024), 9–14 September 2024, Tbilisi, Georgia. LIPIcs, vol. 309, pp. 5:1–5:19. Schloss Dagstuhl - Leibniz-Zentrum für Informatik (2024). https://doi.org/10.4230/LIPICS.ITP.2024.5
8. Audebaud, P., Paulin-Mohring, C.: Proofs of randomized algorithms in Coq. Sci. Comput. Program. **74**(8), 568–589 (2009). https://doi.org/10.1016/j.scico.2007.09.002
9. Avigad, J., Hölzl, J., Serafin, L.: A formally verified proof of the central limit theorem. J. Autom. Reason. **59**(4), 389–423 (2017). https://doi.org/10.1007/S10817-017-9404-X
10. Bingham, E., et al.: Pyro: deep universal probabilistic programming. J. Mach. Learn. Res. **20**, 28:1–28:6 (2019)
11. Boldo, S., Lelay, C., Melquiond, G.: Coquelicot: a formalization of real analysis for Coq. http://coquelicot.saclay.inria.fr/html/Coquelicot.Coquelicot.html. Accessed 19 Mar 2025
12. Eddy, S.R.: What is Bayesian statistics? Nat. Biotechnol. **22**(9), 1177–1178 (2004)
13. Gouëzel, S.: A formalization of the change of variables formula for integrals in mathlib. In: 15th International Conference on Intelligent Computer Mathematics (CICM 2022), Tbilisi, Georgia, 19–23 September 2022. Lecture Notes in Computer Science, vol. 13467, pp. 3–18. Springer (2022). https://doi.org/10.1007/978-3-031-16681-5_1
14. Haselwarter, P.G., et al.: SSProve: a foundational framework for modular cryptographic proofs in Coq. ACM Trans. Program. Lang. Syst. **45**(3), 15:1–15:61 (2023). https://doi.org/10.1145/3594735
15. Heimerdinger, M., Shan, C.: Verified equational reasoning on a little language of measures. In: Workshop on Languages for Inference (LAFI 2019), Cascais, Portugal, 15 January 2019 (2019)
16. Heunen, C., Kammar, O., Staton, S., Yang, H.: A convenient category for higher-order probability theory. In: 32nd Annual ACM/IEEE Symposium on Logic in Computer Science (LICS 2017), Reykjavik, Iceland, 20–23 June 2017, pp. 1–12. IEEE Computer Society (2017). https://doi.org/10.1109/LICS.2017.8005137
17. Hirata, M., Minamide, Y., Sato, T.: Program logic for higher-order probabilistic programs in Isabelle/HOL. Sci. Comput. Program. **230**, 102993 (2023). https://doi.org/10.1016/J.SCICO.2023.102993

18. Hirata, M., Minamide, Y., Sato, T.: Semantic foundations of higher-order probabilistic programs in Isabelle/HOL. In: 14th International Conference on Interactive Theorem Proving (ITP 2023), 31 July–4 August 2023, Białystok, Poland. LIPIcs, vol. 268, pp. 18:1–18:18. Schloss Dagstuhl - Leibniz-Zentrum für Informatik (2023). https://doi.org/10.4230/LIPICS.ITP.2023.18
19. Hurd, J.: Formal verification of probabilistic algorithms. Ph.D. thesis, Computer Laboratory, University of Cambridge (2001)
20. Ishiguro, Y., Affeldt, R.: The Radon-Nikodým theorem and the Lebesgue-Stieltjes measure in Coq. Comput. Softw. **41**(2), 41–49 (2024). https://doi.org/10.11309/jssst.41.2_41
21. Kadets, V.: A Course in Functional Analysis and Measure Theory. Universitext, Springer (2018)
22. Mahboubi, A., Melquiond, G., Sibut-Pinote, T.: Formally verified approximations of definite integrals. J. Autom. Reason. **62**(2), 281–300 (2018). https://doi.org/10.1007/s10817-018-9463-7
23. MathComp-Analysis: MathComp-Analysis: Mathematical Components compliant analysis library (2017). https://github.com/math-comp/analysis. Authors: Reynald Affeldt, Yves Bertot, Alessandro Bruni, Cyril Cohen, Marie Kerjean, Assia Mahboubi, Damien Rouhling, Pierre Roux, Kazuhiko Sakaguchi, Zachary Stone, Pierre-Yves Strub, and Laurent Théry. Last stable version: 1.13.0 (2025)
24. Monae: Monadic effects and equational reasonig in Rocq (2018). https://github.com/affeldt-aist/monae. Authors: Reynald Affeldt, David Nowak, Takafumi Saikawa, Jacques Garrigue, Ayumu Saito, Celestine Sauvage, and Kazunari Tanaka. Last stable release: 0.9.1 (2025)
25. Narayanan, P.: Verifiable and reusable conditioning. Ph.D. thesis, Indiana University (2019)
26. Narayanan, P., Carette, J., Romano, W., Shan, C., Zinkov, R.: Probabilistic inference by program transformation in Hakaru (system description). In: Kiselyov, O., King, A. (eds.) FLOPS 2016. LNCS, vol. 9613, pp. 62–79. Springer, Cham (2016). https://doi.org/10.1007/978-3-319-29604-3_5
27. Rouhling, D.: Formalisation Tools for Classical Analysis—A Case Study in Control Theory. Ph.D. thesis, Université Côte d'Azur (2019)
28. Rudin, W.: Principles of Mathematical Analysis, 3rd edn. McGraw-Hill (1976)
29. Saito, A., Affeldt, R.: Experimenting with an intrinsically-typed probabilistic programming language in Coq. In: 21st Asian Symposium on Programming Languages and Systems (APLAS 2023), Taipei, Taiwan, 26–29 November. Lecture Notes in Computer Science, vol. 14405, pp. 182–202. Springer (2023). https://doi.org/10.1007/978-981-99-8311-7_9
30. Sakaguchi, K., Roux, P.: Algebra tactics: ring, field, lra, nra, and psatz tactics for Mathematical Components (2021). https://github.com/math-comp/algebra-tactics. Last stable release: 1.2.6 (2025)
31. Shan, C.: Calculating distributions. In: 20th International Symposium on Principles and Practice of Declarative Programming (PPDP 2018), Frankfurt am Main, Germany, 3–5 September 2018, pp. 2:1–2:5. ACM (2018). https://doi.org/10.1145/3236950.3236973
32. Shan, C.C.: Equational reasoning for probabilistic programming. POPL 2018 TutorialFest (2018). https://homes.luddy.indiana.edu/ccshan/rational/equational-handout.pdf
33. Staton, S.: Commutative semantics for probabilistic programming. In: Yang, H. (ed.) ESOP 2017. LNCS, vol. 10201, pp. 855–879. Springer, Heidelberg (2017). https://doi.org/10.1007/978-3-662-54434-1_32

34. Tassarotti, J., Tristan, J.: Verified density compilation for a probabilistic programming language. Proc. ACM Program. Lang. **7**(PLDI), 615–637 (2023). https://doi.org/10.1145/3591245
35. Tassarotti, J., Vajjha, K., Banerjee, A., Tristan, J.: A formal proof of PAC learnability for decision stumps. In: 10th ACM SIGPLAN International Conference on Certified Programs and Proofs (CPP 2021), Virtual Event, Denmark, 17–19 January 2021, pp. 5–17. ACM (2021). https://doi.org/10.1145/3437992.3439917
36. The MathComp development team: Mathematical components (2005). https://github.com/math-comp/math-comp. Last stable version: 2.4.0 (2025)
37. The Rocq Development Team: Custom entries. Inria (2025). Chapter "Syntax extensions and notation scopes" of [38]
38. The Rocq Development Team: The Rocq Proof Assistant Reference Manual. Inria (2025). https://rocq-prover.org/doc/V9.0.0/refman/index.html. Version 9.0.0
39. The Stan Development Team: Stan modeling language users guide and reference manual (2024). https://mc-stan.org/
40. Wikipedia: Fundamental theorem of calculus (2025). https://en.wikipedia.org/wiki/Fundamental_theorem_of_calculus. Accessed 24 Mar 2025
41. Wood, F.D., van de Meent, J., Mansinghka, V.: A new approach to probabilistic programming inference. In: 7th International Conference on Artificial Intelligence and Statistics (AISTATS 2014), Reykjavik, Iceland, 22–25 April 2014. JMLR Workshop and Conference Proceedings, vol. 33, pp. 1024–1032. JMLR.org (2014)
42. Zhang, Y., Amin, N.: Reasoning about "reasoning about reasoning": semantics and contextual equivalence for probabilistic programs with nested queries and recursion. Proc. ACM Program. Lang. **6**(POPL), 1–28 (2022). https://doi.org/10.1145/3498677

Control, Effects, and Decidability

Reachability is Decidable for ATM-Typable Finitary PCF with Effect Handlers

Ryunosuke Endo[1,2] and Tachio Terauchi[1(✉)]

[1] Waseda University, Tokyo, Japan
minerva@ruri.waseda.jp, terauchi@waseda.jp
[2] Mizuho Bank, Ltd., Tokyo, Japan

Abstract. It is well known that the reachability problem for simply-typed lambda calculus with recursive definitions and finite base-type values (finitary PCF) is decidable. A recent paper by Dal Lago and Ghyselen has shown that the same problem becomes undecidable when the language is extended with algebraic effect and handlers (effect handlers). We show that, perhaps surprisingly, the problem becomes decidable even with effect handlers when the type system is extended with answer type modification (ATM). A natural intuition may find the result contradictory, because one would expect allowing ATM makes more programs typable. Indeed, this intuition is correct in that there are programs that are typable with ATM but not without it, as we shall show in the paper. However, a corollary of our decidability result is that the converse is true as well: there are programs that are typable without ATM but becomes untypable with ATM, and we will show concrete examples of such programs in the paper. Our decidability result is proven by a novel continuation passing style (CPS) transformation that transforms an ATM-typable finitary PCF program with effect handlers to a finitary PCF program without effect handlers. Additionally, as another application of our CPS transformation, we show that every recursive-function-free ATM-typable finitary PCF program with effect handlers terminates, while there are (necessarily ATM-untypable) recursive-function-free finitary PCF programs with effect handlers that may diverge. Finally, we disprove a claim made in a recent work that proved a similar but strictly weaker decidability result. We foresee our decidability result to lay a foundation for developing verification methods for programs with effect handlers, just as the decidability result for reachability of finitary PCF has done such for programs without effect handlers.

1 Introduction

A popular approach to the verification of infinite-state programs is to abstract the programs so that their base-type values are over finite domains, as seen in,

---

The original version of the chapter has been revised. The Chapter 4 Fig 5 has been corrected. A correction to this chapter can be found at
https://doi.org/10.1007/978-981-95-3585-9_14

for example, predicate abstraction with CEGAR [3,4,7–9,19,20,26,28,34,36,39,42]. Importantly, the reachability problem, which asks whether there exists an execution of the program reaching a certain program state (typically a designated "error" state), is known to be decidable for such programs when they are simply-typable, even when the programs contain higher-order and recursive functions. That is, reachability for finitary PCF is decidable [17,27,41].[1]

Meanwhile, algebraic effects and handlers (*effect handlers* henceforth) are a programming language feature for expressing computational effects such as mutable state, exception, and non-determinism [35]. They have a theoretical origin, stemming from the research on denotational semantics [5,29–33], but are also practically popular and have been incorporated into many popular programming languages such as C, C++, Java, OCaml, and Haskell [1,6,13,22,38,44]. Unfortunately, a recent paper [21] has shown that reachability, which is decidable for finitary PCF as mentioned above, becomes undecidable when the language is extended with effect handlers.

In this paper, we show that this undecidability stems from the way the standard type systems for effect handlers are designed. More concretely, we show that, perhaps surprisingly, extending the standard type system to allow answer type modification (ATM) [2,10,16] recovers decidability. A natural intuition may find the result contradictory because one would expect allowing ATM makes more programs typable. Indeed, this intuition is correct in that there are programs that are typable with ATM but not without it, as we shall show in the paper (cf. Example 5). However, a corollary of our decidability result is that the converse is true as well: there are programs that are typable without ATM but becomes untypable with ATM, and we will show concrete examples of such programs in the paper (cf. Sects. 3.2 and 3.3).

Our decidability result is proven by a novel continuation passing style (CPS) transformation that transforms an ATM-typable finitary PCF program with effect handlers to a finitary PCF program without effect handlers. Then, our decidability result follows from the fact that the target of the CPS transformation, finitary PCF, has decidable reachability as mentioned in the first paragraph of this section.

Additionally, as another application of our CPS transformation, we show that every recursive-function-free ATM-typable finitary PCF program with effect handlers terminates, while there are (necessarily ATM-untypable) recursive-function-free finitary PCF programs with effect handlers that may diverge. Finally, we disprove in a claim made in a recent work that proved a similar but strictly weaker decidability result [37]. In summary, the main contributions of the paper are as follows.

- We show that reachability for ATM-typable finitary PCF with effect handlers is decidable. A novel CPS transformation is introduced to prove the result.

---

[1] The result can be seen as an extension of the decidability result for reachability of pushdown systems [12], which correspond to first-order recursive programs, to higher-order recursive programs. Also, the result should not be confused with the result that observational equivalence for finitary PCF is undecidable [24].

$$v ::= x \mid () \mid \top \mid \bot \mid \lambda x.c \mid \text{rec } x = v$$
$$c ::= \text{return } v \mid op\ v \mid v_1\ v_2 \mid \text{if } v \text{ then } c_1 \text{ else } c_2 \mid \text{let } x = c_1 \text{ in } c_2 \mid \text{with } h \text{ handle } c$$
$$h ::= \{\text{return } x = c, \overline{op_i\ x_i\ k_i = c_i}\}$$

Fig. 1. The syntax of $\text{FPCF}_{\mathit{eff}}$.

- A corollary of our decidability result is that there are finitary PCF programs typable without ATM but untypable with it, and we show concrete examples of such programs.
- As another application of the CPS transformation, we show that recursive-function-free ATM-typable finitary PCF programs with effect handlers always terminate, while there are (ATM-untypable) recursive-function-free finitary PCF programs with effect handlers that may diverge.
- We disprove a claim made in a recent paper [37] regarding what the paper calls the number of "active effect handlers".

The rest of the paper is organized as follows. Section 2 defines preliminary notions. Section 3 contains the main results mentioned above. Section 4 discusses related work. Section 5 concludes the paper. For space, some materials are deferred to the extended report [11].

2 Preliminaries

Figure 1 shows the syntax of untyped finitary PCF with effect handlers $\text{FPCF}_{\mathit{eff}}$. As in many presentations of effect handlers [16,35], we adopt the approach of call-by-push-value λ calculus [23] to separate the syntax of expressions into *values*, ranged over by meta variables v, and *computations*, ranged over by c. A *handler*, ranged over by h, consists of a single *return clause* of the form $\text{return } x = c$ and finitely many *operation clauses* of the form $op_i\ x_i\ k_i = c_i$. The parameter k_i in an operation clause is called the *continuation parameter*. Recursive definitions are given by the syntax $\text{rec } x = v$ which recursively binds x in v.

Note that functions, arguments, and conditional expressions are restricted to values. This does not reduce expressivity because, for example, a function application $c\ v$ can be expressed as $\text{let } x = c \text{ in } x\ v$ using a fresh variable x. For convenience, we often assume this convention and allow computations to appear at positions where values are expected. For example, we may write $x\ y\ z$ for $\text{let } w = x\ y \text{ in } w\ z$, adopting the usual convention that function application is left associative. Conversely, when a value v appears at a position where a computation in expected, we read it as $\text{return } v$. For example, we may write $\lambda x.\lambda y.x$ for $\lambda x.\text{return } \lambda y.\text{return } x$. We also write $c_1; c_2$ for $\text{let } x = c_1 \text{ in } c_2$ where x is not free in c_2. As usual, a *program* is a closed expression.

For concreteness, $\text{FPCF}_{\mathit{eff}}$ uses Booleans and unit as base-type values, but our results can be easily adopted to other finite base-type domains such as variant types and integers modulo a constant. Note that $\text{FPCF}_{\mathit{eff}}$ is untyped. Later in the paper, we present two type systems for it, an ordinary simple type system

$$\frac{c_1 \to c_2}{\texttt{let } x = c_1 \texttt{ in } c \to \texttt{let } x = c_2 \texttt{ in } c} \text{ (E-LET)} \qquad \frac{}{\texttt{let } x = \texttt{return } v \texttt{ in } c \to c[v/x]} \text{ (E-RET)}$$

$$\frac{}{(\lambda x.c)\, v \to c[v/x]} \text{ (E-LAMAPP)} \qquad \frac{}{(\texttt{rec } x = v)\, v' \to v[(\texttt{rec } x = v)/x]\, v'} \text{ (E-RECAPP)}$$

$$\frac{}{\texttt{if } \top \texttt{ then } c_1 \texttt{ else } c_2 \to c_1} \text{ (E-IFTRUE)} \qquad \frac{}{\texttt{if } \bot \texttt{ then } c_1 \texttt{ else } c_2 \to c_2} \text{ (E-IFFALSE)}$$

$$\frac{c \to c'}{\texttt{with } h \texttt{ handle } c \to \texttt{with } h \texttt{ handle } c'} \text{ (E-HAN)}$$

$$\frac{\texttt{return } x = c \in h}{\texttt{with } h \texttt{ handle return } v \to c[v/x]} \text{ (E-HRET)}$$

$$\frac{\texttt{op } x\, k = c \in h}{\texttt{with } h \texttt{ handle } E[\texttt{op } v] \to c[v/x, \lambda y.\texttt{with } h \texttt{ handle } E[\texttt{return } y]/k]} \text{ (E-OP)}$$

Fig. 2. The semantics of $\text{FPCF}_{\mathit{eff}}$.

$\vdash_{\text{st}}$ and a type system with answer-type modification $\vdash_{\text{atm}}$, and investigate how they affect the decidability of reachability.

Figure 2 shows the operational semantics of $\text{FPCF}_{\mathit{eff}}$. Here, the *evaluation context* E is defined by: $E ::= [] \mid \texttt{let } x = E \texttt{ in } c$. The semantics is standard for a language with effect handlers. A key rule is (E-OP) which invokes an operation. An operation invocation is quite different from an ordinary function call, and replaces the current context up to and including the nearest with-handle block with the body of the operation clause c. The actual argument v gets bound to the formal parameter x and the continuation parameter k gets the captured *delimited continuation* $\lambda y.\texttt{with } h \texttt{ handle } E[\texttt{return } y]$. The behavior is similar to that of the *shift* operation from delimited control [2,10]. Note that the evaluation context E in the delimited continuation is wrapped in the with-handle block, following the standard *deep-handler* semantics [15]. Another important rule is (E-HRET) which processes a return clause invocation. Note that unlike the ordinary return of (E-RET), a return at a tail position of a with-handle block invokes the return clause so that the returned result is (the evaluation result of) $c[v/x]$ rather than v. As standard, we write $\to^*$ to denote the reflexive transitive closure of $\to$. The *reachability problem* is defined as follows.

Definition 1 (Reachability). The *reachability problem* is to decide, given a program c, if $c \to^* \texttt{return } \top$.

We note that the choice of $\top$ is arbitrary. We could have alternatively chosen any other base-type value as the final value that we would like to decide if the program returns or not.

Example 1. Let c_{ex1} be the following program.[2]

(with h_{state} handle (rec $loop = \lambda_{\_}$.
      let $n = get\ ()$ in
      if $v_{fst}\ n$ then if $v_{snd}\ n$ then $c_{incr}; loop\ ()$ else $()$
      else $c_{incr}; loop\ ())\ (v_{tup} \perp \perp))$; return $\top$

where

$$v_{tup} \triangleq \lambda x.\lambda y.\lambda f.f\ x\ y \quad v_{fst} \triangleq \lambda p.p\ \lambda x.\lambda y.x \quad v_{snd} \triangleq \lambda p.p\ \lambda x.\lambda y.y$$
$$c_{inc} \triangleq \text{let } n = get\ ()\ \text{in}$$
    if $v_{fst}\ n$ then if $v_{snd}\ n$ then $()$ else $set\ (v_{tup} \perp \top)$
    else if $v_{snd}\ n$ then $set\ (v_{tup}\ \top\ \top)$ else $set\ (v_{tup}\ \top \perp)$
$$h_{state} \triangleq \{\text{return } x = \lambda s.x, set\ x\ k = \lambda s.k\ ()\ x, get\ x\ k = \lambda s.k\ s\ s\}$$

The handler h_{state} adopts the standard state-passing approach for expressing mutable states with effect handlers [35]. Namely, the operation *set* updates the current state with the given argument and the operation *get* returns the current state. In this program, a state is a pair of Booleans encoding a 2-bit non-negative integer. We use the standard λ calculus encoding of pairs: v_{tup}, v_{fst}, and v_{snd} respectively creates a pair, projects the first element, and the projects the second element. The computation c_{inc} is effectful and uses *get* and *set* to increment the current state by one. The initial state is set to be zero (i.e., the pair $(\perp, \perp)$), and the recursive function defined by rec $loop = \ldots$ repeatedly increments the state until the value becomes one (i.e., $(\top, \perp)$). Because the initial state is zero, one is eventually reached and the program c_{ex1} terminates returning $\top$. The same program would also terminate and return $\top$ if the state was initialized to be one, but it would diverge if the state was initialized to be two (i.e., $(\perp, \top)$) or three (i.e., $(\top, \top)$). Therefore, the answer to the reachability problem for this program would be yes in the first two cases and be no in the latter two cases.

Example 2. Next, let c_{ex2} be the following program, also adopted from [35].

let $r =$ (with h_{nd} handle let $x =$ if $dec\ ()$ then v_0 else v_1 in
          let $y =$ if $dec\ ()$ then v_2 else v_3 in $v_{xor}\ x\ y$) in
if r then (rec $f = \lambda_{\_}.f\ ())\ ()$ else return $\top$

where

$$v_{xor} \triangleq \lambda x.\lambda y.\text{if } x \text{ then (if } y \text{ then } \perp \text{ else } \top) \text{ else (if } y \text{ then } \top \text{ else } \perp)$$
$$v_{or} \triangleq \lambda x.\lambda y.\text{if } x \text{ then } \top \text{ else if } y \text{ then } \top \text{ else } \perp$$
$$h_{nd} \triangleq \{\text{return } x = x, dec\ x\ k = v_{or}\ (k\ \top)\ (k \perp)\}$$

Here, $v_0, v_1, v_2, v_3 \in \{\perp, \top\}$. The handler h_{nd} implements non-deterministic choice by the *dec* operation whose clause executes the given delimited continuation k, which is expected to take and return Booleans, with both $\top$ an $\perp$, and

---

[2] Recall the syntactic sugar such as the notation $c_1; c_2$ remarked earlier.

returns the disjunction of the two results. Therefore, the with-handle block will, for each of the four possibilities where x is bound to v_0 or v_1 and y is bound to v_2 or v_3, computes the exclusive-or of x and y, and takes the disjunction of the four results. Therefore, the with-handle block returns $\bot$ if the Booleans v_0, v_1, v_2, v_3 are all equal and otherwise returns $\top$, and the program c_{ex2} returns $\top$ in the former cases and diverges in the later cases (due to the infinite loop ($\text{rec } f = \lambda\_.f \, () \, ()$). Thus, the answer to the reachability problem would be true in the former two cases (i.e., the four Booleans are all $\top$ or all $\bot$) and be no in the latter 14 cases.

Figure 3 defines the simple types. The base types are denoted by b. As usual, the function type constructor $\to$ associates to the right. Figure 4 shows the typing rules of the simple type system $\vdash_{\text{st}}$. The type system is parameterized by a *signature* Σ that assigns types to the operation names. The rules (ST-UNIT) to (ST-LET) are standard. The last four rules concern effect handlers, and they are also standard, matching those studied in prior work [18,21,35].[3] Importantly, (ST-HDLR) checks if a handler is well-typed by checking the well-typedness of the return clause as well as that of each operation clause. Note that the type of the return clause body, the types of the operation clause bodies, and the return types of the continuation parameters, are the same type σ'. This type σ' is called the *answer type*, and the fact that all the answer types in a handler are the same signifies that $\vdash_{\text{st}}$ lacks *answer-type modification* (ATM). We shall show in Sect. 3 a type system that has ATM, $\vdash_{\text{atm}}$, and show that the feature makes reachability decidable.

$b ::= \text{unit} \mid \text{bool}$
$\sigma ::= b \mid \sigma_1 \to \sigma_2$

Fig. 3. The simple types.

Example 3. Recall c_{ex1} and c_{ex2} from Examples 1 and 2. Both programs are $\vdash_{\text{st}}$-typable. For c_{ex1}, the types of some subexpressions are as follows:

$v_{tup} : \text{bool} \to \text{bool} \to \sigma_t \qquad v_{fst}, v_{snd} : \sigma_t \to \text{bool} \qquad c_{inc} : \text{unit}$

where $\sigma_t = (\text{bool} \to \text{bool} \to \text{bool}) \to \text{bool}$. And, the typing for the handler can be given by $x : \sigma_t \vdash_{\text{st}} \lambda s.x : \sigma_a$ for the return clause, and $x : \sigma_t, k : \text{unit} \to \sigma_a \vdash_{\text{st}} \lambda s.k \, () \, x : \sigma_a$ and $x : \text{unit}, k : \sigma_t \to \sigma_a \vdash_{\text{st}} \lambda s.k \, s \, s : \sigma_a$ for the clauses of *set* and *get* respectively, where $\sigma_a = \sigma_t \to \text{unit}$. Note that the answer type is σ_a in all clauses, indicating that ATM is not needed to type the example. Similarly, c_{ex2} can be typed by typing the return clause as $x : \text{bool} \vdash_{\text{st}} x : \text{bool}$, and the *dec* clause as $x : \text{unit}, k : \text{bool} \to \text{bool} \vdash_{\text{st}} v_{or} \, (k \, \top) \, (k \, \bot) : \text{bool}$. Note that the answer type is bool in all clauses in this typing, again indicating that ATM is not needed for typing the example.

We say that a FPCF$_{eff}$ program c is $\vdash_{\text{st}}$-*typable* if $\vdash_{\text{st}} c : \sigma$ for some σ. We define untyped finitary PCF (without effect handlers) as the fragment of

---

[3] Technically, [18,21] use weaker type systems that restrict (non-continuation) parameters of operations to base types. Our main result shows that ATM-typability makes reachability decidable even when no such restriction is imposed (cf. Sect. 3.4 and 4 for further discussion).

$$\frac{}{\Gamma \vdash_{st} () : \text{unit}} \text{ (St-Unit)} \quad \frac{v \in \{\top, \bot\}}{\Gamma \vdash_{st} v : \text{bool}} \text{ (St-Bool)} \quad \frac{x : \sigma \in \Gamma}{\Gamma \vdash_{st} x : \sigma} \text{ (St-Var)}$$

$$\frac{\Gamma, x : \sigma \vdash_{st} c : \sigma'}{\Gamma \vdash_{st} \lambda x.c : \sigma \to \sigma'} \text{ (St-Lam)} \quad \frac{\Gamma, x : \sigma \vdash_{st} v : \sigma}{\Gamma \vdash_{st} \text{rec } x = v : \sigma} \text{ (St-Rec)}$$

$$\frac{\Gamma \vdash_{st} v : \text{bool} \quad \Gamma \vdash_{st} c_1 : \sigma \quad \Gamma \vdash_{st} c_2 : \sigma}{\Gamma \vdash_{st} \text{if } v \text{ then } c_1 \text{ else } c_2 : \sigma} \text{ (St-If)}$$

$$\frac{\Gamma \vdash_{st} v_1 : \sigma \to \sigma' \quad \Gamma \vdash_{st} v_2 : \sigma}{\Gamma \vdash_{st} v_1 \, v_2 : \sigma'} \text{ (St-App)} \quad \frac{\Gamma \vdash_{st} c_1 : \sigma \quad \Gamma, x : \sigma \vdash_{st} c_2 : \sigma'}{\Gamma \vdash_{st} \text{let } x = c_1 \text{ in } c_2 : \sigma'} \text{ (St-Let)}$$

$$\frac{\Gamma \vdash_{st} v : \sigma}{\Gamma \vdash_{st} \text{return } v : \sigma} \text{ (St-Ret)} \quad \frac{\Sigma(op) = \sigma \to \sigma' \quad \Gamma \vdash_{st} v : \sigma}{\Gamma \vdash_{st} op \, v : \sigma'} \text{ (St-Op)}$$

$$\frac{\Gamma, x : \sigma \vdash_{st} : c : \sigma' \quad \Gamma, x_i : \sigma_i, k_i : \sigma'_i \to \sigma' \vdash_{st} c_i : \sigma' \quad \Sigma(op_i) = \sigma_i \to \sigma'_i}{\Gamma \vdash_{st} \{\text{return } x = c, op_i \, x_i \, k_i = c_i\} : \sigma \to \sigma'} \text{ (St-Hdlr)}$$

$$\frac{\Gamma \vdash_{st} h : \sigma \to \sigma' \quad \Gamma \vdash_{st} c : \sigma}{\Gamma \vdash_{st} \text{with } h \text{ handle } c : \sigma'} \text{ (St-Han)}$$

Fig. 4. The typing rules of the simple type system $\vdash_{st}$.

FPCF$_{eff}$ without with h handle c or op v, and we refer to the fragment by FPCF. As mentioned in the introduction, the reachability problem for $\vdash_{st}$-typable FPCF is decidable [17,27,41].

Theorem 1 ([17,27,41]). *Reachability is decidable for $\vdash_{st}$-typable FPCF.*

By contrast, as also mentioned in the introduction, a recent paper [21] has shown that the reachability problem is undecidable for $\vdash_{st}$-typable FPCF$_{eff}$.[4]

Theorem 2 ([18,21]). *Reachability is undecidable for $\vdash_{st}$-typable FPCF$_{eff}$.*

3 Main Results

Figure 5 shows the ATM types. The base types, b, remain unchanged from those of ordinary simple types. A *value type*, denoted by τ, is either a basetype or a function type of the form $\tau' \to \rho$ where ρ is a *computation type*. A computation type is either of the form $\tau/\Box$ expressing a *pure* computation that returns a value of type τ, or of the form $\tau/\rho_1 \Rightarrow \rho_2$ expressing an *effectful* computation that changes the answer type from ρ_1 to ρ_2 and returns a value of type τ.

$$\tau ::= b \mid \tau \to \rho$$
$$\rho ::= \tau/\Box \mid \tau/\rho_1 \Rightarrow \rho_2$$

Fig. 5. The ATM types.

---

[4] An alternative proof is given in [18].

$$\frac{\Gamma \vdash_{\text{atm}} c_1 : \tau_1/\square \quad \Gamma, x : \tau_1 \vdash_{\text{atm}} c_2 : \tau_2/\square}{\Gamma \vdash_{\text{atm}} \text{let } x = c_1 \text{ in } c_2 : \tau_2/\square} \quad \text{(T-LETP)}$$

$$\frac{\Gamma \vdash_{\text{atm}} c_1 : \tau_1/\rho_1 \Rightarrow \rho_1' \quad \Gamma, x : \tau_1 \vdash_{\text{atm}} c_2 : \tau_2/\rho_2 \Rightarrow \rho_1}{\Gamma \vdash_{\text{atm}} \text{let } x = c_1 \text{ in } c_2 : \tau_2/\rho_2 \Rightarrow \rho_1'} \quad \text{(T-LETIP)}$$

$$\frac{\Gamma \vdash_{\text{atm}} v : \tau}{\Gamma \vdash_{\text{atm}} \text{return } v : \tau/\square} \quad \text{(T-RET)} \qquad \frac{\Sigma(op) = \tau \to \tau'/\rho_1 \Rightarrow \rho_2 \quad \Gamma \vdash_{\text{atm}} v : \tau}{\Gamma \vdash_{\text{atm}} op\ v : \tau'/\rho_1 \Rightarrow \rho_2} \quad \text{(T-OP)}$$

$$\frac{\Sigma(op_i) = \tau_i \to \tau_i'/\rho_i \Rightarrow \rho_i' \quad \Gamma, x_i : \tau_i, k_i : \tau_i' \to \rho_i \vdash_{\text{atm}} c_i : \rho_i'}{\Gamma \vdash_{\text{atm}} \{\text{return } x = c, \overline{op_i\ x_i\ k_i = c_i}\}} \quad \text{(T-HDLR)}$$

$$\frac{\Gamma \vdash_{\text{atm}} h \quad \Gamma \vdash_{\text{atm}} c : \tau/\rho \Rightarrow \rho' \quad \Gamma, x : \tau \vdash_{\text{atm}} c' : \rho \quad \text{return } x = c' \in h}{\Gamma \vdash_{\text{atm}} \text{with } h \text{ handle } c : \rho'} \quad \text{(T-HAN)}$$

$$\frac{\Gamma \vdash_{\text{atm}} v : \tau \quad \tau \leq \tau'}{\Gamma \vdash_{\text{atm}} v : \tau'} \quad \text{(T-VSUB)} \qquad \frac{\Gamma \vdash_{\text{atm}} c : \rho \quad \rho \leq \rho'}{\Gamma \vdash_{\text{atm}} c : \rho'} \quad \text{(T-CSUB)}$$

Fig. 6. Representative typing rules of the ATM type system $\vdash_{\text{atm}}$.

Figure 6 shows representative typing rules of the ATM type system $\vdash_{\text{atm}}$. We refer to the extended report [11] for the complete set. The type system is essentially the ATM refinement type system proposed in [16], but without the refinement types aspect that is orthogonal to our paper. (T-LETP) stipulates that if both c_1 and c_2 are pure computations then the entire computation is also a pure one. By contrast, (T-LETIP) says that if c_1 is an effectful computation that changes the answer type from ρ_1 to ρ_1' and c_2 is an effectful computation that changes the answer type from ρ_2 to ρ_1, then the entire computation is an effectful computation that changes the answer type from ρ_2 to ρ_1'. Note that the answer types of the sub-computations are composed in a backward manner (cf. [16] for the explanation). (T-RET) and (T-OP) are analogous to the corresponding rules (ST-RET) and (ST-OP) of $\vdash_{\text{st}}$. In particular, the latter looks up the type of the operation in the signature Σ whose return computation type $\tau'/\rho_1 \Rightarrow \rho_2$ is an effectful one that changes the answer type from ρ_1 to ρ_2. (T-HDLR) checks that a handler is well-typed. Note that, unlike (ST-HDLR) of $\vdash_{\text{st}}$, the rule allows the operation clause bodies and their continuation parameters to have different answer types, signifying that $\vdash_{\text{atm}}$ allows ATM. The return clause is typed in (T-HAN) and it too is allowed to have a different answer type. Additionally, (T-HAN) stipulates that the type of the with-handle block is changed from that of the return clause body, ρ, to ρ' by ATM. The last two rules, (T-VSUB) and (T-CSUB), are subsumption rules for the subtyping relation $\leq$.

A key subtyping rule is the following one that allows "embedding" a pure computation type into an effectful computation type:

$$\frac{\tau_1 \leq \tau_2 \quad \rho_1 \leq \rho_2}{\tau_1/\square \leq \tau_2/\rho_1 \Rightarrow \rho_2} \quad \text{(S-Embed)}$$

The rule signifies that a pure computation can always be used where an effectful one is expected. The remaining subtyping rules are defined inductively on the structure of the types. We refer to the extended report [11] for the complete set of subtyping rules. We say that a program c is $\vdash_{\text{atm}}$-*typable* if $\vdash_{\text{atm}} c : \tau/\square$ for some τ.[5]

Example 4. Recall c_{ex1} and c_{ex2} from Examples 1 and 2. Recall that both programs are $\vdash_{\text{st}}$-typable as shown in Example 3. We show that both programs are also $\vdash_{\text{atm}}$-typable. For c_{ex1}, the typing for the handler can be given by $x : \tau_t \vdash_{\text{atm}} \lambda s.x : \rho_a$ for the return clause, $x : \sigma_t, k : \text{unit} \to \rho_a \vdash_{\text{atm}} \lambda s.k \ () \ x : \rho_a$ for the *set* clause, and $x : \text{unit}, k : \tau_t \to \rho_a \vdash_{\text{atm}} \lambda x.k \ s \ s : \rho_a$ for the *get* clause, where

$$\tau_t = (\text{bool} \to (\text{bool} \to \text{bool}/\square)/\square) \to \text{bool}/\square$$
$$\rho_a = (\tau_t \to \text{unit}/\square)/\square$$

Typing these clauses does not need (T-LetIp) but only (T-LetP) because the computation in the clauses are all pure.[6] By contrast, the operation invocations of *get* and *set* will respectively be given effectful computation types $\tau_t/\rho_a \Rightarrow \rho_a$ and $\text{unit}/\rho_a \Rightarrow \rho_a$ by (T-OP). The body of the with-handle block will also be given an effectful computation type $\text{unit}/\rho_a \Rightarrow \rho_a$ by using (T-LetIp) to compose effectful computation types and giving the recursive function *loop* the type $\text{unit} \to \text{unit}/\rho_a \Rightarrow \rho_a$. Therefore, $\vdash_{\text{atm}} c_{ex1} : \text{bool}/\square$. Similarly, c_{ex2} can be $\vdash_{\text{atm}}$-typed by typing the return clause and the *dec* clause as $x : \text{bool} \vdash_{\text{atm}} x : \rho_b$ and $x : \text{unit}, k : \text{bool} \to \rho_b \vdash_{\text{atm}} v_{or} \ (k \ \top) \ (k \ \bot) : \rho_b$, respectively, where $\rho_b = \text{bool}/\square$. The invocations of *dec* in the with-handle-block body can be given the type $\text{bool}/\rho_b \Rightarrow \rho_b$ and so can the body itself.

Example 5. The previous example programs c_{ex1} and c_{ex2} were both $\vdash_{\text{st}}$-typable and $\vdash_{\text{atm}}$-typable. Here, we show an example of a program that *needs* ATM to be typed. That is, the program is $\vdash_{\text{atm}}$-typable but not $\vdash_{\text{st}}$-typable. Consider the following program c_{ex3}.

    let r = with $\{$return $x = x$, op $x \ k = k \ x$; $\top\}$ handle $(op \ (); ())$ in
    if r then $\top$ else $\bot$

Note that the program is semantically type safe. In particular, note that the value that gets bound to r is the Boolean value $\top$ rather than unit. The program is

---

[5] The restriction to pure types for $\vdash_{\text{atm}}$-typable programs is for simplicity. It lets us disregard the case the source program gets stuck with an unhandled operation when showing the correctness of the CPS transformation. It can be shown that reachability remains decidable for $\vdash_{\text{atm}}$-typable programs even without the restriction.

[6] (T-LetP) is used when the trivial let bindings hidden by the notational convention are expanded (cf. Sect. 2).

$\vdash_{atm}$-typable by giving the invocation of op the type unit/(unit/$\square$ $\Rightarrow$ bool/$\square$) and giving the variable r the type bool. However, it is not $\vdash_{st}$-typable because, in that type system, the return clause body needs to be given the type unit whereas the op clause body needs to be given the type bool and the rule for typing a handler (ST-HDLR) asserts that these types need to be the same.

As shown in the above example, there are programs typable with ATM but not without it. In fact, one may naturally expect allowing ATM makes more programs typable because it allows an operation invocation to change the type of a with-handle block from that of the return clause body to that of an operation clause body. Therefore, the following main result of the paper may come as a surprise because, as remarked before, reachability is undecidable for $\vdash_{st}$-typable $FPCF_{eff}$.

Theorem 3 (Decidability). *Reachability is decidable for $\vdash_{atm}$-typable $FPCF_{eff}$.*

The rest of this section is organized as follows. We prove Theorem 3 in Sect. 3.1 by presenting a novel typing-derivation-directed CPS transformation that transforms an $\vdash_{atm}$-typable $FPCF_{eff}$ program to a $\vdash_{st}$-typable FPCF program. A corollary of Theorem 3 is the existence of a $FPCF_{eff}$ program that is $\vdash_{st}$-typable but not $\vdash_{atm}$-typable, and we present a concrete example of such a program in Sect. 3.2 (Sect. 3.3 also has such an example). Section 3.3 describes another application of our CPS transformation. That is, we show there that every $\vdash_{atm}$-typable recursive-definition-free $FPCF_{eff}$ program terminates while the same does not hold for $\vdash_{st}$-typable ones. Section 3.4 disproves a claim made in a recent paper [37] regarding what the paper calls *active effect handlers*.

3.1 Typing-Derivation-Directed CPS Transformation and the Proof of Theorem 3

We prove Theorem 3 by presenting a CPS transformation that transforms an $\vdash_{atm}$-typable $FPCF_{eff}$ program to a $\vdash_{st}$-typable FPCF program. Then, Theorem 3 follows from the fact that reachability is decidable for $\vdash_{st}$-typable FPCF programs.

We note that a CPS transformation for a language with effect handlers and ATM has already been proposed in a recent work by Kawamata et al. [16]. However, their CPS transformation requires higher-rank parametric polymorphism in an essential way to type the target of the transformation, and therefore, it is insufficient for our purpose because reachability for FPCF programs typable with a higher-rank parametric polymorphic type system is undecidable [40].

Our key observation is that the CPS transformation of [16] uses parametric polymorphism to allow a pure computation to be used in contexts where an effectful computation is expected. This is what subtyping is used for in $\vdash_{atm}$. Based on the observation, and inspired by the CPS transformation proposed in a paper by Materzok and Biernacki [25], we propose a new CPS transformation for effect handlers that is subtyping-aware so that the target of the transformation

$$\llbracket b \rrbracket = b \quad \llbracket \tau \to \rho \rrbracket = \llbracket \tau \rrbracket \to \llbracket \rho \rrbracket \quad \llbracket \tau / \square \rrbracket = \llbracket \tau \rrbracket$$
$$\llbracket \tau / \rho_1 \Rightarrow \rho_2 \rrbracket = \llbracket \Sigma \rrbracket \to (\llbracket \tau \rrbracket \to \llbracket \rho_1 \rrbracket) \to \llbracket \rho_2 \rrbracket$$
$$\llbracket \{op_i : \tau_i \to \tau_i'/\rho_i \Rightarrow \rho_i' \rrbracket = \{op_i : \llbracket \tau_i \rrbracket \to (\llbracket \tau_i' \rrbracket \to \llbracket \rho_i \rrbracket) \to \llbracket \rho_i' \rrbracket\}$$

Fig. 7. The CPS transformation of types.

can be typed without parametric polymorphism. The key idea, like that of [25], is to make the transformation be directed by the *typing derivation* of the source expression, instead of being only *type*-directed as more commonly seen for a CPS transformation.

For convenience, we extend $\vdash_{st}$-typed FPCF with records. That is, we extend the syntax of expressions and simple types as follows.

$$v ::= \cdots \mid \{\overline{l_i = v_i}\} \qquad c ::= \cdots \mid v.l \qquad \sigma ::= \cdots \mid \{\overline{l_i : \sigma_i}\}$$

The extension to the operational semantics and the typing rules is standard and is given in the extended report [11]. We note that the reachability for FPCF remains decidable with the record extension.[7]

Figure 7 shows the CPS transformation of types. As seen in the second to the last rule, an effectful computation is transformed to a function that takes a transformed signature (i.e., a record of the type $\llbracket \Sigma \rrbracket$), a transformed continuation of the type $\llbracket \tau \rrbracket \to \llbracket \rho_1 \rrbracket$, and returns a value of the type $\llbracket \rho_2 \rrbracket$. For a type environment Γ, we denote by $\llbracket \Gamma \rrbracket$ the CPS transformed environment $\{x : \llbracket \tau \rrbracket \mid x : \tau \in \Gamma\}$.

Next, we define the CPS transformation of subtyping derivations, which is of the form $\llbracket \tau_1 \leq \tau_2 \rrbracket$ for subtyping of value types and $\llbracket \rho_1 \leq \rho_2 \rrbracket$ for subtyping of computation types. An important case is the transformation of a derivation whose root is an instance of (S-EMBED) shown below.

$$\llbracket \tau_1/\square \leq \tau_2/\rho_1 \Rightarrow \rho_2 \rrbracket = \lambda x.\lambda h.\lambda k.\llbracket \rho_1 \leq \rho_2 \rrbracket @ (k @ (\llbracket \tau_1 \leq \tau_2 \rrbracket @ x))$$

where @ denotes a *static application* that is processed during the CPS transformation [14,16]. The complete set of the CPS transformation rules that concern subtyping derivations is given in the extended report [11].

Finally, we define the CPS transformation of typing derivations, which is of the form $\llbracket \Gamma \vdash_{atm} v : \tau \rrbracket$ for value expression typing and $\llbracket \Gamma \vdash_{atm} c : \rho \rrbracket$ for computation expression typing. An interesting rule is one concerning the subsumption rule (T-CSUB) shown below.

$$\left\llbracket \frac{\Gamma \vdash_{atm} c : \rho \quad \rho \leq \rho'}{\Gamma \vdash_{atm} c : \rho'} \right\rrbracket = \llbracket \rho \leq \rho' \rrbracket @ \llbracket \Gamma \vdash_{atm} c : \rho \rrbracket$$

Note that it uses the transformation obtained from the subtyping $\rho \leq \rho'$ to properly CPS transform the source computation expression c that has been

---

[7] This can be shown, for example, by encoding records as functions similarly to how it was done for tuples in Example 1.

CPS transformed with respect to the sub-derivation $\Gamma \vdash_{atm} c : \rho$. Another exemplifying transformation rule is one concerning the (T-HDLR) rule for typing a handler shown below.

$$\left[\!\!\left[\frac{\Sigma(op_i) = \tau_i \to \tau_i'/\rho_i \Rightarrow \rho_i' \quad \overline{\Gamma, x_i : \tau_i, k_i : \tau_i' \to \rho_i \vdash_{atm} c_i : \rho_i'}}{\Gamma \vdash_{atm} \{\texttt{return } x = c, \overline{op_i \ x_i \ k_i = c_i}\}} \right]\!\!\right] = \left\{ \overline{op_i = \lambda x_i.\lambda k_i.[\![\Gamma, x_i : \tau_i, k_i : \tau_i' \to \rho_i \vdash_{atm} c_i : \rho_i']\!]} \right\}$$

Note that the transformed result is a record mapping each operation name op_i to a function obtained by transforming the typing derivation for the operation clause body c_i. The rule is used in the CPS transformation corresponding to the typing rule (T-HAN) for typing a with-handle block shown below.

$$\left[\!\!\left[\frac{\Gamma \vdash_{atm} h \quad \Gamma \vdash_{atm} c : \tau/\rho \Rightarrow \rho' \quad \Gamma, x : \tau \vdash_{atm} c' : \rho \quad \texttt{return } x = c' \in h}{\Gamma \vdash_{atm} \texttt{with } h \texttt{ handle } c : \rho'} \right]\!\!\right]$$
$$= [\![\Gamma \vdash_{atm} c : \tau/\rho \Rightarrow \rho']\!] @ [\![\Gamma \vdash_{atm} h]\!] @ \lambda x. [\![\Gamma, x : \tau \vdash_{atm} c' : \rho]\!]$$

The rule uses the transformation rule corresponding to (T-HDLR) mentioned above to transform the handler typing derivation $\Gamma \vdash_{atm} h$ to a record of operations, transform the return clause typing derivation $\Gamma, x : \tau \vdash_{atm} c' : \rho$, and apply the transformation of the typing derivation for the with-handle block body $\Gamma \vdash_{atm} c : \tau/\rho \Rightarrow \rho'$, which would be a function of the type $[\![\Sigma]\!] \to ([\![\tau]\!] \to [\![\rho]\!]) \to [\![\rho']\!]$, to the former and the λ abstraction of the latter. The passed record will be looked up in the transformation of an operation invocation, as seen in the following transformation rule corresponding to (T-OP).

$$\left[\!\!\left[\frac{\Sigma(op) = \tau \to \tau'/\rho_1 \Rightarrow \rho_2 \quad \Gamma \vdash_{atm} v : \tau}{\Gamma \vdash_{atm} op \ v : \tau'/\rho_1 \Rightarrow \rho_2} \right]\!\!\right] = \lambda h.\lambda k.h.op \ [\![\Gamma \vdash_{atm} v : \tau]\!] \ k$$

We refer to the extended report [11] for the complete set of transformation rules that concern typing derivations.

We show the correctness of our CPS transformation. First, we show that the transformed program is a $\vdash_{st}$-typable FPCF program, which follows immediately from the following theorem that can be proven by induction on (sub)typing derivations, and the fact that the right hands of the transformation rules do not contain effect handlers.

Theorem 4 (Typability Preservation). *The following holds.*

1. *If $\tau \leq \tau'$ then $\vdash_{st} [\![\tau \leq \tau']\!] : [\![\tau]\!] \to [\![\tau']\!]$.*
2. *If $\rho \leq \rho'$ then $\vdash_{st} [\![\rho \leq \rho']\!] : [\![\rho]\!] \to [\![\rho']\!]$.*
3. *If $\Gamma \vdash_{atm} v : \tau$ then $[\![\Gamma]\!] \vdash_{st} [\![\Gamma \vdash_{atm} v : \tau]\!] : [\![\tau]\!]$.*
4. *If $\Gamma \vdash_{atm} c : \rho$ then $[\![\Gamma]\!] \vdash_{st} [\![\Gamma \vdash_{atm} c : \rho]\!] : [\![\rho]\!]$.*

Next, we show that the transformation preserves reachability. That is, if c is $\vdash_{atm}$-typable by a derivation $\vdash_{atm} c : \tau/\square$, then the answer to the reachability problem for c is the same as that for $[\![\vdash_{atm} c : \tau/\square]\!]$. This is shown by the following simulation theorem. Let $\to^+$ denote the transitive closure of $\to$.

Theorem 5 (Simulation). *Suppose* $\vdash_{atm} c : \tau/\square$. *The following holds.*

1. *If* $c \rightarrow^*$ return v *then* $\vdash_{atm} v : \tau$ *and* $[\![\vdash_{atm} c : \tau/\square]\!] \rightarrow^+ [\![\vdash_{atm} v : \tau]\!]$.
2. *If* $[\![\vdash_{atm} c : \tau/\square]\!] \rightarrow^+$ return v' *then there is v such that* $\vdash_{atm} v : \tau$, $[\![\vdash_{atm} v : \tau]\!] = v'$, *and* $c \rightarrow^*$ return v.

We refer to the extended report [11] for the proof. Therefore, given an $\vdash_{atm}$-typable c, we can decide the reachability of c by deciding the reachability of $[\![\vdash_{atm} c : \tau/\square]\!]$, because $[\![\vdash_{atm} c : \tau/\square]\!]$ is a $\vdash_{st}$-typable FPCF program by Theorem 4 and the reachability problem of $\vdash_{st}$-typable FPCF is decidable. Thus, reachability for $\vdash_{atm}$-typable FPCF$_{eff}$ is decidable. This completes the proof of Theorem 3.

3.2 A Concrete Example of a $\vdash_{st}$-Typable but $\vdash_{atm}$-Untypable Program

A corollary of our decidability result (Theorem 3) is that there are $\vdash_{st}$-typable programs that are not $\vdash_{atm}$-typable, which may seem counter-intuitive because one may naturally think that allowing ATM can only make more programs typable. We give a concrete example of such a program. Let

$$c_{ex4} \triangleq \text{rec } f = \lambda z.\text{with } h \text{ handle } f\,()$$
$$h \triangleq \{\text{return } x = op\,(), op\,x\,k = ()\}$$

This program c_{ex4} is $\vdash_{st}$-typable. Namely, $\vdash_{st} c_{ex4}$: unit $\rightarrow$ unit with $\Sigma(op) =$ unit $\rightarrow$ unit. The recursively defined function f would also be given the type unit $\rightarrow$ unit. We now show that c_{ex4} is $\vdash_{atm}$-untypable. Suppose for contradiction that it is $\vdash_{atm}$-typable. It must be the case that the recursive function f is given the type unit $\rightarrow \rho_f$ for some ρ_f. Because the body of the with-handle block is $f\,()$, by (T-HAN), this ρ_f must satisfy $\rho_f \leq \tau/\rho_1 \Rightarrow \rho_2$ for some τ, ρ_1, and ρ_2. However, by (T-HAN) again, ρ_2 must be a subtype of the with-handle block and thus a subtype of ρ_f by (T-REC). That is, we have the subtyping relation $\rho_2 \leq \tau/\rho_1 \Rightarrow \rho_2$. We state the following general property of ATM subtyping, which will be used in our argument.

Lemma 1. *If* $\rho \leq \tau/\rho' \Rightarrow \rho$ *then ρ' is pure.*

Proof. By induction on the structure of ρ. □

Therefore, ρ_1 must be pure. This is not possible because ρ_1 must be a supertype of the type of the return clause, but the return clause invokes the operation op and therefore must be given an effectful type. Thus, c_{ex4} is not $\vdash_{atm}$-typable.

3.3 Termination and Non-termination for $\vdash_{atm}$-Typable and $\vdash_{st}$-Typable Programs

The example of a $\vdash_{st}$-typable but $\vdash_{atm}$-untypable program given in Sect. 3.2 used a recursive definition in an essential way. A natural question is whether this is always the case, that is, recursive definitions are necessary for a program to be $\vdash_{\text{st}}$-typable but not $\vdash_{\text{atm}}$-typable. We answer the question negatively by presenting a recursive-definition-free program that is $\vdash_{\text{st}}$-typable but not $\vdash_{\text{atm}}$-typable. We do this by presenting a result that may be of independent interest and says that any $\vdash_{\text{atm}}$-typable recursive-definition-free program terminates whereas the same is not true for the $\vdash_{\text{st}}$-typable ones.

Consider the following recursive-definition-free program c_{ex5}:

$$(\text{with } h_{state} \text{ handle let } f = \lambda x.get\ ()\ ()\ \text{in } (set\ f; f\ ())) \ \lambda x.()$$

where h_{state} is the mutable state handler from Example 1. This program essentially implements the textbook encoding of an infinite loop by a mutable state (i.e., Landin's knot), and is non-terminating. Indeed, we have

$$\begin{aligned}
c_{ex5} &\to^+ (\lambda s.(\lambda y.\text{with } h_{state} \text{ handle } y; v_f\ ())\ ()\ v_f)\ \lambda x.() \\
&\to^+ (\lambda y.\text{with } h_{state} \text{ handle } y; v_f\ ())\ ()\ v_f \\
&\to^+ (\text{with } h_{state} \text{ handle } v_f\ ())\ v_f \\
&\to^+ (\text{with } h_{state} \text{ handle } get\ ()\ ())\ v_f \\
&\to^+ (\lambda s.(\lambda x.\text{with } h_{state} \text{ handle } x\ ()) \ s\ s)\ v_f \\
&\to^+ (\lambda x.\text{with } h_{state} \text{ handle } x\ ())\ v_f\ v_f \\
&\to^+ (\text{with } h_{state} \text{ handle } v_f\ ())\ v_f
\end{aligned}$$

where $v_f = \lambda_-.get\ ()\ ()$. Because the last line is the same as the third line, the evaluation diverges. The program c_{ex5} is $\vdash_{\text{st}}$-typable. Namely, it can be $\vdash_{\text{st}}$-typed by giving get the type $\text{unit} \to \sigma_t$ and set the type $\sigma_t \to \text{unit}$ in the operation signature, where $\sigma_t = \text{unit} \to \text{unit}$. The typing of the return, get, and set clauses can be done in the same way as in Example 3 except for using the above σ_t for the σ_t there. The with-handle block can be given the type unit with these types of get and set. However, c_{ex5} is not $\vdash_{\text{atm}}$-typable. This follows from the theorem below which can be easily shown by using our CPS transformation.

Theorem 6. *Every $\vdash_{\text{atm}}$-typable $FPCF_{eff}$ program without recursive definitions terminates.*

Proof. Let c be an $\vdash_{\text{atm}}$-typable $FPCF_{eff}$ program without recursive definitions, and let $c' = [\![\vdash_{\text{atm}} c : \tau / \square]\!]$. Because our CPS transformation does not add new recursive definitions, c' also does not contain recursive definitions (in addition to not containing effect handlers). By the results shown in Sect. 3.1, c' is $\vdash_{\text{st}}$-typable and c' terminates iff c terminates. Because simply-typed λ calculus (without recursive definitions or effect handlers) is terminating, c' must terminate and therefore so must c. □

3.4 Number of Active Effect Handlers Does Not Capture Decidability

A recent paper [37] introduced a notion called *active effect handlers*. Their paper claims that the boundedness of the number of active effect handlers characterizes the decidability of reachability, and that the reason why ATM ensures the decidability is because it ensures that this number is bounded. In this section, we disprove this claim by presenting a class of programs with only a bounded number of active effect handlers (in fact, with only at most one active effect handler) but whose reachability is nonetheless undecidable.

Let $succ$ be an operation, and $x_0, x_1, f_0, \ldots, f_n$ be variables where $n \geq 0$. Let us define the set of computation expressions $Inst^n \triangleq \{c_{inc}^{i,j} \mid i \in \{0,1\}, j \in \{0,\ldots,n\}\} \cup \{c_{dec}^{i,j,m} \mid i \in \{0,1\}, j, m \in \{0,\ldots,n\}\} \cup \{()\}$ where

$$c_{inc}^{i,j} \triangleq \texttt{let } x_i = \lambda y.succ\ x_i \texttt{ in } f_j\ x_0\ x_1$$
$$c_{dec}^{i,j,m} \triangleq \texttt{with } \{\texttt{return } x = f_j\ x_0\ x_1, succ\ x_i\ k = f_m\ x_0\ x_1\} \texttt{ handle } x_i\ ()$$

Then, let MM^n be the class of programs of the form

$$\texttt{mrec } f_0 = \lambda x_0.\lambda x_1.c_0 \texttt{ and } \ldots \texttt{ and } f_n = \lambda x_0.\lambda x_1.c_n \texttt{ in } (f_0\ (\lambda x.()) \ \lambda x.());\top$$

where each $c_i \in Inst^n$, and the mutual recursive definition $\texttt{mrec } f_0 = v_0$ and $\ldots$ and $f_n = v_n$ in c is syntactic sugar defined inductively by:

$$\texttt{let } f_0 = \texttt{rec } f_0 = (\texttt{mrec } f_1 = v_1 \texttt{ and } \ldots \texttt{ and } f_n = v_n \texttt{ in } v_0) \texttt{ in}$$
$$\vdots$$
$$\texttt{let } f_n = \texttt{rec } f_n = (\texttt{mrec } f_0 = v_0 \texttt{ and } \ldots \texttt{ and } f_{n-1} = v_{n-1} \texttt{ in } v_n) \texttt{ in } c$$

Let $MM = \bigcup_{n \in \mathbb{N}} MM^n$. We refer to the extended report [11] for the proof of the following theorem.

Theorem 7. *Reachability for MM is undecidable.*

We note that MM is $\vdash_{st}$-typable. Indeed, any program in MM can be $\vdash_{st}$-typed by giving the operation $succ$ the type $\sigma_{nat} \to \texttt{unit}$ and each recursive function f_i the type $\sigma_{nat} \to \sigma_{nat} \to \texttt{unit}$ where $\sigma_{nat} = \texttt{unit} \to \texttt{unit}$.

Next, we recall the notion of *active effect handlers* from [37]. Concretely, the number of active effect handlers is said to be *bounded* for a program if there is a non-negative integer n such that the evaluation of the program only yields intermediate expressions of the form

$$\ldots (\texttt{with } h_1 \texttt{ handle} \ldots (\texttt{with } h_m \texttt{ handle } c) \ldots) \ldots$$

for $m \leq n$ where c does not contain a with-handle block. Roughly, the number of active effect handlers measures the number of pending effect handlers on the call stack (when effect handlers are implemented by using a call stack, as often done in real implementations).

It is easy to see that the number of active effect handlers for any program in MM is bounded (in fact, by one), because a with-handle block will only appear in the evaluation by a calling a recursive function whose body is some c_{dec}, but then a subsequent recursive function call can happen only by replacing this with-handle block by the body of the return clause or the $succ$ clause. Because reachability for MM is undecidable as shown in Theorem 7, this disproves the claim that the boundedness of the number of active effect handlers characterizes the decidability of reachability for finitary PCF with effect handlers.

Additionally, a recent paper [21] contains a result stating that the reachability problem becomes decidable when the operation clauses are restricted to only use the given delimited continuation at tail positions. This may appear to contradict Theorem 7 because the operation (i.e., *succ*) clause in *MM* does not use the given delimited continuation. But it actually does not, because [21] restricts the (non-continuation) parameters of operations to base types and thus disallows programs like *MM*.[8] The main result of our paper (Theorem 3) shows that such restrictions on operation parameter types or delimited continuation usage are not need for ATM to ensure the decidability of reachability.

4 Related Work

As mentioned in the introduction, our work is inspired by the prior research on reachability for finitary PCF (without effect handlers). The problem was shown to be decidable [17,27,41], and the result has served as a foundation of methods for verifying infinite-state higher-order-recursive programs by incorporating techniques like predicate abstraction and CEGAR to abstract infinite data to finite domains [3,4,7,19,28,36,39,42]. It is worth noting that such studies have extended beyond just reachability (i.e., safety properties) and have also lead to methods for verifying liveness properties by incorporating techniques like binary reachability analysis and automata-theoretic verification method [8,9,20,26,34,43].

Inspired by this success and the popularity of effect handlers, a recent paper by Dal Lago and Ghyselen [21] has investigated the decidability of reachability for finitary PCF extended with effect handlers, and has found that the problem is undecidable. An alternative proof of this undecidability is also given in a recent paper by Kobayashi [18]. In this paper, we have shown that this undecidability comes from the way the standard type systems for effect handlers are designed, and that, surprisingly, the problem becomes decidable when the type system is extended to allow ATM. As remarked in Sect. 3.4, [21] contains a result stating that the reachability problem becomes decidable if the operation clauses are restricted to only use the captured delimited continuation at tail positions. However, as we have shown there, this decidability result crucially relies on the fact that operation parameters are restricted to base types in [21] because allowing arbitrary (simple) types for operation parameters makes reachability undecidable even with the restriction on the delimited continuation usage. The decidability result of our paper shows that such restrictions on operation parameter types or delimited continuation usage are not needed for ATM to ensure the decidability of reachability.

Our decidability result was proven by a novel typing-derivation-directed CPS transformation that transforms an ATM-typable program with effect handlers to a simply-typable program without effect handlers. Our CPS transformation is

---

[8] The same restriction is used in [18].

based on the one proposed by Kawamata et al. [16] but using typing-derivation dependency to eliminate parametric polymorphism. The elimination was crucial for reducing the problem to the decidable problem of reachability for (non-polymorphic) finitary PCF. As mentioned before, [16] used higher-rank parametric polymorphism in an essential way to allow pure computations to be used in contexts where effectful ones are expected, and we have observed that this is precisely what subtyping is used for by the ATM type system. We have adopted the ideas from the (sub)typing-derivation-directed CPS transformation for delimited control presented in the paper by Materzok and Biernacki [25] to design a new (sub)typing-derivation-directed CPS transformation for effect handlers. The CPS transformation of [25] does not consider effect handlers, and, as mentioned above, the CPS transformation of [16] requires parametric polymorphism. Our new CPS transformation makes a novel combination of the ideas from these prior CPS transformations.

A recent paper by Sekiyama and Unno [37] proves a similar but strictly weaker decidability result which essentially says that the typability in an ATM type system lacking subtyping is sufficient for decidability of the reachability for finitary PCF with effect handlers. Our paper proves a stronger result that says that typability in the ATM type system that supports subtyping is sufficient for the decidability, and their result follows as an easy corollary of our result. We note that subtyping makes a significant difference for an ATM type system. Indeed, without subtyping, an ATM type system cannot, for example, type a program that uses a pure function in contexts expecting effectful computations with different answer-type modifications. The lack of subtyping allowed their paper to use a more straightforward CPS transformation obtained by simply dropping parametric polymorphism from the CPS transformation of [16]. By contrast, our CPS transformation makes a novel use of the ideas from the (sub)typing-derivation-driven CPS transformation of [25] to eliminate parametric polymorphism without losing the support for subtyping. Additionally, we have disproved an erroneous claim made in [37] regarding active effect handlers. Namely, we have shown that the notion does not capture the decidability of reachability for programs with effect handlers, and that boundedness of their number is not the reason why ATM ensures the decidability of reachability.

5 Conclusion

We have studied the reachability problem for finitary PCF extended with effect handlers. Recent work [18,21] have shown that the problem is undecidable, in stark contrast to the case without effect handlers for which the problem is known to be decidable [17,27,41]. In this paper, we have shown that the undecidability comes from the way the standard type systems for effect handlers are designed. Concretely, we have shown that, perhaps surprisingly, extending the type system to allow ATM recovers decidability. A corollary of our decidability result is that, perhaps counter-intuitively, there are program that are typable without ATM but untypable with it, and we have shown concrete examples of such programs. Our decidability result was proven by a novel typing-derivation-driven CPS transformation, and as another application of the CPS transformation, we have shown that every ATM-typable recursive-definition-free finitary PCF programs terminates while the same does not hold for the simply-typable ones. Finally, we have disproved a claim made in a recent paper [37] by showing that active effect handlers do not characterize the decidability of reachability for finitary PCF with effect handlers. We foresee our decidability result to lay a foundation for developing verification methods for programs with effect handlers, just as the decidability result for reachability of finitary PCF has done such for programs without effect handlers.

Acknowledgments. We thank the anonymous reviewers for their suggestions. We thank Yukiyoshi Kameyama, Naoki Kobayashi, Taro Sekiyama, and Hiroshi Unno for discussions on the work. This work was supported by JSPS KAKENHI Grant Numbers JP23K24826 and JP20K20625.

References

1. Alvarez-Picallo, M., Freund, T., Ghica, D.R., Lindley, S.: Effect handlers for C via coroutines. Proc. ACM Program. Lang. **8**(OOPSLA2), 2462–2489 (2024). https://doi.org/10.1145/3689798
2. Asai, K.: On typing delimited continuations: three new solutions to the printf problem. High. Order Symb. Comput. **22**(3), 275–291 (2009). https://doi.org/10.1007/s10990-009-9049-5
3. Ball, T., Majumdar, R., Millstein, T.D., Rajamani, S.K.: Automatic predicate abstraction of C programs. In: Proceedings of the 2001 ACM SIGPLAN Conference on Programming Language Design and Implementation (PLDI), Snowbird, Utah, USA, 20–22 June 2001, pp. 203–213. ACM (2001). https://doi.org/10.1145/378795.378846
4. Ball, T., Rajamani, S.K.: The SLAM project: debugging system software via static analysis. In: Conference Record of POPL 2002: The 29th SIGPLAN-SIGACT Symposium on Principles of Programming Languages, Portland, OR, USA, 16–18 January 2002, pp. 1–3. ACM (2002). https://doi.org/10.1145/503272.503274
5. Bauer, A.: What is algebraic about algebraic effects and handlers? CoRR **abs/1807.05923** (2018). http://arxiv.org/abs/1807.05923
6. Brachthäuser, J.I., Schuster, P., Ostermann, K.: Effect handlers for the masses. Proc. ACM Program. Lang. **2**(OOPSLA), 111:1–111:27 (2018). https://doi.org/10.1145/3276481
7. Clarke, E., Grumberg, O., Jha, S., Lu, Y., Veith, H.: Counterexample-guided abstraction refinement. In: Emerson, E.A., Sistla, A.P. (eds.) CAV 2000. LNCS, vol. 1855, pp. 154–169. Springer, Heidelberg (2000). https://doi.org/10.1007/10722167_15
8. Cook, B., Gotsman, A., Podelski, A., Rybalchenko, A., Vardi, M.Y.: Proving that programs eventually do something good. In: Proceedings of the 34th ACM SIGPLAN-SIGACT Symposium on Principles of Programming Languages, POPL 2007, Nice, France, 17–19 January 2007, pp. 265–276. ACM (2007). https://doi.org/10.1145/1190216.1190257

9. Cook, B., Podelski, A., Rybalchenko, A.: Termination proofs for systems code. In: Proceedings of the ACM SIGPLAN 2006 Conference on Programming Language Design and Implementation, Ottawa, Ontario, Canada, 11–14 June 2006, pp. 415–426. ACM (2006). https://doi.org/10.1145/1133981.1134029
10. Danvy, O., Filinski, A.: Abstracting control. In: Proceedings of the 1990 ACM Conference on LISP and Functional Programming, LFP 1990, Nice, France, 27–29 June 1990, pp. 151–160. ACM (1990). https://doi.org/10.1145/91556.91622
11. Endo, R., Terauchi, T.: Reachability is decidable for ATM-typable finitary PCF with effect handlers. CoRR abs/2508.12572 (2025). https://arxiv.org/abs/2508.12572
12. Esparza, J., Hansel, D., Rossmanith, P., Schwoon, S.: Efficient algorithms for model checking pushdown systems. In: Emerson, E.A., Sistla, A.P. (eds.) CAV 2000. LNCS, vol. 1855, pp. 232–247. Springer, Heidelberg (2000). https://doi.org/10.1007/10722167_20
13. Ghica, D.R., Lindley, S., Bravo, M.M., Piróg, M.: High-level effect handlers in C++. Proc. ACM Program. Lang. 6(OOPSLA2), 1639–1667 (2022). https://doi.org/10.1145/3563445
14. Hillerström, D., Lindley, S., Atkey, R., Sivaramakrishnan, K.C.: Continuation passing style for effect handlers. In: 2nd International Conference on Formal Structures for Computation and Deduction, FSCD 2017, Oxford, UK, 3–9 September 2017. LIPIcs, vol. 84, pp. 18:1–18:19. Schloss Dagstuhl - Leibniz-Zentrum für Informatik (2017). https://doi.org/10.4230/LIPIcs.FSCD.2017.18
15. Kammar, O., Lindley, S., Oury, N.: Handlers in action. In: ACM SIGPLAN International Conference on Functional Programming, ICFP 2013, Boston, MA, USA, 25–27 September 2013, pp. 145–158. ACM (2013). https://doi.org/10.1145/2500365.2500590
16. Kawamata, F., Unno, H., Sekiyama, T., Terauchi, T.: Answer refinement modification: refinement type system for algebraic effects and handlers. Proc. ACM Program. Lang. 8(POPL), 115–147 (2024). https://doi.org/10.1145/3633280
17. Kobayashi, N.: Types and higher-order recursion schemes for verification of higher-order programs. In: Proceedings of the 36th ACM SIGPLAN-SIGACT Symposium on Principles of Programming Languages, POPL 2009, Savannah, GA, USA, 21–23 January 2009, pp. 416–428. ACM (2009). https://doi.org/10.1145/1480881.1480933
18. Kobayashi, N.: On decidable and undecidable extensions of simply typed lambda calculus. Proc. ACM Program. Lang. 9(POPL), 1136–1166 (2025). https://doi.org/10.1145/3704875
19. Kobayashi, N., Sato, R., Unno, H.: Predicate abstraction and CEGAR for higher-order model checking. In: Proceedings of the 32nd ACM SIGPLAN Conference on Programming Language Design and Implementation, PLDI 2011, San Jose, CA, USA, 4–8 June 2011, pp. 222–233. ACM (2011). https://doi.org/10.1145/1993498.1993525
20. Kuwahara, T., Terauchi, T., Unno, H., Kobayashi, N.: Automatic termination verification for higher-order functional programs. In: Shao, Z. (ed.) ESOP 2014. LNCS, vol. 8410, pp. 392–411. Springer, Heidelberg (2014). https://doi.org/10.1007/978-3-642-54833-8_21
21. Lago, U.D., Ghyselen, A.: On model-checking higher-order effectful programs. Proc. ACM Program. Lang. 8(POPL), 2610–2638 (2024). https://doi.org/10.1145/3632929

22. Leijen, D.: Implementing algebraic effects in C. In: Chang, B.-Y.E. (ed.) APLAS 2017. LNCS, vol. 10695, pp. 339–363. Springer, Cham (2017). https://doi.org/10.1007/978-3-319-71237-6_17
23. Levy, P.B.: Call-By-Push-Value: A Functional/Imperative Synthesis, Semantics Structures in Computation, vol. 2. Springer, Dordrecht (2004). https://doi.org/10.1007/978-94-007-0954-6
24. Loader, R.: Finitary PCF is not decidable. Theor. Comput. Sci. **266**(1-2), 341–364 (2001). https://doi.org/10.1016/S0304-3975(00)00194-8
25. Materzok, M., Biernacki, D.: Subtyping delimited continuations. In: Proceeding of the 16th ACM SIGPLAN International Conference on Functional Programming, ICFP 2011, Tokyo, Japan, 19–21 September 2011, pp. 81–93. ACM (2011). https://doi.org/10.1145/2034773.2034786
26. Murase, A., Terauchi, T., Kobayashi, N., Sato, R., Unno, H.: Temporal verification of higher-order functional programs. In: Proceedings of the 43rd Annual ACM SIGPLAN-SIGACT Symposium on Principles of Programming Languages, POPL 2016, St. Petersburg, FL, USA, 20–22 January 2016, pp. 57–68. ACM (2016). https://doi.org/10.1145/2837614.2837667
27. Ong, C.L.: On model-checking trees generated by higher-order recursion schemes. In: 21th IEEE Symposium on Logic in Computer Science (LICS 2006), Seattle, WA, USA, 12–15 August 2006, Proceedings, pp. 81–90. IEEE Computer Society (2006). https://doi.org/10.1109/LICS.2006.38
28. Ong, C.L., Ramsay, S.J.: Verifying higher-order functional programs with pattern-matching algebraic data types. In: Proceedings of the 38th ACM SIGPLAN-SIGACT Symposium on Principles of Programming Languages, POPL 2011, Austin, TX, USA, 26–28 January 2011, pp. 587–598. ACM (2011). https://doi.org/10.1145/1926385.1926453
29. Plotkin, G., Power, J.: Adequacy for algebraic effects. In: Honsell, F., Miculan, M. (eds.) FoSSaCS 2001. LNCS, vol. 2030, pp. 1–24. Springer, Heidelberg (2001). https://doi.org/10.1007/3-540-45315-6_1
30. Plotkin, G., Power, J.: Notions of computation determine monads. In: Nielsen, M., Engberg, U. (eds.) FoSSaCS 2002. LNCS, vol. 2303, pp. 342–356. Springer, Heidelberg (2002). https://doi.org/10.1007/3-540-45931-6_24
31. Plotkin, G.D., Power, J.: Algebraic operations and generic effects. Appl. Categorical Struct. **11**(1), 69–94 (2003). https://doi.org/10.1023/A:1023064908962
32. Plotkin, G.D., Pretnar, M.: A logic for algebraic effects. In: Proceedings of the Twenty-Third Annual IEEE Symposium on Logic in Computer Science, LICS 2008, Pittsburgh, PA, USA, 24–27 June 2008, pp. 118–129. IEEE Computer Society (2008). https://doi.org/10.1109/LICS.2008.45
33. Plotkin, G., Pretnar, M.: Handlers of algebraic effects. In: Castagna, G. (ed.) ESOP 2009. LNCS, vol. 5502, pp. 80–94. Springer, Heidelberg (2009). https://doi.org/10.1007/978-3-642-00590-9_7
34. Podelski, A., Rybalchenko, A.: Transition invariants. In: 19th IEEE Symposium on Logic in Computer Science (LICS 2004), Turku, Finland, 14–17 July 2004, Proceedings, pp. 32–41. IEEE Computer Society (2004). https://doi.org/10.1109/LICS.2004.1319598
35. Pretnar, M.: An introduction to algebraic effects and handlers. invited tutorial paper. In: The 31st Conference on the Mathematical Foundations of Programming Semantics, MFPS 2015, Nijmegen, The Netherlands, 22–25 June 2015. Electronic Notes in Theoretical Computer Science, vol. 319, pp. 19–35. Elsevier (2015). https://doi.org/10.1016/j.entcs.2015.12.003

36. Ramsay, S.J., Neatherway, R.P., Ong, C.L.: A type-directed abstraction refinement approach to higher-order model checking. In: The 41st Annual ACM SIGPLAN-SIGACT Symposium on Principles of Programming Languages, POPL 2014, San Diego, CA, USA, 20–21 January 2014, pp. 61–72. ACM (2014). https://doi.org/10.1145/2535838.2535873
37. Sekiyama, T., Unno, H.: Higher-order model checking of effect-handling programs with answer-type modification. Proc. ACM Program. Lang. **8**(OOPSLA2), 2662–2691 (2024). https://doi.org/10.1145/3689805
38. Sivaramakrishnan, K.C., Dolan, S., White, L., Kelly, T., Jaffer, S., Madhavapeddy, A.: Retrofitting effect handlers onto OCaml. In: PLDI 2021: 42nd ACM SIGPLAN International Conference on Programming Language Design and Implementation, Virtual Event, Canada, 20–25 June 2021, pp. 206–221. ACM (2021). https://doi.org/10.1145/3453483.3454039
39. Terauchi, T.: Dependent types from counterexamples. In: Proceedings of the 37th ACM SIGPLAN-SIGACT Symposium on Principles of Programming Languages, POPL 2010, Madrid, Spain, 17–23 January 2010, pp. 119–130. ACM (2010). https://doi.org/10.1145/1706299.1706315
40. Tsukada, T., Kobayashi, N.: Untyped recursion schemes and infinite intersection types. In: Ong, L. (ed.) FoSSaCS 2010. LNCS, vol. 6014, pp. 343–357. Springer, Heidelberg (2010). https://doi.org/10.1007/978-3-642-12032-9_24
41. Tsukada, T., Kobayashi, N.: Complexity of model-checking call-by-value programs. In: Muscholl, A. (ed.) FoSSaCS 2014. LNCS, vol. 8412, pp. 180–194. Springer, Heidelberg (2014). https://doi.org/10.1007/978-3-642-54830-7_12
42. Unno, H., Terauchi, T., Kobayashi, N.: Automating relatively complete verification of higher-order functional programs. In: The 40th Annual ACM SIGPLAN-SIGACT Symposium on Principles of Programming Languages, POPL 2013, Rome, Italy, 23–25 January 2013, pp. 75–86. ACM (2013). https://doi.org/10.1145/2429069.2429081
43. Vardi, M.Y.: Verification of concurrent programs: the automata-theoretic framework. Ann. Pure Appl. Log. **51**(1-2), 79–98 (1991). https://doi.org/10.1016/0168-0072(91)90066-U
44. Xie, N., Leijen, D.: Effect handlers in Haskell, evidently. In: Proceedings of the 13th ACM SIGPLAN International Symposium on Haskell, Haskell@ICFP 2020, Virtual Event, USA, 7 August 2020, pp. 95–108. ACM (2020). https://doi.org/10.1145/3406088.3409022

Expressive Power of One-Shot Control Operators and Coroutines

Kentaro Kobayashi[✉] and Yukiyoshi Kameyama

University of Tsukuba, Ibaraki, Japan
{kentaro.kobayashi,kameyama}@acm.org

Abstract. Control operators, such as exceptions and effect handlers, provide a means of representing computational effects in programs abstractly and modularly. While most theoretical studies have focused on multi-shot control operators, one-shot control operators – which restrict the use of captured continuations to at most once – are gaining attention for their balance between expressiveness and efficiency. This study aims to fill the gap. We present a mathematically rigorous comparison of the expressive power among one-shot control operators, including effect handlers, delimited continuations, and even asymmetric coroutines. Following previous studies on multi-shot control operators, we adopt Felleisen's macro-expressiveness as our measure of expressiveness. We verify the folklore that one-shot effect handlers and one-shot delimited-control operators can be macro-expressed by asymmetric coroutines, but not vice versa. We explain why a previous informal argument fails, and how to revise it to make a valid macro-translation.

Keywords: One-shot continuation · Effect handler & Delimited continuation · Asymmetric coroutine · Macro-expressibility

1 Introduction

Control operators are powerful tools for representing computational effects. Exceptions and coroutines are classic control operators, implemented in many languages. Delimited-control operators (e.g., shift/reset) have been extensively studied in the literature. The last decade has seen growing interest in effect handlers, which support modular abstraction of computational effects [13,14].

This paper studies the theoretical foundation of *one-shot* variants of control operators, where captured continuations are restricted to at most one use. While most studies[1] on control operators focused on unrestricted (i.e., *multi-shot*) control operators, one-shot variants have been recently gaining attention. There are several reasons to consider one-shot variants: First, they can be implemented more efficiently than multi-shot, as they avoid stack copying [3]. Second, they may alleviate the verification burden by reducing the complexity of reasoning

---

[1] A notable exception is Berdine et al., who proposed linearly-used continuations [2].

about sensitive resources [15]. Third, one-shotness is key to relating control operators based on continuations to classic ones found in many dynamic languages. For instance, a recent example in the former category is one-shot effect handlers in OCaml Version 5.x,[2] while the latter category includes coroutines and the yield operator, both of which are intrinsically one-shot.[3]

Despite these advantages, few authors have studied the theoretical foundation of one-shot control operators. Indeed, it is folklore that results for multi-shot control operators carry over easily to their one-shot counterparts; however, this is not the case. Since one-shotness is a dynamic property, a formal calculus for one-shot control operators should track the validity of each continuation, complicating both the semantics and precise reasoning about them. Among the few authors, de Moura and Ierusalimschy demonstrated a connection between one-shot delimited-control operators and coroutines [12]. However, this correspondence relies heavily on mutable states that can store higher-order functions, which, in our view, obscures the raw expressive power of these control operators.

We note that comparing the expressiveness of control operators is surprisingly difficult. For the case of one-shot control operators, the expressiveness results in the literature often lacked correctness proofs (e.g., [9]), or were incorrect. In this paper, we explain why a simple and seemingly correct translation from delimited-control operators to coroutines fails to preserve semantics.

This paper studies the relative expressiveness among three one-shot control operators: one-shot effect handlers, one-shot delimited-control operators, and asymmetric coroutines [12]. We adopt macro-expressibility [5] as the basis for our comparison, since it is well-established in the literature, particularly in the study of control operators, such as Forster, Kammar, Lindley, and Pretnar [7]. To our knowledge, this is the first systematic study to rigorously analyze the expressiveness of one-shot control operators.

Our contributions are threefold:

1. We prove that one-shot delimited-control operators can be macro-expressed by asymmetric coroutines.
2. We also prove that one-shot effect handlers can be macro-expressed by asymmetric coroutines.
3. We show that the converse direction does not hold: asymmetric coroutines cannot be macro-expressed by either one-shot delimited-control operators or one-shot effect handlers.

Figure 1 illustrates the macro-expressibility results established in this paper.

The remainder of this paper is organized as follows. Section 2 introduces macro-translations and the core calculus. Sections 3 and 4 present three extensions to the core calculus and establish the macro-expressibility results, while Sect. 5 disproves the macro-expressibility of the converse direction. Section 6 concludes the paper.[4]

---

[2] https://ocaml.org.
[3] James and Sabry argued that a multi-shot variant of the yield operator is as expressive as delimited-control operators [8].
[4] The full version of this paper is available on arXiv.

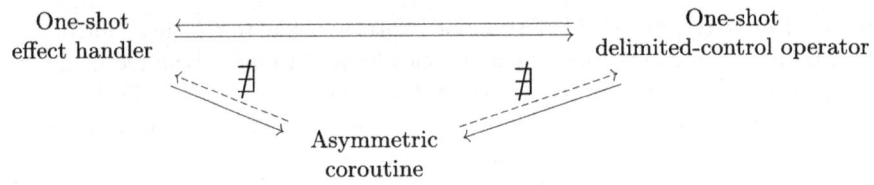

Fig. 1. Macro-expressibility among control operators. Solid lines indicate the existence of a macro-translation; dashed lines indicate its non-existence.

2 Macro-expressibility and Core Calculus

2.1 Macro-expressibility

Felleisen [5] formalized the notion of *macro-expressibility* to compare the expressive power of two programming languages when one is an extension of the other. The notion has later been adjusted to compare two languages when both are extensions of a common language [7]. Below, we show a definition based on operational semantics, in the spirit of Felleisen's formalization.

We assume that a programming language $\mathscr{L}$ is equipped with a set of $\mathscr{L}$-phrases, a set of $\mathscr{L}$-programs, which is a non-empty subset of $\mathscr{L}$-phrases, and an evaluation function $\mathrm{Eval}_{\mathscr{L}}(\cdot)$ that maps $\mathscr{L}$-programs to (suitably defined) values. Phrases and programs may be distinct in some languages. For instance, phrases can contain runtime values such as references. An n-hole syntactic abstraction in $\mathscr{L}$ is an $\mathscr{L}$-phrase that has n holes.

Definition 1. *Let $\mathscr{L}_1$ and $\mathscr{L}_2$ be conservative extensions[5] of $\mathscr{L}$. A partial map ϕ from $\mathscr{L}_1$-phrases to $\mathscr{L}_2$-phrases is a macro-translation if and only if all the following conditions are satisfied:*

1. *If M is an $\mathscr{L}_1$-program, $\phi(M)$ is defined and an $\mathscr{L}_2$-program.*
2. *If F is an n-ary function symbol of $\mathscr{L}$, for any $\mathscr{L}_1$-phrases $M_1, \ldots, M_n$, $\phi(F(M_1, \ldots, M_n)) = F(\phi(M_1), \ldots, \phi(M_n))$.*
3. *For each n-ary function symbol $F \in \mathscr{L}_1 \setminus \mathscr{L}$, there is an n-hole syntactic abstraction A in $\mathscr{L}_2$ such that $\phi(F(M_1, \ldots, M_n)) = A[\phi(M_1), \ldots, \phi(M_n)]$ for any $\mathscr{L}_1$-phrases $M_1, \ldots, M_n$.*
4. *$\mathrm{Eval}_{\mathscr{L}_1}(M)$ terminates if and only if $\mathrm{Eval}_{\mathscr{L}_2}(\phi(M))$ terminates.*

We say $\mathscr{L}_1$ is (strongly) macro-expressible in $\mathscr{L}_2$ if a macro-translation from $\mathscr{L}_1$ to $\mathscr{L}_2$ exists. We can define a weak macro-translation by replacing the "if and only if"-clause in the last condition by "only if".

An example of macro-expressibility is the let-construct in call-by-value lambda calculus. We can define a macro-translation ϕ in such a way that $\phi(\mathbf{let}\ x = M\ \mathbf{in}\ N) = (\lambda x.\ \phi(N))\ \phi(M)$ holds. Macro-expressibility is transitive: the composition of macro-translations is also a macro-translation.

---

[5] The formal definition of a conservative extension is provided in the full version.

$V, W ::=$		value	$\mid (V, W)$		pairing
	$\mid x \in \mathscr{V}$	variable	$\mid \mathbf{inj}_{\mathrm{L}} V$	$(\mathrm{L} \in \mathscr{C})$	variant
	$\mid ()$	unit	$\mid \{M\}$		thunk

$M, N ::=$		computation	$\mid \mathbf{let}\ x = M\ \mathbf{in}\ N$	sequencing
	$\mid \mathbf{case}\ V\ \mathbf{of}\ (x_1, x_2) \mapsto M$	product matching	$\mid \lambda x.\ M$	abstraction
	$\mid \mathbf{case}\ V\ \mathbf{of}\ \{(\mathbf{inj}_{\mathrm{L}_i} x_i \mapsto M_i)_i\}$	variant matching	$\mid M\ V$	application
	$\mid V!$	force	$\mid \langle M, N \rangle$	pairing
	$\mid \mathbf{return}\ V$	returner	$\mid \mathbf{prj}_i\ M$	projection

Fig. 2. Syntax of **MAM**

$$\begin{aligned}
\text{pure frame } \mathcal{P} &::= \mathbf{let}\ x = [\,]\ \mathbf{in}\ N \mid [\,]\ V \mid \mathbf{prj}_i\ [\,] \\
\text{computational frame } \mathcal{F} &::= \mathcal{P} \\
\text{pure context } \mathcal{H} &::= [\,] \mid \mathcal{P}[\mathcal{H}[\,]] \\
\text{evaluation context } \mathcal{C} &::= [\,] \mid \mathcal{F}[\mathcal{C}[\,]]
\end{aligned}$$

Fig. 3. Frames and Contexts of **MAM**

2.2 Core Calculus MAM

We use the language **MAM** (multi-adjunctive language) by Forster et al. [7], which was designed after Levy's Call-By-Push-Value calculus [10]. It serves as the common core calculus for our extensions.

Figure 2 gives the syntax of **MAM**. **MAM** differs from the untyped lambda calculus in that values and computations are clearly separated, and its own constructs are as follows: The pairing of computations $\langle M, N \rangle$ is *lazy*, a thunk freezes a computation, and a force thaws the thunk out: $\{M\}! \rightarrow^{\beta}_{\mathbf{M}} M$.

We consider terms modulo renaming of bound variables as usual. We define **MAM**-Phrases as the union of the set of values and that of computations. **MAM**-Programs are the set of computations.

To present the operational semantics of **MAM**, we define frames and contexts in Fig. 3, and the beta reduction rules $\rightarrow^{\beta}_{\mathbf{M}}$ on computations in Fig. 4.

We define the transition relation $\rightarrow_{\mathbf{M}}$ on computations by using evaluation contexts [6] as follows:

$$\frac{M \rightarrow^{\beta}_{\mathbf{M}} M'}{\mathcal{C}[M] \rightarrow_{\mathbf{M}} \mathcal{C}[M']}$$

($\times$) $\mathbf{case}\ (V_1, V_2)\ \mathbf{of}\ (x_1, x_2) \mapsto M$ $\rightarrow^{\beta}_{\mathbf{M}} M[V_1/x_1, V_2/x_2]$
($+$) $\mathbf{case}\ \mathbf{inj}_{\mathrm{L}_k} V\ \mathbf{of}\ \{(\mathbf{inj}_{\mathrm{L}_i} x_i \mapsto M_i)_i\}$ $\rightarrow^{\beta}_{\mathbf{M}} M_k[V/x_k]$
(F) $\mathbf{let}\ x = \mathbf{return}\ V\ \mathbf{in}\ M \rightarrow^{\beta}_{\mathbf{M}} M[V/x]$
(U) $\{M\}! \rightarrow^{\beta}_{\mathbf{M}} M$
($\rightarrow$) $(\lambda x.\ M)\ V \rightarrow^{\beta}_{\mathbf{M}} M[V/x]$
(&) $\mathbf{prj}_i \langle M_1, M_2 \rangle \rightarrow^{\beta}_{\mathbf{M}} M_i$

Fig. 4. Beta Reduction Rules of **MAM**

$V, W ::= \ldots$ value
$\quad | \; l \in \mathscr{L}_{\mathbf{D}}$ continuation label

$M, N ::= \ldots$ computation $| \; \langle M | x.N \rangle$ dollar
$\quad | \; \mathbf{S_0} k. \; M$ shift0 $\quad | \;$ **throw** $V \; W$ throw

pure frame $\mathcal{P} ::= \ldots$
computational frame $\mathcal{F} ::= \ldots | \; \langle [\;] | x.N \rangle$

pure context $\mathcal{H} ::= \ldots$
evaluation context $\mathcal{C} ::= \ldots$

Fig. 5. Syntax of $\mathbf{DEL}_{\text{one}}$

Evaluation of a program is defined by: $\text{Eval}_{\mathbf{MAM}}(M) := V$ if $M \to^*_{\mathbf{M}}$ **return** V. $\text{Eval}_{\mathbf{MAM}}(M)$ is a well-defined partial function, since $\to^{\mathbf{M}}$ is deterministic.

3   One-Shot Delimited Continuations as Asymmetric Coroutines

This section investigates the macro-expressibility of one-shot delimited continuations in terms of asymmetric coroutines, which has been considered folklore, but turns out unexpectedly complicated. We first introduce two calculi: $\mathbf{DEL}_{\text{one}}$ for one-shot delimited continuations and $\mathbf{AC}$ for asymmetric coroutines, then present a macro-translation from $\mathbf{DEL}_{\text{one}}$ to $\mathbf{AC}$.

3.1   The Calculus for One-Shot Delimited Continuations

We present the calculus $\mathbf{DEL}_{\text{one}}$, which incorporates a one-shot version of the control operator $shift_0/dollar$. The $shift_0/dollar$ operator, proposed by Materzok and Biernacki [11], is a variant of $shift_0/reset_0$ [4] and has the same macro-expressive power. We adopt the calculus $\mathbf{DEL}$ defined by Forster et al. [7], restricting each captured continuation to one-shot use.

Figure 5 shows the syntax of $\mathbf{DEL}_{\text{one}}$ as an extension of $\mathbf{MAM}$, where the ellipses $(\ldots)$ indicate the syntax from $\mathbf{MAM}$. $\mathscr{L}_{\mathbf{D}}$ is a countable set of continuation labels, where l is a dynamically generated label for a continuation. The dollar term $\langle M | x.N \rangle$ is similar to reset0: when evaluated, it installs a delimiter for continuations captured in M. Unlike reset0, it has an additional part $x.N$ where x is bound in N. When M evaluates to a value, its result is bound to x, and N is evaluated. When the term $\mathbf{S_0} k. \; M$ is evaluated, a continuation delimited by the nearest dollar term is captured, k is bound to the continuation, and the body M is evaluated. If there is no surrounding dollar term, the evaluation gets stuck. **throw** $l \; V$ invokes the continuation represented by l, passing V as an argument. $\mathbf{DEL}_{\text{one}}$-Phrases is the set of all $\mathbf{DEL}_{\text{one}}$-values and $\mathbf{DEL}_{\text{one}}$-computations, and $\mathbf{DEL}_{\text{one}}$-Programs is the set of computations without continuation labels.

In $\mathbf{DEL}_{\text{one}}$, continuations can be invoked at most once. Consider the example:

$$\left\langle \begin{array}{l} \mathbf{S_0} k. \; \mathbf{let} \; a = \mathbf{throw} \; k \; 1 \; \mathbf{in} \\ \quad \mathbf{let} \; b = \mathbf{throw} \; k \; 2 \; \mathbf{in} \; \mathbf{return} \; (a, b) \end{array} \middle| \; x.\mathbf{return} \; x \right\rangle$$

$$
\begin{array}{ll}
\textbf{(MAM)} & \dfrac{M \to^{\beta}_{\mathbf{M}} M'}{\langle M;\theta\rangle \to^{\beta}_{\mathbf{D}} \langle M';\theta\rangle} \\[2ex]
\textbf{(ret)} & \langle\langle\textbf{return}\ V|x.M\rangle;\theta\rangle \to^{\beta}_{\mathbf{D}} \langle M[V/x];\theta\rangle \\[2ex]
\textbf{(shift)} & \dfrac{l \text{ is a fresh label}}{\langle\langle\mathcal{H}[\mathbf{S_0}k.\ M]|x.N\rangle;\theta\rangle \to^{\beta}_{\mathbf{D}} \langle M[l/k];\theta[l := \lambda y.\ \langle\mathcal{H}[\textbf{return}\ y]|x.N\rangle]\rangle} \\[2ex]
\textbf{(throw)} & \dfrac{\theta(l) = \lambda y.\ \langle\mathcal{H}[\textbf{return}\ y]|x.N\rangle}{\langle\textbf{throw}\ l\ V;\theta\rangle \to^{\beta}_{\mathbf{D}} \langle\langle\mathcal{H}[\textbf{return}\ V]|x.N\rangle;\theta[l := \textbf{nil}]\rangle} \\[2ex]
\textbf{(fail)} & \dfrac{\theta(l) = \textbf{nil}}{\langle\textbf{throw}\ l\ V;\theta\rangle \to^{\beta}_{\mathbf{D}} \bot}
\end{array}
$$

Fig. 6. Beta reduction rules of $\mathbf{DEL}_{\text{one}}$

The term attempts to use the continuation k twice, first to compute a and then to compute b. Such usage violates the one-shotness constraint, and to detect it, we use a *store* to record the content and the status of continuations.

A store is a partial function $\theta : \mathscr{L}_{\mathbf{D}} \rightharpoonup \text{computation} \sqcup \{\textbf{nil}\}$. $\text{Dom}(\theta)$ is the set of continuation labels l such that $\theta(l)$ is defined. Note that $\textbf{nil}$ is not an undefined element, and the complement of $\text{Dom}(\theta)$ is *not* equal to $\theta^{-1}(\textbf{nil})$. If $\theta(l) = \textbf{nil}$, it means that the continuation labeled l has already been invoked. The empty set $\emptyset$ represents the store with no bindings.

We introduce *configurations* to describe the runtime states of programs. A configuration C is a pair of a $\mathbf{DEL}_{\text{one}}$-computation M and a store θ, or the error state $\bot$. The beta reduction rules $\to^{\mathbf{D}}_{\beta}$ on configurations are defined in Fig. 6.[6]

The reduction rules of $\mathbf{DEL}_{\text{one}}$ are defined as follows:

$$
\dfrac{\langle M;\theta\rangle \to^{\beta}_{\mathbf{D}} \langle M';\theta'\rangle}{\langle \mathcal{C}[M];\theta\rangle \to_{\mathbf{D}} \langle \mathcal{C}[M'];\theta'\rangle} \qquad \dfrac{\langle M;\theta\rangle \to^{\beta}_{\mathbf{D}} \bot}{\langle \mathcal{C}[M];\theta\rangle \to_{\mathbf{D}} \bot}
$$

Evaluation of a $\mathbf{DEL}_{\text{one}}$-program is defined by: $\text{Eval}_{\mathbf{DEL}_{\text{one}}}(M) := V$ if there exists a store θ such that $\langle M;\emptyset\rangle \to^{*}_{\mathbf{D}} \langle\textbf{return}\ V;\theta\rangle$. $\text{Eval}_{\mathbf{DEL}_{\text{one}}}(M)$ is a well-defined partial function, since $\to_{\mathbf{D}}$ is deterministic.

3.2 The Calculus for Asymmetric Coroutines

De Moura and Ierusalimschy [12] studied several variations of coroutines and introduced two calculi, symmetric coroutines and asymmetric coroutines. In this paper, we present the calculus **AC** for asymmetric coroutines, which are prevalent in modern programming languages.

Figure 7 presents the syntax of **AC**. Besides the constructors of **MAM**, **AC** has coroutine labels as values, and four constructs to manipulate coroutines as computations: labeled computation, **create**, **resume**, and **yield**. $\mathscr{L}_{\mathbf{AC}}$ is a

---

[6] In (shift), we assume that y does not freely occur in the context $\mathcal{H}$. Similarly, throughout the rest of this paper, we assume that the same condition holds for variables that are freshly generated, whether in reduction rules or in translations.

$V, W ::= \ldots$ value $\quad M, N ::= \ldots$ computation | **yield** V yield
$\quad\quad | \; l \in \mathscr{L}_{\mathbf{AC}}$ coroutine label $\quad\quad$ | **create** V create $\quad$ | **resume** $V\;W$ resume
$\quad\quad\quad\quad\quad\quad\quad\quad\quad\quad\quad\quad\quad\quad\quad\quad\quad$ | $l : M$ labeled computation
$\quad\quad\quad\quad\quad$ pure frame $\mathcal{P} ::= \ldots$ $\quad\quad\quad\quad\quad\quad$ pure context $\mathcal{H} ::= \ldots$
computational frame $\mathcal{F} ::= \ldots | \; l : [\;]$ $\quad\quad$ evaluation context $\mathcal{C} ::= \ldots$

Fig. 7. Syntax of **AC**

(MAM) $\quad \dfrac{M \to^{\beta}_{\mathbf{M}} M'}{\langle M; \theta \rangle \to^{\beta}_{\mathbf{AC}} \langle M'; \theta \rangle}$

(create) $\quad \dfrac{l \text{ is a fresh label}}{\langle \mathbf{create}\; V; \theta \rangle \to^{\beta}_{\mathbf{AC}} \langle \mathbf{return}\; l; \theta[l := V] \rangle}$

(resume) $\quad \dfrac{l \in \mathrm{Dom}(\theta) \quad \theta(l) \neq \mathbf{nil}}{\langle \mathbf{resume}\; l\; V; \theta \rangle \to^{\beta}_{\mathbf{AC}} \langle l : (\theta(l)!\; V); \theta[l := \mathbf{nil}] \rangle}$

(fail) $\quad \dfrac{\theta(l) = \mathbf{nil}}{\langle \mathbf{resume}\; l\; V; \theta \rangle \to^{\beta}_{\mathbf{AC}} \bot}$

(ret) $\quad \langle l : \mathbf{return}\; V; \theta \rangle \to^{\beta}_{\mathbf{AC}} \langle \mathbf{return}\; V; \theta \rangle$

(yield) $\quad \langle l : \mathcal{H}[\mathbf{yield}\; V]; \theta \rangle \to^{\beta}_{\mathbf{AC}} \langle \mathbf{return}\; V; \theta[l := \{\lambda y.\; \mathcal{H}[\mathbf{return}\; y]\}] \rangle$

$\dfrac{\langle M; \theta \rangle \to^{\beta}_{\mathbf{AC}} \langle M'; \theta' \rangle}{\langle \mathcal{C}[M]; \theta \rangle \to_{\mathbf{AC}} \langle \mathcal{C}[M']; \theta' \rangle} \quad\quad \dfrac{\langle M; \theta \rangle \to^{\beta}_{\mathbf{AC}} \bot}{\langle \mathcal{C}[M]; \theta \rangle \to_{\mathbf{AC}} \bot}$

Fig. 8. Semantics of **AC**

countable set of coroutine labels. The labeled computation $l : M$ represents the coroutine l executing the computation M. **create** V produces a new coroutine whose computation is V, and **resume** $V\;W$ starts (or resumes) a coroutine whose label is V with a parameter W. **yield** V suspends the current coroutine, yielding V to its caller. **AC**-Phrases are the values and computations of **AC**, and **AC**-Programs are the computations without coroutine labels.

A store θ is a partial function that maps labels to *values* or $\mathbf{nil}$. Note the difference from the store in $\mathbf{DEL}_{\mathrm{one}}$, which maps labels to *computations* or $\mathbf{nil}$. As in $\mathbf{DEL}_{\mathrm{one}}$, a configuration in **AC** is a pair $\langle M; \theta \rangle$ of a computation M and a store θ, or the error state $\bot$.

Figure 8 defines the operational semantics of **AC** which includes the beta reduction rules $\to^{\beta}_{\mathbf{AC}}$ and the reduction rules $\to_{\mathbf{AC}}$. Note that coroutines are inherently one-shot: while a coroutine may be called multiple times by suspending and resuming it, it cannot be duplicated or reused.

Evaluation of an **AC**-program is defined by: $\mathrm{Eval}_{\mathbf{AC}}(M) := V$ if there exists a store θ such that $\langle M; \emptyset \rangle \to^{*}_{\mathbf{AC}} \langle \mathbf{return}\; V; \theta \rangle$. Since $\to_{\mathbf{AC}}$ is deterministic, $\mathrm{Eval}_{\mathbf{AC}}$ is a well-defined partial function.

$$\overline{\langle M | x.N \rangle} := \begin{pmatrix} \textbf{let } z = \textbf{create } \{\lambda\_.\ \textbf{let } x = \underline{M} \textbf{ in return } \{\lambda\_.\ \underline{N}\}\} \textbf{ in} \\ \textbf{let } \textit{res} = \textbf{resume } z\ ()\ \textbf{in} \\ \textit{res}!\ z \end{pmatrix}$$

$$\overline{\textbf{S}_0 k.\ L} := \textbf{yield } \{\lambda k.\ \underline{L}\}$$

$$\overline{\textbf{throw } V\ W} := \begin{pmatrix} \textbf{let } \textit{res} = \textbf{resume } \underline{V}\ \underline{W} \textbf{ in} \\ \textit{res}!\ \underline{V} \end{pmatrix}$$

Fig. 9. Naive translation from $\textbf{DEL}_{\text{one}}$ to $\textbf{AC}$

3.3 Naive Translation and Its Failure

Given the similarity between delimited continuations and coroutines, one may think that it is straightforward to macro-translate $\textbf{DEL}_{\text{one}}$ to $\textbf{AC}$ with the following correspondence: a dollar term in $\textbf{DEL}_{\text{one}}$ is translated to a create term in $\textbf{AC}$, a shift0 term to a yield term, and a throw term to a resume term. Based on this intuition, we can define the naive translation from $\textbf{DEL}_{\text{one}}$ to $\textbf{AC}$ in Fig. 9. Note that on the right-hand side of $\overline{\langle M | x.N \rangle}$, x corresponds to the binding occurrence of x in the original term $\overline{\langle M | x.N \rangle}$. Figure 9 only shows non-trivial cases. Other cases are translated homomorphically except for continuation labels, whose translations are not defined. This is not problematic, since a macro-translation only has to translate all $\textbf{DEL}_{\text{one}}$-programs, which do not contain continuation labels.

The naive translation works for simple expressions. However, we found a counterexample to it. Consider the following $\textbf{DEL}_{\text{one}}$-program M.

$$M := \left\langle \begin{array}{l} \textbf{let } j = (\textbf{S}_0 k_1.\ \textbf{let } r_1 = \textbf{throw } k_1\ 10 \textbf{ in} \\ \qquad\qquad\qquad \textbf{let } r_2 = \textbf{throw } k_1\ 20 \textbf{ in return } r_1)\ \textbf{in} \\ \textbf{S}_0 k_2.\ \textbf{return } 30 \end{array} \middle| \ i.\,\textbf{return } i \right\rangle$$

In $\textbf{DEL}_{\text{one}}$, M is evaluated as follows: First, the shift0 term $\textbf{S}_0 k_1.\ \cdots$ is invoked, then the pure context surrounding it is captured and stored under a fresh label l_1:[7]

$$M \to_{\textbf{D}} \textbf{let } r_1 = \textbf{throw } l_1\ 10 \textbf{ in let } r_2 = \textbf{throw } l_1\ 20 \textbf{ in return } r_1 \qquad (1)$$

Next, **throw** l_1 10 invokes the captured continuation labeled l_1, rendering it invalid:

$$\cdots \to_{\textbf{D}}^+ \begin{pmatrix} \textbf{let } r_1 = \left\langle \begin{array}{l} \textbf{let } j = \textbf{return } 10 \textbf{ in} \\ \textbf{S}_0 k_2.\ \textbf{return } 30 \end{array} \middle| \ i.\,\textbf{return } i \right\rangle \textbf{ in} \\ \textbf{let } r_2 = \textbf{throw } l_1\ 20 \textbf{ in return } r_1 \end{pmatrix} \qquad (2)$$

$$\to_{\textbf{D}} \begin{pmatrix} \textbf{let } r_1 = \langle \textbf{S}_0 k_2.\ \textbf{return } 30 \mid i.\,\textbf{return } i \rangle \textbf{ in} \\ \textbf{let } r_2 = \textbf{throw } l_1\ 20 \textbf{ in return } r_1 \end{pmatrix}$$

---

[7] For brevity, the full content of the store is omitted from the evaluation trace. We will only mention the changes relevant to the main computation.

$$M \to^+_{\mathbf{AC}} \begin{pmatrix} \text{let } r_1 = \underline{\mathbf{throw}} \ (l, l_c, 0) \ 10 \ \mathbf{in} \\ \text{let } r_2 = \underline{\mathbf{throw}} \ (l, l_c, 0) \ 20 \ \mathbf{in} \\ \mathbf{return} \ r_1 \end{pmatrix} \begin{bmatrix} \text{where} \\ l \mapsto \left\{ \lambda y. \ \mathcal{P} \begin{bmatrix} \text{let } j = \mathbf{return} \ y \ \mathbf{in} \\ \mathbf{yield} \ \{\lambda k_2. \ \mathbf{return} \ 30\} \end{bmatrix} \right\} \\ l_c \mapsto \{RefCell(0)\} \end{bmatrix}$$

(**throw** increments l_c and resumes l.)

$$\to^+_{\mathbf{AC}} \begin{pmatrix} \text{let } r_1 = \begin{pmatrix} \text{let } res = l : \\ res! \ \underbrace{(l, l_c, 1)}_{\text{valid}} \end{pmatrix} \left(\mathcal{P} \begin{bmatrix} \text{let } j = \mathbf{return} \ 10 \ \mathbf{in} \\ \mathbf{yield} \ \{\lambda k_2. \ \mathbf{return} \ 30\} \end{bmatrix} \right) \mathbf{in} \\ \text{let } r_2 = \underline{\mathbf{throw}} \ \underbrace{(l, l_c, 0)}_{\text{invalid}} \ 20 \ \mathbf{in} \\ \mathbf{return} \ r_1 \end{pmatrix} \mathbf{in} \quad (3)$$

$$\begin{bmatrix} \text{where} \\ l \mapsto \mathbf{nil} \\ l_c \mapsto \{RefCell(1)\} \end{bmatrix}$$

(The coroutine labeled l is suspended by **yield**.)

$$\to^+_{\mathbf{AC}} \begin{pmatrix} \text{let } r_1 = \{\lambda k_2. \ \mathbf{return} \ 30\}! \ (l, l_c, 1) \ \mathbf{in} \\ \text{let } r_2 = \underline{\mathbf{throw}} \ (l, l_c, 0) \ 20 \ \mathbf{in} \\ \mathbf{return} \ r_1 \end{pmatrix} \begin{bmatrix} \text{where} \\ l \mapsto \{\lambda y. \ \mathcal{P}[\mathbf{return} \ y]\} \\ l_c \mapsto \{RefCell(1)\} \end{bmatrix} \quad (4)$$

(The continuation $(l, l_c, 1)$ is not used and l remains active)

$$\to^+_{\mathbf{AC}} \begin{pmatrix} \text{let } r_2 = \underline{\mathbf{throw}} \ (l, l_c, 0) \ 20 \ \mathbf{in} \\ \mathbf{return} \ 30 \end{pmatrix} \begin{bmatrix} \text{where} \\ l \mapsto \{\lambda y. \ \mathcal{P}[\mathbf{return} \ y]\} \\ l_c \mapsto \{RefCell(1)\} \end{bmatrix} \quad (5)$$

Fig. 10. Evaluation of $\underline{M}$ where $\mathcal{P} \equiv \mathbf{let} \ i = [\ ] \ \mathbf{in \ return} \ \{\lambda\_. \ \mathbf{return} \ i\}$. The black parts show the evaluation using the naive translation; the red parts are additions by our refined translation in Fig. 11. (Color figure online)

Then, the shift0 term $\mathbf{S_0} k_2. \ \cdots$ is invoked. This captures the context and stores it under another fresh label l_2. The evaluation then continues as follows (note that the continuation labeled l_2 is not used):

$$\cdots \to^+_{\mathbf{D}} \mathbf{let} \ r_1 = \mathbf{return} \ 30 \ \mathbf{in \ let} \ r_2 = \mathbf{throw} \ l_1 \ 20 \ \mathbf{in \ return} \ r_1$$
$$\to_{\mathbf{D}} \mathbf{let} \ r_2 = \mathbf{throw} \ l_1 \ 20 \ \mathbf{in \ return} \ 30$$

Finally, **throw** l_1 20 is invoked, but since the continuation labeled l_1 has already been consumed, the evaluation fails.

Therefore, in **AC**, $\underline{M}$ must not successfully terminate since macro-translations preserve semantics; however, this is not the case. To understand the reason, consider the evaluation trace shown in the black parts of Fig. 10 (ignore the red[8] parts for the moment). First, after applying the translation, $\underline{M}$ reduces to the term on the first line (corresponding to (1)) where the continuation captured by $\mathbf{S_0} k_1. \ \cdots$ in M is represented by a coroutine labeled

---

[8] In the printed (monochrome) version, the red parts may appear as gray.

l. Next, **throw** l 10 is evaluated. This resumes the coroutine labeled l and invalidates l by mapping it to **nil**. The evaluation then reaches (3), which corresponds to (2). Then, **let** $j =$ **return** 10 **in** $\cdots$ is evaluated and the term **yield** $\{\lambda k_2.$ **return** $30\}$ ($\equiv \mathbf{S_0} k_2.$ **return** 30) is invoked. This suspends the coroutine labeled l, *reactivating* it in the store, as shown in (4).

This reactivation is the source of the failure. In the evaluation of M in $\mathbf{DEL}_{\text{one}}$, the two shift0 invocations result in two distinct continuation labels, l_1 and l_2. Our naive translation, however, maps both of these labels to the same coroutine label l. Because of this, the reactivation of l makes the stale continuation (corresponding to l_1) available again. This would be harmless if the thunk returned by **yield** eventually resumed l, as that would invalidate l again. In our counterexample, however, this thunk does not resume l. Therefore, the coroutine labeled l remains active and the final **throw** in (5) succeeds incorrectly.

This phenomenon had been overlooked for years. In fact, there was folklore that a simple macro-translation from $\mathbf{DEL}_{\text{one}}$ to $\mathbf{AC}$ should exist. For example, Kawahara and Kameyama proposed such a translation from one-shot effect handlers to asymmetric coroutines, which has been implemented in Lua, Go, and several other languages [9]. Our analysis, however, reveals that these simple translations fail to preserve semantics and therefore cannot be macro-translations. The problem becomes apparent when we examine a dollar term that contains more than one occurrence of shift0.[9]

3.4 Refined Translation from $\mathbf{DEL}_{\text{one}}$ to $\mathbf{AC}$

Our key idea to handle this problem is to introduce a counter mechanism into the translation so that one can distinguish valid continuations from stale ones. The red parts of Fig. 10 illustrate how these counters are introduced: l_c is a counter associated with a coroutine l, and holds a counter object in the form of $\mathit{RefCell}(n)$, where n is a natural number. Each counter is incremented every time the continuation associated with the corresponding coroutine is used. Each continuation also carries an index – a natural number. If this index does not match the counter's value, it indicates that the continuation has already been used, causing the computation to fail. In the second use of k_1, k_1's index is 0 while l_c's value is 1, correctly invalidating the invocation.

Realizing this idea as a macro-translation requires a bit of programming: First, we encode natural numbers by regarding $\mathbf{inj}_{\text{Zero}}\,()$ as 0 and $\mathbf{inj}_{\text{Succ}}$ as the successor function, then we can write increment and comparison functions in $\mathbf{AC}$. Second, we encode counters as mutable cells that are expressible by coroutines (see Sect. 5). Figure 11 shows the complete translation. A dollar term is translated into a term that creates a new counter by $\mathit{ref}!\,\mathbf{inj}_{\text{Zero}}\,()$, and makes a pair (z, zc) consisting of the coroutine and the corresponding counter. The last element in the argument passed to $\mathit{res}!$ is $\mathbf{inj}_{\text{Zero}}\,()$, indicating that the first continuation label to be generated should have index 0. A throw term is translated

---

[9] It can be shown that Kawahara and Kameyama's translation fails to preserve semantics by considering a similar counterexample.

$S_0 k. \underline{M} := \text{yield } \{\lambda k. \underline{M}\}$
$\langle M | x.N \rangle :=$
$\left(\begin{array}{l} \text{let } z = \text{create} \\ \quad \left\{ \begin{array}{l} \lambda\_. \text{ let } x = M \text{ in} \\ \quad \text{return } \{\lambda\_. \underline{N}\} \end{array} \right\} \text{ in} \\ \text{let } zc = ref! \, 0 \text{ in} \\ \text{let } res = \text{resume } z \, () \text{ in} \\ res! \, ((z, zc), 0) \end{array} \right)$

$\text{throw } \underline{V} \; \underline{W} :=$
$\left(\begin{array}{l} \text{case } \underline{V} \text{ of } \{ \\ \quad ((z, zc), i) \mapsto \\ \quad\quad \text{let } j = get! \, zc \text{ in} \\ \quad\quad \text{let } b = compare! \, i \, j \text{ in} \\ \quad\quad \text{case } b \text{ of } \{ \\ \quad\quad\quad (\text{inj}_{\text{True}} \, ()) \mapsto \\ \quad\quad\quad\quad \text{let } i' = incr! \, i \text{ in} \\ \quad\quad\quad\quad \text{let } () = set! \, zc \, i' \text{ in} \\ \quad\quad\quad\quad \text{let } res = \text{resume } z \, \underline{W} \text{ in} \\ \quad\quad\quad\quad res! \, ((z, zc), i') \\ \quad\quad\quad (\text{inj}_{\text{False}} \, ()) \mapsto fail! \\ \quad\quad \} \\ \} \end{array} \right)$

where
$fail :=$
$\left\{ \begin{array}{l} \text{let } z = \text{create } \{\lambda\_. \text{ return } ()\} \text{ in} \\ \text{let } \_ = \text{resume } z \, () \text{ in} \\ \text{resume } z \, () \end{array} \right\}$

$0 := \text{inj}_{\text{Zero}} \, ()$
$Succ := \text{inj}_{\text{Succ}}$
$incr := \{\lambda n. \text{ return } (Succ \, n)\}$
$compare :=$
$\{(\lambda x. \, cmp! \, \{x! \, x\}) \, \{\lambda x. \, cmp! \, \{x! \, x\}\}\}$
$cmp :=$
$\left\{ \begin{array}{l} \lambda f.\lambda n.\lambda m. \text{ case } (n, m) \text{ of } \{ \\ \quad (0, 0) \mapsto \text{inj}_{\text{True}} \, () \\ \quad (0, Succ \, n') \mapsto \text{inj}_{\text{False}} \, () \\ \quad (Succ \, n', 0) \mapsto \text{inj}_{\text{False}} \, () \\ \quad (Succ \, n', Succ \, m') \mapsto f! \, n' \, m' \} \end{array} \right\}$

$ref := \{\lambda v. \text{ create } RefCell(v)\}$
$RefCell(v) :=$
$\left\{ \begin{array}{l} \lambda y. \text{ let } q' = \text{return } y \text{ in} \\ \quad \{(\lambda x. \, th! \, \{x! \, x\}) \, \{\lambda x. \, th! \, \{x! \, x\}\}\}! \, v \, q' \end{array} \right\}$
$th :=$
$\left\{ \begin{array}{l} \lambda f.\lambda s.\lambda q. \text{ case } q \text{ of } \{ \\ \quad (\text{inj}_{\text{Set}} \, v) \mapsto \text{let } q' = \text{yield } () \text{ in } f! \, v \, q' \\ \quad (\text{inj}_{\text{Get}} \, ()) \mapsto \text{let } q' = \text{yield } s \text{ in } f! \, s \, q' \} \end{array} \right\}$
$get := \{\lambda c. \text{ resume } c \text{ inj}_{\text{Get}} \, ()\}$
$set := \{\lambda c. \, \lambda v. \text{ resume } c \text{ inj}_{\text{Set}} \, v\}$

Fig. 11. Refined translation from $\mathbf{DEL}_{\text{one}}$ to $\mathbf{AC}$

into a term whose first argument V is the tuple $((z, zc), i)$. The translated term checks whether the value of the counter zc matches i using $compare! \, i \, j$. If it holds, the counter is incremented, and the continuation stored in z is resumed with the argument W. Otherwise, an invalidated continuation is about to be invoked, and the execution fails.

3.5 Simulation

To prove that the translation in Fig. 11 is a valid macro-translation, we use *simulation*. For two transition systems $\mathscr{L}$ and $\mathscr{L}'$, a binary relation on $\mathscr{L}$-terms and $\mathscr{L}'$-terms is a simulation relation if the following condition holds:

If $M \to_{\mathscr{L}} M'$ and $M \sim N$ hold, there exists an N' such that $N \to^*_{\mathscr{L}'} N'$ and $M' \sim N'$ hold.

If such a simulation relation exists, we say $\mathscr{L}'$ *simulates* $\mathscr{L}$. In our case, we shall construct a simulation relation $\sim$ on $\mathbf{DEL}_{\text{one}}$-configurations and $\mathbf{AC}$-configurations that respects the translation in Fig. 11. We then use this to show that the translation preserves the semantics.

To establish the simulation, we must resolve the fundamental mismatch between $\mathbf{DEL_{one}}$ and $\mathbf{AC}$: the former generates a fresh label for each continuation capture, while the latter reuses the same coroutine labels. In our translation, this mismatch is addressed by the counter mechanism. Therefore, the simulation relation must incorporate the logic of the counter mechanism.

We introduce several auxiliary notions that are necessary to define a simulation relation. First, since configurations may contain runtime labels, we must extend the translation $\underline{\cdot}$, which is only defined for label-free $\mathbf{DEL_{one}}$-programs. For this purpose, we introduce a mapping η as a partial function from $\mathscr{L}_\mathbf{D}$ to $\mathscr{L}_\mathbf{AC} \times \mathscr{L}_\mathbf{AC} \times \mathbb{N}$. The extended translation $\underline{\cdot}_\eta$ is then defined by $\underline{l}_\eta := \eta(l)$ for continuation labels l, while acting identically to $\underline{\cdot}$ for all other terms. For convenience, we identify the $\mathbf{AC}$-representations of Peano numbers with natural numbers ($\mathbb{N}$).

Second, to track the association between a coroutine and its dedicated counter, we use a partial function κ from $\mathscr{L}_\mathbf{AC}$ to $\mathscr{L}_\mathbf{AC}$. With the partial functions η and κ, we define a binary relation $\overset{\eta}{\underset{\kappa}{\sim}}$ between configurations. We only present two crucial cases, and the complete definition can be found in the full version.

Definition 2 (excerpt). *Let C be a $\mathbf{DEL_{one}}$-configuration and D be an $\mathbf{AC}$-configuration. We inductively define a binary relation $C \overset{\eta}{\underset{\kappa}{\sim}} D$, which is parameterized by η and κ, as follows:*

(Case: return term)

$$\langle \mathbf{return}\ V; \theta \rangle \overset{\eta}{\underset{\kappa}{\sim}} \langle \underline{\mathbf{return}\ V}_\eta; \tau \rangle$$

(Case: dollar term)

$$\frac{\langle M_1; \theta \rangle \overset{\eta}{\underset{\kappa}{\sim}} \langle N_1; \tau \rangle \quad \mathrm{get}\,(\kappa(m), \tau) = i \quad \tau(m) = \mathbf{nil} \quad \eta^{-1}(m, \kappa(m), \_) \subseteq \theta^{-1}(\mathbf{nil})}{\langle\langle\, M_1 \,|\, x.M_2 \rangle; \theta \rangle \overset{\eta}{\underset{\kappa}{\sim}} \left\langle \begin{array}{l} \mathbf{let}\ res = m : (\mathbf{let}\ x = N_1\ \mathbf{in\ return}\ \{\lambda_\_.\ \underline{M_2}_\eta\})\ \mathbf{in} \\ res!\,(m, \kappa(m), i) \end{array} ; \tau \right\rangle}$$

$C \overset{\eta}{\underset{\kappa}{\sim}} D$ relates each $\mathbf{DEL_{one}}$-computation to one or more corresponding $\mathbf{AC}$-computations. In most of the cases, it does so structurally; that is, $\langle M; \theta \rangle \overset{\eta}{\underset{\kappa}{\sim}} \langle \underline{M}_\eta; \tau \rangle$. However, the case for a dollar term is an exception: it involves an active coroutine label m, which lacks a corresponding continuation label. This imposes a few constraints on stores and labels. For example, $\mathrm{get}\,(\kappa(m), \tau) = i$ specifies that the index of the continuation label to be generated must equal the value of its counter; and $\eta^{-1}(m, \kappa(m), \_) \subseteq \theta^{-1}(\mathbf{nil})$ requires that all continuation labels corresponding to m be invalid.

Finally, we lift the relation $\overset{\eta}{\underset{\kappa}{\sim}}$ to the simulation relation $\sim$. The relation $\overset{\eta}{\underset{\kappa}{\sim}}$ checks if the structures of two configurations correspond to each other. However, it is not sufficient; we also need to ensure that the global properties for the counter mechanism are satisfied.

For example, a label for an invalidated continuation in $\mathbf{DEL}_{\mathrm{one}}$ must correspond to a triple in $\mathbf{AC}$ whose index is strictly smaller than its counter's value, but this property is not ensured by the relation $\overset{\eta}{\underset{\kappa}{\sim}}$. To capture such properties, we define $C \sim D$ as a binary relation that holds if and only if there exist partial functions η and κ such that $C \overset{\eta}{\underset{\kappa}{\sim}} D$ holds and certain *invariant conditions* are satisfied. A key invariant condition is "$\theta(l) = \mathbf{nil} \implies \mathrm{get}\,(\mathrm{pr}_2(\eta(l)), \tau) > \mathrm{pr}_3(\eta(l))$", which formalizes exactly the rule mentioned above. For the complete definition, see the full version. We remark that $C \sim D$ has the following property.

Lemma 1. *1. For any $\mathbf{DEL}_{\mathrm{one}}$ computation M, $\langle M; \emptyset \rangle \overset{\emptyset}{\underset{\emptyset}{\sim}} \langle \underline{M}; \emptyset \rangle$. Therefore, $\langle M; \emptyset \rangle \sim \langle \underline{M}; \emptyset \rangle$.*

2. If $\langle \mathbf{return}\ V; \theta \rangle \sim \langle N; \tau \rangle$, then there exist a partial function $\eta : \mathscr{L}_{\mathbf{DEL}_{\mathrm{one}}} \rightharpoonup \mathscr{L}_{\mathbf{AC}} \times \mathscr{L}_{\mathbf{AC}} \times \mathbb{N}$ such that $N \equiv \mathbf{return}\ \underline{V}_\eta$.

We can prove that the relation $\sim$ is a simulation relation from $\mathbf{DEL}_{\mathrm{one}}$ to $\mathbf{AC}$.

Theorem 1. *Let C be a $\mathbf{DEL}_{\mathrm{one}}$-configuration and D be an $\mathbf{AC}$-configuration and assume that $C \sim D$ and $C \to_{\mathbf{D}} C'$. Then, there exists an $\mathbf{AC}$-configuration D' such that $D \to_{\mathbf{AC}}^{+} D'$ and $C' \sim D'$ hold.*

Proof. We can prove this theorem by induction on case analysis on $C \to_{\mathbf{D}} C'$. See the full version for the complete proof.

Theorem 2. $\mathbf{DEL}_{\mathrm{one}}$ *is macro-expressible in* $\mathbf{AC}$.

Proof. We show that $A \mapsto \underline{A}$ is a valid macro-translation. Here, we only prove semantic preservation, i.e., $\mathrm{Eval}_{\mathbf{DEL}_{\mathrm{one}}}(M)$ terminates if and only if $\mathrm{Eval}_{\mathbf{AC}}(\underline{M})$ does, since the other conditions are straightforward to check. We first prove the "only if" direction. Suppose that there exist a value V and a store θ such that $\langle M; \emptyset \rangle \to_{\mathbf{D}}^{+} \langle \mathbf{return}\ V; \theta \rangle$. By Lemma 1, we have $\langle M; \emptyset \rangle \sim \langle \underline{M}; \emptyset \rangle$. By repeatedly applying Theorem 1, we obtain $\langle \underline{M}; \emptyset \rangle \to_{\mathbf{AC}}^{+} \langle N; \tau \rangle$ and $\langle \mathbf{return}\ V; \theta \rangle \sim \langle N; \tau \rangle$ for some N and τ. By Lemma 1, we have $N \equiv \mathbf{return}\ \underline{V}_\eta$, which completes the "only if" direction. The proof of the "if" direction is provided in the full version.

The complexity of the simulation arises from the fundamental mismatch between $\mathbf{DEL}_{\mathrm{one}}$ and $\mathbf{AC}$. The naive translation may suffice for establishing weak macro-expressibility of $\mathbf{DEL}_{\mathrm{one}}$ in $\mathbf{AC}$; however, its simulation proof must still address the mismatch. In particular, it must track the correspondence between continuation labels and coroutine labels, via η and certain invariant conditions. This reflects the intrinsic difficulty of translating one-shot delimited continuations to asymmetric coroutines.

$$
\begin{array}{ll}
V, W ::= \ldots & \text{value} \\
\quad \mid \; l_H \quad (l \in \mathscr{L}_\mathbf{E}) & \text{continuation label} \\
M, N ::= \ldots & \text{computation} \\
\quad \mid \; \mathsf{op}\; V \quad (\mathsf{op} \in \mathscr{O}) & \text{operation call} \\
\quad \mid \; \mathbf{with}\; H \;\mathbf{handle}\; M & \text{handle} \\
\quad \mid \; \mathbf{throw}\; V\; W & \text{throw} \\
H ::= \{\mathbf{return}\; x \mapsto M_{\mathrm{ret}},\; (\mathsf{op}_i\; p_i\; k_i \mapsto M_i)_i\} \;\text{handler}
\end{array}
$$

$$
\begin{array}{ll}
\text{pure frame } \mathcal{P} ::= \ldots & \text{pure context } \mathcal{H} ::= \ldots \\
\text{computational frame } \mathcal{F} ::= \ldots \mid \mathbf{with}\; H\; \mathbf{handle}\; [\,] & \text{evaluation context } \mathcal{C} ::= \ldots
\end{array}
$$

Fig. 12. Syntax of $\mathbf{EFF}_{\mathrm{one}}$ (Note that x is bound in M_{ret}, and p_i and k_i are bound in their respective M_i.)

4 One-Shot Effect Handlers as Asymmetric Coroutines

Since Plotkin and Pretnar's proposal [14], effect handlers have been actively studied in recent years. This section extends our results to effect handlers, namely, we establish macro-expressibility of one-shot effect handlers in terms of asymmetric coroutines. Since macro-translations are composable, it suffices to show that one-shot effect handlers are macro-expressible by one-shot delimited-control operators.

4.1 The Calculus for One-Shot Effect Handlers

Figure 12 presents the syntax of $\mathbf{EFF}_{\mathrm{one}}$, the calculus for one-shot effect handlers. $\mathscr{L}_\mathbf{E}$ denotes a countable set of labels. A continuation label l_H is a pair of its name $l \in \mathscr{L}_\mathbf{E}$ and a handler H, and serves as a runtime representation of a one-shot continuation delimited by the handler H. The term $\mathsf{op}\; V$ is an operation invocation with an argument V, where the operation op is an element of a countable set $\mathscr{O}$. The term $\mathbf{with}\; H\; \mathbf{handle}\; M$ installs a handler H and evaluates M under it. The term $\mathbf{throw}\; V\; W$ invokes the continuation represented by V, which should be a continuation label.

We assume that every handler handles all operations that appear in programs. This is not an essential restriction, as any handler can be rewritten to satisfy this condition.[10] $\mathbf{EFF}_{\mathrm{one}}$-Phrases are the values and computations, and $\mathbf{EFF}_{\mathrm{one}}$-Programs are the computations without continuation labels.

Similarly to $\mathbf{DEL}_{\mathrm{one}}$, captured continuations can be invoked at most once during program execution, hence handling the operation E under the following handler raises a runtime error:

$$
H \equiv \left\{ \begin{array}{l} \mathbf{return}\; x \mapsto \mathbf{return}\; x, \\ \mathsf{E}\; p\; k \mapsto \mathbf{let}\; a = \mathbf{throw}\; k\; 1\; \mathbf{in}\; \mathbf{let}\; b = \mathbf{throw}\; k\; 2\; \mathbf{in}\; \mathbf{return}\; (a, b) \end{array} \right\}
$$

$\mathbf{EFF}_{\mathrm{one}}$ uses a store to detect one-shotness, which is a partial function: $\theta : \mathscr{L}_\mathbf{E} \times \text{handler} \rightharpoonup \text{computation} \sqcup \{\mathbf{nil}\}$.

---

[10] For each unhandled operation op, we add a clause $\mathsf{op}\; p\; k \mapsto \mathbf{let}\; r = \mathsf{op}\; p\; \mathbf{in}\; \mathbf{throw}\; k\; r$ to the handler.

$$\text{(MAM)} \quad \frac{M \to_{\mathbf{M}}^{\beta} M'}{\langle M; \theta \rangle \to_{\mathbf{E}}^{\beta} \langle M'; \theta \rangle}$$

$$\text{(ret)} \quad \frac{H \equiv \{\textbf{return } x \mapsto M_{\text{ret}}, \ldots\}}{\langle \textbf{with } H \textbf{ handle } (\textbf{return } V); \theta \rangle \to_{\mathbf{E}}^{\beta} \langle M_{\text{ret}}[V/x]; \theta \rangle}$$

$$\text{(op)} \quad \frac{H \equiv \{\textbf{return } x \mapsto M_{\text{ret}}, (\textbf{op}_i\ p_i\ k_i \mapsto M_i)_i\} \quad l_H \text{ is a fresh label}}{\langle \textbf{with } H \textbf{ handle } (\mathcal{H}[\textbf{op}_j\ V]); \theta \rangle}$$
$$\to_{\beta}^{\mathbf{E}} \langle M_j[V/p_j, l_H/k_j]; \theta[l_H := \lambda x.\ \textbf{with } H \textbf{ handle } \mathcal{H}[\textbf{return } x]] \rangle$$

$$\text{(throw)} \quad \frac{\theta(l_H) = \lambda x.\ \textbf{with } H \textbf{ handle } \mathcal{H}[\textbf{return } x]}{\langle \textbf{throw } l_H\ V; \theta \rangle \to_{\mathbf{E}}^{\beta} \langle \textbf{with } H \textbf{ handle } \mathcal{H}[\textbf{return } V]; \theta[l_H := \textbf{nil}] \rangle}$$

$$\text{(fail)} \quad \frac{\theta(l_H) = \textbf{nil}}{\langle \textbf{throw } l_H\ V; \theta \rangle \to_{\mathbf{E}}^{\beta} \bot}$$

Fig. 13. Beta Reduction Rules of $\mathbf{EFF}_{\text{one}}$

$$\begin{aligned}
\textbf{op } V &:= \quad \mathbf{S}_0 k.\ \lambda h.\ h!\ \textbf{inj}_{\text{op}}\ (\underline{V}, \{\lambda y.\ \textbf{throw } k\ y\ h\}) \\
\textbf{throw } \underline{V_1}\ \underline{V_2} &:= \quad \underline{V_1}!\ \underline{V_2} \\
\textbf{with } H \textbf{ handle } M &:= \quad \langle \underline{M} | H^{\text{ret}} \rangle \{H^{\text{ops}}\} \\
&\quad \text{where } (\{\textbf{return } x \mapsto M_{\text{ret}}, \ldots\})^{\text{ret}} = x.\lambda_{\_}.\ \underline{M_{\text{ret}}} \\
&\qquad (\{\textbf{return } x \mapsto M_{\text{ret}}, (\textbf{op}_i\ p_i\ k_i \mapsto M_i)_i\})^{\text{ops}} \\
&\qquad = \lambda c.\ \textbf{case } c \textbf{ of } \{(\textbf{inj}_{\text{op}_i}\ (p_i, k_i) \mapsto \underline{M_i})_i\}
\end{aligned}$$

Fig. 14. Translation from $\mathbf{EFF}_{\text{one}}$ to $\mathbf{DEL}_{\text{one}}$

A configuration C is a pair of an $\mathbf{EFF}_{\text{one}}$-computation M and a store θ, or the error state $\bot$. The beta reduction rules $\to_{\mathbf{E}}^{\beta}$ on configurations are defined in Fig. 13. The reduction of $\mathbf{EFF}_{\text{one}}$ is defined as follows:

$$\frac{\langle M; \theta \rangle \to_{\mathbf{E}}^{\beta} \langle M'; \theta' \rangle}{\langle \mathcal{C}[M]; \theta \rangle \to_{\mathbf{E}} \langle \mathcal{C}[M']; \theta' \rangle} \qquad \frac{\langle M; \theta \rangle \to_{\mathbf{E}}^{\beta} \bot}{\langle \mathcal{C}[M]; \theta \rangle \to_{\mathbf{E}} \bot}$$

Evaluation of an $\mathbf{EFF}_{\text{one}}$-program is defined by: $\text{Eval}_{\mathbf{EFF}_{\text{one}}}(M) := V$ if there exists a store θ such that $\langle M; \emptyset \rangle \to_{\mathbf{E}}^{*} \langle \textbf{return } V; \theta \rangle$. $\text{Eval}_{\mathbf{EFF}_{\text{one}}}(M)$ is a well-defined partial function, since $\to_{\mathbf{E}}$ is deterministic.

4.2 Macro-translation from $\mathbf{EFF}_{\text{one}}$ to $\mathbf{DEL}_{\text{one}}$

We present a translation from $\mathbf{EFF}_{\text{one}}$ to $\mathbf{DEL}_{\text{one}}$ in Fig. 14, which is based on the translation by Forster et al. [7].

Theorem 3. $\mathbf{EFF}_{\text{one}}$ *is macro-expressible in* $\mathbf{DEL}_{\text{one}}$.

Proof. First, this translation maps $\mathbf{EFF}_{\text{one}}$-Programs to $\mathbf{DEL}_{\text{one}}$-Programs since it introduces no continuation labels. The translation does not alter **MAM** constructors, so it homomorphically acts on them. Also, Fig. 14 clearly shows

$V, W ::= \ldots$ value $M, N ::= \ldots$ computation | **set** $V\ W$ set
     | $l \in \mathscr{L}_\mathbf{R}$ reference cell | **create** V create | **get** V get

Fig. 15. Syntax of **REF**

that the program constructs specific to $\mathbf{EFF}_{one}$ are expressed by syntactic abstractions of $\mathbf{DEL}_{one}$. We prove the preservation of semantics in the full version.

From Theorem 3 together with Theorem 2 and the compositionality of macro-translations, we get the following theorem.

Theorem 4. $\mathbf{EFF}_{one}$ *is macro-expressible in* **AC**.

4.3 Macro-translation from $\mathbf{DEL}_{one}$ to $\mathbf{EFF}_{one}$

We can also show the macro-expressibility of $\mathbf{DEL}_{one}$ to $\mathbf{EFF}_{one}$, using Forster et al.'s translation for the multi-shift $shift_0/dollar$. See the full version for the proof.

Theorem 5. *Assume that* shift0 *is contained in the set of operations $\mathcal{O}$. Then, the following translation is a macro-translation from* $\mathbf{DEL}_{one}$ *to* $\mathbf{EFF}_{one}$.

$$\underline{\mathbf{S}_0 k.\, M} := \mathtt{shift0}\ \{\lambda k.\, \underline{M}\}$$
$$\underline{\mathtt{throw}\ V\ W} := \mathtt{throw}\ \underline{V}\ \underline{W}$$
$$\underline{\langle M \mid x.N \rangle} := \mathtt{with}\ \{\mathtt{return}\ x \mapsto \underline{N},\ \mathtt{shift0}\ p\ k \mapsto p!\ k\}\ \mathtt{handle}\ \underline{M}$$

5 One-Shot Effect Handlers Cannot Macro-express Asymmetric Coroutines

When asymmetric coroutines macro-express one-shot effect handlers, it is natural to ask whether the converse direction also holds. In this section, we prove that the converse direction does not hold.

To show this, we introduce **REF**, a calculus with ML-style reference cells, defined in Fig. 15. The definition of **REF**-frames is omitted since it is the same as that of **MAM**-frames. **REF**-Phrases are the values and the computations of **REF**, and **REF**-Programs are the values and the computations which contain no reference cells. As in the previous calculi, we use stores and configurations: a store is a partial function that maps reference cells to *values*, and a configuration is a pair of a **REF**-computation and a store. Figure 16 presents the semantics of **REF**.

First, we prove that $\mathbf{EFF}_{one}$ cannot macro-express **REF**:

Theorem 6. *There is no valid macro-translation from* **REF** *to* $\mathbf{EFF}_{one}$.

$$\text{(MAM)} \quad \frac{M \to_{\mathbf{M}}^{\beta} M'}{\langle M; \theta \rangle \to_{\mathbf{R}}^{\beta} \langle M'; \theta \rangle}$$

$$\text{(create)} \quad \frac{l \text{ is a fresh reference cell}}{\langle \mathbf{create}\ V; \theta \rangle \to_{\mathbf{R}}^{\beta} \langle \mathbf{return}\ l; \theta[l := V] \rangle}$$

$$\text{(set)} \quad \frac{l \in \mathrm{Dom}(\theta)}{\langle \mathbf{set}\ l\ V; \theta \rangle \to_{\mathbf{R}}^{\beta} \langle \mathbf{return}\ (); \theta[l := V] \rangle}$$

$$\text{(get)} \quad \frac{\theta(l) = V}{\langle \mathbf{get}\ l; \theta \rangle \to_{\mathbf{R}}^{\beta} \langle \mathbf{return}\ V; \theta \rangle}$$

$$\boxed{\frac{\langle M; \theta \rangle \to_{\mathbf{R}}^{\beta} \langle M'; \theta' \rangle}{\langle \mathcal{C}[M]; \theta \rangle \to_{\mathbf{R}} \langle \mathcal{C}[M']; \theta' \rangle}}$$

Fig. 16. Semantics of **REF**

Proof Sketch. Suppose there is a macro-translation from **REF** to **EFF**$_{\text{one}}$, and consider the following term M in **REF**.

$$M := \begin{pmatrix} \mathbf{let}\ r = \mathbf{create}\ \mathrm{inj}_A\ ()\ \mathbf{in} \\ \mathbf{let}\ i = \mathbf{get}\ r\ \mathbf{in} \\ \mathbf{let}\ \_ = \mathbf{set}\ r\ \mathrm{inj}_B\ ()\ \mathbf{in} \\ \mathbf{let}\ k = \mathbf{get}\ r\ \mathbf{in} \\ \mathbf{return}\ (i, k) \end{pmatrix} \mapsto \underline{M} = \begin{pmatrix} \mathbf{let}\ r = \underline{\mathbf{create}}\ (\mathrm{inj}_A\ ())\ \mathbf{in} \\ \mathbf{let}\ i = \underline{\mathbf{get}\ r}\ \mathbf{in} \\ \mathbf{let}\ \_ = \underline{\mathbf{set}}\ r\ (\mathrm{inj}_B\ ())\ \mathbf{in} \\ \mathbf{let}\ k = \underline{\mathbf{get}\ r}\ \mathbf{in} \\ \mathbf{return}\ (i, k) \end{pmatrix}$$

In **REF**, M evaluates to $(\mathrm{inj}_A\ (), \mathrm{inj}_B\ ())$. In **EFF**$_{\text{one}}$, however, $\underline{M}$ ought to evaluate to $(\mathrm{inj}_A\ (), \mathrm{inj}_A\ ())$. This is because a macro-translation must be local and compositional, which prevents $\underline{M}$ from being enclosed by any handler in **EFF**$_{\text{one}}$, forcing the two evaluations of **get** r in $\underline{M}$ to yield the same value. See the full version for the complete proof.

On the other hand, **AC** can macro-express **REF**:

Theorem 7. **REF** *is macro-expressible in* **AC**.

Proof. The following translation is a valid macro-translation from **REF** to **AC**.[11]

$$\begin{aligned}
\underline{\mathbf{create}\ V} &:= \mathbf{create}\ RefCell(\underline{V}) \\
\underline{\mathbf{set}\ V\ W} &:= \mathbf{resume}\ \underline{V}\ (\mathrm{inj}_{\text{Set}}\ \underline{W}) \\
\underline{\mathbf{get}\ V} &:= \mathbf{resume}\ \underline{V}\ (\mathrm{inj}_{\text{Get}}\ ())
\end{aligned}$$

We prove the details in the full version.

Corollary 1. **EFF**$_{\text{one}}$ *cannot macro-express* **AC**.

Proof. Suppose that a macro-translation from **AC** to **EFF**$_{\text{one}}$ exists. Then we have a macro-translation from **REF** to **EFF**$_{\text{one}}$ by Theorem 7, which contradicts Theorem 6.

Corollary 1 is counter-intuitive, since effect handlers are considered a universal tool for expressing various computational effects, such as coroutines. This gap arose due to the strictness of macro-translations, which adheres to Felleisen's

---

[11] $RefCell(\cdot)$ is defined in Fig. 11.

original notion. We conjecture that, under a suitably relaxed definition of macro-translations, **EFF**$_{one}$ can macro-express **REF** and **AC**. One possible relaxation is to allow macro-translations to insert a fixed context at the root of each translated term in order to represent global effects. Such relaxed macro-translations would establish that **REF** and **AC** are macro-expressible in **EFF**$_{one}$, while preserving the compositionality of the translations. We leave the formalization and verification of this idea for future work.

6 Conclusion

This study investigated the relative macro-expressiveness of one-shot control operators, resulting in several key findings: (1) One-shot delimited-control operators and one-shot effect handlers can be macro-expressed by asymmetric coroutines, and (2) The converse direction does not hold. Previously, the former was considered trivial; however, we spotted a gap in the literature and fixed the problem by devising the counter mechanism. As our results demonstrate, establishing such a connection requires a precise mathematical analysis.

To our knowledge, this work is the first study to conduct a systematic comparison of the expressiveness of one-shot control operators. James and Sabry claimed that the one-shot yield operator can be seen as a one-shot variant of delimited-control operators [8], but they did not provide a formal justification. Forster et al. studied multi-shot control operators – effect handlers, monadic reflection, and delimited-control operators – from operational and denotational semantics, and analyzed their macro-expressibility with and without types [7]. Following their approach but adopting a purely operational viewpoint, we have revealed certain aspects of one-shot control operators that cannot be directly derived from prior multi-shot results. Meanwhile, earlier work by de Moura and Ierusalimschy examined the expressiveness of symmetric coroutines, asymmetric coroutines, and one-shot subcontinuations in the presence of mutable states [12]. In contrast, we study the calculi without mutable states, which clarifies the expressive power of control operators.

There are a number of directions for future work. Proposing a type system for coroutines and proving that our translation preserves types would be an important extension to our results. Although Anton and Thiemann proposed a type system for coroutines [1], it remains unclear whether their system aligns with our translations. Introducing affine types to statically guarantee that each continuation may be invoked at most once, in the spirit of linearly used continuations [2], is another interesting future topic.

Acknowledgments. We would like to thank anonymous reviewers for their constructive comments. This work was supported by JSPS KAKENHI Grant Number JP23K24819.

References

1. Anton, K., Thiemann, P.: Typing coroutines. In: Page, R., Horváth, Z., Zsók, V. (eds.) TFP 2010. LNCS, vol. 6546, pp. 16–30. Springer, Heidelberg (2011). https://doi.org/10.1007/978-3-642-22941-1_2
2. Berdine, J., O'Hearn, P.W., Reddy, U.S., Thielecke, H.: Linear continuation-passing. High. Order Symb. Comput. **15**(2–3), 181–208 (2002). https://doi.org/10.1023/A:1020891112409
3. Bruggeman, C., Waddell, O., Dybvig, R.K.: Representing control in the presence of one-shot continuations. In: Fischer, C.N. (ed.) Proceedings of the ACM SIGPLAN 1996 Conference on Programming Language Design and Implementation (PLDI), Philadephia, Pennsylvania, USA, 21–24 May 1996, pp. 99–107. ACM (1996). https://doi.org/10.1145/231379.231395
4. Danvy, O., Filinski, A.: A functional abstraction of typed contexts. BRICS 89/12 (1989)
5. Felleisen, M.: On the expressive power of programming languages. Sci. Comput. Program. **17**(1–3), 35–75 (1991). https://doi.org/10.1016/0167-6423(91)90036-W
6. Felleisen, M., Friedman, D.P.: A reduction semantics for imperative higher-order languages. In: de Bakker, J.W., Nijman, A.J., Treleaven, P.C. (eds.) PARLE 1987. LNCS, vol. 259, pp. 206–223. Springer, Heidelberg (1987). https://doi.org/10.1007/3-540-17945-3_12
7. Forster, Y., Kammar, O., Lindley, S., Pretnar, M.: On the expressive power of user-defined effects: effect handlers, monadic reflection, delimited control. J. Funct. Program. **29**, e15 (2019). https://doi.org/10.1017/S0956796819000121
8. James, R.P., Sabry, A.: Yield: mainstream delimited continuations. In: Proceedings of the 1st International Workshop on Theory and Practice of Delimited Continuations (TPDC 2011), 12 pages (2011)
9. Kawahara, S., Kameyama, Y.: One-shot algebraic effects as coroutines. In: Byrski, A., Hughes, J. (eds.) TFP 2020. LNCS, vol. 12222, pp. 159–179. Springer, Cham (2020). https://doi.org/10.1007/978-3-030-57761-2_8
10. Levy, P.B.: Call-By-Push-Value: A Functional/Imperative Synthesis, Semantics Structures in Computation, vol. 2. Springer, Dordrecht (2004). https://doi.org/10.1007/978-94-007-0954-6
11. Materzok, M., Biernacki, D.: A dynamic interpretation of the CPS hierarchy. In: Jhala, R., Igarashi, A. (eds.) APLAS 2012. LNCS, vol. 7705, pp. 296–311. Springer, Heidelberg (2012). https://doi.org/10.1007/978-3-642-35182-2_21
12. de Moura, A.L., Ierusalimschy, R.: Revisiting coroutines. ACM Trans. Program. Lang. Syst. **31**(2), 6:1–6:31 (2009). https://doi.org/10.1145/1462166.1462167
13. Plotkin, G.D., Power, J.: Algebraic operations and generic effects. Appl. Categorical Struct. **11**(1), 69–94 (2003). https://doi.org/10.1023/A:1023064908962
14. Plotkin, G., Pretnar, M.: Handlers of algebraic effects. In: Castagna, G. (ed.) ESOP 2009. LNCS, vol. 5502, pp. 80–94. Springer, Heidelberg (2009). https://doi.org/10.1007/978-3-642-00590-9_7
15. de Vilhena, P.E., Pottier, F.: A separation logic for effect handlers. Proc. ACM Program. Lang. **5**(POPL), 1–28 (2021). https://doi.org/10.1145/3434314

Positive Sharing and Abstract Machines

Beniamino Accattoli[1]($\boxtimes$), Claudio Sacerdoti Coen[2], and Jui-Hsuan Wu[3]

[1] Inria and LIX, École Polytechnique, Palaiseau, France
beniamino.accattoli@inria.fr
[2] Alma Mater Studiorum - Università di Bologna, Bologna, Italy
[3] CNRS, LIP, ENS de Lyon, Lyon, France

Abstract. Wu's positive λ-calculus is a recent call-by-value λ-calculus with sharing coming from Miller and Wu's study of the proof-theoretical concept of focalization. Accattoli and Wu showed that it simplifies a technical aspect of the study of sharing; namely it rules out the recurrent issue of renaming chains, that often causes a quadratic time slowdown.

In this paper, we define the natural abstract machine for the positive λ-calculus and show that it suffers from an inefficiency: the quadratic slowdown somehow reappears when analyzing the cost of the machine. We then design an optimized machine for the positive λ-calculus, which we prove efficient. The optimization is based on a new slicing technique which is dual to the standard structure of machine environments.

Keywords: λ-calculus · abstract machines · complexity analyses

1 Introduction

The λ-calculus is a minimalistic abstract setting that does not come with a fixed implementation schema. This is part of its appeal as a theoretical framework. Yet, for the very same reason, many different implementation techniques have been developed along the decades. How to implement the λ-calculus is in fact a surprisingly rich problem with no absolute best answer.

Recently, a proof theoretical study about focusing by Miller and Wu [28] led to a new λ-calculus with sharing—Wu's positive λ-calculus λ_{pos} [35]—that provides a fresh perspective on, and an improvement of a recurrent efficiency issue as shown by Accattoli and Wu [19]. The present paper studies a somewhat surprising fact related to the efficiency of the positive λ-calculus.

Similar to the ordinary λ-calculus, Wu's calculus is a minimalistic abstract setting. Its sharing mechanism, however, decomposes β-reduction in micro steps and makes it closer to implementations than the ordinary λ-calculus. It is, in fact, almost an abstract machine.

This work stems from the observation that the natural refinement of λ_{pos} as an abstract machine suffers from an inefficiency. Intuitively, the efficiency issue improved by λ_{pos} resurfaces at the lower level of machines. After pointing out the problem, we design an optimized abstract machine and prove it efficient, solving the issue. The adopted *slicing* optimization is new and based on a dual of the standard environment data structure for abstract machines. We believe it to be an interesting new implementation schema.

The Positive λ-Calculus. In [28], Miller and Wu decorate focalized proofs for minimal intuitionistic logic with proof terms. Minimal intuitionistic logic is the proof-theoretical counterpart of the λ-calculus via the Curry-Howard correspondence. Focalization is a technique that constrains the shape of proofs depending on a polarity assignment to atomic formulas. Miller and Wu show that uniformly adopting the negative polarity induces the ordinary λ-calculus, while the positive polarity induces an alternative syntax with (sub-term) sharing, where sharing is represented via let-expressions or, equivalently, explicit substitutions.

An important aspect of this new positive syntax is its *compactness property*, also referred to as *positive sharing*: the shape of terms is highly constrained, more than in most other calculi with let-expressions or explicit substitutions. In particular, applications cannot be nested, arguments can only be variables, applications and abstractions are always shared, and variables cannot be shared. Some of these constraints are also at work in Sabry and Felleisen's *A-normal forms* [23,31], of which positive sharing can be seen as an even more constrained variant; see the introduction of Accattoli and Wu [19] for extended discussions about similar formalisms. Intuitively, the constrained syntax somewhat forces a maximal sharing of sub-terms by ruling out redundant cases of sharing from the grammar for terms.

In [35], Wu endows the positive syntax with rewriting rules. Because of the compact syntax, there is not much freedom for defining the rules: they have to be call-by-value, and they have to be micro-step, that is, the granularity of the substitution process is the one of abstract machines, that replace one variable occurrence at a time. Call-by-name or meta-level substitution on all occurrences of a variable are indeed ruled out because they do not preserve compactness. The outcome is the positive λ-calculus λ_{pos}. The difference between λ_{pos} and an abstract machine is only that λ_{pos} does not have rules searching for redexes.

Renaming Chains. In [19], Accattoli and Wu show two things. Firstly, compactness rules out a recurrent issue in the study of sharing and abstract machines, namely *renaming chains*. In general, when one adds to the λ-calculus an explicit substitution construct, noted here $t[x \leftarrow u]$ (equivalent to let $x = u$ in t, and sharing u for x in t), then one can have chains of shared variables of the following form: $t[x_1 \leftarrow x_2] \ldots [x_{n-1} \leftarrow x_n]$.

These renaming, or indirection chains, are a recurrent burden of sharing-based systems, as they lead to both time and space inefficiencies—typically a quadratic time slowdown—and need optimizations to avoid their creations, as done for instance by Sands et al. [32], Wand [34], Friedman et al. [24], and Sestoft [33]. In the literature on sharing and abstract machines, the issue tended to receive little attention, until Accattoli and Sacerdoti Coen focused on it [17]. Removing renaming chains is also essential in the study of reasonable logarithmic space for the λ-calculus, see Accattoli et al. [10].

In the positive λ-calculus, variables cannot be shared. Therefore, renaming chains simply cannot be expressed, ruling out the issue. It is important to point out, however, that forbidding the sharing of variables requires tuning the rewriting rules by adding some meta-level renamings.

Useful Sharing. Secondly, Accattoli and Wu show that the compactness and the removal of renaming chains of the positive λ-calculus have the effect of drastically simplifying *useful sharing*, a sophisticated implementation technique introduced by Accattoli and Dal Lago in the study of reasonable time cost models [9]. Intuitively, useful sharing aims at preventing the useless unfolding of sharing, which is exactly what is achieved by compactness via the restriction of the grammar of terms. That is, positive sharing captures the essence of useful sharing.

To be precise, Accattoli and Wu show that compactness simplifies the *specification* of useful sharing, but they do not provide precise cost analyses—that are an essential aspect of useful sharing—for the positive λ-calculus.

The Inefficiency. The inception of the present work is exactly the desire to develop a cost analysis of λ_{pos}. Cost analyses are usually done via a study of an abstract machine for the calculus of interest. The somewhat surprising fact is that the natural abstract machine associated to the positive λ-calculus—first given here, and dubbed Natural POsitive Machine, or *Natural POM*—is inefficient. The culprit is the mentioned meta-level renamings added to compensate for the fact that variables cannot be shared. The implementation of these renamings induces a quadratic (rather than linear) overhead in the number of β-steps. Essentially, the inefficiency of renaming chains reappears at the lower level of the Natural POM even if the chains themselves have disappeared.

Useful sharing is meant to reduce the overhead from exponential to polynomial, so the inefficiency does not invalidate the value of λ_{pos} for specifying useful sharing. The literature however contains abstract machines for useful sharing having only a *linear* overhead (by Accattoli and co-authors [7,8,13,16]), thus the Natural POM compares poorly, despite the fact that the positive λ-calculus is a better specification of useful sharing than those in the literature.

The Solution: Sub-term Property and Slices. We then design an optimized abstract machine, the *Sliced POM*, that solves the issue and recovers linearity in the number of β-steps. To give a hint of the solution, we need to say a bit more about the problem. Complexity analyses of abstract machines are based on their crucial *sub-term property*, stating that all the terms duplicated along the run of the machine are sub-terms of the initial term. The property allows one to bound the cost of each transition using the initial term, which is essential in order to express the cost of the run as a function of the size of the initial term.

Now, the Natural POM does verify the sub-term property *with respect to duplications*; the source of the inefficiency for once is not the duplication process. The source is nonetheless related to a lack of sub-term property *for renamings*: the additional meta-level renamings act over a scope that might not be a sub-term of the initial term. The solution amounts to *slicing* such scopes in slices that are sub-terms of the initial term, and in noting that each meta-level renaming is always confined to exactly one slice. The slicing technique is managed very easily, via an additional basic data structure, the slice stack.

Slices vs Environments. A pleasant aspect is that the slicing stack can be seen as *dual* to the environment data structure used to manage sharing:

- an environment entry $[x \leftarrow t]$ stores the delayed substitution of t for x waiting for the evaluation of active term to expose occurrences of x to replace;
- an entry $t[x \leftarrow \cdot]$ of the slice stack waits for the active term to become a variable z to be substituted for x in the slice t.

This duality suggests that the slicing technique exposes a new natural structure. The meta-level renamings of the calculus are similar to the ones generated by β-redexes. In traditional settings with sharing, indeed, the optimizations to remove renaming chains act on the environment. We find it interesting that positive sharing *disentangles* meta-level renamings from the usual substitution process, and manages them via a sort of dual mechanism.

On the Value of Positive Sharing. The reader might wonder what the value of positive sharing is, given that the issue that it is supposed to solve does reappear at the level of machines and forces the design of a new solution. In our opinion, the value of positive sharing is in re-structuring the study of sharing techniques. The study by Accattoli and Wu [19] suggests that positive sharing *removes* the issue of renaming chains, but our work provides a refined picture. Namely, positive sharing enables a neater theory of sharing, disentangling renaming chains from the treatment of explicit substitutions, and encapsulating their inefficiency at the lower level of implementations choices. Additionally, it brings to the fore the concept of slice stack, which we believe is an interesting addition to the theory of implementations of the λ-calculus.

OCaml Implementation. For lack of space we overview in Appendix A of the technical report [18] an implementation in OCaml of the Sliced POM, to be found at https://github.com/sacerdot/PositiveAbstractMachine. The implementation is meant to provide further evidence on the cost of the atomic operations of the machine. Moreover, it allows the interested reader to enter ordinary λ-terms and see how they are transformed into positive terms (via the transformation studied by Accattoli and Wu in [19]) and then run by the Sliced POM.

The implementation is a prototype: it does not attempt to further optimize space usage or to recover garbage memory, nor does it optimize the code that is unrelated to running the machine (*e.g.* the pretty-printing of machine states).

Proofs. Most proofs are omitted. They can be found in the appendix of the technical report on arXiv [18].

2 The Positive λ-Calculus

In this section, we present Wu's positive λ-calculus [35]. Precisely, we adopt the *explicit open* variant from Accattoli and Wu [19]. For simplicity, we simply refer to it as the positive λ-calculus, and note it λ_{pos}. We depart slightly from the

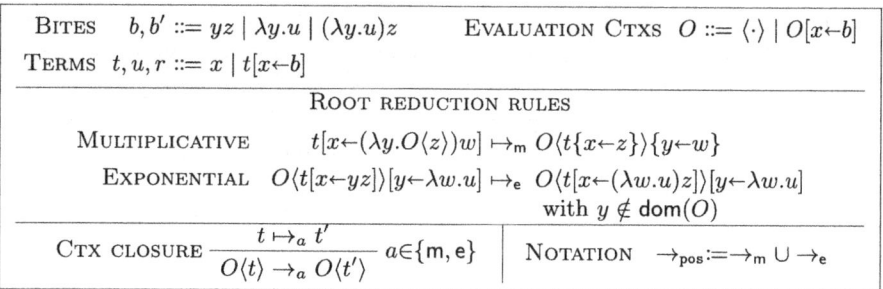

Fig. 1. The positive λ-calculus λ_{pos}.

presentation in [19], omitting the garbage collection rule because it can always be postponed, as shown in [19], and changing some notations. The definition is in Fig. 1.

Terms. The positive λ-calculus uses let-expressions, similarly to Moggi's CbV calculus [29,30]. We do however write a let-expression let $x = u$ in t as a more compact *explicit substitution* $t[x{\leftarrow}u]$ (ES for short), which binds x in t. Moreover, for the moment our let/ES does not fix an order of evaluation between t and u, in contrast to many papers in the literature (*e.g.* Levy et al. [27]) where u is evaluated first. The evaluation order shall be fixed in the next section.

While we borrow the terminology *explicit substitution* from the seminal work of Abadi et al. [1], the way we employ the construct is deeply different, since the theory of ESs has progressed considerably since that first work. In particular, we do use variable names instead of de Bruijn indices, and our ESs do not move through the structure of the term, instead they act *at a distance* (explained below). The positive λ-calculus is rather reminiscent of Sabry and Felleisen's *A-normal forms* [23,31], or of the calculi for call-by-need by Lunchbury [26] and Sestoft [33], of which it can be thought as a more constrained variant.

In fact, ESs are here used in a slightly unusual way even with respect to more recent work on ESs. In λ_{pos}, as in the λ-calculus, there are only three constructors, variables, applications, and abstractions. There are however, various differences, namely:

- Applications have either shape yz or $(\lambda y.t)z$, that is, arguments can only be variables and the left sub-term cannot be an application;
- Applications and abstractions are dubbed *bites* (following the terminology of Accattoli et al. [7]) and are always shared, that is, standalone applications and abstractions are not allowed by the grammar. They can only be introduced by the ESs constructs $[x{\leftarrow}yz]$, $[x{\leftarrow}(\lambda y.t)z]$, and $[x{\leftarrow}\lambda y.u]$;
- Positive sharing is peculiar as positive terms are *not* shared in general, that is, $t[x{\leftarrow}u]$ is not a positive term. There is no construct for sharing variables or applications/abstractions with top-level sharing, *i.e.* $t[x{\leftarrow}y]$ or $t[x{\leftarrow}yz[y{\leftarrow}\lambda w.u]]$ are not terms of λ_{pos}. In particular, the absence of $t[x{\leftarrow}y]$ is what forbids renaming chains.

The set of free variables of a term t is denoted by $\mathsf{fv}(t)$ and it is defined as expected. Terms are identified up to α-renaming. We use $t\{x\mathord{\leftarrow}y\}$ for the capture-avoiding substitution of y for each free occurrence of x in t; in this paper we never need the more general operation $t\{x\mathord{\leftarrow}u\}$ substituting terms. The meta-level renamings mentioned in the introduction, to be used to compensate for the absence of $t[x\mathord{\leftarrow}y]$, shall be instances of $t\{x\mathord{\leftarrow}y\}$.

Open Setting. Evaluation in λ_{pos} shall be open in the sense promoted by Accattoli and Guerrieri [12], that is, it does not go under abstraction (also referred to as *weak*) and terms *can* be open (but do not have to). As discussed at length by Accattoli and Guerrieri, this is a more general framework than the standard for functional programming languages of weak evaluation and *closed* terms. The increased generality enables the developed theory to scale up to evaluation under abstraction, which is needed to model proof assistants, by iterating evaluation under abstraction—this is done for instance by Grégoire and Leroy for Coq [25]—because the body of abstractions cannot be assumed to be closed. See [12] for more discussions.

Open Contexts. Contexts are terms with exactly one occurrence of the *hole* $\langle\cdot\rangle$, an additional constant, standing for a removed sub-term. We shall use various notions of contexts. The most general ones in this paper are *open contexts* O, that are simply lists of ESs. The main operation about contexts is *plugging* $O\langle t\rangle$ where the hole $\langle\cdot\rangle$ in context O is replaced by t. Plugging, as usual with contexts, can capture variables—for instance $(\langle\cdot\rangle[x\mathord{\leftarrow}b])\langle x\rangle = x[x\mathord{\leftarrow}u]$.

The domain $\mathsf{dom}(O)$ of a context is the set of variables possibly captured by O (i.e., on which O has an ES scoping over $\langle\cdot\rangle$); example: setting $O := \langle\cdot\rangle[x\mathord{\leftarrow}\lambda y.y[y'\mathord{\leftarrow}y''y'']][z\mathord{\leftarrow}z'z'']$ one obtains $\mathsf{dom}(O) = \{x, z\}$. When $x \in \mathsf{dom}(O)$, we also use the notation $O(x)$ to denote the bite associated to x in O; in the example, $O(z) = z'z''$.

As it is immediately seen from the grammar of positive terms, every positive term t can be written uniquely as $O\langle x\rangle$ for some x and O, with O possibly capturing x. If $t = O\langle x\rangle$ then x is referred to as the *head variable* of t.

Rewriting Rules. There are two rewriting rules, following the *at a distance* style promoted by Accattoli and Kesner [14], which involves contexts in the definition of the rules, even before the contextual closure. The rules names come from the connection with linear logic proof nets, which is omitted here.

The multiplicative rule $\to_\mathsf{m}$ reduces a shared β-redex. The rule is forced to decompose the body of the abstraction as $O\langle z\rangle$ in order to write the reduct. The point is that the simpler rule $t[x\mathord{\leftarrow}(\lambda y.u)w] \mapsto_\mathsf{m} t[x\mathord{\leftarrow}u[y\mathord{\leftarrow}w]]$ does not respect the grammars of the positive λ-calculus, since ESs such as $[x\mathord{\leftarrow}u]$ and $[y\mathord{\leftarrow}w]$, as well as their nesting, are forbidden. Let us show an example of multiplicative step stressing the action of renamings:

$$z[x\mathord{\leftarrow}yz][z\mathord{\leftarrow}(\lambda w.z'[x'\mathord{\leftarrow}wz'])y'] \to_\mathsf{m} z[x\mathord{\leftarrow}yz]\{z\mathord{\leftarrow}z'\}[x'\mathord{\leftarrow}wz']\{w\mathord{\leftarrow}y'\}$$
$$= z'[x\mathord{\leftarrow}yz'][x'\mathord{\leftarrow}y'z']$$

The exponential rule $\to_e$ simply replaces an applied variable with the associated abstraction. Note that arguments, that are variables, are never replaced, because their replacement would—once more—step out of the grammar of the positive λ-calculus.

Both rules are closed by open contexts and together form the rewriting relation $\to_{pos}$ of the positive λ-calculus.

Translating λ-Terms. In [19], Accattoli and Wu show how to translate λ-terms to positive terms in a way that induces a simulation of call-by-value evaluation. We refer the interested reader to their work, because in this paper we only deal with positive terms.

Diamond. The defined calculus is non-deterministic. Consider for instance $t := z[x {\leftarrow} yy][z {\leftarrow} (\lambda w.w)y'][y {\leftarrow} \lambda x'.u]$. One has for instance the following diagram:

$$\begin{array}{ccc} t & \xrightarrow{m} & y'[x{\leftarrow}yy][y{\leftarrow}\lambda x'.u] \\ {\scriptstyle e}\downarrow & & \vdots {\scriptstyle e} \\ z[x{\leftarrow}(\lambda x'.u)y][z{\leftarrow}(\lambda w.w)y'][y{\leftarrow}\lambda x'.u] & \xdashrightarrow{m} & y'[x{\leftarrow}(\lambda x'.u)y][y{\leftarrow}\lambda x'.u] \end{array}$$

The calculus however is confluent, and even more than confluent, it has the diamond property. According to Dal Lago and Martini [20], a relation $\to$ is *diamond* if $u_1 \leftarrow t \to u_2$ imply $u_1 = u_2$ or $u_1 \to r \leftarrow u_2$ for some r. The diamond property expresses a relaxed form of determinism, since it states that different choices cannot change the result *nor the length of evaluation sequences* (note that the diagram closes in either zero or one steps on both sides).

Theorem 1 (Positive diamond, [19]). *Relation $\to_{pos}$ is diamond.*

Sub-term Property. When the substitution process is decomposed in micro steps, usually it is possible to bound the cost of each duplication along an evaluation sequence using the size of the initial term of the sequence—this is the sub-term property. It is crucial in order to analyze the cost of evaluation sequences as a function of the size of the initial term and the number of steps, since the main danger of excessive cost usually comes from duplications. The property does not hold, for instance, for the ordinary λ-calculus (see Accattoli [2, Section 3]) that relies on meta-level (rather than micro-step) substitution. The positive λ-calculus has the sub-term property, that is expressed for values, because they are what is duplicated by the exponential rule.

Lemma 1 (Sub-term property). *Let $t \to_{pos}^* u$ be a reduction sequence. Then $|\lambda x.r| \leq |t|$ for every bite $\lambda x.r$ duplicated by a e-step of the sequence.*

Proof. Formally, the proof is a straightforward induction on the length of the reduction sequence, by looking at the last step and using the i.h. The following informal observations however are probably enough. Evaluation duplicates variables (in $\to_m$) and abstractions (in $\to_e$). The substitution of variables cannot change the size of abstractions. For abstractions, note that replaced variables are out of abstractions, and open contexts never enter abstractions, so that all abstractions of the sequence can be traced back to t (up to α-renaming). □

3 The Right Strategy

Usually, abstract machines are deterministic and implement a deterministic evaluation strategy. Therefore, in this section, we define a deterministic strategy for the positive λ-calculus and prove its basic properties.

We adopt the right(-to-left) strategy $\to_r$ that picks redexes from right to left. It is a standard approach but it turns out that defining it in λ_{pos} is a bit tricky, because of e-steps, where two ESs interact at a distance.

Redex Positions. For calculi at a distance, the notion of position of a redex—which is mandatory to determine the rightmost redex—might not be as expected. For us, a position in a term is simply an open context.

Definition 1 (Redex positions). *When taking into account the contextual closure, m-steps and e-steps have the following shapes:*

$$t = O'\langle r[x{\leftarrow}(\lambda y.O\langle z\rangle)w]\rangle \to_m O'\langle O\langle r\{x{\leftarrow}z\}\rangle\{y{\leftarrow}w\}\rangle = u$$
$$t = O'\langle O\langle r[x{\leftarrow}yz]\rangle[y{\leftarrow}\lambda w.q]\rangle \to_e O'\langle O\langle r[x{\leftarrow}(\lambda w.q)z]\rangle[y{\leftarrow}\lambda w.q]\rangle = u$$

The position of the m-step is simply given by the surrounding context O'. The position of the e-step is the context $O'\langle O[y{\leftarrow}\lambda w.q]\rangle$.

The rationale behind the position of e-steps is the idea that they are triggered when one finds the variable to substitute, and not when one finds the abstraction—this is indeed how abstract machines work. This approach is standard in the literature about ESs at a distance, see *e.g.* Accattoli et al. [6].

Example: in $x[x{\leftarrow}yz][x'{\leftarrow}y'z][y'{\leftarrow}\lambda w'.r][y{\leftarrow}\lambda w.u]$ there are two redexes (on y and y') and the rightmost one is on y', despite the ES on y' occurring to the left of the one on y.

Right Contexts. We specify the strategy via the notion of right contexts, itself specified via the notion of applied free variable. In fact, there are two dual ways of defining right contexts. We present them both and prove their equivalence.

Definition 2 (Applied free variables, right contexts). *The set of applied (and out of abstraction bodies) free variables $\mathsf{afv}(O)$ of an open context O is defined as:*

SET OF APPLIED FREE VARIABLES

$$\mathsf{afv}(\langle\cdot\rangle) := \emptyset \quad\quad \mathsf{afv}(O[x{\leftarrow}yz]) := (\mathsf{afv}(O) \setminus \{x\}) \cup \{y\}$$
$$\mathsf{afv}(O[x{\leftarrow}(\lambda y.t)z]) := \mathsf{afv}(O) \setminus \{x\} \quad\quad \mathsf{afv}(O[x{\leftarrow}\lambda y.t]) := \mathsf{afv}(O) \setminus \{x\}$$

The two definitions of right contexts (we use on purpose the same meta-variable, since they shall be proved equivalent right next) are given by:

OUTSIDE-IN RIGHT CONTEXTS
$$R ::= \langle \cdot \rangle \mid R[x \leftarrow yz] \mid R[x \leftarrow \lambda y.u] \text{ if } x \notin \mathsf{afv}(R)$$
INSIDE-OUT RIGHT CONTEXTS
$$R ::= \langle \cdot \rangle \mid R\langle\langle \cdot \rangle [x \leftarrow yz]\rangle \text{ if } R(y) \neq \lambda w.t \mid R\langle\langle \cdot \rangle [x \leftarrow \lambda y.u]\rangle$$

Lemma 2. *Outside-in and inside-out right contexts coincide.*

Because of the lemma, we only speak of right contexts, and adopt the most convenient definition in each case.

Right Strategy. We now have all the ingredients to define the right strategy and prove its basic properties.

Definition 3 (Right strategy). *A $\to_{\mathsf{pos}}$ step is right when its position is a right context. The right strategy $\to_\mathsf{r}$ reduces at each step a right redex, if any. We write $t \to_{\mathsf{rm}} u$ (resp. $t \to_{\mathsf{re}} u$) for a right m-step (resp. e-step).*

Lemma 3 (Basic properties of the right strategy).

1. *Determinism: if $t \to_\mathsf{r} t_1$ and $t \to_\mathsf{r} t_2$ then $t_1 = t_2$;*
2. *No premature stops: if $t \to_{\mathsf{pos}} u$ then $t \to_\mathsf{r} r$ for some r.*

4 A Natural but Inefficient Positive Machine

In this section, we give the natural abstract machine implementing the right strategy of the previous section, obtained by adding a basic mechanism for searching redexes, discuss the (in)efficiency of the machine, and explain how to modify it as to make it efficient. The tone is slightly informal. The next sections shall formally define and study the modified machine.

Typical abstract machines for the λ-calculus in the literature are the Krivine abstract machine (KAM) or Felleisen and Friedman's CEK machine [22] that use many environments, closures, and never α-rename. Here we rely on a different and simpler approach, having only one global environment (represented as a context), no closures, and using α-renaming. For comparisons between the two approaches, see Accattoli and Barras [5].

The Natural POM. States of the Natural POsitive Machine (Natural POM[1]) are pairs $t \triangleleft R$ denoting a pointer $\triangleleft$ inside the structure of the term $u := R\langle t \rangle$ represented by the state. The pointer represents the current position of the machine over u. Initially, the pointer is at the rightmost position, that is, initial states have shape $t \triangleleft \langle \cdot \rangle$. The Natural POM has the four transitions in Fig. 2. The differences with respect to the positive λ-calculus are that:

---

[1] Acronyms for abstract machines tend to end with AM for Abstract Machine. We avoided PAM, however, because there already is a PAM (Pointer Abstract Machine) in the literature, introduced by Danos et al. [21].

TRANSITIONS					
ACTIVE CODE	RIGHT CTX		ACTIVE CODE	RIGHT CTX	
$t[x{\leftarrow}\lambda y.u]$	$\lhd R$	$\leadsto_{\mathsf{sea}_1}$	t	$\lhd R\langle\langle\cdot\rangle[x{\leftarrow}\lambda y.u]\rangle$	
$t[x{\leftarrow}yz]$	$\lhd R$	$\leadsto_{\mathsf{sea}_2}$	t	$\lhd R\langle\langle\cdot\rangle[x{\leftarrow}yz]\rangle$	(*)
$t[x{\leftarrow}yz]$	$\lhd R$	$\leadsto_{\mathsf{e}}$	$t[x{\leftarrow}(\lambda w.u)^\alpha z]$	$\lhd R$	(#)
$t[x{\leftarrow}(\lambda y.O\langle z\rangle)w]$	$\lhd R$	$\leadsto_{\mathsf{m}}$	$O\langle t\{x{\leftarrow}z\}\rangle\{y{\leftarrow}w\}$	$\lhd R$	

(*) if $y \notin \mathsf{dom}(R)$ or $R(y) \neq \lambda w.u$; (#) if $R(y) = \lambda w.u$.

Fig. 2. The Natural Positive Machine (Natural POM).

- *Search*: there are two search transitions sea_1 and sea_2 to move the pointer, in order to search for redexes, that move $\lhd$ right-to-left (hence the symbol);
- *Names*: there is a more controlled management of α-conversion, which is performed only on the exponential step, when copying abstractions.

Transition sea_1 moves the abstraction from the active code to the right context. Transition sea_2 moves $[x{\leftarrow}yz]$ when y is a free variable (that is, $y \notin \mathsf{dom}(R)$) or when it is bound by an ES in R but not one that contains an abstraction, so that the application yz does not give rise to a multiplicative redex. Note that these two cases are exactly the inside-out definition of right contexts in Definition 2.

Example of Run. As an example of execution of the Natural POM, we consider the first few transitions of the infinite run for the positive representation $x[x{\leftarrow}yy][y{\leftarrow}\lambda z.w[w{\leftarrow}zz]]$ of the paradigmatic looping λ-term $\Omega := (\lambda y.yy)(\lambda z.zz)$:

ACTIVE CODE	RIGHT CTX	
$x[x{\leftarrow}yy][y{\leftarrow}\lambda z.w[w{\leftarrow}zz]]$	$\lhd \langle\cdot\rangle$	$\leadsto_{\mathsf{sea}_1}$
$x[x{\leftarrow}yy]$	$\lhd [y{\leftarrow}\lambda z.w[w{\leftarrow}zz]]$	$\leadsto_{\mathsf{e}}$
$x[x{\leftarrow}(\lambda z'.w'[w'{\leftarrow}z'z'])y]$	$\lhd [y{\leftarrow}\lambda z.w[x{\leftarrow}zz]]$	$\leadsto_{\mathsf{m}}$
$w'[w'{\leftarrow}yy]$	$\lhd [y{\leftarrow}\lambda z.w[x{\leftarrow}zz]]$	$\leadsto_{\mathsf{e}}$ ...

Basics of the Complexity of Abstract Machines. The problem with the Natural POM concerns the complexity of its overhead with respect to the calculus. Let us first recall the basics of the topic. For abstract machines, the complexity of the overhead for a machine run r of initial term t is measured with respect to two parameters: the number of steps of the underlying calculus and the size $|t|$ of the initial term. A large number of machines has complexity linear in both parameters—shortened to *bi-linear*—as first shown by Accattoli et al. [3], and repeatedly verified after that for even more machines [4,7,8,13,16]. The bi-linearity of the overhead then becomes a design principle, or, when it fails, a strong indication of an inefficiency, and that the machine can be improved.

The key property enabling complexity analyses of machines is the sub-term property already discussed for λ_{pos}. It ensures that the size of states cannot grow more than the size of the initial term at each transition. In turn, this fact usually implies that the time cost is also linearly bounded.

The Inefficiency of the Natural POM. The natural POM inherits the sub-term property from the calculus. Its inefficiency is related to the multiplicative transition $\leadsto_m$, namely to the meta-level renaming $t\{x\leftarrow z\}$ (referring to Fig. 2). Meta-level substitutions are possibly costly. Usually, the danger is the time spent in making copies of the term to duplicate, which might be big and/or because many copies of it might be required. The size of the term to duplicate is not the problem here, since the involved term is a simple variable z.

The culprit actually is the *size of the scope* over which the renaming can take place, rather than the number of copies. There are two renamings. The renaming $\{y\leftarrow w\}$ is harmless: its scope seems to be $O\langle t\{x\leftarrow z\}\rangle$ but in fact y can occur only in $O\langle z\rangle$ (which is the body of the abstraction of y in the source state of the transition), and the sub-term property guarantees that the size of $O\langle z\rangle$ is bound by the size of the initial term. Therefore, one can propagate $\{y\leftarrow w\}$ on $O\langle z\rangle$ before computing the full reduct, staying within a linear cost.

For the renaming $t\{x\leftarrow z\}$, however, there is in general no connection between t and the initial term. For the first multiplicative step of the run, t is a sub-term of the initial term. But the step itself re-combines O and t as to create a new term unrelated to the initial one. Consider for instance the following run, where we assume that O captures z and that $(\lambda y.(O\langle z\rangle[z'\leftarrow b]))^\alpha = \lambda y'.(O'\langle z'\rangle[z''\leftarrow b'])$:

	Active code	Right ctx	
	$t[x\leftarrow x'w][x'\leftarrow \lambda y.(O\langle z\rangle[z'\leftarrow b])]$	$\triangleleft \langle\cdot\rangle$	
$\leadsto_{sea_1}$	$t[x\leftarrow x'w]$	$\triangleleft [x'\leftarrow \lambda y.(O\langle z\rangle[z'\leftarrow b])]$	(1)
$\leadsto_e$	$t[x\leftarrow (\lambda y'.(O'\langle z'\rangle[z''\leftarrow b']))w]$	$\triangleleft [x'\leftarrow \lambda y.(O\langle z\rangle[z'\leftarrow b])]$	
$\leadsto_m$	$O'\langle t\{x\leftarrow z'\}\rangle[z''\leftarrow b']\{y'\leftarrow w\}$	$\triangleleft [x'\leftarrow \lambda y.(O\langle z\rangle[z'\leftarrow b])]$	

Now, if the bite b' is a β-redex then the next transition is multiplicative and it is going to rename over $O'\langle t\{x\leftarrow z'\}\rangle$ which is not a sub-term of the initial term.

How Big is the Inefficiency? When the time cost depends on something that is not a sub-term of the initial term, things can easily escalate up to exponential costs, as in the paradigmatic case of size explosion, see Accattoli [2, Section 3]. Luckily, here things do not go sideways, there is only a mild inefficiency. The key point is that the sub-term property for duplications *does hold*: it ensures that the size of the whole state grows bi-linearly with the number of transitions, so there is no exponential growth. The problematic renaming—and thus each multiplicative transition—might then have to scan a scope that is at worst bi-linear in the length of the preceding run and the size of the initial term. A standard argument then gives a quadratic bound (in the number of steps and the size of the initial term) on the global cost of all multiplicative steps.

Let us give an example. We use a diverging term because it is the simplest example showcasing the phenomenon. We define the positive representation of $\Omega_3 := \delta_3 \delta_3$ where $\delta_3 := \lambda x.x(xx)$. Let $\tau_3 := x[x\leftarrow yz][z\leftarrow yy]$ and let

$\tau_3' := x'[x' {\leftarrow} y'z'][z' {\leftarrow} y'y']$ and so on. The analogous of Ω_3 is $\tau_3[y {\leftarrow} \lambda y.\tau_3]$, that runs as follows:

Active code	Right ctx	
$x[x {\leftarrow} yz][z {\leftarrow} yy][y {\leftarrow} \lambda y.\tau_3]$	$\lhd \langle \cdot \rangle$	$\leadsto_{\mathsf{sea}_1}$
$x[x {\leftarrow} yz][z {\leftarrow} yy]$	$\lhd [y {\leftarrow} \lambda y.\tau_3]$	$\leadsto_{\mathsf{e}}$
$x[x {\leftarrow} yz][z {\leftarrow} (\lambda y'.\tau_3')y]$	$\lhd [y {\leftarrow} \lambda y.\tau_3]$	$=$
$x[x {\leftarrow} yz][z {\leftarrow} (\lambda y'.x'[x' {\leftarrow} y'z'][z' {\leftarrow} y'y'])y]$	$\lhd [y {\leftarrow} \lambda y.\tau_3]$	$\leadsto_{\mathsf{m}}$
$x[x {\leftarrow} yx'][x' {\leftarrow} yz'][z' {\leftarrow} yy]$	$\lhd [y {\leftarrow} \lambda y.\tau_3]$	$\leadsto_{\mathsf{e}}$
$x[x {\leftarrow} yx'][x' {\leftarrow} yz'][z' {\leftarrow} (\lambda y''.\tau_3'')y]$	$\lhd [y {\leftarrow} \lambda y.\tau_3]$	$\leadsto_{\mathsf{m}}$
$x[x {\leftarrow} yx'][x' {\leftarrow} yx''][x'' {\leftarrow} yz''][z'' {\leftarrow} yy]$	$\lhd [y {\leftarrow} \lambda y.\tau_3]$	$\leadsto_{\mathsf{e}} \;\ldots$

It is clear that the scopes of the renamings keep growing, even if the number of renamed occurrences by each renaming is constant.

Removing the Inefficiency: Slices. An observation about the run (1) above suggests how to improve the situation. The idea is to delay the merging of t and $O'\langle z' \rangle$ as $O'\langle t\{x {\leftarrow} z'\} \rangle$ (similarly to how ESs delay meta-level substitutions) by putting the pair (t, x)—dubbed *slice* and that shall actually be denoted with $t[x {\leftarrow} \cdot]$—in a new stack storing delayed merges, and keeping as active code $O'\langle z' \rangle$. The observation is that if b' is a β-redex and generates a renaming of z'' then one only needs to inspect $O'\langle z' \rangle$—which, crucially, is a sub-term of the initial term—because z'' cannot occur in t, given that it comes from the body of an abstraction out of t.

Before defining the Sliced POM, and prove that slices do solve the problem, we start over with a more formal approach to abstract machines.

5 Preliminaries About Abstract Machines

In this section, we fix the terminology about abstract machines. We follow Accattoli and co-authors [4,7,8,13,16], adapting their notions to our framework. We mostly stay abstract. In the next section, we shall instantiate the abstract notions on a specific machine.

Abstract Machines Glossary. Abstract machines manipulate *pre-terms*, that is, terms without implicit α-renaming. In this paper, an *abstract machine* is a quadruple $\mathsf{M} = (\mathtt{States}, \leadsto, \cdot \lhd \cdot, \overline{\cdot})$ the components of which are as follows.

- *States.* A state $\mathtt{Q} \in \mathtt{States}$ is composed by the *active term* t, plus some data structures; the machine of the next section shall have two data structures. Terms in states are actually pre-terms.
- *Transitions.* The pair $(\mathtt{States}, \leadsto)$ is a transition system with transitions $\leadsto$ partitioned into *principal transitions*, whose union is noted $\leadsto_{\mathsf{pr}}$ and that are meant to correspond to rewriting steps on the calculus, and *search transitions*, whose union is noted $\leadsto_{\mathsf{sea}}$, that take care of searching for (principal) redexes.

- *Initialization.* The component $\triangleleft \subseteq \Lambda \times \mathtt{States}$ is the *initialization relation* associating terms to initial states. It is a *relation* and not a function because $t \triangleleft \mathsf{Q}$ maps a term t (considered modulo α) to a state Q having a *pre-term representant* of t (which is not modulo α) as active term. Intuitively, any two states Q and Q' such that $t \triangleleft \mathsf{Q}$ and $t \triangleleft \mathsf{Q}'$ are α-equivalent. A state Q is *reachable* if it can be reached starting from an initial state, that is, if $\mathsf{Q}' \rightsquigarrow^* \mathsf{Q}$ where $t \triangleleft \mathsf{Q}'$ for some t and Q', shortened as $t \triangleleft \mathsf{Q}' \rightsquigarrow^* \mathsf{Q}$.
- *Read-back.* The read-back function $\overline{\cdot} : \mathtt{States} \to \Lambda$ turns reachable states into terms and satisfies the *initialization constraint*: if $t \triangleleft \mathsf{Q}$ then $\overline{\mathsf{Q}} =_\alpha t$.

Further Terminology and Notations. A state is *final* if no transitions apply. A *run* $r : \mathsf{Q} \rightsquigarrow^* \mathsf{Q}'$ is a possibly empty finite sequence of transitions, the length of which is noted $|r|$; note that the first and the last states of a run are not necessarily initial and final. If a and b are transitions labels (that is, $\rightsquigarrow_a \subseteq \rightsquigarrow$ and $\rightsquigarrow_b \subseteq \rightsquigarrow$) then $\rightsquigarrow_{a,b} := \rightsquigarrow_a \cup \rightsquigarrow_b$ and $|r|_a$ is the number of a transitions in r.

Well-Boundness and Renamings. For the machine in this paper, the pre-terms in initial states shall be *well-bound*, that is, they have pairwise distinct bound names; for instance $w[w{\leftarrow}\lambda z.z][x{\leftarrow}\lambda y.y]$ is well-bound while $w[w{\leftarrow}\lambda y.y][x{\leftarrow}\lambda y.y]$ is not. We shall write also t^α in a state Q for a *fresh well-bound renaming* of t, i.e. t^α is α-equivalent to t, well-bound, and its bound variables are fresh with respect to those in t and in the other components of Q.

Mechanical Bismulations. Machines are usually showed to be correct with respect to a strategy via some form of bisimulation relating terms and states. The notion that we adopt is here dubbed *mechanical bisimulation*. The definition, tuned towards complexity analyses, requires a perfect match between the steps of the evaluation sequence and the principal transitions of the machine run.

Definition 4 (Mechanical bisimulation). *A machine* $\mathsf{M} = (\mathtt{States}, \rightsquigarrow, \triangleleft, \cdot, \overline{\cdot})$ *and a strategy* $\to_{\mathrm{str}}$ *on terms are mechanical bisimilar when, given an initial state* $t \triangleleft \mathsf{Q}$:

1. *Runs to evaluations: for any run* $r : t \triangleleft \mathsf{Q} \rightsquigarrow^* \mathsf{Q}'$ *there exists an evaluation* $e : t \to_{\mathrm{str}}^* \overline{\mathsf{Q}'}$;
2. *Evaluations to runs: for every evaluation* $e : t \to_{\mathrm{str}}^* u$ *there exists a run* $r : t \triangleleft \mathsf{Q} \rightsquigarrow^* \mathsf{Q}'$ *such that* $\overline{\mathsf{Q}'} = u$;
3. *Principal matching: for every principal transition* $\rightsquigarrow_a$ *of label* a *of* M, *in both previous points the number* $|r|_a$ *of* a-*transitions in* r *is exactly the number* $|e|_a$ *of of* a-*steps in the evaluation* e, *i.e.* $|e|_a = |r|_a$.

The proof that a machine and a strategy are in a mechanical bisimulation follows from some basic properties, grouped under the notion of *distillery*, following Accattoli et al. [3] (but removing their use of structural equivalence, that here is not needed). The intuition behind the notion of distillery is that the calculus

Slice stacks	Environments	States	Initialization
S ::= ϵ | S : t[x←·]	E ::= ϵ | [x←b] : E	Q ::= (S, t, E)	t ◁ (ϵ, t^α, ϵ) (∗)

			Transitions			
Sl. st.	Active slice	Env		Sl. st.	Active slice	Env
S	$t[x{\leftarrow}\lambda y.u]$	E	$\leadsto_{\mathsf{sea}_1}$	S	t	$[x{\leftarrow}\lambda y.u] : E$	
S	$t[x{\leftarrow}yz]$	E	$\leadsto_{\mathsf{sea}_2}$	S	t	$[x{\leftarrow}yz] : E$	(%)
S	$t[x{\leftarrow}yz]$	E	$\leadsto_{\mathsf{e}}$	S	$t[x{\leftarrow}(\lambda w.u)^\alpha z]]$	E	(#)(∗)
S	$t[x{\leftarrow}(\lambda y.u)w]$	E	$\leadsto_{\mathsf{m}}$	S : t[x←·]	$u\{y{\leftarrow}w\}$	E
S : t[x←·]	z	E	$\leadsto_{\mathsf{sea}_3}$	S	$t\{x{\leftarrow}z\}$	E

(∗) t^α is any well-bound code α-equivalent to t such that its bound names are fresh with respect to those in the rest of the state;

(%) if $y \notin \mathsf{dom}(E)$ or $E(y) \neq \lambda w.u$; (#) if $E(y) = \lambda w.u$.

	Read back		
Envs (to ctxs)	$\overline{\epsilon} := \langle \cdot \rangle$		$\overline{[x{\leftarrow}b] : E} := \overline{E}\langle\langle\cdot\rangle[x{\leftarrow}b]\rangle$
States (to terms)	$\overline{(\epsilon, t, E)} := \overline{E}\langle t \rangle$		$\overline{(S : t[x{\leftarrow}\cdot], O\langle y \rangle, E)} := \overline{(S, O\langle t\{x{\leftarrow}y\}\rangle, E)}$

Fig. 3. The Sliced Positive Machine (Sliced POM).

distils the machine in that it removes the search mechanism—as captured by the search transparency property below—as well as the organization of states in data structures, while it faithfully mimics the underlying dynamics, as captured by the principal projection and halt properties. At the meta-level, the technique is also meant to distil the reasoning behind bisimulation proofs: the mechanical bisimulation theorem after the definition is proved abstractly by relying solely on the properties defining a distillery.

Definition 5 (Distillery). *A machine* M = (States, $\leadsto, \cdot \triangleleft \cdot, \overline{\cdot}$) *and a strategy* $\to_{\mathsf{str}}$ *are a* distillery *if the following conditions hold:*

1. *Principal projection:* Q $\leadsto_{\mathsf{a}}$ Q' *implies* $\overline{Q} \to_{\mathsf{a}} \overline{Q'}$ *for every principal transition of label* a;
2. *Search transparency:* Q $\leadsto_{\mathsf{sea}}$ Q' *implies* $\overline{Q} = \overline{Q'}$;
3. *Search transitions terminate:* $\leadsto_{\mathsf{sea}}$ *terminates;*
4. *Determinism:* $\to_{\mathsf{str}}$ *is deterministic;*
5. *Halt:* M *final states decode to* $\to_{\mathsf{str}}$-*normal terms.*

Theorem 2 (Sufficient condition for mechanical bisimulations). *Let a machine* M *and a strategy* $\to_{\mathsf{str}}$ *be a distillery. Then, they are mechanical bisimilar.*

6 The Sliced Positive Machine

In this section, we present the optimized machine for the positive λ-calculus and establish the bisimulation between the new machine and the right strategy $\to_{\mathsf{r}}$.

The Sliced POM: Data Structures. The Sliced POsitive Machine (Sliced POM) is defined in Fig. 3. The machine has two data structures, the environment E and the slice stack S. The active code is re-dubbed *active slice*.

Environments E are nothing else but encodings of right contexts R. We prefer to change the representation for two reasons. Firstly, it is closer to how contexts are represented in the OCaml implementation. Secondly, it is a bit more precise: environments are free structures, and an invariant shall prove that they decode to right contexts (which are defined via some additional conditions).

The slice stack is simply a list of slices $t[x{\leftarrow}\cdot]$. Note the duality between environments and slice stacks: the entries of both are pairs of a term t and a variable x, but environment entries are meant to substitute t for x on some other term, while slices are meant to receive a variable and substitute it for x in t.

The Sliced POM: New Transition. The Sliced POM inherits the same four transitions of the Natural POM, but note that in transition $\leadsto_m$ now it is no longer necessary to decompose the body u of the abstraction as $O\langle z \rangle$ (please note that u is a meta-variable for *terms*, and not for variables). Additionally, the Sliced POM has a new search transition sea_3. When the evaluation of the active slice is over, which happens when one is left only with the head variable z of the slice, the new transitions sea_3 pops the first slice on the slice stack and replaces z for x in t. An invariant shall guarantee that t is a sub-term of the initial term, so that the cost of the renaming now is under control.

A Technical Point. The attentive reader might wonder why $\leadsto_m$ and $\leadsto_{\mathsf{sea}_3}$ are not reformulated in the following eager way (with slices reduced to be simply terms), where the head of the abstraction is substituted when the slice is *pushed* on the slice stack, and not when it is popped:

Sl. st.	Active slice	Env		Sl. st.	Active slice	Env
S	$t[x{\leftarrow}(\lambda y.O\langle z\rangle)w]$	E	$\leadsto_m$	S : $t\{x{\leftarrow}z\}$	$O\langle z\rangle\{y{\leftarrow}w\}$	E
S : t	z	E	$\leadsto_{\mathsf{sea}_3}$	S	t	E

We do not adopt the eager approach because the evaluation of the active slice might change its head variable (thus making it unsound to substitute eagerly), as it is demonstrated by the following run of the standard Sliced POM:

Slice stack	Active slice	Env	
ϵ	$t[x{\leftarrow}(\lambda y.z[z{\leftarrow}(\lambda x'.x')w'])w]$	ϵ	$\leadsto_m$
$\epsilon : t[x{\leftarrow}\cdot]$	$z[z{\leftarrow}(\lambda x'.x')w']$	ϵ	$\leadsto_m$
$\epsilon : t[x{\leftarrow}\cdot] : z[z{\leftarrow}\cdot]$	w'	ϵ	$\leadsto_{\mathsf{sea}_3}$
$\epsilon : t[x{\leftarrow}\cdot]$	w'	ϵ	

Invariants. To establish the bisimulation between the strategy $\to_r$ of the positive λ-calculus and the Sliced POM, we shall prove that the two form a distillery, that, in turn, is proved using the following invariants of the machine.

Lemma 4 (Qualitative invariants). *Let* $Q = (S, t, E)$ *be a reachable state.*

1. *Contextual read-back:* $\overline{E}$ *is a right context.*
2. *Well-bound:*
   - *Bound names in terms: if $\lambda x.u$ or $u[x \leftarrow b]$ occurs in Q then any other occurrence of x in Q, if any, is a free variable occurrence of u;*
   - *ES names of environment entries: for any ES $[y \leftarrow b]$ in E the name y can occur (in any form) only on the left of that ES in Q.*

Proof. By induction on the length of the run reaching Q. For both points, the base case trivially holds, and the inductive case is by analysis of the last transition, which is always a straightforward inspection of the transitions using the *i.h.* For contextual read-back, the proof relies on the inside-out definition of right contexts (see Definition 2). □

The well-bound invariant has two consequences that might not be evident. Firstly, there cannot be two ESs $[x \leftarrow b]$ and $[x \leftarrow b']$ on the same variable. This fact implies the determinism of the machine, that however shall not be proved because it is not necessary (determinism of the strategy is enough for proving the bisimulation). Secondly, the name x of an environment entry $[x \leftarrow b]$ can occur both in the active slice and in the slice stack, while the names of ESs in slices can occur only within the slice. In particular, x cannot occur in S in $(S, t[x \leftarrow b], E)$.

Theorem 3 (Distillery).

1. *Principal projection:*
   (a) *if $Q \rightsquigarrow_e Q'$ then $\overline{Q} \rightarrow_e \overline{Q'}$.*
   (b) *if $Q \rightsquigarrow_m Q'$ then $\overline{Q} \rightarrow_m \overline{Q'}$.*
2. *Search transparency: if $Q \rightsquigarrow_{sea_1, sea_2, sea_3} Q'$ then $\overline{Q} = \overline{Q'}$.*
3. *Search terminates: $\rightsquigarrow_{sea_1, sea_2, sea_3}$ is terminating.*
4. *Halt: if Q is final then it is of the form (ϵ, x, E) and $\overline{Q} = \overline{E}\langle x \rangle$ is $\rightarrow_{pos}$-normal.*

The points of the proved theorem together with determinism of the right strategy (Lemma 3) provide all the requirements for a distillery. Then, the abstract theorem about distilleries (Thorem 2) gives the following corollary.

Corollary 1 (Mechanical bisimulation). *The Sliced POM and the right strategy $\rightarrow_r$ are in a mechanical bisimulation.*

7 Complexity Analysis

In this section, we show that the Sliced POM can be concretely implemented within a bi-linear overhead, that is, linear in the number of m-steps/transitions and the size of the initial term.

Sub-term Property. As it is standard, the complexity analysis crucially relies on the sub-term property. In CbV settings, the property is usually expressed saying that all values are sub-terms of the initial terms, as in Lemma 1. The Sliced POM only duplicates values too, but (as we have discussed for the Natural POM) we also want to know that the terms to which renamings are applied are sub-terms of the initial term, and these terms are not values. Thus, the property is given with respect to *all* terms in a state.

There is in fact a very minor exception. The substitution performed by an exponential transition takes two sub-terms of the initial term, namely $t[x\leftarrow yz]$ and $\lambda w.u$, and creates a term $t[x\leftarrow(\lambda w.u)^\alpha z]$ that is not a sub-term of the initial one. The new term, however, is very short lived: the next transition is multiplicative and decomposes that term in sub-terms of the initial term (up to renaming).

Lemma 5 (Sub-term property). *Let $t \triangleleft Q \leadsto^* Q' = (S, u, E)$ be a Sliced POM run. Then:*

1. *If Q' is not the target of a e-transition then $|r| \leq |t|$ for any term r in Q';*
2. *Otherwise, $|r| \leq |t|$ for any term r in Q' except u.*

Proof. By induction on the length of the run, inspecting the last transition and using the *i.h.* □

Number of Transitions. Some basic observations about the transitions, together with the sub-term property, allow us to bound their number using the two key parameters (that is, number of m-steps/transitions and size of the initial term).

Lemma 6 (Number of transitions). *Let $r : t \triangleleft Q \leadsto^* Q'$ be a Sliced POM run.*

1. $|r|_{\mathsf{e},\mathsf{sea}_3} \in \mathcal{O}(|r|_\mathsf{m})$;
2. $|r|_{\mathsf{sea}_1,\mathsf{sea}_2} \in \mathcal{O}(|t| \cdot (|r|_\mathsf{m} + 1))$.

Proof. 1. $|r|_\mathsf{e} \leq |r|_\mathsf{m} + 1$ because exponential transitions can only be followed by multiplicative transitions.
$|r|_{\mathsf{sea}_3} \leq |r|_\mathsf{m}$ because every sea_3 transition consumes one entry from the slice stack, which are created only by m transitions.

2. Note that $\mathsf{sea}_1/\mathsf{sea}_2$ transitions decrease the size of the active slice, which is increased only by transitions e and sea_3. By the sub-term property (Lemma 5), the size increase of the active slice by transitions e and sea_3 is bounded by the size $|t|$ of the initial term. By Point 1, $|r|_{\mathsf{e},\mathsf{sea}_3} = \mathcal{O}(|r|_\mathsf{m})$. Then $|r|_{\mathsf{sea}_1,\mathsf{sea}_2} \in \mathcal{O}(|t| \cdot (|r|_{\mathsf{e},\mathsf{sea}_2} + 1)) = \mathcal{O}(|t| \cdot (|r|_\mathsf{m} + 1))$. □

Cost of Single Transitions. Lastly, we need some assumptions on how the Sliced POM can be concretely implemented. Transition sea_2 can evidently be done in $\mathcal{O}(1)$. Our OCaml implementation—overviewed in Appendix A of the technical report [18]—represents variables as memory locations and variable occurrences as pointers to those locations, obtaining random access to environment entries in

$\mathcal{O}(1)$.[2] Therefore, also transition sea_1 can be done in $\mathcal{O}(1)$. The cost of transition e is bound by the size of the value to copy, itself bound by the sub-term property. The cost of transitions m and sea_3 is bound by the size of the term to rename, itself bound by the sub-term property. The next lemma sums it up.

Lemma 7 (Cost of single transitions). *Let* $t \triangleleft \mathsf{Q} \leadsto^* \mathsf{Q}'$ *be a Sliced POM run. Implementing* sea_1 *and* sea_2 *transitions from* Q' *costs* $\mathcal{O}(1)$ *each while implementing* e, m, *and* sea_3 *transitions costs* $\mathcal{O}(|t|)$ *each.*

Putting all together, we obtain our main result: a bilinear bound for the Sliced POM, showing that it is an efficient machine for the right strategy.

Theorem 4 (Sliced POM is bi-linear). *Let* $r : t \triangleleft \mathsf{Q} \leadsto^* \mathsf{Q}'$ *be a Sliced POM run. Then* r *can be implemented on random access machines in* $\mathcal{O}(|t| \cdot (|r|_\mathsf{m} + 1))$.

Proof. The cost of implementing r is obtained by multiplying the number of each kind of transitions (Lemma 6) by the cost of that kind of transition (Lemma 7), and summing over all kinds of transition. □

8 Conclusions

In λ-calculi with sharing, renaming chains are a recurrent issue that causes both time and space inefficiencies. The recently introduced positive λ-calculus removes renaming chains, while adding some meta-level renamings. This paper stems from the observation that the added meta-level renamings reintroduce a time inefficiency if implemented naively.

The problem is analyzed via the sub-term property, showing that the culprit is the fact that the scope of renamings is not a sub-term of the initial term. The analysis leads to the design of an optimized machine, the new Sliced POM, that removes once and for all the inefficiency. The key tool is a new decomposition in slices of the scopes of renamings, via a new stack for slices playing a role dual to that of environments. We also provide a prototype OCaml implementation of the Sliced POM, described in Appendix A of the technical report [18].

---

[2] Assuming that memory accesses take $\mathcal{O}(1)$ is an idealized abstraction. In real computer architectures, that cost is highly dependent on where the data is stored, but it is bounded nonetheless. To be theoretically precise, the cost of accessing an *unbound* memory should be instead assumed to be logarithmic in the size of the memory in use. In the analyses of polynomial algorithms, and of abstract machines in particular, it is standard to assume an underlying random access machine model with constant-time access, since the logarithmic factor is somewhat negligible. The index of the location does instead play a more relevant role in the study of lower time and space complexities.

Future Work. At the theoretical level, we plan to adapt the positive λ-calculus and the Sliced POM to call-by-need evaluation. At the practical level, it would be interesting to see how the schema of the Sliced POM combines with other techniques such as closure conversion or skeletal call-by-need; these techniques were in fact recasted in the same abstract machine framework of the present work, and also analyzed from a complexity point of view, in two parallel works involving Accattoli and Sacerdoti Coen [11,15]. We also suspect that the Sliced POM can be used to simplify the sophisticated machine for Strong Call-by-Value by Accattoli et al. in [8].

Acknowledgments. The second author is funded by the INdAM/GNCS project MARQ and the third by the ANR project RECIPROG (ANR-21-CE48-019).

References

1. Abadi, M., Cardelli, L., Curien, P., Lévy, J.: Explicit substitutions. J. Funct. Program. **1**(4), 375–416 (1991). https://doi.org/10.1017/S0956796800000186
2. Accattoli, B.: Exponentials as substitutions and the cost of cut elimination in linear logic. Log. Methods Comput. Sci. **19**(4) (2023). https://doi.org/10.46298/LMCS-19(4:23)2023
3. Accattoli, B., Barenbaum, P., Mazza, D.: Distilling abstract machines. In: 19th ACM SIGPLAN International Conference on Functional Programming, ICFP 2014, pp. 363–376. ACM (2014). https://doi.org/10.1145/2628136.2628154
4. Accattoli, B., Barenbaum, P., Mazza, D.: A strong distillery. In: Feng, X., Park, S. (eds.) APLAS 2015. LNCS, vol. 9458, pp. 231–250. Springer, Cham (2015). https://doi.org/10.1007/978-3-319-26529-2_13
5. Accattoli, B., Barras, B.: Environments and the complexity of abstract machines. In: Vanhoof, W., Pientka, B. (eds.) Proceedings of the 19th International Symposium on Principles and Practice of Declarative Programming, Namur, Belgium, October 09 - 11, 2017, pp. 4–16. ACM (2017). https://doi.org/10.1145/3131851.3131855
6. Accattoli, B., Bonelli, E., Kesner, D., Lombardi, C.: A nonstandard standardization theorem. In: Jagannathan, S., Sewell, P. (eds.) The 41st Annual ACM SIGPLAN-SIGACT Symposium on Principles of Programming Languages, POPL '14, San Diego, CA, USA, January 20-21, 2014. pp. 659–670. ACM (2014). https://doi.org/10.1145/2535838.2535886
7. Accattoli, B., Condoluci, A., Guerrieri, G., Sacerdoti Coen, C.: Crumbling abstract machines. In: Komendantskaya, E. (ed.) Proceedings of the 21st International Symposium on Principles and Practice of Programming Languages, PPDP 2019, Porto, Portugal, October 7-9, 2019. pp. 4:1–4:15. ACM (2019). https://doi.org/10.1145/3354166.3354169
8. Accattoli, B., Condoluci, A., Sacerdoti Coen, C.: Strong call-by-value is reasonable, implosively. In: 36th Annual ACM/IEEE Symposium on Logic in Computer Science, LICS 2021, Rome, Italy, June 29 - July 2, 2021. pp. 1–14. IEEE (2021). https://doi.org/10.1109/LICS52264.2021.9470630
9. Accattoli, B., Dal Lago, U.: (leftmost-outermost) beta reduction is invariant, indeed. Log. Methods Comput. Sci. **12**(1) (2016). https://doi.org/10.2168/LMCS-12(1:4)2016

10. Accattoli, B., Dal Lago, U., Vanoni, G.: Reasonable space for the λ-calculus, logarithmically. In: Baier, C., Fisman, D. (eds.) LICS '22: 37th Annual ACM/IEEE Symposium on Logic in Computer Science, Haifa, Israel, August 2 - 5, 2022. pp. 47:1–47:13. ACM (2022). https://doi.org/10.1145/3531130.3533362
11. Accattoli, B., Ghica, D., Guerrieri, G., Lourenço, C.B., Sacerdoti Coen, C.: Closure conversion, flat environments, and the complexity of abstract machines. CoRR **abs/2507.15843** (2025). https://doi.org/10.48550/ARXIV.2507.15843, accepted at PPDP 2025
12. Accattoli, B., Guerrieri, G.: Open call-by-value. In: Igarashi, A. (ed.) Programming Languages and Systems - 14th Asian Symposium, APLAS 2016, Hanoi, Vietnam, November 21-23, 2016, Proceedings. Lecture Notes in Computer Science, vol. 10017, pp. 206–226 (2016). https://doi.org/10.1007/978-3-319-47958-3_12
13. Accattoli, B., Guerrieri, G.: Abstract machines for open call-by-value. Sci. Comput. Program. **184** (2019). https://doi.org/10.1016/J.SCICO.2019.03.002
14. Accattoli, B., Kesner, D.: The structural λ-calculus. In: Dawar, A., Veith, H. (eds.) CSL 2010. LNCS, vol. 6247, pp. 381–395. Springer, Heidelberg (2010). https://doi.org/10.1007/978-3-642-15205-4_30
15. Accattoli, B., Magliocca, F., Peyrot, L., Sacerdoti Coen, C.: The cost of skeletal call-by-need, smoothly. In: Fernández, M. (ed.) 10th International Conference on Formal Structures for Computation and Deduction, FSCD 2025, July 14-20, 2025, Birmingham, UK. LIPIcs, vol. 337, pp. 5:1–5:22. Schloss Dagstuhl - Leibniz-Zentrum für Informatik (2025). https://doi.org/10.4230/LIPICS.FSCD.2025.5
16. Accattoli, B., Sacerdoti Coen, C.: On the relative usefulness of fireballs. In: 30th Annual ACM/IEEE Symposium on Logic in Computer Science, LICS 2015, Kyoto, Japan, July 6-10, 2015, pp. 141–155. IEEE Computer Society (2015). https://doi.org/10.1109/LICS.2015.23
17. Accattoli, B., Sacerdoti Coen, C.: On the value of variables. Inf. Comput. **255**, 224–242 (2017). https://doi.org/10.1016/j.ic.2017.01.003
18. Accattoli, B., Sacerdoti Coen, C., Wu, J.: Positive sharing and abstract machines. CoRR abs/2506.14131 (2025). https://doi.org/10.48550/ARXIV.2506.14131
19. Accattoli, B., Wu, J.H.: Positive focusing is directly useful. Electronic Notes in Theoretical Informatics and Computer Science, Volume 4 - Proceedings of MFPS XL, 3 (2024). https://doi.org/10.46298/entics.14758
20. Dal Lago, U., Martini, S.: The weak lambda calculus as a reasonable machine. Theor. Comput. Sci. **398**(1–3), 32–50 (2008). https://doi.org/10.1016/J.TCS.2008.01.044
21. Danos, V., Herbelin, H., Regnier, L.: Game semantics & abstract machines. In: Proceedings, 11th Annual IEEE Symposium on Logic in Computer Science, New Brunswick, New Jersey, USA, July 27-30, 1996. pp. 394–405. IEEE Computer Society (1996). https://doi.org/10.1109/LICS.1996.561456
22. Felleisen, M., Friedman, D.P.: Control operators, the SECD-machine, and the λ-calculus. In: Wirsing, M. (ed.) Formal Description of Programming Concepts - III: Proceedings of the IFIP TC 2/WG 2.2 Working Conference on Formal Description of Programming Concepts - III, Ebberup, Denmark, 25-28 August 1986. pp. 193–222. North-Holland (1987)
23. Flanagan, C., Sabry, A., Duba, B.F., Felleisen, M.: The essence of compiling with continuations. In: Cartwright, R. (ed.) Proceedings of the ACM SIGPLAN'93 Conference on Programming Language Design and Implementation (PLDI), Albuquerque, New Mexico, USA, June 23-25, 1993. pp. 237–247. ACM (1993). https://doi.org/10.1145/155090.155113

24. Friedman, D.P., Ghuloum, A., Siek, J.G., Winebarger, O.L.: Improving the lazy Krivine machine. High. Order Symb. Comput. **20**(3), 271–293 (2007). https://doi.org/10.1007/S10990-007-9014-0
25. Grégoire, B., Leroy, X.: A compiled implementation of strong reduction. In: Wand, M., Jones, S.L.P. (eds.) Proceedings of the Seventh ACM SIGPLAN International Conference on Functional Programming (ICFP '02), Pittsburgh, Pennsylvania, USA, October 4-6, 2002, pp. 235–246. ACM (2002). https://doi.org/10.1145/581478.581501
26. Launchbury, J.: A natural semantics for lazy evaluation. In: Deusen, M.S.V., Lang, B. (eds.) Conference Record of the Twentieth Annual ACM SIGPLAN-SIGACT Symposium on Principles of Programming Languages, Charleston, South Carolina, USA, January 1993, pp. 144–154. ACM Press (1993). https://doi.org/10.1145/158511.158618
27. Levy, P.B., Power, J., Thielecke, H.: Modelling environments in call-by-value programming languages. Inf. Comput. **185**(2), 182–210 (2003). https://doi.org/10.1016/S0890-5401(03)00088-9
28. Miller, D., Wu, J.H.: A positive perspective on term representation (invited talk). In: Klin, B., Pimentel, E. (eds.) 31st EACSL Annual Conference on Computer Science Logic, CSL 2023, February 13-16, 2023, Warsaw, Poland. LIPIcs, vol. 252, pp. 3:1–3:21. Schloss Dagstuhl - Leibniz-Zentrum für Informatik (2023). https://doi.org/10.4230/LIPICS.CSL.2023.3
29. Moggi, E.: Computational λ-Calculus and Monads. LFCS report ECS-LFCS-88-66, University of Edinburgh (1988). http://www.lfcs.inf.ed.ac.uk/reports/88/ECS-LFCS-88-66/ECS-LFCS-88-66.pdf
30. Moggi, E.: Computational lambda-calculus and monads. In: Proceedings of the Fourth Annual Symposium on Logic in Computer Science (LICS '89), Pacific Grove, California, USA, June 5-8, 1989. pp. 14–23. IEEE Computer Society (1989). https://doi.org/10.1109/LICS.1989.39155
31. Sabry, A., Felleisen, M.: Reasoning about programs in continuation-passing style. In: White, J.L. (ed.) Proceedings of the Conference on Lisp and Functional Programming, LFP 1992, San Francisco, California, USA, 22–24 June 1992, pp. 288–298. ACM (1992). https://doi.org/10.1145/141471.141563
32. Sands, D., Gustavsson, J., Moran, A.: Lambda calculi and linear speedups. In: Mogensen, T.Æ., Schmidt, D.A., Sudborough, I.H. (eds.) The Essence of Computation. LNCS, vol. 2566, pp. 60–82. Springer, Heidelberg (2002). https://doi.org/10.1007/3-540-36377-7_4
33. Sestoft, P.: Deriving a lazy abstract machine. J. Funct. Program. **7**(3), 231–264 (1997). https://doi.org/10.1017/S0956796897002712
34. Wand, M.: On the correctness of the krivine machine. High. Order Symb. Comput. **20**(3), 231–235 (2007). https://doi.org/10.1007/S10990-007-9019-8
35. Wu, J.H.: Proofs as terms, terms as graphs. In: Hur, C. (ed.) APLAS 2023. LNCS, vol. 14405, pp. 91–111. Springer, Cham (2023). https://doi.org/10.1007/978-981-99-8311-7_5

Quantum Programming and Logic

IMALL with a Mixed-State Modality: A Logical Approach to Quantum Computation

Kinnari Dave[1,2(✉)], Alejandro Díaz-Caro[2,3], and Vladimir Zamdzhiev[1]

[1] Université Paris-Saclay, CNRS, ENS Paris-Saclay, Inria, Laboratoire Méthodes Formelles, 91190 Gif-sur-Yvette, France
[2] Université de Lorraine, CNRS, Inria, LORIA, 54000 Nancy, France
[3] Universidad Nacional de Quilmes, Bernal, Buenos Aires, Argentina

Abstract. We introduce a proof language for Intuitionistic Multiplicative Additive Linear Logic (IMALL), extended with a modality $\mathcal{B}$ to capture mixed-state quantum computation. The language supports algebraic constructs such as linear combinations, and embeds pure quantum computations within a mixed-state framework via $\mathcal{B}$, interpreted categorically as a functor from a category of Hilbert Spaces to a category of finite-dimensional C*-algebras. Measurement arises as a definable term, not as a constant, and the system avoids the use of quantum configurations, which are part of the theory of the quantum lambda calculus. Cut-elimination is defined via a composite reduction relation, and shown to be sound with respect to the denotational interpretation. We prove that any linear map on $\mathbb{C}^{2^n}$ can be represented within the system, and illustrate this expressiveness with examples such as quantum teleportation and the quantum switch.

Keywords: quantum computation · linear logic · algebraic lambda calculus · mixed states · proof theory · categorical semantics

1 Introduction

Quantum programming languages typically adopt either *classical control* or *quantum control* as a guiding principle. Each paradigm offers advantages but also entails limitations. The former enables measurement and branching over classical data, yet typically restricts quantum computation to a fixed set of unitary operations [21,22]. The latter, by contrast, supports higher-order manipulation of quantum data and richer linear-algebraic structure, but often lacks native support for measurement and, consequently, mixed-state computation [10,12].

In parallel with the development of quantum programming languages, a complementary line of research seeks to understand the logical structure underlying quantum computation. Just as intuitionistic logic, λ-calculus, and Cartesian closed categories are linked via the Curry–Howard–Lambek correspondence [16,

17,23], one may ask whether there exists a natural logical system whose proof language corresponds to quantum computation. This perspective motivates the study of *quantum computational logic*, where proofs denote quantum processes and the type system reflects the constraints and structure of quantum theory.

From this viewpoint, the challenge is not to build yet another quantum programming language, but to construct a logical framework with a well-defined proof theory that aligns with the operational and denotational semantics of quantum computation. Such a framework should ideally support superposition and linear combinations natively, provide a proof-theoretic foundation for unitary transformations and entangled systems, and admit a natural account of measurement and mixed states.

This paper presents a proof language for Intuitionistic Multiplicative Additive Linear Logic (IMALL), extended with a modality $\mathcal{B}$ that captures the transition from pure to mixed states. Our system is based on quantum control and supports both pure and mixed-state computation within a unified logical setting, with a compositional and adequate semantics.

Our approach offers three major advantages over the typical approach adopted by quantum lambda calculi (QLCs) [3,6,22,25]. First, our approach enables a richer linear-algebraic structure: instead of treating unitary transformations as fixed constants, they can be defined and composed as first-class terms, allowing precise descriptions of quantum operations as linear maps. Second, it allows the expression of genuinely quantum control flows, such as the *quantum switch* [19], where the order of operations is conditioned on the state of a qubit—a behaviour not efficiently representable in QLCs. Third, quantum control dispenses with the need for an external global configuration—such as the "quantum configurations" in the QLC—to carry quantum state alongside the program. In our system, both state and program are encoded in the same proof language, and measurement is not a fixed constant with special semantics, but a proof term built from the same algebraic structure as the rest of the language.

Contributions. Our main contributions are as follows:

- We define the logic $\mathcal{B}$-IMALL by extending IMALL with a modality $\mathcal{B}$ in a *transparent* way: every provable formula in $\mathcal{B}$-IMALL remains provable in IMALL when occurrences of $\mathcal{B}$ are erased. Our system does not include LL exponentials, because we want to keep it simple while still being able to demonstrate the main point. There can be interaction between the $\mathcal{B}$ functor and the LL exponentials in the model (see [18] which requires complicated analytic structure), but it is unclear how to do this in a simple way on the logical side. This is interesting future work.
- The proof language supports linear combinations of terms through the operators $\cdot$ and $+$, which preserve the structure of a complex vector space (Corollary 5.1). Our system is thus *algebraically linear* in a precise sense.
- Unlike the algebraic λ-calculi [1,2,26], our language integrates both pure and mixed-state computation. The syntax accommodates superpositions and measurements within the same framework.
- Unlike the Lambda-S family of calculi [9–12], which introduce a new logic based on a dedicated modality S to manage quantum superpositions, our

system builds directly on the well-established logic IMALL. This ensures that
the logical foundations are familiar, modular, and reusable, while still being
expressive enough to represent both pure and mixed-state computation.
- The modality $\mathcal{B}$ embeds the pure fragment into the mixed one, allowing transitions from pure-state vectors to density matrices. This resolves a limitation of earlier approaches using the $\odot$ connective [7], which were well suited to probabilistic settings but lacked a clear quantum denotational semantics [13].
- The cut-elimination process is defined via a composite reduction relation, obtained by interleaving a linear-algebraic equivalence ($\leftrightarrows$) with a deterministic evaluation ($\rightarrow$), as formalised in Sect. 2.1. This approach combines ideas from other frameworks: the relation $\rightarrow$ captures the interaction between algebraic constructors and logical connectives, as in the $\odot$ and $\mathcal{L}\odot$ calculi [7,8], and is here extended to handle the $\mathcal{B}$ modality. The symmetric relation $\leftrightarrows$ ensures canonical vector forms, in the style of algebraic λ-calculi [1,2,26].
- Measurement is expressible as a program, not as a constant: rather than requiring a dedicated syntactic construct with external semantics, it emerges naturally as a proof term within the language.
- The language avoids the need for quantum lambda configurations (QLCs) [3,6,22,25], by encoding both program and quantum state uniformly as terms.
- We provide a denotational model inspired by [4]. Our model defines a functor $\mathcal{B}$ mapping pure-state morphisms to completely positive maps. A similar functor also denoted with the same symbol first appeared in [6]. This model validates the design of the language and supports an adequacy theorem.
- Finally, we show that every linear transformation over $\mathbb{C}^{2^n}$ can be encoded in the pure fragment of our language (Sect. 5), and demonstrate the expressiveness of the language through examples such as quantum teleportation and the quantum switch—highlighting its ability to naturally capture paradigmatic quantum phenomena.

Taken together, these results yield a novel proof language that can express both pure and mixed-state quantum computation, grounded in a transparent logical system with a compositional and adequate semantics.

Compared to previous systems, our approach treats quantum computation not merely as a programming discipline but as a logical theory with intrinsic proof-theoretic content. Rather than relying on external control structures or dedicated constants, we encode quantum data, operations, and measurements uniformly as logical terms. This design bridges foundational insights from logic with the practical demands of quantum computation.

Structure of the Paper. Section 2 introduces the syntax of the proof terms, the derivation rules for both pure and mixed fragments, and the cut-elimination procedure. We also establish standard meta-theoretic properties such as preservation under reduction, progress, and strong normalisation. Section 3 presents a categorical model based on the categories **FHilb** and **FC***, which motivates the interpretation of the $\mathcal{B}$ modality as a transition from pure to mixed-state computation. Section 4 defines the denotational semantics of the language and proves that it is sound and adequate with respect to cut-elimination. Section 5 shows the expressive power of the language by encoding quantum notions such as qubits, gates, measurements, higher-order quantum control, quantum teleportation, and the quantum switch. Section 6 summarises our contributions and gives directions for future work.

2 The $\mathcal{L}_\mathcal{B}$-calculus

2.1 Syntax, Derivation Rules, and Cut-Elimination

The calculus $\mathcal{L}_\mathcal{B}$ is an extension of the linear lambda calculus, viewed as a proof system for an extension of IMALL. This extension consists of adding a new modality, $\mathcal{B}$, to the language, which enables the embedding of pure-state quantum computations into the mixed-state fragment of the calculus. As a result, the language is divided into two fragments: one for pure-state quantum computation and another for mixed-state quantum computation. Accordingly, the logic $\mathcal{B}$-IMALL has the following grammar.

$$\boldsymbol{P} := \boldsymbol{\top} \mid \boldsymbol{1} \mid \boldsymbol{P} \multimap \boldsymbol{P} \mid \boldsymbol{P} \mathbin{\&} \boldsymbol{P} \mid \boldsymbol{P} \otimes \boldsymbol{P} \qquad \text{(Pure Propositions)}$$
$$A := 0 \mid 1 \mid A \multimap A \mid A \oplus A \mid A \otimes A \mid \mathcal{B}(\boldsymbol{P}) \qquad \text{(Mixed Propositions)}$$

We denote pure propositions by bold capital Latin letters, and mixed propositions by regular capital Latin letters.

Notice that, by removing the modality $\mathcal{B}$ and ignoring the distinction between bold and non-bold connectives, the two fragments collapse into IMALL. For example, $\boldsymbol{\top} \oplus \boldsymbol{1}$ is not a valid proposition in $\mathcal{B}$-IMALL, whereas $\mathcal{B}(\boldsymbol{\top}) \oplus 1$ is. Removing the modality from the latter, and identifying $\boldsymbol{1}$ with 1, yields the syntactically valid IMALL proposition $\top \oplus 1$.

The proposition $\mathcal{B}(\boldsymbol{P})$ represents a mixed-state quantum computation on the Hilbert space represented by the proposition $\boldsymbol{P}$. The notation $\mathcal{B}(\cdot)$ is inspired by our denotational model, where $\mathcal{B}(H)$ denotes the C^*-algebra of linear operators on a finite-dimensional Hilbert space H. Readers may consult the model (Sect. 3) to get better intuition and understanding of this.

Note that the split between pure and mixed propositions is not justified by logical polarities or any other well-established logical criteria. Indeed, the status of logical polarities in relation to quantum theory was recently investigated in [18], but only in the sense of mixed-state quantum information and entirely done in a semantic model of LL. In contrast, our work focuses on the combination of both pure and mixed quantum primitives and a large part of our work is focused on the logical treatment, not just the semantic model. Thus, the split between pure/mixed propositions used here is novel and inspired by the specifics of the quantum model.

The proof terms of the calculus are also divided into two fragments: one for pure-state quantum computation, corresponding to pure propositions, and another for mixed-state quantum computation, corresponding to mixed ones.

$$\boldsymbol{m} := \boldsymbol{x} \mid \boldsymbol{m} \boldsymbol{+} \boldsymbol{m} \mid a \cdot \boldsymbol{m} \mid \langle\rangle \mid * \mid \delta_1(\boldsymbol{m}, \boldsymbol{m}) \mid \lambda x.\boldsymbol{m} \mid \boldsymbol{m}\, \boldsymbol{m} \qquad \text{(Pure Terms)}$$
$$\mid \langle \boldsymbol{m}, \boldsymbol{m}\rangle \mid \delta^1_{\&}(\boldsymbol{m}, x.\boldsymbol{m}) \mid \delta^2_{\&}(\boldsymbol{m}, x.\boldsymbol{m}) \mid \boldsymbol{m} \otimes \boldsymbol{m} \mid \delta_\otimes(\boldsymbol{m}, xy.\boldsymbol{m})$$

$m := x \mid m + m \mid p \cdot m \mid \delta_0(m) \mid * \mid \delta_1(m, m) \mid \lambda x.m \mid m\ m$ (Mixed Terms)
$\mid inl(m) \mid inr(m) \mid \delta_\oplus(m, x.m, y.m) \mid m \otimes m \mid \delta_\otimes(m, xy.m) \mid \mathcal{B}(m) \mid \tau(m)$

Pure and mixed variables–denoted by $\boldsymbol{x}, \boldsymbol{y}, \boldsymbol{z}$ and x, y, z, respectively–belong to an enumerable set VARS. The α-equivalence relation and the free variables of a term are defined as usual. Terms are defined modulo α-equivalence. Closed terms are the ones that do not contain free variables.

Most terms in $\mathcal{L}_\mathcal{B}$ are standard for the linear lambda calculus. As before, to highlight the distinction between pure and mixed terms, pure terms are represented by bold letters $\boldsymbol{m}, \boldsymbol{n}, \boldsymbol{o}$, while mixed terms are represented by the letters m, n, o. Each construction corresponds to a rule of the logic.

Starting with the pure fragment, the symbols $+$ and $\cdot$ denote sums and scalar multiplication, which correspond to the following rules introduced in [8].

$$\frac{\Gamma \vdash \boldsymbol{P} \quad \Gamma \vdash \boldsymbol{P}}{\Gamma \vdash \boldsymbol{P}} \qquad \frac{\Gamma \vdash \boldsymbol{P}}{\Gamma \vdash \boldsymbol{P}}$$

Scalars in the pure fragment range over the field of complex numbers and are denoted by the letters a, b, c. We work with unnormalized vectors, since the techniques required to restrict the calculus to normalized vectors are similar to those used in [10], and would make the calculus even more complex.

The other constructions are standard: The connective ⊤ has only an introduction rule, as usual, which is $\langle\rangle$. The connective $\boldsymbol{1}$ has an introduction rule, given by $*$, and also an elimination rule, $\delta_1(\boldsymbol{m}, \boldsymbol{n})$, intended to be understood as sequencing. While not always necessary, it is useful in the presence of scalars. The connective $\multimap$ has the standard introduction and elimination rules: $\lambda \boldsymbol{x}.\boldsymbol{m}$ and $\boldsymbol{m}\ \boldsymbol{n}$, respectively. The connective & has an introduction rule given by $\langle \boldsymbol{m}, \boldsymbol{n} \rangle$, and, since we present all rules in their extended version, it has the extended elimination rule $\delta^i_\&(\boldsymbol{m}, \boldsymbol{x}.\boldsymbol{n})$ for $i \in \{1, 2\}$. The connective ⊗ has an introduction rule given by $\boldsymbol{m} \otimes \boldsymbol{n}$, and an elimination rule given by $\delta_\otimes(\boldsymbol{m}, \boldsymbol{xy}.\boldsymbol{n})$.

Similarly, the symbols $+$ and $\cdot$ in the mixed fragment denote sums and scalar multiplication. However, scalars in the mixed fragment range over the non-negative real numbers and are denoted by the letters p, q. Again, we work with unnormalized vectors, thus a generalization of probability distributions.

The connectives $\boldsymbol{1}$, $\multimap$, and $\otimes$ are completely analogous to those in the pure fragment. The connectives $\boldsymbol{0}$ and $\oplus$ are standard: $\boldsymbol{0}$ has only an elimination rule, as usual, given by $\delta_0(m)$; $\oplus$ has two introduction rules, $inl(m)$ and $inr(n)$, and an elimination rule given by $\delta_\oplus(m, x.n, y.o)$.

Finally, there are two other constructions specific to the mixed fragment, which do not correspond to any logical connective:

- The modality $\mathcal{B}(\boldsymbol{m})$, which embeds pure terms into the mixed fragment. It has a rule that allows the inclusion of closed pure terms. Thus, a pure term $\boldsymbol{m}$ can be embedded as $\mathcal{B}(\boldsymbol{m})$. The rule $\mathcal{B}^m$ behaves analogously to a modal introduction in necessity logic: from a closed derivation of $\boldsymbol{P}$ one derives $\mathcal{B}(\boldsymbol{P})$. The other rules involving $\mathcal{B}$ ($\mathcal{B}(\multimap)^m_e$ and $\mathcal{B}(\otimes)^m$) are not eliminations of the modality, but rather structural rules describing how logical connectives behave under the embedding. This reflects the behaviour of the categorical functor $\mathcal{B}$, which maps between two distinct semantic domains: from pure-state morphisms in **FHilb** to completely positive maps in **FC*** (see Sect. 3). $\mathcal{B}$ can be understood as a structural operation that reflects a change of logical layer. In this sense, $\mathcal{B}(P)$ should be read as "the mixed version of P". Its behaviour is better captured by its categorical semantics, where $\mathcal{B}$ corresponds to a functor between categories representing different computational paradigms (from pure to mixed quantum computation).

- The construction $\tau(m)$ is a *coercion* operator that enables switching from the proposition $\mathcal{B}(P) \otimes \mathcal{B}(Q)$ to the proposition $\mathcal{B}(P \otimes Q)$. This operator is crucial for the interaction between the pure and mixed fragments.

The pure and mixed values in this calculus are defined as follows:

$$v_b := * \mid \boldsymbol{x} \mid \boldsymbol{v}_n \otimes \boldsymbol{v}_n$$
$$v_n := \langle\rangle \mid \boldsymbol{\lambda x}.m \mid \langle \boldsymbol{v}, \boldsymbol{v} \rangle \mid v_b$$
$$v := v_n \mid \sum_{i=1}^n \boldsymbol{a}_i \cdot \boldsymbol{v}_{bi} + \sum_{j=1}^l \boldsymbol{v}_{bj} \mid \sum_{i=1}^n \boldsymbol{0} \cdot \boldsymbol{v}_{bi} \qquad \text{(Pure Values)}$$

$$v_b := * \mid x \mid inl(v_n) \mid inr(v_n) \mid v_n \otimes v_n \mid \mathcal{B}(v)$$
$$v_n := \lambda x.m \mid v_b$$
$$v := v_n \mid \sum_{i=1}^n p_i \cdot v_{bi} + \sum_{j=1}^l v_{bj} \mid \sum_{i=1}^n 0 \cdot v_{bi} \qquad \text{(Mixed Values)}$$

where, in the summations, each $\boldsymbol{v}_{bi}, \boldsymbol{v}_{bj}$ (resp. v_{bi}, v_{bj}) is assumed to be a distinct value, and $\boldsymbol{a}_i \neq \boldsymbol{0}, \boldsymbol{1}$ (resp. $p_i > 0, p_i \neq 1$).

From now on, we will always assume that the summation symbol $\sum$ is used in the context of values, and that the summands are distinct.

Pure values $\boldsymbol{v}$ are composed of linear combinations of the values $\boldsymbol{v}_b$, and of values $\boldsymbol{v}_n$, which are not linear combinations. The values $\boldsymbol{v}_n$ correspond to the connectives $\top$, $\multimap$, and $\&$, for which linear combinations commute with the introduction rules and can be distributed internally. For example, the term $\langle \boldsymbol{m}_1, \boldsymbol{n}_1 \rangle + \langle \boldsymbol{m}_2, \boldsymbol{n}_2 \rangle$ can be rewritten as $\langle \boldsymbol{m}_1 + \boldsymbol{m}_2, \boldsymbol{n}_1 + \boldsymbol{n}_2 \rangle$. In contrast, the values $\boldsymbol{v}_b$ correspond to the connectives $\boldsymbol{1}$ and $\otimes$, where such commutation is not possible. For instance, the term $(\boldsymbol{m}_1 \otimes \boldsymbol{n}_1) + (\boldsymbol{m}_2 \otimes \boldsymbol{n}_2)$ cannot be rewritten by commuting $+$ with $\otimes$.

Similarly, mixed values v are composed of linear combinations of the values v_b, and of values v_n, which are not linear combinations.

Henceforth, we may use the letters M, N, O to denote *both* mixed and pure terms, the letters U, V, W to denote both mixed and pure values, and S, T to denote both mixed and pure propositions. Additionally, we use the Greek letters α, β to denote scalars from either fragment.

For simplicity, we may use the same symbols for connectives in both fragments when using capital letters. For example, we may write $\otimes$ to refer to either $\otimes$ or $\otimes$, depending on context. Similarly, we may write x instead of $\boldsymbol{x}$, $*$ instead of $*$, and so on, when the distinction is clear.

Whenever we use metavariables like M, N, or S in place of concrete terms or propositions, we assume that all components belong to the same fragment. For instance, since $\delta_1(t, r)$ is not a valid term—because δ_1 and t belong to the pure fragment and r to the mixed one—expressions like $\delta_1(M, N)$ implicitly assume that M, N, and the connective itself all belong to the same fragment.

The logic $\mathcal{B}$-IMALL is defined by the syntax given above, together with a set of derivation rules, presented in Fig. 1. The rules are formulated in natural deduction style, with proof terms annotating the derivations.

A context is a list of variable declarations, where each variable is associated with a proposition. A pure context is denoted by Γ or Δ, while a mixed context is denoted by $\varGamma$ or $\varDelta$. As before, we simply write Γ or Δ when the distinction is clear or when referring to both fragments. The notation Γ, Δ denotes the concatenation of the two disjoint contexts Γ and Δ.

The names of the rules include a superscript p indicating it belongs to the pure fragment or a superscript m for the mixed fragment. The absence of a superscript indicates that the rule applies to both fragments. In such cases, we may optionally add the superscript later when specifying one of the fragments.

All the rules are standard, except for the rules sum and $\text{prod}(\alpha)$, which correspond to sums and scalar multiplication, respectively, and the rules related to the $\mathcal{B}$ modality. Notice that the rules sum and $\text{prod}(\alpha)$ do not change the provability associated with formulae.

The rules related to $\mathcal{B}$ are the following:

- The rule $\mathcal{B}^m$ allows the introduction of *closed* pure terms into the mixed fragment. There are two reasons for this being restricted to closed terms. First, the design and construction of proof terms for propositions $\mathcal{B}(P)$ are inspired by the denotational model, where $\mathcal{B}$ is interpreted as a functor between two categories. As such, it cannot be composed directly with morphisms from the domain category. Second, allowing open proof terms of propositions P to be promoted to proof terms of $\mathcal{B}(P)$ would permit arbitrary transformations from pure to mixed propositions to be expressed as valid terms in $\mathcal{L}_\mathcal{B}$. This goes against the intended design, which views the pure fragment as a subsystem of $\mathcal{L}_\mathcal{B}$ dedicated to pure-state quantum computation. In contrast, the mixed fragment is regarded as the "main" language of the calculus, with the pure fragment *included* into it to provide expressive power for encoding pure-state quantum computation.
- The rule $\mathcal{B}(\multimap)_e^m$ allows the elimination of an embedded pure arrow.
- The rule $\mathcal{B}(\otimes)^m$ is a coercion rule. It allows one to transition from the proposition $\mathcal{B}(P) \otimes \mathcal{B}(Q)$ to the less informative proposition $\mathcal{B}(P \otimes Q)$—just as type-casting an integer to a real "forgets" its integer nature.

Cut-elimination in $\mathcal{L}_\mathcal{B}$ is defined via a reduction relation $\hookrightarrow$ (Definition 2.1), formulated in terms of two auxiliary relations: an equivalence relation $\leftrightarrows$, capturing basic algebraic identities between proof terms, and a cut-reduction relation $\rightarrow$. Contexts are defined by the following grammar:

$$K := [.] \mid K + M \mid \alpha \cdot K \mid \delta_0(K) \mid \delta_1(K, M) \mid K\,M \mid V\,K$$

$$\frac{}{x:S \vdash x:S}\,\text{ax} \qquad \frac{\Gamma \vdash M:S \quad \Gamma \vdash N:S}{\Gamma \vdash M + N:S}\,\text{sum} \qquad \frac{\Gamma \vdash M:S}{\Gamma \vdash \alpha \cdot M:S}\,\text{prod}(\alpha)$$

$$\frac{}{\Gamma \vdash \langle\rangle:\top}\,\top_i^p \qquad \frac{\Gamma \vdash m:0}{\Gamma, \Delta \vdash \delta_0(m):A}\,0_e^m \qquad \frac{}{\vdash *:1}\,1_i \qquad \frac{\Gamma \vdash M:1 \quad \Delta \vdash N:S}{\Gamma, \Delta \vdash \delta_1(M,N):S}\,1_e$$

$$\frac{\Gamma, x:S \vdash M:T}{\Gamma \vdash \lambda x.M : S \multimap T}\,\multimap_i \qquad \frac{\Gamma \vdash M : S \multimap T \quad \Delta \vdash N:S}{\Gamma, \Delta \vdash M\,N:T}\,\multimap_e$$

$$\frac{\Gamma \vdash m:P \quad \Gamma \vdash n:Q}{\Gamma \vdash \langle m,n\rangle : P \& Q}\,\&_i^p$$

$$\frac{\Gamma \vdash m:P\&Q \quad \Delta, x:P \vdash n:R}{\Gamma, \Delta \vdash \delta_\&^1(m,x.n):R}\,\&_{e_1}^p \qquad \frac{\Gamma \vdash m:P\&Q \quad \Delta, x:Q \vdash n:R}{\Gamma, \Delta \vdash \delta_\&^2(m,x.n):R}\,\&_{e_2}^p$$

$$\frac{\Delta \vdash m:A}{\Delta \vdash inl(m): A \oplus B}\,\oplus_{i1}^m \qquad \frac{\Delta \vdash n:B}{\Delta \vdash inr(n): A \oplus B}\,\oplus_{i2}^m$$

$$\frac{\Delta \vdash m: A \oplus B \quad \Gamma, x:A \vdash n:C \quad \Gamma, y:B \vdash o:C}{\Delta, \Gamma \vdash \delta_\oplus(m, x.n, y.o):C}\,\oplus_e^m$$

$$\frac{\Delta \vdash M:S_1 \quad \Gamma \vdash N:S_2}{\Delta, \Gamma \vdash M \otimes N : S_1 \otimes S_2}\,\otimes_i \qquad \frac{\Delta \vdash M:S_1 \otimes S_2 \quad \Gamma, x:S_1, y:S_2 \vdash N:T}{\Delta, \Gamma \vdash \delta_\otimes(M, xy.N):T}\,\otimes_e$$

$$\frac{\vdash m:P}{\vdash \mathcal{B}(m):\mathcal{B}(P)}\,\mathcal{B}^m$$

$$\frac{\Gamma \vdash m:\mathcal{B}(P \multimap Q) \quad \Delta \vdash n:\mathcal{B}(P)}{\Gamma, \Delta \vdash m\,n : \mathcal{B}(Q)}\,\mathcal{B}(\multimap)_e^m \qquad \frac{\Gamma \vdash m: \mathcal{B}(P) \otimes \mathcal{B}(Q)}{\Gamma \vdash \tau(m):\mathcal{B}(P \otimes Q)}\,\mathcal{B}(\otimes)^m$$

$$\frac{\Delta, y:S_1, x:S_2, \Gamma \vdash M:T}{\Delta, x:S_2, y:S_1, \Gamma \vdash M:T}\,\text{ex}$$

Fig. 1. Derivation rules.

$$\mid \langle K,m \rangle \mid \langle v,K \rangle \mid \delta_\&^1(K,x.m) \mid \delta_\&^2(K,x.t)$$
$$\mid inl(K) \mid inr(K) \mid \delta_\oplus(K,x.m,y.m)$$
$$\mid K \otimes M \mid V \otimes K \mid \delta_\otimes(K,xy.M) \mid \mathcal{B}(K) \mid \tau(K)$$

The equivalence relation $\leftrightarrows$ on terms is defined in Fig. 2 (top part). The rules are divided into two groups: the left column corresponds to the rules usually seen in algebraic lambda calculi [1,2,10,26], while the right column corresponds to rules involving the $\otimes$ connective.

Definition 2.1 ($\hookrightarrow$). *The relation* $\hookrightarrow$ *is defined as:*

$$\frac{M \to N}{M \hookrightarrow N} \qquad \frac{M \leftrightarrows V}{M \hookrightarrow V} \qquad \frac{M \not\to \quad M \leftrightarrows \mathfrak{a}(M) \quad \mathfrak{a}(M) \to N}{M \hookrightarrow N}$$

We denote by $\equiv$ *the reflexive, transitive, and symmetric closure of* $\hookrightarrow$.

The relation $\leftrightarrows$ gives rise to the possibility of defining a canonical form for terms. To this end, we introduce the notion of *algebraic form* of a term, which is a linear combination of distinct *base forms* of terms. These concepts

$$1 \cdot M \leftrightarrows M$$
$$M_1 + M_2 \leftrightarrows M_2 + M_1$$
$$M_1 + (M_2 + M_3) \leftrightarrows (M_1 + M_2) + M_3$$
$$\alpha \cdot M + \beta \cdot M \leftrightarrows (\alpha + \beta) \cdot M$$
$$\alpha \cdot (\beta \cdot M) \leftrightarrows \alpha\beta \cdot M$$
$$\alpha \cdot (M_1 + M_2) \leftrightarrows \alpha \cdot M_1 + \alpha \cdot M_2$$
$$\text{If } M \neq 0 \cdot M', \; M + 0 \cdot N \leftrightarrows M$$

$$M_1 \otimes (\alpha \cdot M_2) \leftrightarrows \alpha \cdot M_1 \otimes M_2$$
$$(\alpha \cdot M_1) \otimes M_2 \leftrightarrows \alpha \cdot M_1 \otimes M_2$$
$$(M_1 + M_2) \otimes N \leftrightarrows M_1 \otimes N + M_2 \otimes N$$
$$M \otimes (N_1 + N_2) \leftrightarrows M \otimes N_1 + M \otimes N_2$$

$$\delta_1(\alpha \cdot *, M) \to \alpha \cdot M \tag{1}$$
$$(\lambda x.M)\, V \to (V/x)M \tag{2}$$
$$\delta^1_\&(\langle v, w\rangle, x.t) \to (v/x)t \tag{3}$$
$$\delta^2_\&(\langle v, w\rangle, y.t) \to (w/y)t \tag{4}$$
$$\delta_\oplus(inl(v), x.m, y.n) \to (v/x)m \tag{5}$$
$$\delta_\oplus(inr(v), x.m, y.n) \to (v/y)n \tag{6}$$
$$\delta_\otimes(V_n \otimes W_n, xy.M) \to (V_n/x, W_n/y)M \tag{7}$$
$$a \cdot \langle\rangle \to \langle\rangle \tag{8}$$
$$\sum_{i=1}^n \alpha_i \cdot \lambda x.M_i \to \lambda x.(\sum_{i=1}^n \alpha_i \cdot M_i) \tag{9}$$
$$\sum_{i=1}^n a_i \cdot \langle v_i, w_i\rangle \to \langle \sum_{i=1}^n a_i \cdot v_i, \sum_{i=1}^n a_i \cdot w_i\rangle \tag{10}$$
$$\delta_\oplus(\sum_{i=1}^n p_i \cdot v_{bi}, x.o, y.s) \to \sum_{i=1}^n p_i \cdot \delta_\oplus(v_{bi}, x.o, y.s) \tag{11}$$
$$\delta_\otimes(\sum_{i=1}^n \alpha_i \cdot V_{bi}, xy.M) \to \sum_{i=1}^n \alpha_i \cdot \delta_\otimes(V_{bi}, xy.M) \tag{12}$$
$$inl(\sum_{i=1}^n p_i \cdot v_{bi}) \to \sum_{i=1}^n p_i \cdot inl(v_{bi}) \tag{13}$$
$$inr(\sum_{i=1}^n p_i \cdot v_{bi}) \to \sum_{i=1}^n p_i \cdot inr(v_{bi}) \tag{14}$$
$$\tau(\mathcal{B}(v) \otimes \mathcal{B}(w)) \to \mathcal{B}(v \otimes w) \tag{15}$$
$$\tau(\sum_{i=1}^n p_i \cdot v_{bi}) \to \sum_{i=1}^n p_i \cdot \tau(v_{bi}) \tag{16}$$
$$\text{If } a \neq 1, \; \mathcal{B}(a \cdot v_b) \to |a|^2 \cdot \mathcal{B}(v_b) \tag{17}$$
$$(\sum_{i=1}^n p_i \cdot \mathcal{B}(v_i))(\sum_{j=1}^k q_j \cdot \mathcal{B}(w_j)) \to \sum_{i,j} p_i q_j \cdot \mathcal{B}(v_i\, w_j) \tag{18}$$

$$\frac{M \leftrightarrows N}{K[M] \leftrightarrows K[N]} \qquad \frac{M \to N}{K[M] \to K[N]}$$

Fig. 2. Reduction relations $\leftrightarrows$ and $\to$.

are defined by the following grammar. As before, the symbols correspond to both fragments unless otherwise specified. We recall that, as per our earlier convention, all summations are assumed to involve pairwise distinct summands.

$\mathfrak{b} := x \mid \langle\rangle \mid \delta_0(\mathfrak{a}) \mid * \mid \delta_1(\mathfrak{a},\mathfrak{a}) \mid \lambda x.\mathfrak{a} \mid \mathfrak{a}\,\mathfrak{a} \mid \langle\mathfrak{a},\mathfrak{a}\rangle \mid \delta^i_\&(\mathfrak{a}, x.\mathfrak{a})$ (Base Form)
$\phantom{\mathfrak{b} :=} \mid inl(\mathfrak{a}) \mid inr(\mathfrak{a}) \mid \delta_\oplus(\mathfrak{a}, x.\mathfrak{a}, y.\mathfrak{a}) \mid \mathfrak{b} \otimes \mathfrak{b} \mid \delta_\otimes(\mathfrak{a}, xy.\mathfrak{a}) \mid \mathcal{B}(\mathfrak{a}) \mid \tau(\mathfrak{a})$
$\mathfrak{a} := \sum_{i=1}^n 0 \cdot \mathfrak{b}_i \mid \sum_{i=1}^n \alpha_i \cdot \mathfrak{b}_i \ (\alpha_i \neq 0)$ (Algebraic Form)

Note that the choice of a symmetric relation and the use of algebraic forms are made purely for convenience. The rules could be oriented, following [2], so that canonical forms coincide with normal forms.

Theorem 2.2 (Uniqueness). *If $\Gamma \vdash M : T$, then there is a unique algebraic form $\mathfrak{a}$ such that $M \leftrightarrows \mathfrak{a}$. We denote the algebraic form of M by $\mathfrak{a}(M)$.*

Proof. Proof is by induction on M. See the appendix of [5] for details.

Note that the values given in Sect. 2.1 are in their algebraic forms.

The rewrite relation $\to$ is also defined in Fig. 2. As usual, we write $(N/x)M$ for the substitution of N for x in M. In the rules involving summations, we assume—as per our earlier convention—that all summands are pairwise distinct. The rules are divided into three groups:

- Rules (1) to (7) correspond to cut-elimination steps: an introduction rule followed by an elimination rule for each connective. The only non-standard case is the rule for 1 (and **1**), which carries a scalar α in the elimination.
- Rules (8) to (12), consist of commutation rules that allow the proof constructors $+$ and · to commute with each connective. In some cases, commutation applies to introduction rules (for $\top$, $\multimap$, and &); in others, to elimination rules (for $\oplus$ and $\otimes$). There is no commutation rule for 0, and no need for one for 1, which is already handled by Rule (1). The last two rules of this group, Rules (13) and (14), are not strictly necessary, as they are subsumed by Rule (11). However, they are useful for obtaining better normal forms. For instance, the term $inl(p \cdot *) + inl(q \cdot *)$ reduces, using $\to$ and $\leftrightarrows$, to $(p+q) \cdot inl(*)$.
- Rule (15) is a coercion rule to transition from proposition $\mathcal{B}(P) \otimes \mathcal{B}(Q)$ to proposition $\mathcal{B}(P \otimes Q)$. Rule (16) is a commutation rule for the coercion operator τ. Rule (17) allows a scalar to commute with the $\mathcal{B}$ operator. Note that $\mathcal{B}$ is not a linear operator. Intuitively, if v_b represents a quantum state in vector form, then $\mathcal{B}(v_b)$ represents the same state in its density matrix form. As a consequence, the scalar a is multiplied by $\overline{a}$ when commuting with $\mathcal{B}$. Finally, Rule (18) distributes applications over the $\mathcal{B}$ operator.

Intuitively, $\hookrightarrow$ interleaves $\leftrightarrows$ and $\to$: it rewrites any term via $\leftrightarrows$ until it either reduces under $\to$ or reaches normal form. For instance, the term $\delta_\oplus(inl(*) + inl(*), x.m, y.n)$ does not reduce under $\to$ alone (because $inl(*) + inl(*)$ is not a value), but rewriting it via $\leftrightarrows$ to $\delta_\oplus(2 \cdot inl(*), x.m, y.n)$ makes it reducible. Each step of $\leftrightarrows$ is a purely algebraic manipulation. In the following section, we show that $\hookrightarrow$ satisfies the standard properties of a well-behaved reduction system.

2.2 Correctness

We state the standard correctness theorems. See [5] for omitted proofs.

Theorem 2.3 (Progress). $\vdash M : T$ *implies* $T \neq 0$, *and either* M *is a value* V, *or there exists* N *such that* $M \hookrightarrow N$. □

Theorem 2.4 (Preservation). $\Gamma \vdash M : T$ *and* $M \hookrightarrow N$ *imply* $\Gamma \vdash N : T$. □

Theorem 2.5 (Strong Normalisation). $\Gamma \vdash M : T$ *implies* M *terminates.*

Proof. The proof uses Girard's ultra-reduction technique [14], extending the relation with $+$-elimination and scalar erasure rules. Strong normalisation of the extended system implies that of the original. See [5] for more details. □

Theorem 2.6 (Confluence). *Let* $\Gamma \vdash M : T$. *If* $M \hookrightarrow^* M_1$ *and* $M \hookrightarrow^* M_2$, *then there exists a value* V *such that* $M_1 \hookrightarrow^* V \;^*\!\hookleftarrow M_2$.

Proof. The confluence of $\hookrightarrow$ follows from its structure as an interleaving of a deterministic reduction ($\rightarrow$) and the equivalence $\leftrightarrows$. The relation $\leftrightarrows$ is applied only when $\rightarrow$ is blocked, serving as an algebraic normalisation step to enable further reduction. By Theorems 2.2 and 2.3, the normal forms of $\hookrightarrow$ are unique, so any two reduction sequences from M must converge. □

3 Categorical Model

This section introduces the categorical model used for our denotational semantics, structured in two parts. The first, described in Subsect. 3.1, consists of finite-dimensional Hilbert spaces and linear maps—a standard setting for pure-state quantum computation—and is used to interpret the pure fragment of $\mathcal{L}_\mathcal{B}$. The second, presented in Subsect. 3.2, consists of finite-dimensional C*-algebras and completely positive maps, which model the mixed fragment. We describe the relevant categorical structure in Subsect. 3.3.

3.1 Finite-Dimensional Hilbert Spaces

Finite-dimensional Hilbert spaces are ubiquitous and well-known in quantum information theory, so we mostly use this subsection to fix notation.

Definition 3.1. *A finite-dimensional Hilbert space is a vector space* H *equipped with an inner-product* $\langle \cdot | \cdot \rangle \colon H \times H \rightarrow \mathbb{C}$ *that is anti-linear in the first argument and linear in the second one.*

If H_1 and H_2 are two finite-dimensional Hilbert spaces, we write $H_1 \otimes H_2$ for their *Hilbert space tensor product* and we write $H_1 \oplus H_2$ for their *Hilbert space direct sum*, both defined in the standard way. The maps that are relevant for our development are the linear maps $f \colon H_1 \to H_2$ between finite-dimensional Hilbert spaces. Since H_1 and H_2 are finite-dimensional, every such map f is necessarily bounded, or equivalently, continuous with respect to the usual topology. The *adjoint* of f is the (bounded) linear map $f^\dagger \colon H_2 \to H_1$ that is uniquely determined by the property: $\langle f(h_1)|h_2\rangle = \langle h_1|f^\dagger(h_2)\rangle$ for every $h_1 \in H_1$ and $h_2 \in H_2$. If we choose orthonormal bases of H_1 and H_2, then the matrix representation of $f^\dagger$ is given by taking the conjugate transpose of the matrix representation of f. We say that a linear map $f \colon H_1 \to H_2$ is *unitary* if $f \circ f^\dagger = \mathrm{id}_{H_2}$ and $f^\dagger \circ f = \mathrm{id}_{H_1}$.

3.2 Finite-Dimensional C*-Algebras

Finite-dimensional C*-algebras [24] have sufficient structure to allow us to describe completely-positive maps and to model the quantum operations (also known as channels) that are used for mixed-state quantum computation in finite dimensions. We begin by recalling the relevant definitions.

Definition 3.2. *A finite-dimensional C^*-algebra is a complex vector space A together with: a binary operation $(-\cdot-) \colon A \times A \to A$, called multiplication, and written via juxtaposition, i.e. $ab := a \cdot b$, which is associative and linear in both components; a multiplicative unit $1 \in A$, such that $1a = a1 = a$ for all $a \in A$; a unary operation $(\cdot)^* \colon A \to A$, called involution, such that $(a^*)^* = a$, $(ab)^* = b^* a^*$, $(\lambda a)^* = \bar{\lambda} a^*$, and $(a+b)^* = a^* + b^*$, for all $a, b \in A$ and $\lambda \in \mathbb{C}$; a norm $\|\cdot\| \colon A \to [0, \infty)$ that satisfies certain additional conditions.*

Remark 3.3. We do not make essential use of C*-algebra norms in this paper, so we omit the details of this part of the definition. In order to avoid repetition, we often say "C*-algebra" instead of "finite-dimensional C*-algebra".

Let A be a C*-algebra. An element $a \in A$ is called *self-adjoint* if $a = a^*$. We say that $a \in A$ is *positive* if there exists an element $b \in A$, such that $a = bb^*$. Note that every positive element is self-adjoint.

Example 3.4. One important example of a C*-algebra is given by the matrix algebra M_n, consisting of the $n \times n$ complex matrices. The vector space structure is obvious and multiplication is given by multiplication of matrices. The involution is given by the conjugate transpose and the unit element 1 is the identity matrix 1_n. The norm on M_n is the usual operator norm. The complex numbers $\mathbb{C}$ is a C*-algebra which may be identified with M_1.

Example 3.5. If H is a Hilbert space, then the space $\mathcal{B}(H)$ of bounded linear operators on H, has the structure of a C*-algebra. The vector space structure is obvious, the involution is given by taking adjoints, the multiplication by composition of functions, the multiplicative unit is id_H and the norm is the usual operator norm. When H is finite-dimensional, as assumed in this paper, with dimension n, then $\mathcal{B}(H) \cong M_n$ as C*-algebras, so the two may be often identified.

Definition 3.6. *Let A and B be C*-algebras. The direct sum of A and B is the C*-algebra $A \oplus B$ defined in the following way: the vector space structure is the vector space direct sum $A \oplus B$; the involution, multiplication and unit are defined pointwise; the norm is defined as $\|(a,b)\| := \max(\|a\|, \|b\|)$.*

Definition 3.7. *Given two finite-dimensional C*-algebras A and B, we write $A \otimes B$ for their C*-algebra tensor product which is defined in the following way: the underlying vector space is $A \otimes B$; the multiplication map is determined by the assignment $(a_1 \otimes b_1)(a_2 \otimes b_2) = a_1 a_2 \otimes b_1 b_2$; the multiplicative unit is $1_A \otimes 1_B$; the involution is determined by the assignment $(a \otimes b)^* = a^* \otimes b^*$; there is a unique way to assign a C*-algebra norm [20, pp. 231], but we elide the details.*

We can now define the C*-algebra morphisms that we use in our semantics.

Definition 3.8. *Given C*-algebras A and B, we say that a linear map $f: A \to B$ is* positive *when f preserves positive elements and* completely-positive *when the map $\mathrm{id}_{M_n} \otimes f : M_n \otimes A \to M_n \otimes B$ is positive for every $n \in \mathbb{N}$.*

Example 3.9. For every C*-algebra A, the identity map id_A is completely-positive. If H, K are finite-dimensional Hilbert spaces and $f: H \to K$ is a linear map, then the map $f(\cdot)f^\dagger : B(H) \to B(K)$ is a completely-positive map.

3.3 Categorical Structure

We write **FHilb** for the category of finite-dimensional Hilbert spaces with linear maps as morphisms and we write **FC*** for the category of finite-dimensional C*-algebras and completely-positive maps as morphisms. Both categories enjoy similar categorical properties that we now recall and for which we use similar notation. See [4,15] for more information. Throughout the remainder of the subsection, let X, Y, Z be finite-dimensional Hilbert spaces (C*-algebras).

Symmetric Monoidal Structure. The category **FHilb** (**FC***) has a symmetric monoidal structure with tensor unit given by the Hilbert space (C*-algebra) $\mathbb{C}$ and monoidal product given by the Hilbert space (C*-algebra) tensor product $X \otimes Y$. The left (right) unitors λ (ρ), the associator α, and symmetry σ natural isomorphisms are defined in the same way as for vector spaces.

Compact Closed Structure. The category **FHilb** (**FC***) is also compact closed. We write $\eta_X : \mathbb{C} \to X^* \otimes X$ for the unit and $\epsilon_X : X \otimes X^* \to \mathbb{C}$ for the counit of the compact closed structure, where X^* indicates the dual of X (in the sense of compact closure). It follows that **FHilb** (**FC***) is a closed symmetric monoidal category with internal hom given by $[X, Y] := X^* \otimes Y$. We write $\Phi : \mathbf{C}(X \otimes Y, Z) \cong \mathbf{C}(X, [Y, Z])$ for the currying natural isomorphism, where **C** stands for **FHilb** or **FC***, and we write $\mathrm{eval}_{X,Y} : [X, Y] \otimes X \to Y$ for the canonically induced evaluation morphism of **C**.

Finite Biproducts. The category **FHilb** (**FC***) also has finite biproducts. Binary biproducts are given by the Hilbert space (C*-algebra) direct sum $X \oplus Y$ and the zero object is given by the zero-dimensional Hilbert space (C*-algebra) 0. We write $!_{X,Y} : X \to Y$ for the unique morphism that factors through 0. We write $\pi_1\colon X \oplus Y \to X$ and $\pi_2\colon X \oplus Y \to Y$ for the canonical projections, which are defined as $\pi_1(x,y) = x$ and $\pi_2(x,y) = y$. Given morphisms $f\colon Z \to X$ and $g\colon Z \to Y$ in **FHilb** (**FC***), $\langle f,g \rangle\colon Z \to X \oplus Y$ is the canonical morphism induced by the categorical product and defined by $\langle f,g \rangle(z):=(f(z),g(z))$. We write $i_1\colon X \to X \oplus Y$ and $i_2\colon Y \to X \oplus Y$ for the canonical coproduct injections defined by $i_1(x):=(x,0)$ and $i_2(y) = (0,y)$. Given morphisms $f\colon X \to Z$ and $g\colon Y \to Z$ in **FHilb** (**FC***), we write $[f,g]\colon X \oplus Y \to Z$ for the canonical map induced by the couniversal property of $X \oplus Y$ and defined by $[f,g](x,y) = f(x)+g(y)$. Since **FHilb** (**FC***) is symmetric monoidal closed, it follows that the monoidal product distributes over coproducts and we write $d_{X,Y,Z}\colon X \otimes (Y \oplus Z) \cong (X \otimes Y) \oplus (X \otimes Z)$ for the canonical natural isomorphism.

Linear Combinations. The homsets **FHilb**(X,Y) are closed under finite $\mathbb{C}$-linear combinations, i.e. for $f_i \in$ **FHilb**(X,Y), $\alpha_i \in \mathbb{C}$ complex scalars, $i \in I$ with I a finite set, $\sum_{i \in I} \alpha_i f_i \in$ **FHilb**(H,K), where the sum is defined pointwise in the usual way. However, the homsets **FC**$^*(X,Y)$ are *not* closed under such linear combinations, because if $f\colon X \to Y$ is a completely-positive map, the map $(-1)f$ need not be one. Instead, homsets in **FC**$^*(X,Y)$ are closed under finite $\mathbb{R}_{\geq 0}$-linear combinations, again defined pointwise, so that $\sum_{i \in I} r_i f_i \in$ **FC**$^*(X,Y)$, where $r_i \geq 0$ for all $i \in I$. Linear combinations behave well with these categorical constructions, as the next lemma shows.

Lemma 3.10. *Given compatible morphisms f, f', g, g', h in* **FHilb** (**FC***) *and a scalar $a \in \mathbb{C}$ ($a \in \mathbb{R}_{\geq 0}$), the following equations hold:*

$$\Phi(f + g) = \Phi(f) + \Phi(g) \qquad \Phi(a \cdot f) = a \cdot \Phi(f)$$
$$\langle f, g \rangle + \langle f', g' \rangle = \langle f + f', g + g' \rangle \qquad a \cdot \langle f, g \rangle = \langle a \cdot f, a \cdot g \rangle$$
$$[f, g] + [f', g'] = [f + f', g + g'] \qquad a \cdot [f, g] = [a \cdot f, a \cdot g]$$
$$(f + g) \otimes h = f \otimes h + g \otimes h \qquad a \cdot (f \otimes h) = (a \cdot f) \otimes h = f \otimes (a \cdot h)$$
$$h \otimes (f + g) = h \otimes f + h \otimes g$$

Proof. Straightforward verification. □

The assignment $\mathcal{B}(-)$ from Example 3.5 can be extended functorially by defining $\mathcal{B}(f):=f(\cdot)f^\dagger$ for a linear map $f\colon H \to K$, see Example 3.9. This allows us to lift functions acting on pure states to ones acting on mixed states.

Lemma 3.11. *The assignment $\mathcal{B}(-)\colon$ **FHilb** $\to$ **FC*** can be equipped with the structure of a strong monoidal functor. We write $\tau_{H,K}\colon \mathcal{B}(H) \otimes \mathcal{B}(K) \cong \mathcal{B}(H \otimes K)$ and $\tau_\mathbb{C}\colon \mathbb{C} \cong \mathcal{B}(\mathbb{C})$ for the obvious natural isomorphisms.* □

4 Denotational Semantics

With the model in place, we now describe the denotational semantics of $\mathcal{L}_\mathcal{B}$. Pure and mixed propositions are interpreted as objects in **FHilb** and **FC***, respectively.

$$[\![\top]\!]:=0_{\mathbf{FHilb}}, \quad [\![\mathbf{1}]\!]:=\mathbb{C}, \quad [\![P \multimap Q]\!]:=[[\![P]\!],[\![Q]\!]], \quad [\![P \& Q]\!]:=[\![P]\!] \oplus [\![Q]\!],$$

$$[\![x : S \vdash x : S]\!] := id$$
$$[\![\Gamma \vdash M + N : S]\!] := [\![M]\!] + [\![N]\!]$$
$$[\![\Gamma \vdash \alpha \cdot M : S]\!] := \alpha \cdot [\![M]\!]$$
$$[\![\boldsymbol{\Gamma \vdash \langle \rangle : \top}]\!] := \;!$$
$$[\![\Gamma, \Delta \vdash \delta_0(m) : A]\!] := \;! \circ ([\![m]\!] \otimes id)$$
$$[\![\vdash * : \mathbf{1}]\!] := id$$
$$[\![\Gamma, \Delta \vdash \delta_1(M, N) : S]\!] := \lambda \circ ([\![M]\!] \otimes [\![N]\!])$$
$$[\![\Gamma \vdash \lambda x.M : S \multimap T]\!] := \Phi([\![M]\!])$$
$$[\![\Gamma, \Delta \vdash M\; N : T]\!] := \mathrm{eval} \circ ([\![M]\!] \otimes [\![N]\!])$$
$$[\![\boldsymbol{\Gamma \vdash \langle m, n \rangle : P\; \&\; Q}]\!] := \langle [\![\boldsymbol{m}]\!], [\![\boldsymbol{n}]\!] \rangle$$
$$[\![\boldsymbol{\Gamma, \Delta \vdash \delta^i_\&(m, x.n) : R}]\!] := [\![\boldsymbol{n}]\!] \circ \sigma \circ (\pi_i \otimes id) \circ ([\![\boldsymbol{m}]\!] \otimes id)$$
$$[\![\Delta \vdash inl(m) : A \oplus B]\!] := i_1 \circ [\![m]\!]$$
$$[\![\Delta \vdash inr(n) : A \oplus B]\!] := i_2 \circ [\![n]\!]$$
$$[\![\Gamma, \Delta \vdash \delta_\oplus(m, x.n, y.o) : C]\!] := [\![[\![n]\!], [\![o]\!]]\!] \circ d \circ \sigma \circ ([\![m]\!] \otimes id)$$
$$[\![\Gamma, \Delta \vdash M \otimes N : S_1 \otimes S_2]\!] := [\![M]\!] \otimes [\![N]\!]$$
$$[\![\Gamma, \Delta \vdash \delta_\otimes(M, xy.N) : T]\!] := [\![N]\!] \circ (id \otimes [\![M]\!])$$
$$[\![\vdash \mathcal{B}(t) : \mathcal{B}(P)]\!] := \mathcal{B}([\![t]\!])$$
$$[\![\Gamma, \Delta \vdash m\; n : \mathcal{B}(Q)]\!] := \mathcal{B}(\mathrm{eval}) \circ \tau \circ ([\![m]\!] \otimes [\![n]\!])$$
$$[\![\Gamma \vdash \tau(m) : \mathcal{B}(P \otimes Q)]\!] := \tau \circ [\![m]\!]$$
$$[\![\Delta, x : S_2, y : S_1, \Gamma \vdash M : T]\!] := [\![M]\!] \circ (id \otimes \sigma \otimes id)$$

Fig. 3. Interpretation of judgements.

$$[\![P \otimes Q]\!] := [\![P]\!] \otimes [\![Q]\!], \quad [\![0]\!] := 0_{\mathbf{FC^*}}, \quad [\![1]\!] := \mathbb{C}, \quad [\![A \multimap B]\!] := [[\![A]\!], [\![B]\!]],$$
$$[\![A \oplus B]\!] := [\![A]\!] \oplus [\![B]\!], \quad [\![A \otimes B]\!] := [\![A]\!] \otimes [\![B]\!], \quad [\![\mathcal{B}(P)]\!] := \mathcal{B}([\![P]\!]).$$

A pure context $\Gamma = x_1 : P_1, \ldots, x_n : P_n$ is interpreted as $[\![\Gamma]\!] := [\![P_1]\!] \otimes [\![P_2]\!] \otimes \cdots \otimes [\![P_n]\!]$. Similarly, a mixed context $\Gamma = x_1 : A_1, \ldots, x_n : A_n$ is interpreted as $[\![\Gamma]\!] := [\![A_1]\!] \otimes [\![A_2]\!] \otimes \cdots \otimes [\![A_n]\!]$. Pure judgements $\boldsymbol{\Gamma \vdash m : P}$ are interpreted as morphisms $[\![\boldsymbol{\Gamma \vdash m : P}]\!] : [\![\boldsymbol{\Gamma}]\!] \to [\![\boldsymbol{P}]\!]$ in **FHilb** and mixed judgements $\Gamma \vdash m : A$ are interpreted as morphisms $[\![\Gamma \vdash m : A]\!] : [\![\Gamma]\!] \to [\![A]\!]$ in **FC***. The denotational interpretation of judgements from both fragments is given in Fig. 3. We sometimes write $[\![M]\!]$ as a shorthand for $[\![\Gamma \vdash M : T]\!]$. For simplicity, we often suppress some of the coherent natural isomorphisms related to the monoidal structure (e.g. the α monoidal associator).

Our interpretation is sound with respect to the cut-elimination process (Theorem 4.1), and complete (Theorem 4.4) with respect to a notion of contextual equivalence (Definition 4.3). Since this completeness is established with respect to a different relation than the one used for soundness, the result is usually referred to as *adequacy*. The omitted proofs can be found in the appendix of [5].

Theorem 4.1 (Soundness). *If $M \hookrightarrow^* N$ then $[\![M]\!] = [\![N]\!]$.* □

Definition 4.2 (Elimination context). *An elimination context E is a term with exactly one free variable, denoted by $[.]$, defined by the following grammar:*

$$E := [.] \mid \delta_0(E) \mid \delta_1(E, M) \mid E\, M$$
$$\mid \delta^1_\&(E, x.m) \mid \delta^2_\&(E, x.m) \mid \delta_\oplus(E, x.m, y.n) \mid \delta_\otimes(E, xy.M)$$

The substitution of $[.]$ by a term M in E is denoted by $E[M]$.

Definition 4.3 (Contextual equivalence). *Two terms M and N are contextually equivalent ($M \sim N$) if, for every elimination context $[.] \vdash E : T$, with $T \in \{1, 1, \mathcal{B}(1)\}$, there exists a value V such that $E[M] \hookrightarrow^* V$ iff $E[N] \hookrightarrow^* V$.*

Theorem 4.4 (Adequacy). *If $[\![\vdash M : T]\!] = [\![\vdash N : T]\!]$ then $M \sim N$.* □

5 Encoding Quantum Computing

The fact that our calculus is linear in a linear algebraic sense follows as a straightforward corollary of adequacy (Theorem 4.4).

Corollary 5.1 (Linearity). *Let $x : S \vdash M : T$, $\Delta \vdash N_1 : S$, $\Delta \vdash N_2 : S$, and $\Delta \vdash N : S$ (all in the same fragment), then $(\lambda x.M)\,(\alpha \cdot N_1 + \beta \cdot N_2) \sim \alpha \cdot (\lambda x.M)\,N_1 + \beta \cdot (\lambda x.M)\,N_2$.*

Remark that Corollary 5.1 excludes $\mathcal{B}$, since those terms are always closed.

Let Q be the set of closed proof terms $\boldsymbol{m}$ of $\boldsymbol{1\&1}$, modulo the equivalence relation $\equiv$. From now on, we write **qubit** for $\boldsymbol{1\&1}$.

Theorem 5.2 (One-to-one correspondence [8, Lemmas 3.7 and 3.8]). *The set Q forms a finite-dimensional vector space, with vector addition and scalar multiplication given by $+$ and $\cdot$, respectively.*

*For every element $[\boldsymbol{m}] \in Q$, there is a vector $\overline{[\boldsymbol{m}]} \in \mathbb{C}^2$. Conversely, for any vector $\vec{v} \in \mathbb{C}^2$, there is a closed term $\vdash \overline{\vec{v}} :$ **qubit**. Moreover, this correspondence preserves the structure: $\overline{[\boldsymbol{m_1} + \boldsymbol{m_2}]} = \overline{[\boldsymbol{m_1}]} + \overline{[\boldsymbol{m_2}]}$ and $\overline{[\boldsymbol{a \cdot m}]} = \boldsymbol{a} \cdot \overline{[\boldsymbol{m}]}$.* □

Example 5.3 (Qubit encoding). A single qubit $a|0\rangle + b|1\rangle \in \mathbb{C}^2$ is encoded by the term $\langle \boldsymbol{a \cdot *, b \cdot *} \rangle$. In particular, we define the basis vectors as: $|0\rangle := \langle \boldsymbol{*, 0 \cdot *} \rangle$ and $|1\rangle := \langle \boldsymbol{0 \cdot *, *} \rangle$. An n-qubit is a vector in $\mathbb{C}^{2^n}$, and it is encoded as a linear combination of n-fold tensor products of 1-qubit encodings. As usual, we write $|b_1 \cdots b_n\rangle$ for the n-qubit $|b_1\rangle \otimes \cdots \otimes |b_n\rangle$. For example, the 2-qubit entangled state $\frac{|00\rangle + |11\rangle}{\sqrt{2}}$ is encoded as: $\vdash \frac{1}{\sqrt{2}} \cdot |00\rangle + \frac{1}{\sqrt{2}} \cdot |11\rangle :$ **qubit** $\otimes$ **qubit**, that is, $\vdash \frac{1}{\sqrt{2}} \cdot (\langle \boldsymbol{*, 0 \cdot *} \rangle \otimes \langle \boldsymbol{*, 0 \cdot *} \rangle) + \frac{1}{\sqrt{2}} \cdot (\langle \boldsymbol{0 \cdot *,*} \rangle \otimes \langle \boldsymbol{0 \cdot *,*} \rangle) : (\boldsymbol{1\&1}) \otimes (\boldsymbol{1\&1})$.

Remark 5.4. In [8], 2^n-dimensional vectors are encoded as proof terms of $\boldsymbol{1}^{\&2^n}$. Here we prefer to use the tensor notation, which provides finer control over term structure—in particular, allowing for a more direct encoding of constructs such as the Quantum Switch (see Example 5.8).

We first show how to encode 2×2 matrices (Theorem 5.5), and then generalise the construction to $n \times n$ matrices (Corollary 5.6).

Theorem 5.5 (2×2 **matrices** [8, Theorem 3.10]). *Let M be a 2×2 complex matrix. Then there exists a closed proof term f of* **qubit** $\multimap$ **qubit** *such that for any vector $\vec{v} \in \mathbb{C}^2$, we have: $M\vec{v} = \boldsymbol{f}(\overline{\vec{v}})$.*

Proof. Let $M := a|0\rangle\langle 0| + b|0\rangle\langle 1| + c|1\rangle\langle 0| + d|1\rangle\langle 1|$ be a 2×2 matrix, and let $\boldsymbol{f} := \lambda x.\delta^1_{\&}(x, x_1.\boldsymbol{f_1}x_1) \mathbin{+\!\!\!+} \delta^2_{\&}(x, x_2.\boldsymbol{f_2}x_2)$, where $\boldsymbol{f_1} := \lambda x.\delta_1(x, \langle a \cdot *, c \cdot * \rangle)$ and $\boldsymbol{f_2} := \lambda x.\delta_1(x, \langle b \cdot *, d \cdot * \rangle)$. Let $\vec{v} := a_1|0\rangle + b_1|1\rangle \in \mathbb{C}^2$. Notice that $\boldsymbol{f}(\overline{\vec{v}}) \hookrightarrow^* \boldsymbol{f_1}(a_1 \cdot *) \mathbin{+\!\!\!+} \boldsymbol{f_2}(b_1 \cdot *) \hookrightarrow^* \langle (a_1 a + b_1 b) \cdot *, (a_1 c + b_1 d) \cdot * \rangle$. Thus, $M\vec{v} = \boldsymbol{f}(\overline{\vec{v}})$. □

Corollary 5.6. *Let M be a linear transformation on $\mathbb{C}^{2^n}$. Then there exists a closed term $\boldsymbol{f}$ such that: $\boldsymbol{f}(\overline{\vec{v}}) = M\vec{v}$ for all $\vec{v} \in \mathbb{C}^{2^n}$.*

Proof. Let $\boldsymbol{f_1}$ and $\boldsymbol{g_1}$ encode two matrices M_1 and N_1 respectively. The the tensor product $M_1 \otimes N_1$ can be encoded by: $\lambda z.\, \delta_\otimes(z, xy.\boldsymbol{f_1}x \otimes \boldsymbol{g_1}y)$. Thus, the result follows from Theorem 5.5 and the fact that any linear transformation on a finite-dimensional space $V \otimes W$ can be written as a linear combination of operators of the form $f \otimes g$, with $f : V \to V$ and $g : W \to W$. □

Example 5.7 (CNOT gate). The $CNOT$ gate can be written as a linear combination of tensor products of Pauli matrices X, Z, and the identity I: $\frac{1}{2}(I \otimes I + Z \otimes I + I \otimes X - Z \otimes X)$. Let $\boldsymbol{f_x}$, $\boldsymbol{f_z}$ be the proof terms representing X and Z, respectively. Then, by Corollary 5.6, a proof term representing the $CNOT$ gate for proposition **qubit** $\otimes$ **qubit** $\multimap$ **qubit** $\otimes$ **qubit** is:
$\lambda z.\delta_\otimes \Big(z, xy.\frac{1}{2} \cdot (x \otimes y) \mathbin{+\!\!\!+} \frac{1}{2} \cdot (\boldsymbol{f_z}\, x \otimes y) \mathbin{+\!\!\!+} \frac{1}{2} \cdot (x \otimes \boldsymbol{f_x}\, y) \mathbin{+\!\!\!+} \frac{-1}{2} \cdot (\boldsymbol{f_z}\, x \otimes \boldsymbol{f_x}\, y) \Big)$.

Example 5.8 (Quantum switch). The quantum switch is a higher-order construction that applies two proofs $\boldsymbol{f}, \boldsymbol{g} : \boldsymbol{P} \multimap \boldsymbol{P}$ in opposite order depending on the value of a control qubit. It can be represented in $\mathcal{L}_\mathcal{B}$ as the proof term:
$\lambda h.\lambda z.\delta_\otimes \Big(h,\, fg.\delta_\otimes(z, xy.\delta^1_{\&}(x, x_1.x_1 \otimes f(g\,y)) \mathbin{+\!\!\!+} \delta^2_{\&}(x, x_2.x_2 \otimes g(f\,y))) \Big)$
proving the proposition $((\boldsymbol{P} \multimap \boldsymbol{P}) \otimes (\boldsymbol{P} \multimap \boldsymbol{P})) \multimap (\textbf{qubit} \otimes \boldsymbol{P}) \multimap (\textbf{qubit} \otimes \boldsymbol{P})$.

The mixed-state fragment allows us to represent quantum measurements. Let $m : M_2 \to M_2$ be the measurement map
$$m(\rho) := \sum_{i=1}^n P_i \rho P_i^\dagger,$$
determined by a choice of positive elements $P_i \in M_2$ that sum to the identity, i.e. a POVM. Let $\boldsymbol{m_i}$ denote the encoding in $\mathcal{L}_\mathcal{B}$ of the linear map P_i. Then $\mathcal{B}(\boldsymbol{m_i})$ encodes the map $P_i(\cdot)P_i^\dagger$ in a way that allows us to recover its action on positive elements (which is sufficient considering our choice of morphisms). Therefore the encoding of m in $\mathcal{L}_\mathcal{B}$ is

$$\vdash \mathcal{B}(m_1) + \mathcal{B}(m_2) + \cdots + \mathcal{B}(m_n) : \mathcal{B}(\mathbf{qubit} \multimap \mathbf{qubit}).$$

This construction naturally generalises to measurements on finitely many qubits by applying Corollary 5.6.

Example 5.9 (Measurement in the computational basis). Consider the 2×2 projection matrices $|0\rangle\langle 0|$ and $|1\rangle\langle 1|$. Let m_1, m_2 denote the encoding of these matrices in $\mathcal{L}_\mathcal{B}$. Then, the measurement of a single qubit in the computational basis is given by the term $\vdash \mathcal{B}(m_1) + \mathcal{B}(m_2) : \mathcal{B}(\mathbf{qubit} \multimap \mathbf{qubit})$. Consider, for example, the term $|+\rangle := \langle \frac{1}{\sqrt{2}} \cdot *, \frac{1}{\sqrt{2}} \cdot * \rangle$. Then:

$$(\mathcal{B}(m_1) + \mathcal{B}(m_2)) \, \mathcal{B}(|+\rangle) \hookrightarrow \mathcal{B}(m_1 \, |+\rangle) + \mathcal{B}(m_2 \, |+\rangle)$$
$$\hookrightarrow^* \mathcal{B}(\langle \tfrac{1}{\sqrt{2}} \cdot *, 0 \cdot * \rangle) + \mathcal{B}(\langle 0 \cdot *, \tfrac{1}{\sqrt{2}} \cdot * \rangle).$$

This is, as expected, the representation of the density matrix $\frac{1}{2} \cdot |0\rangle\langle 0| + \frac{1}{2} \cdot |1\rangle\langle 1|$.

Example 5.10 (Bell measurement). The Bell basis is given by $\{\beta_{00}, \beta_{01}, \beta_{10}, \beta_{11}\}$, with $\beta_{ij} := CNOT((H|i\rangle) \otimes |j\rangle)$. Let m_{ij} be the encoding of the projector $|\beta_{ij}\rangle\langle\beta_{ij}|$. Then, Bell measurement is represented by:

$$\vdash \mathcal{B}(m_{00}) + \mathcal{B}(m_{01}) + \mathcal{B}(m_{10}) + \mathcal{B}(m_{11}) : \mathcal{B}(\mathbf{qubit} \otimes \mathbf{qubit} \multimap \mathbf{qubit} \otimes \mathbf{qubit})$$

Example 5.11 (Teleportation). Quantum teleportation transfers the state of a qubit $|\psi\rangle$ using shared entanglement and classical communication. Let f_i be the proof terms representing the unitary corrections U_i, and h_i the proof terms for the projectors P_i used in a Bell measurement. Then, consider the proof term:

$$U := \mathcal{B}(\lambda z. \delta_\otimes(z, xy.f_1 \, x \otimes h_1 \, y)) + \mathcal{B}(\lambda z. \delta_\otimes(z, xy.f_2 \, x \otimes h_2 \, y)) +$$
$$\mathcal{B}(\lambda z. \delta_\otimes(z, xy.f_3 \, x \otimes h_3 \, y)) + \mathcal{B}(\lambda z. \delta_\otimes(z, xy.f_4 \, x \otimes h_4 \, y))$$

of the proposition $\mathcal{B}(\mathbf{qubit} \otimes (\mathbf{qubit} \otimes \mathbf{qubit})) \multimap \mathcal{B}(\mathbf{qubit} \otimes (\mathbf{qubit} \otimes \mathbf{qubit}))$. Teleportation is then encoded as the proof term for the proposition $\mathcal{B}(\mathbf{qubit}) \multimap \mathcal{B}(\mathbf{qubit} \otimes \mathbf{qubit} \otimes \mathbf{qubit})$ given by

$$\text{Telep} := \lambda z. \, U \, (\tau(\mathcal{B}(\beta_{00}) \otimes z)).$$

Here, τ is used to encode the Bell state and the state to be teleported into a single density matrix.

6 Conclusion

We introduced a proof language for Intuitionistic Multiplicative Additive Linear Logic (IMALL), extended with a modality $\mathcal{B}$ to integrate both pure and mixed-state quantum computation in a unified setting. The language is equipped with a categorical model that serves two key roles in our development: (1) the design of the logical system was inspired and largely extracted from the categorical/mathematical model; (2) this model is relevant for the mathematical formulation of finite-dimensional quantum theory and we use it to justify design choices in the logical system. Our logical system enables the expression of the pure-state quantum switch (Example 5.8), which can, in principle, be applied in a mixed-state context subsequently. This requires combining pure-state primitives with mixed-state primitives and cannot be easily achieved in most other logical/type systems.

Future work includes extending the model to full Intuitionistic Linear Logic (ILL) and clarifying the connection with Lambda-S, whose semantics is based on the same adjunction used to interpret the exponential modality of linear logic [11,12].

Acknowledgements. We thank Cole Comfort, James Hefford, and Bert Lindenhovius for discussions. This work has been partially funded by the French National Research Agency (ANR) within the framework of "Plan France 2030", under the research projects EPIQ ANR-22-PETQ-0007, HQI-Acquisition ANR-22-PNCQ-0001 and HQI-R&D ANR-22-PNCQ-0002, by the European Union through the MSCA SE project QCOMICAL (Grant Agreement ID: 101182520), and by the Uruguayan CSIC grant 22520220100073UD.

References

1. Arrighi, P., Dowek, G.: Lineal: a linear algebraic lambda-calculus. Log. Meth. Comput. Sci. **13**(1:8) (2017)
2. Assaf, A., Díaz-Caro, A., Perdrix, S., Tasson, C., Valiron, B.: Call-by-value, call-by-name and the vectorial behaviour of the algebraic λ-calculus. Log. Meth. Comput. Sci. **10** (2014)
3. Clairambault, P., de Visme, M., Winskel, G.: Game semantics for quantum programming. Proc. ACM Program. Lang. **3**(POPL), 32:1–32:29 (2019)
4. Coecke, B., Heunen, C., Kissinger, A.: Categories of quantum and classical channels. Quantum Inf. Process. **15**, 5179–5209 (2016)
5. Dave, K., Díaz-Caro, A., Zamdzhiev, V.: IMALL with a mixed-state modality: a logical approach to quantum computation. arXiv:2506.09545 (2025). preprint of this paper with appendix
6. Dave, K., Lemonnier, L., Péchoux, R., Zamdzhiev, V.: Combining quantum and classical control: syntax, semantics and adequacy. In: Abdulla, P.A., Kesner, D. (eds.) FoSSaCS 2025. LNCS, vol. 15691, pp. 155–175. Springer, Cham (2025). https://doi.org/10.1007/978-3-031-90897-2_8
7. Díaz-Caro, A., Dowek, G.: A new connective in natural deduction, and its application to quantum computing. Theoret. Comput. Sci. **957**, 113840 (2023)

8. Díaz-Caro, A., Dowek, G.: A linear linear lambda-calculus. Math. Struct. Comput. Sci. **34**, 1103–1137 (2024)
9. Díaz-Caro, A., Dowek, G., Rinaldi, J.: Two linearities for quantum computing in the lambda calculus. Biosystems **186**, 104012 (2019)
10. Díaz-Caro, A., Guillermo, M., Miquel, A., Valiron, B.: Realizability in the unitary sphere. In: Proceedings of the 34th Annual ACM/IEEE Symposium on Logic in Computer Science (LICS 2019), pp. 1–13 (2019)
11. Díaz-Caro, A., Malherbe, O.: A categorical construction for the computational definition of vector spaces. Appl. Categ. Struct. **28**(5), 807–844 (2020)
12. Díaz-Caro, A., Malherbe, O.: Quantum control in the unitary sphere: Lambda-S_1 and its categorical model. Logical Methods Comput. Sci. **18**(3:32) (2022)
13. Díaz-Caro, A., Malherbe, O.: The sup connective in IMALL: a categorical semantics. arXiv:2205.02142 (2024)
14. Girard, J.Y.: Interprétation fonctionnelle et élimination des coupures dans l'arithmétique d'ordre supérieur. Ph.D. thesis, Université de Paris VII (1972)
15. Heunen, C., Vicary, J.: Categories for Quantum Theory: An Introduction. Oxford University Press (2019)
16. Howard, W.A.: The formulae-as-types notion of construction. In: Curry, H., B., H., Roger, S.J., Jonathan, P. (eds.) To H. B. Curry: Essays on Combinatory Logic, Lambda Calculus, and Formalism, pp. 479–490. Academic Press (1980). Hitherto unpublished note of 1969
17. Lambek, J.: From lambda calculus to Cartesian closed categories. In: Curry, H., B., H., Roger, S.J., Jonathan, P. (eds.) To H. B. Curry: Essays on Combinatory Logic, Lambda Calculus, and Formalism, pp. 375–402. Academic Press (1980)
18. Lindenhovius, B., Zamdzhiev, V.: Operator spaces, linear logic and the Heisenberg-Schrödinger duality of quantum theory (2025). to appear in LICS'25
19. Oreshkov, O., Costa, F., Brunner, N.: Quantum correlations with no causal order. Nat. Commun. **3**, 1092 (2012)
20. Pisier, G.: Introduction to Operator Space Theory. Cambridge University Press (2003)
21. Selinger, P.: Towards a quantum programming language. Math. Struct. Comput. Sci. **14**(4), 527–586 (2004)
22. Selinger, P., Valiron, B.: A lambda calculus for quantum computation with classical control. Math. Struct. Comput. Sci. **16**(3), 527–552 (2006)
23. Sørensen, M.H., Urzyczyn, P.: Lectures on the Curry-Howard isomorphism. Elsevier (2006)
24. Takesaki, M.: Theory of Operator Algebras I. Springer, New York (1979)
25. Tsukada, T., Asada, K.: Enriched presheaf model of quantum FPC. Proc. ACM Program. Lang. **8**(POPL), 13:362–13:392 (2024)
26. Vaux, L.: The algebraic lambda-calculus. Math. Struct. Comput. Sci. **19**(5), 1029–1059 (2009)

A Quantum-Control Lambda-Calculus with Multiple Measurement Bases

Alejandro Díaz-Caro[1,2] and Nicolas A. Monzon[3,4](✉)

[1] Université de Lorraine, CNRS, Inria, LORIA, 54000 Nancy, France
alejandro.diaz-caro@inria.fr
[2] Universidad Nacional de Quilmes, Bernal, BA, Argentina
[3] Universidad Argentina de la Empresa, CABA, Argentina
[4] Universidad de la República, PEDECIBA-Informática, Montevideo, Uruguay
nimonzon@uade.edu.ar

Abstract. We introduce Lambda-SX, a typed quantum lambda-calculus that supports multiple measurement bases. By tracking duplicability relative to arbitrary bases within the type system, Lambda-SX enables more flexible control and compositional reasoning about measurements. We formalise its syntax, typing rules, subtyping, and operational semantics, and establish its key meta-theoretical properties. This proof-of-concept shows that support for multiple bases can be coherently integrated into the type discipline of quantum programming languages.

Keywords: Quantum lambda-calculus · Type systems · Subtyping · Quantum control · Multiple measurement bases

1 Introduction

Quantum computing can be viewed as a computational model for quantum mechanics. In this view, the state of a quantum system represents the state of a computation, and its evolution corresponds to a computational process. This opens the way to studying quantum computation using programming language theory and, in particular, type theory. Developing a type theory for quantum computation also creates connections with logic, following the Curry–Howard isomorphism [24]. Eventually, this approach may lead to a formal logic of quantum mechanics grounded in computer science.

Quantum algorithms are traditionally described using circuits, but the need for higher-level abstractions led to the notion of classical control, where a classical computer drives quantum execution. This idea, rooted in Knill's qRAM model [20], was formalised by Selinger [22] to enable classical control flow over quantum hardware. This approach led to the development of the Quantum Lambda Calculus [23], where programs are expressed by a tuple of a lambda term together with a quantum memory. This calculus has been the basis of languages like Quipper [17] and QWIRE [21].

An alternative paradigm is *quantum control*, introduced by Altenkirch and Grattage in the language QML [1]. Here, the goal is to avoid relying on a classical machine to drive a quantum computer, and instead allow quantum data to control computation directly. Following this paradigm, a quantum-control extension of the lambda calculus—later called Lambda-S_1—was proposed in 2019 [12], using realizability techniques [19], and given a categorical model in [14].

Lambda-S_1 was the result of a long line of research on quantum control, started by Lineal [2]—the first extension of the lambda calculus to embody quantum control. Lineal is an untyped lambda calculus extended with arbitrary linear superpositions. Its rewrite rules ensure confluence and avoid cloning arbitrary terms—a forbidden operation in quantum computing [26]—and terms normalize to canonical vector forms. To prevent cloning, it uses a *call-by-base* strategy: applying a lambda abstraction $\lambda x.t$ to a superposition $(\alpha.v + \beta.w)$ yields $\alpha.(\lambda x.t)v + \beta.(\lambda x.t)w$. This guarantees that all abstractions are linear and supports expressing matrices, vectors, and hence quantum programs. These include non-unitary maps and unnormalised vectors.

However, call-by-base breaks down in the presence of measurement. For instance, if $\lambda x.\pi^1 x$ denotes a measurement on the computational basis, then applying it to a superposition yields $\alpha.(\lambda x.\pi^1 x)v + \beta.(\lambda x.\pi^1 x)w$, which fails to produce a probabilistic collapse and instead behaves like the identity.

To solve this, Lambda-S [11] introduced a type-guided approach. In Lambda-S, a superposed term of type A is marked with $S(A)$, allowing beta-reduction to be guided by the argument's type. If $\mathbb{B}$ is the type of base qubits $|0\rangle$ and $|1\rangle$, then $S(\mathbb{B})$ is the type of arbitrary qubits. Thus, in $(\lambda x^{\mathbb{B}}.t)(\alpha.|0\rangle + \beta.|1\rangle)$, call-by-base applies, whereas in $(\lambda x^{S(\mathbb{B})}.t)(\alpha.|0\rangle + \beta.|1\rangle)$, a call-by-name strategy is used. The latter requires a linearity check on t: the variable must not be duplicated.

This modal distinction is dual to that of linear logic [16], where types $!A$ are duplicable. In Lambda-S, $S(A)$ marks non-duplicable types—and this duality is made explicit by its categorical models [13,15].

Among various quantum lambda-calculus extensions, Lambda-S stands out for its ability to distinguish between superposed states and base states with respect to a given measurement basis.

Lambda-S_1 can be seen as a restriction of Lambda-S in which only unitary matrices and normalized vectors are considered. The technique to enforce this restriction was introduced in [12], and a full definition of the restricted language was given in [14], merging Lambda-S with that technique.

These languages favour the use of the computational basis, which is sufficient for quantum computation. Indeed, a measurement in an arbitrary basis can always be simulated by a rotation, followed by a measurement in the computational basis, and then a rotation back. However, restricting to a single basis introduces two important drawbacks.

First, duplicability is not unique to the computational basis: it is allowed in any basis, as long as the basis is known. Therefore, if we can determine that a quantum state is in a given basis, we can treat it as classical information.

Second, while Lambda-S and Intuitionistic Linear Logic (ILL) can be seen as categorical duals—via an adjunction between a Cartesian closed category and a monoidal category, where Lambda-S is interpreted in the Cartesian side and superpositions are captured by a monad, while ILL is interpreted in the monoidal side with duplicable data captured by a comonad—this duality is not complete. The asymmetry arises from Lambda-S being defined relative to a fixed basis, while ILL does not favour any particular basis.

In this paper, we take a first step toward addressing this limitation by extending Lambda-S to track duplicability with respect to multiple bases. We present a proof-of-concept system that remains first-order for simplicity; the rationale and consequences of this choice are discussed in Sect. 2.2. Furthermore, we restrict attention to single-qubit bases, extended pointwise to non-entangled multi-qubit systems. Supporting entangled measurement bases would require additional complexity, and we leave such extensions for future work. These and other simplifications are intentional: our goal is not to provide a fully general system, but to highlight a specific capability that has not been explored in the literature so far—the ability to track duplicability with respect to multiple bases.

Related works. The most directly related work is Lambda-S [11], which already distinguishes between base states and superpositions relative to a fixed basis. Our contribution extends this idea by making duplicability sensitive to *several* measurement bases, something not addressed in Lambda-S.

Beyond Lambda-S, other formalisms support more than one basis. For example, the ZX-calculus [8] captures computations relative to the computational and diagonal bases, while the Many-Worlds Calculus [5] also accommodates multiple bases. Both are graphical frameworks, whereas Lambda-SX works directly within a typed λ-calculus. Among them, the Many-Worlds Calculus is closest in spirit, since it allows superpositions of entire programs. By contrast, our system demonstrates that this flexibility can be achieved within a term language, with a type discipline that explicitly controls duplicability across bases.

A different perspective is offered by the theory of quantum information effects [18], which uses categorical machinery to model side-effects such as measurement and decoherence. Their focus is on extending semantic models with effectful structure. In contrast, Lambda-SX introduces multiple bases directly into the syntax and type system, making the interaction of measurements with terms explicit rather than implicit in the semantics.

Carette et al. [4] propose Quantum Π, a universal language obtained from two interpretations of a reversible classical calculus Π—one in the computational basis and one in a rotated basis—combined through a categorical effect construction. Unlike this approach, which derives quantum behaviour from a semantic amalgamation of classical languages, Lambda-SX directly extends a quantum λ-calculus with multiple bases and uses types to track their effect on duplicability. The emphasis is not on universality, but on showing how multiple bases can be consistently integrated into the typing discipline.

Voichick et al. [25] develop Qunity, designed to unify classical and quantum programming. Their language generalises familiar constructs, such as try-catch or sum types, and interprets duplication and discarding semantically as entanglement and partial trace. Lambda-SX takes the opposite stance: duplication is syntactically constrained by types, ensuring basis-sensitive linearity. Thus, while Qunity broadens classical constructs to the quantum setting via denotational semantics, Lambda-SX sharpens the syntactic control of measurements across incompatible bases.

Another line of research concerns semantic characterisations. Clairambault and de Visme [7] establish full abstraction for a quantum λ-calculus via game semantics and a relational model. Their contribution is to match operational and denotational equivalence. By contrast, our aim is not a new semantic characterisation but a syntactic system that makes basis transitions explicit in terms and types, thereby serving as a proof-of-concept for coherent type-theoretic treatment of multiple bases.

Finally, Choudhury and Gay [6] study the "duality of lambda-abstraction" by extending the simply typed λ-calculus with covalues and coabstraction, guided by categorical dualities between cartesian closure and cocartesian coclosure. Their focus lies on deepening the foundations of classical computation and logical control. Lambda-SX instead addresses specifically quantum features: it incorporates multiple measurement bases into a quantum λ-calculus and refines duplicability accordingly. Whereas their duality is rooted in classical logic, ours stems directly from quantum principles such as the no-cloning theorem.

Plan of the Paper. Section 2 introduces the Lambda-SX calculus with two measurement bases. The main meta-theoretical results are developed in Sect. 3: type soundness is established in Sect. 3.1, followed by a proof of strong normalisation in Sect. 3.2. Section 4 generalises the system to support an arbitrary number of measurement bases and introduces a refined subtyping mechanism that allows quantum states to be shared across multiple bases. We conclude with a summary and discussion of future work in Sect. 5.

2 Lambda-SX

2.1 Types and Terms

We consider two measurement bases: the computational basis, denoted by the type $\mathbb{B}$, and the Hadamard basis, denoted by the type $\mathbb{X}$. The set **B** of base types is defined as $\{\mathbb{B}, \mathbb{X}\}$, closed under Cartesian product, as shown in Fig. 1.

$\nu := \mathbb{B} \mid \mathbb{X}$ Atomic types (**A**) $\qquad \Psi := \mathbb{M} \mid S(\Psi) \mid \Psi \times \Psi$ Qubit types (**Q**)
$\mathbb{M} := \nu \mid \mathbb{M} \times \mathbb{M}$ Base types (**B**) $\qquad A := \Psi \mid \Psi \Rightarrow A \mid S(A)$ Types (**T**)

Fig. 1. Type Grammar.

Qubit types may be base types, their spans (denoted by the modality S), or Cartesian products. The language is first-order: function types are only allowed over qubit types. We work modulo associativity of the product, and parentheses are therefore omitted. We also use the notation $\prod_{i=1}^{n} \Psi_i$ to denote $\Psi_1 \times \ldots \times \Psi_n$.

We define a subtyping relation, shown in Fig. 2. The intuition behind subtyping is that it corresponds to set inclusion. For example, $A \preceq S(A)$ holds because any set is included in its span, and $S(S(A)) \preceq S(A)$ reflects the fact that the span operation is idempotent. If $A \preceq B$ and $B \preceq A$, then A and B are considered *equivalent types*, and we write $A \approx B$. If A and B are syntactically identical, we write $A = B$.

$$\frac{}{A \preceq A} \qquad \frac{A \preceq B \quad B \preceq C}{A \preceq C} \qquad \frac{}{A \preceq S(A)} \qquad \frac{}{S(S(A)) \preceq S(A)} \qquad \frac{}{\prod_{i=0}^{n} \nu_i \preceq S(\prod_{i=0}^{n} \nu_i')}$$

$$\frac{A \preceq B}{S(A) \preceq S(B)} \qquad \frac{A \preceq B \quad \Psi_1 \preceq \Psi_2}{\Psi_2 \Rightarrow A \preceq \Psi_1 \Rightarrow B} \qquad \frac{\Psi_1 \preceq \Psi_2 \quad \Psi_3 \preceq \Psi_4}{\Psi_1 \times \Psi_3 \preceq \Psi_2 \times \Psi_4}$$

Fig. 2. Subtyping relation.

The set of *preterms* is denoted by Λ and is defined by the grammar shown in Fig. 3.

$$
\begin{aligned}
t := &\; x \mid \lambda x^{\Psi}.t \mid tt & \text{(Lambda calculus)} \\
&\mid |0\rangle \mid |1\rangle \mid |+\rangle \mid |-\rangle \mid \;?t\cdot t \mid \;?_X t\cdot t & \text{(Constants)} \\
&\mid \vec{0} \mid t+t \mid \alpha.t \mid \not{t} \mid \pi^m t \mid \pi_X^m t & \text{(Linear combinations)} \\
&\mid t \otimes t \mid \text{hd } t \mid \text{tl } t \mid \Uparrow^\ell t \mid \Uparrow^r t & \text{(Lists)}
\end{aligned}
$$

Fig. 3. Preterms

As usual in algebraic calculi [2,3,12], the symbol $+$ is treated as associative and commutative, so preterms are considered modulo these equational laws. The grammar includes first-order lambda calculus terms, constants (and their conditionals–we write $t?r\cdot s$ as a shorthand for $(?r\cdot s)t$), linear combinations (with measurement as a destructor), and tensor product terms, written using list notation since product types are considered associative.

The symbol $\not{t}$ denotes an error and is used to handle measurements of the zero vector when normalisation fails. The measurement operations π^m and π_X^m are responsible for normalising their input prior to measurement. The casting operations $\Uparrow^\ell$ and $\Uparrow^r$ allow converting between lists of superpositions and superpositions of lists. Indeed, lists are used to represent tensor products. Consequently, a tensor product of superpositions can be regarded as a superposition of tensor products, which loses information about separability. We may use $\Uparrow$ to denote either $\Uparrow^\ell$ or $\Uparrow^r$, depending on the context.

Free variables are defined as usual, and the set of free variables of a preterm t is denoted by $\mathrm{FV}(t)$. The sets of base terms ($\mathcal{B}$) and values ($\mathcal{V}$) are defined by:

$$b := |0\rangle \mid |1\rangle \mid |+\rangle \mid |-\rangle \mid b \otimes b \qquad \text{Base terms } (\mathcal{B})$$

$$v := x \mid \lambda x^\Psi . t \mid b \mid \vec{0} \mid v + v \mid \alpha . v \mid v \otimes v \qquad \text{Values } (\mathcal{V})$$

The type system is presented in Fig. 4. A *term* is a preterm t for which there exists a context Γ and a type A such that $\Gamma \vdash t : A$ is derivable.

$$\dfrac{}{x^\Psi \vdash x : \Psi}\,\text{Ax} \qquad \dfrac{\Gamma, x^\Psi \vdash t : A}{\Gamma \vdash \lambda x^\Psi . t : \Psi \Rightarrow A}\,{\Rightarrow}_I \qquad \dfrac{\Gamma \vdash t : \Psi \Rightarrow A \quad \Delta \vdash r : \Psi}{\Gamma, \Delta \vdash tr : A}\,{\Rightarrow}_E$$

$$\dfrac{\Gamma \vdash t : S(\Psi \Rightarrow A) \quad \Delta \vdash r : S(\Psi)}{\Gamma, \Delta \vdash tr : S(A)}\,{\Rightarrow}_{ES}$$

$$\dfrac{}{\vdash |0\rangle : \mathbb{B}}\,|0\rangle \qquad \dfrac{}{\vdash |1\rangle : \mathbb{B}}\,|1\rangle \qquad \dfrac{}{\vdash |+\rangle : \mathbb{X}}\,|+\rangle \qquad \dfrac{}{\vdash |-\rangle : \mathbb{X}}\,|-\rangle$$

$$\dfrac{\Gamma \vdash t : A \quad \Gamma \vdash r : A}{\Gamma \vdash ?t \cdot r : \mathbb{B} \Rightarrow A}\,\text{If} \qquad \dfrac{\Gamma \vdash t : A \quad \Gamma \vdash r : A}{\Gamma \vdash ?_{\mathbb{X}} t \cdot r : \mathbb{X} \Rightarrow A}\,\text{If}_\mathbb{X}$$

$$\dfrac{}{\vdash \vec{0} : S(A)}\,\vec{0} \qquad \dfrac{\Gamma \vdash t : A \quad \Delta \vdash r : A}{\Gamma, \Delta \vdash t + r : S(A)}\,S_I^+ \qquad \dfrac{\Gamma \vdash t : A}{\Gamma \vdash \alpha . t : S(A)}\,S_I^\alpha \qquad \dfrac{}{\Gamma \vdash \mbox{\Large$\lightning$} : \Psi}\,e$$

$$\dfrac{\Gamma \vdash t : S\left(\prod_{i=1}^n \nu_i\right) \quad 0 < m \le n}{\Gamma \vdash \pi^m t : \mathbb{B}^m \times S\left(\prod_{i=m+1}^n \nu_i\right)}\,S_E \qquad \dfrac{\Gamma \vdash t : S\left(\prod_{i=1}^n \nu_i\right) \quad 0 < m \le n}{\Gamma \vdash \pi_\mathbb{X}^m t : \mathbb{X}^m \times S\left(\prod_{i=m+1}^n \nu_i\right)}\,S_{E_\mathbb{X}}$$

$$\dfrac{\Gamma \vdash t : \Psi \quad \Delta \vdash r : \Phi}{\Gamma, \Delta \vdash t \otimes r : \Psi \times \Phi}\,\times_I \qquad \dfrac{\Gamma \vdash t : \nu \times M}{\Gamma \vdash \mathrm{hd}\ t : \nu}\,\times_{Er} \qquad \dfrac{\Gamma \vdash t : \nu \times M}{\Gamma \vdash \mathrm{tl}\ t : M}\,\times_{El}$$

$$\dfrac{\Gamma \vdash t : S(\Psi \times S(\Phi)) \quad \Psi \ne S(\Psi')}{\Gamma \vdash {\Uparrow}^\ell t : S(\Psi \times \Phi)}\,{\Uparrow}^\ell \qquad \dfrac{\Gamma \vdash t : S(S(\Phi) \times \Psi) \quad \Psi \ne S(\Psi')}{\Gamma \vdash {\Uparrow}^r t : S(\Phi \times \Psi)}\,{\Uparrow}^r$$

$$\dfrac{\Gamma \vdash t : \mathbb{X}}{\Gamma \vdash {\Uparrow} t : S(\mathbb{B})}\,{\Uparrow}_\mathbb{X} \qquad \dfrac{\Gamma \vdash t : \mathbb{B}}{\Gamma \vdash {\Uparrow} t : \mathbb{B}}\,{\Uparrow}_\mathbb{B}$$

$$\dfrac{\Gamma \vdash t : A \quad A \preceq B}{\Gamma \vdash t : B}\,\preceq \qquad \dfrac{\Gamma \vdash t : A}{\Gamma, x^{\mathrm{M}} \vdash t : A}\,W \qquad \dfrac{\Gamma, x^{\mathrm{M}}, y^{\mathrm{M}} \vdash t : A}{\Gamma, x^{\mathrm{M}} \vdash t[y/x] : A}\,C$$

Fig. 4. Type system.

2.2 Operational Semantics

The operational semantics for terms is defined by the relation $\longrightarrow_p$, presented in Figs. 5 to 10. The parameter $p \in [0,1]$ represents a probability and is primarily used in the probabilistic reduction rule associated with measurement.

Figure 5 presents the reduction rules for standard lambda calculus terms and conditional constructs.

Rule (β_n) is the standard call-by-name beta-reduction rule, which applies when the argument is not basis-typed.

$$
\begin{array}{rl}
\text{If } \Psi \notin \mathbf{B}, \text{ then } (\lambda x^\Psi.t)u \longrightarrow_1 t[u/x] & (\beta_\mathsf{n}) \\
\text{If } b \in \mathcal{B} \text{ has type } \mathbb{M}, \text{ then } (\lambda x^\mathbb{M}.t)b \longrightarrow_1 t[b/x] & (\beta_\mathsf{b}) \\
\text{If } t \text{ has type } \mathbb{M} \Rightarrow A, \text{ then } t(r+s) \longrightarrow_1 tr+ts & (\mathsf{lin}_\mathsf{r}^+) \\
\text{If } t \text{ has type } \mathbb{M} \Rightarrow A, \text{ then } t(\alpha.r) \longrightarrow_1 \alpha.tr & (\mathsf{lin}_\mathsf{r}^\alpha) \\
\text{If } t \text{ has type } \mathbb{M} \Rightarrow A \text{ and } t \neq \natural, \text{ then } t\vec{0} \longrightarrow_1 \vec{0} & (\mathsf{lin}_\mathsf{r}^0) \\
(t+r)s \longrightarrow_1 ts+rs & (\mathsf{lin}_\mathsf{l}^+) \\
(\alpha.t)r \longrightarrow_1 \alpha.tr & (\mathsf{lin}_\mathsf{l}^\alpha) \\
\text{If } t \neq \natural, \text{ then } \vec{0}t \longrightarrow_1 \vec{0} & (\mathsf{lin}_\mathsf{l}^0) \\
|1\rangle?t \cdot r \longrightarrow_1 t & (\mathsf{if}_1) \\
|0\rangle?t \cdot r \longrightarrow_1 r & (\mathsf{if}_0) \\
|+\rangle?_\mathbf{x} t \cdot r \longrightarrow_1 t & (\mathsf{if}_+) \\
|-\rangle?_\mathbf{x} t \cdot r \longrightarrow_1 r & (\mathsf{if}_-)
\end{array}
$$

Fig. 5. Reduction rules for beta-reduction and conditionals.

Rules (β_b), $(\mathsf{lin}_\mathsf{r}^+)$, $(\mathsf{lin}_\mathsf{r}^\alpha)$, and $(\mathsf{lin}_\mathsf{r}^0)$ implement the call-by-base strategy [2], distributing the function over the argument when the bound variable is basis-typed. For example $(\lambda x^\mathbb{B}.x \otimes x)(|0\rangle + |1\rangle)$ reduces first to $(\lambda x^\mathbb{B}.x \otimes x)|0\rangle + (\lambda x^\mathbb{B}.x \otimes x)|1\rangle$ by rule $(\mathsf{lin}_\mathsf{r}^+)$, and then to $|0\rangle \otimes |0\rangle + |1\rangle \otimes |1\rangle$ by rule (β_b).

Rules $(\mathsf{lin}_\mathsf{l}^+)$, $(\mathsf{lin}_\mathsf{l}^\alpha)$, and $(\mathsf{lin}_\mathsf{l}^0)$ distribute a superposition on the left-hand side of an application over its argument. Rules (if_1), (if_0), (if_+), and (if_-) determine the selected branch based on the value of the condition.

We restrict the calculus to first-order terms for simplicity. In a higher-order setting, one could consider the term $\lambda x^{S(\mathbb{B})}.\lambda y^\mathbb{B}.x$, which embed an unknown qubit within a perfectly duplicable lambda abstraction. Several solutions are possible: restricting weakening to non-arrow types, restricting the language to first-order, or introducing annotations that prevent duplication of such terms. In this paper, we adopt the second option, as our goal is to provide a proof-of-concept system for handling multiple measurement bases.

Figure 6 presents the reduction rules corresponding to the vector space axioms, taken directly from [2]. These rules normalise expressions by rewriting linear combinations into a canonical form.

$$
\begin{array}{llll}
\vec{0}+t \longrightarrow_1 t & (\mathsf{zero}) & \alpha.(\beta.t) \longrightarrow_1 (\alpha\beta).t & (\mathsf{assoc}) \\
1.t \longrightarrow_1 t & (\mathsf{one}) & \alpha.(t+r) \longrightarrow_1 \alpha.t+\alpha.r & (\mathsf{dist}) \\
0.t \longrightarrow_1 \vec{0} & (\mathsf{scalar}_0) & \alpha.t+\beta.t \longrightarrow_1 (\alpha+\beta).t & (\mathsf{fact}) \\
\alpha.\vec{0} \longrightarrow_1 \vec{0} & (\mathsf{zero}_\mathsf{arg}) & \alpha.t+t \longrightarrow_1 (\alpha+1).t & (\mathsf{fact}_1) \\
& & t+t \longrightarrow_1 2.t & (\mathsf{fact}_2)
\end{array}
$$

Fig. 6. Vector space axioms.

Figure 7 presents the reduction rules related to lists. Rules (head) and (tail) behave as standard destructors on non-superposed list values. The remaining rules implement explicit cast operations, which allow rearranging the interaction between linear combinations and tensor products.

For example, rule (cast_ℓ^+) transforms the term $|0\rangle \otimes (|0\rangle + |1\rangle)$, which has type $\mathbb{B} \times S(\mathbb{B})$ (and hence, by subtyping, $S(\mathbb{B} \times S(\mathbb{B}))$), into the term $|0\rangle \otimes |0\rangle + |0\rangle \otimes |1\rangle$, of type $S(\mathbb{B} \times \mathbb{B})$. See also the typing rule $\Uparrow^\ell$ in Fig. 4.

If $h \neq u \otimes v$ and $h \in \mathcal{B}$, then $\text{hd}\ (h \otimes t) \longrightarrow_1 h$	(head)
If $h \neq u \otimes v$ and $h \in \mathcal{B}$, then $\text{tl}\ (h \otimes t) \longrightarrow_1 t$	(tail)
$\Uparrow^\ell t \otimes (r+s) \longrightarrow_1 \Uparrow^\ell t \otimes r + \Uparrow^\ell t \otimes s$	(cast_ℓ^+)
$\Uparrow^r (t+r) \otimes s \longrightarrow_1 \Uparrow^r t \otimes s + \Uparrow^r r \otimes s$	(cast_r^+)
$\Uparrow^\ell t \otimes (\alpha.r) \longrightarrow_1 \alpha.\Uparrow^\ell t \otimes r$	$(\text{cast}_\ell^\alpha)$
$\Uparrow^r (\alpha.t) \otimes r \longrightarrow_1 \alpha.\Uparrow^r t \otimes r$	(cast_r^α)
$\Uparrow^\ell v \otimes \vec{0} \longrightarrow_1 \vec{0}$	(cast_ℓ^0)
$\Uparrow^r \vec{0} \otimes v \longrightarrow_1 \vec{0}$	(cast_r^0)
$\Uparrow (t+r) \longrightarrow_1 \Uparrow t + \Uparrow r$	$(\text{cast}_\Uparrow^+)$
$\Uparrow (\alpha.t) \longrightarrow_1 \alpha.\Uparrow t$	$(\text{cast}_\Uparrow^\alpha)$
$\Uparrow \vec{0} \longrightarrow_1 \vec{0}$	$(\text{neut}_0^\Uparrow)$
If $b \in \mathcal{B}$, then $\Uparrow^\ell v \otimes b \longrightarrow_1 v \otimes b$	$(\text{neut}_\ell^\Uparrow)$
If $b \in \mathcal{B}$, then $\Uparrow^r b \otimes v \longrightarrow_1 b \otimes v$	$(\text{neut}_r^\Uparrow)$
$\Uparrow \lvert+\rangle \longrightarrow_1 \frac{1}{\sqrt{2}}.\lvert 0\rangle + \frac{1}{\sqrt{2}}.\lvert 1\rangle$	$(\text{cast}_{\lvert+\rangle})$
$\Uparrow \lvert-\rangle \longrightarrow_1 \frac{1}{\sqrt{2}}.\lvert 0\rangle - \frac{1}{\sqrt{2}}.\lvert 1\rangle$	$(\text{cast}_{\lvert-\rangle})$
$\Uparrow \lvert 0\rangle \longrightarrow_1 \lvert 0\rangle$	$(\text{cast}_{\lvert 0\rangle})$
$\Uparrow \lvert 1\rangle \longrightarrow_1 \lvert 1\rangle$	$(\text{cast}_{\lvert 1\rangle})$

Fig. 7. Reduction rules for destructors and casting over tensor products.

Figure 8 presents the reduction rules *schemas* for measurement: each instantiation depends on the specific shape of the term being measured.

The operation π^m applies to a term of type $S(\prod_{i=1}^n \nu_i)$. Before measurement, the term is implicitly converted to the computational basis, yielding a sum of distinct basis vectors: $\sum_{a=1}^f \beta_a \lvert c_{a1}\rangle \otimes \cdots \otimes \lvert c_{an}\rangle$, with $c_{aj} \in \{0, 1\}$. Measurement is performed on the first m qubits, producing a collapse to $\lvert k\rangle \otimes \lvert \phi_k\rangle$ with probability $p_k = \frac{1}{Z} \sum_{a \in I_k} \lvert\beta_a\rvert^2$, where I_k is the set of indices a such that the prefix $\lvert c_{a1} \cdots c_{am}\rangle$ equals $\lvert k\rangle$, and Z is the squared norm of the original input. The state $\lvert \phi_k\rangle$ is defined by normalising the suffixes of the terms in I_k:

$$\lvert \phi_k\rangle = \sum_{a \in I_k} \frac{\beta_a}{\sqrt{\ell}} \lvert c_{a,m+1}\rangle \otimes \cdots \otimes \lvert c_{an}\rangle, \qquad \text{where } \ell = \sum_{a \in I_k} \lvert\beta_a\rvert^2.$$

A Quantum-Control Lambda-Calculus with Multiple Measurement Bases   159

The rule for measurement in the Hadamard basis, $\pi_{\mathbb{X}}^m$, behaves analogously, with the input expressed in the Hadamard basis and $|k\rangle$ ranging over $\{+,-\}^m$.

We write $[\alpha_i.]$ to indicate that scalar may be omitted. Each b_{hi} ranges over $\{0, 1, +, -\}$, and $e \leq 4^n$ denotes the number of basis vectors of arity n.

If the input to π^m or $\pi_{\mathbb{X}}^m$ is or reduces to $\vec{0}$, the result is $\lightning$.

$$\pi^m \left(\sum_{i=1}^{e} [\alpha_i.] \bigotimes_{h=1}^{n} |b_{hi}\rangle \right) \longrightarrow_{p_k} |k\rangle \otimes |\phi_k\rangle \quad \text{(proy)} \qquad \pi^m \vec{0} \longrightarrow_1 \lightning \quad (\text{proy}^{\vec{0}})$$

$$\pi_{\mathbb{X}}^m \left(\sum_{i=1}^{e} [\alpha_i.] \bigotimes_{h=1}^{n} |b_{hi}\rangle \right) \longrightarrow_{p_k} |k\rangle \otimes |\phi_k\rangle \quad (\text{proy}_{\mathbb{X}}) \qquad \pi_{\mathbb{X}}^m \vec{0} \longrightarrow_1 \lightning \quad (\text{proy}_{\mathbb{X}}^{\vec{0}})$$

Fig. 8. Measurement rules for the computational and Hadamard bases.

Example 2.1. (Measurement). To simplify notation, we write $|abcd\rangle$ instead of $|a\rangle \otimes |b\rangle \otimes |c\rangle \otimes |d\rangle$. Consider the following two semantically equivalent terms: $\pi^2(\alpha |0 + 10\rangle + \beta |10 - 0\rangle)$ and $\pi^2(\frac{\alpha}{\sqrt{2}} |0010\rangle + \frac{\alpha}{\sqrt{2}} |0110\rangle + \frac{\beta}{\sqrt{2}} |1000\rangle - \frac{\beta}{\sqrt{2}} |1010\rangle)$. Both reduce, for instance, to $|10\rangle \otimes (\frac{1}{\sqrt{2}} |00\rangle + \frac{1}{\sqrt{2}} |01\rangle)$ with probability $\frac{|\alpha|^2}{\sqrt{|\alpha|^2+|\beta|^2}}$.

Figure 9 specifies how $\lightning$ propagates. In each case, the presence of $\lightning$ causes the entire expression to reduce to $\lightning$.

$$\lightning t \longrightarrow_1 \lightning \quad (\lightning@) \qquad t \otimes \lightning \longrightarrow_1 \lightning \quad (\lightning_\otimes) \qquad \Uparrow^\ell \lightning \longrightarrow_1 \lightning \quad (\lightning_{\Uparrow}^\ell)$$

$$t\lightning \longrightarrow_1 \lightning \quad (\lightning^@) \qquad \lightning \otimes t \longrightarrow_1 \lightning \quad (\lightning^\otimes) \qquad \Uparrow^r \lightning \longrightarrow_1 \lightning \quad (\lightning_{\Uparrow}^r)$$

$$t + \lightning \longrightarrow_1 \lightning \quad (\lightning_+) \qquad \pi^m \lightning \longrightarrow_1 \lightning \quad (\lightning_\pi) \qquad \text{hd } \lightning \longrightarrow_1 \lightning \quad (\lightning_{\text{hd}})$$

$$\alpha.\lightning \longrightarrow_1 \lightning \quad (\lightning_{\text{scal}}) \qquad \pi_{\mathbb{X}}^m \lightning \longrightarrow_1 \lightning \quad (\lightning_{\pi_{\mathbb{X}}}) \qquad \text{tl } \lightning \longrightarrow_1 \lightning \quad (\lightning_{\text{tl}})$$

Fig. 9. Error propagation rules.

Figure 10 presents the context rules.

2.3 Examples

This section illustrates how the type system supports quantum states, operations, and measurements in a functional style, highlighting its flexibility across multiple measurement bases.

Example 2.2. (Hadamard gate). The Hadamard gate can be implemented in multiple ways, depending on the desired type. For example:

$$\vdash \lambda x^{\mathbb{B}}.x?|-\rangle \cdot |+\rangle : \mathbb{B} \Rightarrow \mathbb{X}$$

$$\vdash \lambda x^{\mathbb{X}}.x?|0\rangle \cdot |1\rangle : \mathbb{X} \Rightarrow \mathbb{B}$$

$$\vdash \lambda x^{\mathbb{B}}.x?(\Uparrow |-\rangle) \cdot (\Uparrow |+\rangle) : \mathbb{B} \Rightarrow S(\mathbb{B})$$

If $t \longrightarrow_p r$, then

$$ts \longrightarrow_p rs \qquad t+s \longrightarrow_p r+s \qquad t \otimes s \longrightarrow_p r \otimes s$$
$$(\lambda x^M.v)\,t \longrightarrow_p (\lambda x^M.v)\,r \qquad \alpha.t \longrightarrow_p \alpha.r \qquad s \otimes t \longrightarrow_p s \otimes r$$
$$t?s_1 \cdot s_2 \longrightarrow_p r?s_1 \cdot s_2 \qquad \pi^m t \longrightarrow_p \pi^m r \qquad \text{hd}\ t \longrightarrow_p \text{hd}\ r$$
$$t?_{\mathbb{X}} s_1 \cdot s_2 \longrightarrow_p r?_{\mathbb{X}} s_1 \cdot s_2 \qquad \pi^m_{\mathbb{X}} t \longrightarrow_p \pi^m_{\mathbb{X}} r \qquad \text{tl}\ t \longrightarrow_p \text{tl}\ r$$
$$\Uparrow t \longrightarrow_p \Uparrow r$$

Fig. 10. Context rules.

All these implementations yield equivalent results on arbitrary inputs (in either basis), but the first preserves duplicability on inputs $|0\rangle$ or $|1\rangle$, and the second does so on $|+\rangle$ or $|-\rangle$.

As an instance, we could write $\lambda x^{\mathbb{B}}.(\lambda y^{\mathbb{X}}.y \otimes y)Hx$ as soon as H is the first implementation of the Hadamard gate. Notice that we are cloning a qubit; however, since the basis is tracked since the beginning, this is perfectly valid.

Example 2.3. (CNOT gate). In the same way, the CNOT gate can be implemented in multiple ways, for example

$$\vdash \lambda x^{\mathbb{B} \times \mathbb{B}}.(\text{hd}\ x) \otimes (\text{hd}\ x?\mathbf{NOT}(\text{tl}\ x) \cdot \text{tl}\ x) : \mathbb{B} \times \mathbb{B} \Rightarrow \mathbb{B} \times \mathbb{B}$$
$$\vdash \lambda x^{\mathbb{X} \times \mathbb{B}}.\,|0\rangle \otimes (\text{tl}\ x)$$
$$+ |1\rangle \otimes ((\text{hd}\ x?_{\mathbb{X}}\mathbf{NOT} \cdot (-1).\mathbf{NOT})(\text{tl}\ x)) : \mathbb{X} \times \mathbb{B} \Rightarrow S(\mathbb{B} \times \mathbb{B})$$

where **NOT** is the NOT gate given by $\vdash \lambda x^{\mathbb{B}}.x?|0\rangle \cdot |1\rangle : \mathbb{B} \Rightarrow \mathbb{B}$.

Example 2.4. (Bell states). The entangled Bell states can be produced by the following term, applied to a pair of computational basis qubits:

$$\vdash \lambda x^{\mathbb{B} \times \mathbb{B}}.\mathbf{CNOT}(\mathbf{H}(\text{hd}\ x) \otimes \text{tl}\ x) : \mathbb{B} \times \mathbb{B} \Rightarrow S(\mathbb{B} \times \mathbb{B})$$

However, there are more interesting implementations. For example, the following term maps $|+\rangle$ to the Bell state β_{00} and $|-\rangle$ to β_{10}:

$$\vdash \lambda x^{\mathbb{X}}.(\lambda y^{\mathbb{B}}.y \otimes y)(\Uparrow x) : \mathbb{X} \Rightarrow S(\mathbb{B} \times \mathbb{B})$$

Example 2.5. (Applying gates to multi-qubit states). In general, we can apply a gate to a qubit in a multi-qubit state, even if entangled, with the same technique as used to apply Hadamard to the first qubit in the Bell state. For example, applying CNOT to the first of three qubits can be done as follows:

$$\mathbf{CNOT}^3_{1,2} = \lambda x^{\mathbb{B} \times \mathbb{B} \times \mathbb{B}}.\mathbf{CNOT}((\text{hd}\ x) \otimes (\text{hd tl}\ x)) \otimes (\text{tl tl}\ x)$$

Example 2.6. (Teleportation). We can use the Bell state to implement teleportation, which allows the transmission of an arbitrary qubit state from Alice to Bob using an entangled pair and classical communication. The term implementing it would be

$$\vdash \lambda x^{S(\mathbb{B})}.\pi^2 \Uparrow^\ell \mathbf{Bob}(\Uparrow^\ell (\mathbf{Alice}(x \otimes \mathbf{Bell}(|0\rangle \otimes |0\rangle)))) : S(\mathbb{B}) \Rightarrow (\mathbb{B} \times \mathbb{B} \times S(\mathbb{B}))$$

where: **Bell** produces the Bell state, as defined earlier; **Alice** implements Alice's part of the protocol, defined as: $\lambda x^{S(\mathbb{B}) \times S(\mathbb{B} \times \mathbb{B})}.\pi^2(\Uparrow^r \mathbf{H}_1^3(\mathbf{CNOT}_{1,2}^3(\Uparrow^\ell (\Uparrow^r x))))$, where $\mathbf{H}_1^3$ is the Hadamard operator on the first qubit: $\lambda x^{\mathbb{B} \times \mathbb{B} \times \mathbb{B}}.\mathbf{H}(\mathtt{hd}\ x) \otimes \mathtt{tl}\ x$. **Bob** implements Bob's part: $\lambda x^{\mathbb{B} \times \mathbb{B} \times \mathbb{B}}.(\mathtt{hd}\ x) \otimes (\mathtt{hd}\ \mathtt{tl}\ x) \otimes (\mathbf{C\text{-}Z}(\mathtt{hd}\ x) \otimes (\mathbf{CNOT}(\mathtt{hd}\ \mathtt{tl}\ x) \otimes (\mathtt{tl}\ \mathtt{tl}\ x)))$, where **C-Z** is: $\lambda x^{\mathbb{B} \times \mathbb{B}}.\mathtt{hd}\ x?\mathbf{Z}(\mathtt{tl}\ x) \cdot \mathtt{tl}\ x$.

3 Correctness

In this section we establish the main meta-theoretical properties of our calculus. These results show that the type system is well-behaved with respect to the operational semantics, and they guarantee consistency.

We begin in Sect. 3.1 with the proof of *subject reduction* (Theorem 3.4), showing that the type of a term is preserved under reduction. We then prove *progress* (Theorem 3.5), ensuring that well-typed terms are either values or can take a reduction step. The *linear casting* property follows (Theorem 3.6), showing that terms of type $S(\mathbb{B}^n)$ can be rewritten—via explicit casting reductions—as linear combinations of terms of type $\mathbb{B}^n$. This result provides a semantic justification for viewing casting as a projection onto a measurement basis.

Finally, we show that all well-typed terms are *strongly normalising* (Sect. 3.2); that is, all well-typed terms always terminate.

3.1 Type Soundness

Subject Reduction. The typing rules are not syntax-directed due to application (which has two typing rules), subtyping, weakening, and contraction. Therefore, a generation lemma—stating the conditions under which a typing judgment $\Gamma \vdash t : A$ can be derived—is needed.

The substitution lemma, which plays a central role in the proof of subject reduction, is stated as follows.

Lemma 3.1. (Substitution). *If $\Gamma, x^A \vdash t : C$ and $\Delta \vdash r : A$, then $\Gamma, \Delta \vdash t[r/x] : C$.* □

The type preservation property is strongly related to subtyping. In its proof, several auxiliary properties of the subtyping relation are repeatedly used. The following lemma states these properties.

Lemma 3.2. (Properties of the subtyping relation). *The subtyping relation $\preceq$ satisfies the following properties:*

1. *If $A \Rightarrow B \preceq C \Rightarrow D$, then $C \preceq A$ and $B \preceq D$.*
2. *If $A \Rightarrow B \preceq S(C \Rightarrow D)$, then $C \preceq A$ and $B \preceq D$.*

3. If $S(A) \preceq B$, then $B = S(C)$ and $A \preceq C$, for some C.
4. If $\Psi_1 \times \Psi_2 \preceq A$, then $A \approx S(\Psi_3 \times \Psi_4)$ or $A \approx \Psi_3 \times \Psi_4$, for some Ψ_3, Ψ_4.
5. If $A \preceq B$, then A and B contain the same number of product constructors.
6. If $A \preceq \Psi_1 \Rightarrow C$ then $A \approx \Psi_2 \Rightarrow D$ for some Ψ_2 and D.
7. If $S(A) \preceq S(\Psi_1 \Rightarrow C)$ then $S(A) \approx S(\Psi_2 \Rightarrow D)$, for some Ψ_2 and D.
8. If $S(\Psi_1 \Rightarrow A) \preceq S(\Psi_2 \Rightarrow B)$, then $\Psi_2 \preceq \Psi_1$ and $B \preceq A$.

Proof. The proof relies on several technical properties. Please, refer to the arXiv extended version for the full proof. □

The following properties are crucial for analysing cast elimination, as they constrain the shape of product-type subtypes and relate them to simpler forms.

Lemma 3.3. (Properties of the subtyping relation on products). *The subtyping relation $\preceq$ satisfies the following properties on product types:*

1. If $\varphi \times \mathbb{M} \preceq S(\Psi_1 \times S(\Psi_2))$, then $\varphi \times \mathbb{M} \preceq S(\Psi_1 \times \Psi_2)$.
2. If $\mathbb{M} \times \varphi \preceq S(S(\Psi_1) \times \Psi_2)$, then $\mathbb{M} \times \varphi \preceq S(\Psi_1 \times \Psi_2)$.

Proof. The proof relies on several technical lemmas. Please, refer to the arXiv extended version for the full proof. □

We are now ready to state the main result of this section: the subject reduction property, which ensures that types are preserved under reduction.

Theorem 3.4. (Subject reduction). $\Gamma \vdash t : A$ and $t \longrightarrow_p r$ imply $\Gamma \vdash r : A$.

Proof. By induction on the reduction $t \longrightarrow_p r$. As an illustrative case, consider rule (lin_1^+), where $t = (t_1 + t_2)t_3$ and $r = t_1 t_3 + t_2 t_3$, with $\Gamma \vdash t : A$. By the generation lemma, we have $\Gamma = \Gamma_1, \Gamma_2, \Xi, \mathsf{T}(\Xi) \subseteq \mathbf{B}, \Gamma_1, \Xi \vdash t_1 + t_2 : S(\Psi_1 \Rightarrow C)$, $\Gamma_2, \Xi \vdash t_3 : S(\Psi_1)$, and $S(C) \preceq A$. By the generation lemma again, $\Gamma_1, \Xi = \Gamma_1', \Gamma_2', \Xi'$ with $\Gamma_1', \Xi' \vdash t_1 : D$, $\Gamma_2', \Xi' \vdash t_2 : D$, and $S(D) \preceq S(\Psi_1 \Rightarrow C)$. Then Lemma 3.2.7 gives $S(D) \approx S(\Psi_2 \Rightarrow E)$ with $S(\Psi_2 \Rightarrow E) \preceq S(\Psi_1 \Rightarrow C)$, and Lemma 3.2.8 yields $\Psi_1 \preceq \Psi_2$ and $E \preceq C$. Hence, from $\Gamma_1', \Xi' \vdash t_1 : S(\Psi_2 \Rightarrow E)$ and $\Gamma_2, \Xi \vdash t_3 : S(\Psi_2)$, we derive $\Gamma \vdash t_1 t_3, t_2 t_3 : S(E)$, and thus $\Gamma \vdash t_1 t_3 + t_2 t_3 : S(S(E))$. Since $S(S(E)) \preceq S(E) \preceq S(C) \preceq A$, by transitivity we conclude $\Gamma \vdash r : A$. □

Progress. The next result is the *progress* theorem, stating that well-typed terms in normal form must be either values or the error term.

Theorem 3.5. (Progress). *If $\vdash t : A$ then t reduces, is a value, or is $\frac{\ell}{\ell}$.* □

Linear Casting. Our system also exhibits a property we call *linear casting*, which expresses the idea that terms of type $S(\mathbb{B}^n)$ can be written using other terms of type $\mathbb{B}^n$, thanks to our linear casting reduction rules. This is not trivial, as by subtyping we have $S(\mathbb{B}^n) = S(\prod_{i=1}^{n} \nu_i)$.

Theorem 3.6. (Linear casting theorem). $\vdash \Uparrow t : S(\mathbb{B}^n)$ *implies* $\Uparrow t \longrightarrow_1^* \sum [\alpha_i.] b_i$ *with* $\vdash b_i : \mathbb{B}^n$.

Proof. By Theorems 3.5 and 3.4, we know that $\Uparrow t \longrightarrow_1^* v$ with $\vdash v : S(\mathbb{B}^n)$. By the generation lemma, we distinguish the following cases:

– If $v = |0\rangle$ or $v = |1\rangle$, then $\vdash v : \mathbb{B}$.
– Note that $v \neq |+\rangle$, since $\Uparrow t \not\longmapsto |+\rangle$: casting can only be eliminated through rules ($\mathsf{cast}_{|+\rangle}$), ($\mathsf{cast}_{|-\rangle}$), ($\mathsf{cast}_{|0\rangle}$), or ($\mathsf{cast}_{|1\rangle}$). Hence, this case cannot occur. Similarly, $v \neq |-\rangle$ for the same reason.
– If v has the form $b_1 \otimes b_2 \otimes \cdots \otimes b_n$ with $n \geq 1$, and each b_i a value, then each b_i must be either $|0\rangle$ or $|1\rangle$ by the same argument.
– If v has the form $\sum [\alpha_i.] b_i$, with the b_i having distinct types, then each b_i has the form $b_1 \otimes b_2 \otimes \cdots \otimes b_n$, where each $b_i \in \{|0\rangle, |1\rangle\}$.

Therefore, $v = \sum [\alpha_i.] b_i$, and $\Uparrow t \longrightarrow_1^* \sum [\alpha_i.] b_i$ with $\vdash b_i : \mathbb{B}^n$. □

3.2 Strong Normalization

We conclude the correctness properties by showing that terms are *strongly normalising*, meaning that every reduction sequence eventually terminates.

Let SN denote the set of strongly normalising terms, and $|t|$ the number of reduction steps in a reduction sequence starting from t. We also write $\mathtt{Red}(t)$ for the set of one-step reducts of t, i.e. $\mathtt{Red}(t) = \{r \mid t \longrightarrow_p r\}$.

We start our proof by observing that, excluding rules (β_n) and (β_b), all other rules strictly decrease a well-defined measure. This measure is invariant under commutativity and associativity of addition, meaning that terms like $t + r$ and $r + t$, or $(t + r) + s$ and $t + (r + s)$, receive the same value. We define this measure in Definition 3.7 and prove these properties in Theorem 3.8.

Definition 3.7. (Measure). *We define the following measure on terms:*

$$\|x\| = 0$$
$$\|\vec{0}\| = 0$$
$$\|\notin\| = 0$$
$$\||0\rangle\| = 0$$
$$\||1\rangle\| = 0$$
$$\||+\rangle\| = 0$$
$$\||-\rangle\| = 0$$
$$\|\mathsf{hd}\ t\| = \|t\| + 1$$
$$\|\mathsf{tl}\ t\| = \|t\| + 1$$
$$\|\pi^m t\| = \|t\| + m$$
$$\|\pi_\mathbb{X}^m t\| = \|t\| + m$$

$$\|\lambda x^\Psi.t\| = \|t\|$$
$$\|tr\| = (3\|t\| + 2)(3\|r\| + 2)$$
$$\|t \otimes r\| = \|t\| + \|r\| + 1$$
$$\|\Uparrow t\| = \|t\| + 5$$
$$\|\alpha.\Uparrow t\| = \|\Uparrow t\|$$
$$\|\alpha.t\| = 2\|t\| + 1$$
$$\|\Uparrow t + \Uparrow r\| = \max\{\|t\|, \|r\|\}$$
$$\|t + r\| = \|t\| + \|r\| + 2 \quad \text{(if not both are casts)}$$
$$\|?t \cdot r\| = \|t\| + \|r\|$$
$$\|?_\mathbb{X} t \cdot r\| = \|t\| + \|r\|$$

Theorem 3.8. (Measure decrease and invariance). *The measure defined in Definition 3.7 satisfies the following properties:*

- *If $t = r$ by the commutativity or associativity properties of $+$, then $\|t\| = \|r\|$.*
- *If $t \longrightarrow_p r$ using a rule other than (β_n) and (β_b), then $\|t\| > \|r\|$.*

Proof. We only provide an example here.
$$\|\alpha.(t+r)\| = 1 + 2\|t+r\| = 5 + 2\|t\| + 2\|r\| = 3 + \|\alpha.t\| + \|\alpha.r\|$$
$$= 1 + \|\alpha.t + \alpha.r\| > \|\alpha.t + \alpha.r\| \qquad \square$$

The previous result shows that all reduction sequences that do not involve β-redexes are strongly normalising. We now combine this with a standard reducibility argument to obtain the general strong normalisation theorem. As a first step, we show that linear combinations of strongly normalising terms are themselves strongly normalising.

Lemma 3.9. (Strong normalisation of linear combinations). *If $r_i \in \mathsf{SN}$ for all $1 \leq i \leq n$, then $\sum_{i=1}^{n} [\alpha_i.]r_i \in \mathsf{SN}$.*

Proof. By induction on the lexicographic order of $(\sum_{i=1}^{n} |r_i|,\ \|\sum_{i=1}^{n} [\alpha_i.]r_i\|)$.
$\square$

We now define the *interpretation of types* used in the strong normalisation argument. From this point onwards, we write $t : A$ to mean that the term t has type A in *any* context.

Definition 3.10. (Type interpretation). *Given a type A, its interpretation $[\![A]\!]$ is defined inductively as follows:*

$$[\![\nu]\!] = \{t : S(\nu) \mid t \in \mathsf{SN}\}$$
$$[\![\Psi_1 \times \Psi_2]\!] = \{t : S(\Psi_1 \times \Psi_2) \mid t \in \mathsf{SN}\}$$
$$[\![\Psi \Rightarrow A]\!] = \{t : S(\Psi \Rightarrow A) \mid \text{for all } r \in [\![\Psi]\!],\ tr \in [\![A]\!]\}$$
$$[\![S(A)]\!] = \{t : S(A) \mid t \in \mathsf{SN},\ \exists p\ \text{s.t.}\ t \longrightarrow_p^* \sum_i [\alpha_i.]r_i,\ r_i \in [\![A]\!]\ \text{on all paths}\}$$

with the convention that $\sum_{i=1}^{0}[\alpha_i.]r_i = \vec{0}$.

Since our language is first-order, this interpretation is sufficient. Traditionally, type interpretations are defined either by introduction or elimination. In our case, however, this distinction is not necessary for product types. This is because we define their interpretation using a superposition type rather than a direct product. This design choice is motivated by the interpretation of function types, which requires certain linearity properties on the argument type—properties that hold only when the type is a superposition.

A term $t \in [\![A]\!]$ is said to be *reducible*, and an application tr is said to be *neutral*. We write $\mathcal{N}$ for the set of neutral terms. In particular, expressions of the form $t?r \cdot s$ are in $\mathcal{N}$, since this is shorthand for $(?r \cdot s)t$.

We now establish the main properties of reducibility. What we refer to as **LIN1** and **LIN2** are in fact specific instances of the more general *adequacy* property (Theorem 3.13).

Lemma 3.11. (Reducibility properties). *For every type A, the following hold:*

(**CR1**) *If $t \in [\![A]\!]$, then $t \in \mathsf{SN}$.*
(**CR2**) *If $t \in [\![A]\!]$, then $\mathtt{Red}(t) \subseteq [\![A]\!]$.*
(**CR3**) *If $t : S(A)$, $t \in \mathcal{N}$, and $\mathtt{Red}(t) \subseteq [\![A]\!]$, then $t \in [\![A]\!]$.*
(**LIN1**) *If $t \in [\![A]\!]$ and $r \in [\![A]\!]$, then $t + r \in [\![A]\!]$.*
(**LIN2**) *If $t \in [\![A]\!]$, then $\alpha.t \in [\![A]\!]$.*
(**HAB**) $\vec{0} \in [\![A]\!]$, $\mathord{\xi} \in [\![A]\!]$, *and for every variable $x : A$, we have $x \in [\![A]\!]$.*

Proof. All of these properties are proved simultaneously by induction on the structure of the type. This unified presentation is essential, as several cases rely on the inductive hypotheses applied to their subcomponents. □

Lemma 3.12. (Compatibility with subtyping). *If $A \preceq B$, then $[\![A]\!] \subseteq [\![B]\!]$.* □

Theorem 3.13. (Adequacy). *If $\Gamma \vdash t : A$ and $\theta \vDash \Gamma$, then $\theta(t) \in [\![A]\!]$.*

Proof. By induction on the derivation of $\Gamma \vdash t : A$. □

Corollary 3.14. (Strong normalisation). *If $\Gamma \vdash t : A$, then $t \in \mathsf{SN}$.*

Proof. By Theorem 3.13, if $\theta \vDash \Gamma$, then $\theta(t) \in [\![A]\!]$. By Lemma 3.11. CR1, we have $[\![A]\!] \subseteq \mathsf{SN}$. Moreover, by Lemma 3.11. HAB, we know that $\mathtt{Id} \vDash \Gamma$. Therefore, $\mathtt{Id}(t) = t \in \mathsf{SN}$. □

4 An Arbitrary Number of Bases

4.1 Extending Lambda-SX with Multiple Distinct Bases

Up to this point, we have introduced Lambda-SX with two measurement bases: the computational basis $\mathbb{B}$ and an alternative basis $\mathbb{X}$. However, the design of the system do not need to be restricted to this choice. In fact, the calculus naturally generalises to an arbitrary collection of orthonormal bases.

Let $\mathbb{B}_i$ for $i = 1, \ldots, n$ denote a set of alternative bases, where each $\mathbb{B}_i = \{|{\uparrow_i}\rangle, |{\downarrow_i}\rangle\}$ is defined by a change of basis from the computational basis: $|{\uparrow_i}\rangle = \alpha_{i1}|0\rangle + \beta_{i1}|1\rangle$ and $|{\downarrow_i}\rangle = \alpha_{i2}|0\rangle + \beta_{i2}|1\rangle$ for some $\alpha_{i1}, \alpha_{i2}, \beta_{i1}, \beta_{i2} \in \mathbb{C}$. We assume that all $\mathbb{B}_i$ are distinct from the computational basis $\mathbb{B}$ (which retains its special role), and that one of them may coincide with $\mathbb{X}$.

We extend the grammar of atomic types as follows:

$$\nu ::= \mathbb{B} \mid \mathbb{B}_i$$

and the grammar of terms with corresponding constants and operations:

$$t ::= \cdots \mid |{\uparrow_i}\rangle \mid |{\downarrow_i}\rangle \mid ?_{\mathbb{B}_i} t \cdot t \mid \pi^m_{\mathbb{B}_i} t$$

Typing rules are extended in the natural way:

$$\frac{}{\vdash |{\uparrow_i}\rangle : \mathbb{B}_i} \, |{\uparrow_i}\rangle \qquad \frac{}{\vdash |{\downarrow_i}\rangle : \mathbb{B}_i} \, |{\downarrow_i}\rangle \qquad \frac{\Gamma \vdash t : S(\prod_{i=1}^n \nu_i) \quad 0 < m \leq n}{\Gamma \vdash \pi^m_{\mathbb{B}_i} t : \mathbb{B}^m_i \times S\left(\prod_{i=m+1}^n \nu_i\right)} \, S_{E_{\mathbb{B}_i}}$$

$$\frac{\Gamma \vdash t : A \quad \Gamma \vdash r : A}{\Gamma \vdash ?_{\mathbb{B}_i} t \cdot r : \mathbb{B}_i \Rightarrow A} \, \mathsf{If}_{\mathbb{B}_i} \qquad \frac{\Gamma \vdash t : \mathbb{B}_i}{\Gamma \vdash \Uparrow t : S(\mathbb{B})} \, \Uparrow_{\mathbb{B}_i}$$

The operational semantics is similarly extended with the following rules:

$$|{\uparrow_i}\rangle ?_{\mathbb{B}_i} t \cdot r \longrightarrow_1 t \qquad \qquad (\mathsf{if}_\uparrow)$$
$$|{\downarrow_i}\rangle ?_{\mathbb{B}_i} t \cdot r \longrightarrow_1 r \qquad \qquad (\mathsf{if}_\downarrow)$$
$$\Uparrow |{\uparrow_i}\rangle \longrightarrow_1 \alpha_{i1} \cdot |0\rangle + \beta_{i1} \cdot |1\rangle \qquad (\mathsf{cast}_{|\uparrow\rangle})$$
$$\Uparrow |{\downarrow_i}\rangle \longrightarrow_1 \alpha_{i2} \cdot |0\rangle + \beta_{i2} \cdot |1\rangle \qquad (\mathsf{cast}_{|\downarrow\rangle})$$
$$\pi^m_{\mathbb{B}_i} \left(\sum_{j=1}^e \alpha_j \cdot \bigotimes_{h=1}^n |b_{hj}\rangle \right) \longrightarrow_{p_k} |k\rangle \otimes |\phi_k\rangle \qquad (\mathsf{proy}_{\mathbb{B}_i})$$
$$\pi^m_{\mathbb{B}_i} \lightning \longrightarrow_1 \lightning \qquad \qquad (\lightning_{\pi_{\mathbb{B}_i}})$$

The definition of $|k\rangle$ and $|\phi_k\rangle$ is analogous to the π and π_X cases.

Such flexibility is crucial for modelling quantum procedures that involve intermediate measurements in different bases—for example, variants of phase estimation or error-correction protocols.

A subtle issue arises when a single quantum state belongs to more than one basis. For instance, consider a basis $\mathbb{B}_1 = \{|0\rangle, -|1\rangle\}$. In this case, the vector $|0\rangle$ may be typed both as $\mathbb{B}$ and $\mathbb{B}_1$, but $\mathbb{B}$ and $\mathbb{B}_1$ are not subtypes of each other. Therefore, it is not safe to allow a term like $|0\rangle$ to be freely assigned both types: one must commit to a single basis when typing such terms.

To avoid ambiguity, in this first extension we assume that no basis $\mathbb{B}_i$ shares any element (or scalar multiple of an element) with the computational basis $\mathbb{B}$ or with any other $\mathbb{B}_j$ for $j \neq i$. This restriction simplifies reasoning and ensures disjointness at the type level.

However, in the next section, we revisit this restriction and propose an alternative typing discipline that allows overlapping bases, by making explicit the relationship between different types for the same state.

All the correctness properties from Sect. 3 generalise straightforwardly to this extended system, and thus, we omit their proofs.

4.2 Extending Subtyping Across Overlapping Bases

Let us return to our earlier example, where $\mathbb{B}_1 = \{|0\rangle, -|1\rangle\}$. In this case, we would like $|0\rangle$ to be typable both as $\mathbb{B}$ and as $\mathbb{B}_1$. To make this possible, we introduce a new type $\mathbb{Q}_{|0\rangle}$, representing the one-dimensional subspace spanned by the vector $|0\rangle$, and require that $\mathbb{Q}_{|0\rangle} \preceq \mathbb{B}$ and $\mathbb{Q}_{|0\rangle} \preceq \mathbb{B}_1$. Such types $\mathbb{Q}_{|\psi\rangle}$ will not correspond to measurement bases, but rather to generators of linear subspaces.

Recall that the type $S(A)$ is interpreted as the linear span of the set denoted by A. Consequently, $S(\mathbb{Q}_{|0\rangle})$ is a strict subspace of $S(\mathbb{B})$, meaning in particular that $S(\mathbb{B}) \not\preceq S(\mathbb{Q}_{|0\rangle})$. This distinction is crucial: throughout the paper we rely on the fact that $S(\mathbb{B}) \approx S(\mathbb{X})$, a property that does not hold in general when introducing $\mathbb{Q}_{|\psi\rangle}$ types. To maintain soundness and consistency, we must refine the subtyping relation accordingly.

Let $\mathbf{L}$ denote the class of linear space generators, indexed up to m. Since there are n alternative bases besides the computational basis $\mathbb{B}$, and each base consists of two orthogonal qubit states, we allow m to range from 3 to $2n+1$ to accommodate all possible subspace generators:

$$\mathbb{Q} := \mathbb{Q}_0 \mid \ldots \mid \mathbb{Q}_m \qquad \text{Generators of linear spaces } (\mathbf{L})$$
$$\nu := \mathbb{B} \mid \mathbb{B}_1 \mid \ldots \mid \mathbb{B}_n \qquad \text{Atomic types } (\mathbf{A})$$
$$\mathbb{M} := \nu \mid \mathbb{M} \times \mathbb{M} \qquad \text{Measurement bases } (\mathbf{B})$$
$$\mathbb{G} := \mathbb{Q} \mid \nu \qquad \text{Single-qubit types } (\mathbf{G})$$
$$\Psi := \mathbb{G} \mid S(\Psi) \mid \Psi \times \Psi \qquad \text{Qubit types } (\mathbf{Q})$$

As explained, the subtyping relation must be refined to reflect that $S(\mathbb{Q}_{|\psi\rangle})$ may be a strict subspace of $S(\nu)$. For arbitrary atomic bases ν_1 and ν_2, we still have $S(\nu_1) \approx S(\nu_2)$; however, this is not the case for spaces generated by $\mathbb{Q}_{|\psi\rangle}$ and $\mathbb{Q}_{|\phi\rangle}$ in general. To accommodate these distinctions, we introduce the following subtyping rules:

$$\prod_{i=0}^{a} \left(\left(\prod_{j=0}^{b_i} \nu_{ij} \right) \times \left(\prod_{k=0}^{c_i} \mathbb{Q}_{ik} \right) \right) \preceq S \left(\prod_{i=0}^{a} \left(\left(\prod_{j=0}^{b_i} \nu'_{ij} \right) \times \left(\prod_{k=0}^{c_i} \mathbb{Q}_{ik} \right) \right) \right)$$

$$\overline{\mathbb{Q}_{|0\rangle} \preceq \mathbb{B}} \qquad \overline{\mathbb{Q}_{|1\rangle} \preceq \mathbb{B}} \qquad \frac{|\psi\rangle \in \mathbb{B}_i}{\mathbb{Q}_{|\psi\rangle} \preceq \mathbb{B}_i}$$

These rules allow each $\mathbb{Q}_{|\psi\rangle}$ to be used in any basis containing $|\psi\rangle$, preserving semantic distinctions across bases. This enables precise typing of states that appear in multiple contexts and supports richer quantum programs involving basis reuse. This extended system preserves the core properties proved for Lambda-SX in Sect. 3. The adaptation is straightforward.

Example 4.1. (Basis-sensitive choice). The type $\mathbb{Q}_{|0\rangle}$, introduced in Sect. 4.2, allows a single quantum state to be treated as belonging to multiple bases. For instance, $|0\rangle$ belongs to both the computational basis $\mathbb{B} = \{|0\rangle, |1\rangle\}$ and the alternative basis $\mathbb{Z} = \{|0\rangle, -|1\rangle\}$, and we have $\mathbb{Q}_{|0\rangle} \preceq \mathbb{B}$ and $\mathbb{Q}_{|0\rangle} \preceq \mathbb{Z}$.

This enables the same state to be interpreted differently in different contexts. Suppose we have: $\mathbf{f} : \mathbb{B} \Rightarrow S(\mathbb{B})$ and $\mathbf{g} : \mathbb{Z} \Rightarrow S(\mathbb{B})$. Then both $\mathbf{choice}_\mathbb{B} = \lambda x^{\mathbb{Q}_{|0\rangle}}.\mathbf{f}(x)$ and $\mathbf{choice}_\mathbb{Z} = \lambda x^{\mathbb{Q}_{|0\rangle}}.\mathbf{g}(x)$ are well-typed. We can also define a basis-sensitive choice controlled by a qubit: $\mathbf{choice} = \lambda y^\mathbb{B}.\lambda x^{\mathbb{Q}_{|0\rangle}}.y?\mathbf{f}(x)\cdot\mathbf{g}(x)$. This term, of type $\mathbb{B} \Rightarrow \mathbb{Q}_{|0\rangle} \Rightarrow S(\mathbb{B})$, illustrates how $\mathbb{Q}_{|\psi\rangle}$ types enable basis-dependent behaviour without unsafe coercions or ad hoc annotations. While the example is simple, it demonstrates how the extended subtyping system supports flexible quantum program structuring, paving the way for optimisations based on contextual basis interpretation.

5 Conclusion and Future Work

We have introduced Lambda-SX, a quantum lambda-calculus that supports control over multiple measurement bases and explicit typing for quantum states shared across them. Through a range of small illustrative examples we have shown that tracking duplicability relative to distinct bases enables concise and compositional encodings of quantum procedures. This expressiveness enables facilitates modular descriptions of basis-sensitive constructs, such as conditional control and Hadamard-based branching, while preserving key meta-theoretical properties like strong normalisation.

While Lambda-SX is presented as a proof-of-concept, it opens avenues for exploring richer type disciplines that more closely mirror quantum semantics. Compared to previous approaches that rely on a single fixed basis, our calculus enables direct reasoning about transformations and measurements involving incompatible bases, without resorting to meta-level annotations. The fine-grained typing system not only enforces safety properties like strong normalisation but also provides a framework for understanding and structuring quantum algorithms in a modular, basis-sensitive way.

As future work, we aim to provide a categorical model for Lambda-SX. The foundational results for Lambda-S and Lambda-S_1 [13–15] already establish a connection between quantum control and adjunctions between Cartesian and monoidal categories. Lambda-SX enriches this picture by integrating multiple measurement bases as first-class citizens in the type system. A natural direction is to explore categorical semantics where each measurement basis corresponds to a distinct comonadic modality, and cast operations are interpreted as morphisms connecting these modalities or embedding subspaces into larger measurement spaces, as formalised by the extended subtyping relation.

This fits into a broader research programme toward a computational quantum logic, as outlined in [9], which aims to provide a Curry-Howard-Lambek-style correspondence for quantum computation. In this programme, Lambda-S represents the computational side of this correspondence, while a linear proof language—such as $\mathcal{L}^S$ [10]—captures the logical side. Preliminary results suggest that quantum computation could be understood as a structural dual to intuitionistic linear logic, with semantic models built on adjunctions between symmetric monoidal categories and their Cartesian or additive counterparts. Extending these models to accommodate the richer structure of Lambda-SX, and even exploring connections to graphical calculi such as ZX, may yield new insights into both the foundations and practical implementation of quantum programming languages.

Lambda-SX opens up a new perspective on how the structure of quantum computation can be captured within a typed lambda-calculus, supporting fine control over duplication, measurement, and basis transition—all of which are essential ingredients in the development of expressive and robust quantum programming formalisms.

Acknowledgment. This work is supported by the European Union through the MSCA SE project QCOMICAL (Grant Agreement ID: 101182520), by the Plan France 2030 through the PEPR integrated project EPiQ (ANR-22-PETQ-0007), and by the Uruguayan CSIC grant 22520220100073UD.

References

1. Altenkirch, T., Grattage, J.: A functional quantum programming language. In: Proceedings of the 20th Annual IEEE Symposium on Logic in Computer Science (LICS 2005), pp. 249–258 (2005)
2. Arrighi, P., Dowek, G.: Lineal: a linear-algebraic Lambda-calculus. Logical Methods Comput. Sci. **13**(1:8) (2017)
3. Assaf, A., Díaz-Caro, A., Perdrix, S., Tasson, C., Valiron, B.: Call-by-value, call-by-name and the vectorial behaviour of the algebraic lambda-calculus. Logical Methods Comput. Sci. **10**(4:8) (2014)
4. Carette, J., Jeunen, C., Kaarsgaard, R., Sabry, A.: How to bake a quantum π. In: Proceedings of the ACM on Programming Languages, vol. 8, pp. 236:1–236:29 (2024)
5. Chardonnet, K., de Visme, M., Valiron, B., Vilmart, R.: The many-worlds calculus. Logical Methods Comput. Sci. **21**(2:13) (2025)
6. Choudhury, V., Gay, S.J.: The duality of λ-abstraction. In: Proceedings of the ACM on Programming Languages, vol. 9, pp. 12:332–12:361 (2025)
7. Clairambault, P., de Visme, M.: Full abstraction for the quantum lambda-calculus. In: Proceedings of the ACM on Programming Languages, vol. 4, pp. 63:1–63:28 (2019)
8. Coecke, B., Duncan, R.: Interacting quantum observables. In: Aceto, L., Damgård, I., Goldberg, L.A., Halldórsson, M.M., Ingólfsdóttir, A., Walukiewicz, I. (eds.) ICALP 2008. LNCS, vol. 5126, pp. 298–310. Springer, Heidelberg (2008). https://doi.org/10.1007/978-3-540-70583-3_25
9. Díaz-Caro, A.: Towards a computational quantum logic: an overview of an ongoing research program. Invited talk at CiE 2025: Computability in Europe. To appear at LNCS (2025)
10. Díaz-Caro, A., Dowek, G.: A linear linear lambda-calculus. Math. Struct. Comput. Sci. **34**(10), 1103–1137 (2024)
11. Díaz-Caro, A., Dowek, G., Rinaldi, J.P.: Two linearities for quantum computing in the lambda calculus. Biosystems **186**, 104012 (2019)

12. Díaz-Caro, A., Guillermo, M., Miquel, A., Valiron, B.: Realizability in the unitary sphere. In: Proceedings of the 34th Annual ACM/IEEE Symposium on Logic in Computer Science (LICS 2019), pp. 1–13 (2019)
13. Díaz-Caro, A., Malherbe, O.: A categorical construction for the computational definition of vector spaces. Appl. Categ. Struct. **28**(5), 807–844 (2020)
14. Díaz-Caro, A., Malherbe, O.: Quantum control in the unitary sphere: Lambda-s_1 and its categorical model. Logical Methods Comput. Sci. **18**(3:32) (2022)
15. Díaz-Caro, A., Malherbe, O.: A concrete model for a typed linear algebraic lambda calculus. Math. Struct. Comput. Sci. **34**(1), 1–44 (2023)
16. Girard, J.Y.: Linear logic. Theoret. Comput. Sci. **50**(1), 1–101 (1987)
17. Green, A.S., Lumsdaine, P.L., Ross, N.J., Selinger, P., Valiron, B.: Quipper: a scalable quantum programming language. ACM SIGPLAN Notices **48**(6), 333–342 (2013)
18. Heunen, C., Kaarsgaard, R.: Quantum information effects. In: Proceedings of the ACM on Programming Languages, vol. 6, pp. 2:1–2:27 (2021)
19. Kleene, S.C.: On the interpretation of intuitionistic number theory. J. Symb. Log. **10**(4), 109–124 (1945)
20. Knill, E.: Conventions for quantum pseudocode. Technical Report LAUR-96-2724, Los Alamos National Laboratory (1996)
21. Paykin, J., Rand, R., Zdancewic, S.: QWIRE: a core language for quantum circuits. ACM SIGPLAN Notices **52**(1), 846–858 (2017)
22. Selinger, P.: Towards a quantum programming language. Math. Struct. Comput. Sci. **14**(4), 527–586 (2004)
23. Selinger, P., Valiron, B.: A lambda calculus for quantum computation with classical control. Math. Struct. Comput. Sci. **16**(3), 527–552 (2006)
24. Sørensen, M.H.B., Urzyczyn, P.: Lectures on the Curry-Howard Isomorphism. Elsevier, Amsterdam; Oxford (2006)
25. Voichick, F., Li, L., Rand, R., Hicks, M.: Qubity: a unified language for quantum and classical computing. In: Proceedings of the ACM on Programming Languages, vol. 7, pp. 32:921–32:951 (2023)
26. Wootters, W.K., Zurek, W.H.: A single quantum cannot be cloned. Nature **299**, 802–803 (1982)

Program Analysis, Specifications, and Decision Procedures

Checking Consistency of Event-Driven Traces

Parosh Aziz Abdulla[1,2], Mohamed Faouzi Atig[1], R. Govind[1(✉)], Samuel Grahn[1], and Ramanathan S. Thinniyam[1]

[1] Uppsala University, Uppsala, Sweden
{parosh.abdulla,mohamed_faouzi.atig,govind.rajanbabu,
samuel.grahn,ramanathan.s.thinniyam}@it.uu.se
[2] Mälardalen University, Västerås, Sweden

Abstract. Event-driven programming is a popular paradigm where the flow of execution is controlled by two features: (1) shared memory and (2) sending and receiving of messages between multiple *handler threads* (just called handler). Each handler has a mailbox (modelled as a queue) for receiving messages, with the constraint that the handler processes its messages sequentially. Executions of messages by different handlers may be interleaved. A central problem in this setting is checking whether a candidate execution is *consistent* with the semantics of event-driven programs. In this paper, we propose an axiomatic semantics for event-driven programs based on the standard notion of *traces* (also known as execution graphs). We prove the equivalence of axiomatic and operational semantics. This allows us to rephrase the consistency problem axiomatically, resulting in the *event-driven consistency problem*: checking whether a given trace is consistent. We analyze the computational complexity of this problem and show that it is NP-complete, even when the number of handler threads is bounded. We then identify a tractable fragment: in the absence of nested posting, where handlers do not post new messages while processing a message, consistency checking can be performed in polynomial time. Finally, we implement our approach in a prototype tool and report on experimental results on a wide range of benchmarks.

Keywords: Event-driven programs · Consistency-checking · Verification

1 Introduction

Event-Driven (ED) programming has emerged as a powerful paradigm for building scalable and responsive systems capable of handling a large number of user interactions concurrently [8,14,19,20,26,32,33,44]. It is widely used across various domains, including file systems [38], high-performance servers [15], systems programming [16], and smartphone applications [39]. Event-driven programs have become so common that they are considered a core topic under *Programming Fundamentals* according to IEEE and ACM computing curricula [34]. ED programming extends multi-threaded shared-memory programming through the use of messages, thus using both shared-memory as well as message-passing.

Verification of ED programs, in addition to the usual challenges associated with shared-memory multi-threaded program verification, has to deal with the non-determinism introduced by the sending and receiving of messages between multiple *handler threads* (just called handler). Each handler has a mailbox (modelled as FIFO queue, following [27,35]) for receiving messages, with the constraint that the handler processes its messages sequentially. Executions of messages by different handlers may be interleaved. A well-established technique for verifying multi-threaded programs is stateless model checking (SMC)[23], which has proven effective for detecting concurrency bugs. SMC has been implemented in several tools - including VeriSoft[24], CHESS[41], Concuerror[12], NIDHUGG [1], rInspect [49], CDSCHECKER [42], RCMC [28], and GENMC [31] - and applied to realistic programs [25,30]. To efficiently explore execution traces, SMC tools often employ dynamic partial order reduction (DPOR) [1,2,6,7,13,22,43,48]. DPOR avoids redundant exploration by recognizing and pruning equivalent executions. DPOR does this by exploring the space of all *traces* (also called execution graphs [28]). Intuitively, a trace is a summary of the important concurrency information contained in a program execution, represented as a directed graph whose edges are the union of certain relations (defined further below).

A central component of DPOR techniques is *consistency checking* (e.g., see Sect. 5 of [5] and Sect. 4 of [29]), which involves determining whether a candidate trace is realizable, i.e., whether there exists an execution of the program that respects all the relations implied by the trace. The consistency checking problem has been extensively studied on its own for different programming models, notably by Gibbons and Korach (for Sequential Consistency) [21] from 1997 and continued in several works (e.g., [10,11,47]).

We refer to the consistency checking in the event-driven setting as the event-driven sequential consistency problem. In this work, we study the event-driven sequential consistency problem. We first propose an axiomatic semantics for ED programs. We then establish the equivalence between the operational and axiomatic semantics of ED programs. Next, we explore the complexity landscape of the event-driven sequential consistency problem.

Concretely, we consider as input a trace represented by a set of events and relations among them. The goal is to determine whether this trace can arise from a valid event-driven execution. These relations include *Program Order* (the order in which instructions are fetched from the code associated with the message), *Read-From* relation (which relates each read to the write that it reads from), *Coherence Order* (which specifies the order between writes on the same variable). The above relations already exist for general multi-threaded shared-memory programs. In addition, our traces contain the *Execution Order* (which fixes the order in which the messages of the same handlers are executed), *Message order* (ordering the posting of messages to the same handler) and *Posted-*

by (relating the instruction posting the message to the instruction starting the execution of the message). We prove that event-driven consistency problem is NP-complete, *even when the number of handler threads is bounded*. On the positive side, we identify a tractable fragment: in the absence of nested posting - where handlers do not post new messages while processing a message - consistency checking can be performed in polynomial time. Finally, we implement our approach in a prototype tool and report on experimental results on a wide range of event-driven benchmarks, both synthetic and from real-world event-driven programs.

Related Work. Race detection in event-driven programs has been studied [37,45]. There has also been work on partial order reduction in this setting [3,35] and stateless model checking [27]. The paper [3] considers the consistency problem in the case of mailboxes modeled as multisets, showing its NP-hardness. In the specialised setting of ED programs for real-time systems, the work [18] shows that checking safety properties is undecidable. The robustness problem, which asks if a given an ED program has the same behaviour as if it were to be run on a single thread, has been studied in [9]. Several efforts have been made to provide language support for ED programming such as Tasks [17] as well as the P programming language [16]. In particular, P programming was built to provide safe asynchronous ED programming from the ground up and used to implement and validate the USB driver in Windows 8. Finally, the consistency problem has been extensively studied for different programming languages (e.g., [3,10,11,21,47]). However, as far as we know, this is first time that the consistency problem is studied in the context of ED programs with FIFO queues as mailboxes.

A full version of the paper is available at [4] with all the missing proofs and more experimental results.

2 Event-Driven Programs: Syntax and Semantics

In the following, we will first give the syntax of Event-driven (ED) programs. Then, we will describe the operational semantics of ED programs. Next, we will define the notion of traces of ED programs and give an equivalent axiomatic definition of traces. Finally, we will define the event-driven consistency problem.

2.1 Syntax of Event-Driven Programs

The syntax of event-driven programs we consider is shown in Fig. 1. An event-driven program $\mathcal{P}$ has a finite set H of *handlers*[1], each $h \in H$ having a finite set R_h of *local registers*. We denote $R = \bigcup_h R_h$. The handlers interact via a finite

---

[1] ED programs often have designated handler threads with mailboxes as well as *non-handler* threads which do not have an associated mailbox. However, we can think of a non-handler thread as a handler to which a message is never posted and hence simplify notation by assuming that all threads are handlers.

set X of *(shared) variables*, as well as via a finite set M_h of *messages* which are posted to the mailbox b_h associated with each handler h. We assume that the local registers and shared variables take values from a data domain D. The message sets of different handlers are assumed to be disjoint with $M = \bigcup_h M_h$ the set of all messages. Each message has a *message name* and comprises of a sequence of instructions, ending in a special instruction *last* which indicates the end of the message.

Each instruction consists of a unique *label* followed by a *statement*. A statement of the form $<var> = <reg>$ in the grammar indicates the writing of a register value into a shared variable. A statement of the form $<reg> = <var>$ indicates the read operation of a shared variable which is then stored in the local register of a handler. More complex manipulations of data domain values are assumed to be performed within handlers through the use of *expressions* as in $<reg> = <exp>$. These expressions are assumed to only use local registers. The **goto** statement moves the program control to the indicated label, with conditional branching allowed using the if construct. The condition *cond* in the if statement uses only the local registers of the handler which executes the statement. The post statement posts a message to the mailbox of the indicated handler. We assume that the labels in $\mathcal{P}$ form a finite set L and there is a successor function $\text{succ} \colon L \mapsto L$ which indicates the flow of program control. Each label $l \in L$ has an associated instruction $\text{inst}(l)$ which is given by the function inst.

$<prog> ::=$ **vars** $<var>^*$ **handlers** $<handler>^*$ **msgs** $<msg>^*$
$<handler> ::= <handlerId>$ **regs** $<reg>^*$
$<msg> ::= <msgname> <inst>^* <label> : <last>$
$<inst> ::= <label> : <stmt>$
$<stmt> ::= <var> = <reg> \mid <reg> = <var> \mid <reg> = <exp>$
$if <cond>$ **goto** $: <label> \mid$ **goto** $: <label>$
$post(<handlerId>, <msgname>)$

Fig. 1. Syntax of Event-Driven Programs.

2.2 Operational Semantics of Event-Driven Programs

We now describe the operational semantics of ED programs, focusing on how handlers interact with mailboxes during the execution of an event-driven program.

Handler. A handler h repeatedly extracts a message from its mailbox, executes the code of the message to completion, then extracts another message and executes its code, and so on. This extraction is modelled as a **get** event. We use a counter at each handler in order to generate unique message IDs. Note that execution of messages by different handlers could be interleaved. Further, while executing the code of a message by a handler, messages could be added to its mailbox. The execution of a message is done one instruction at a time. At any point of time, a handler has at most one *active message* which is being executed. An underlying *nondeterministic scheduler* decides which handler to run at a step.

Mailbox. A mailbox is a labelled transition system MB $= \langle \mathscr{B}, \beta_{\text{init}}, \{\texttt{get}, \texttt{post}\}, \Sigma, \rightarrow \rangle$, where $\mathscr{B}$ is the set of configurations of MB, $\beta_{\text{init}} \in \mathscr{B}$ is the initial configuration, and Σ is the set of messages (including a special symbol $\bot$). We assume that the operations that can be performed on MB are $\{\texttt{get}, \texttt{post}\}$ and the transition relation $\rightarrow \subseteq \mathscr{B} \times \{\texttt{get}, \texttt{post}\} \times \Sigma \times \mathscr{B}$ specifies the semantics of the operations. In this paper, the operations are of two kinds: $\texttt{get}$ which downloads a message from the mailbox, and $\texttt{post}$ which adds a new message into the mailbox. Since the mailbox is modelled as a FIFO queue and follows the first-in-first-out semantics, we have $\mathscr{B} = \Sigma^*$ and $\beta_{\text{init}} = \varepsilon$. We write $\beta \xrightarrow{o,\sigma} \beta'$ to denote that the message σ is returned by (resp. posted by) the operation o if it is a $\texttt{get}$ (resp. $\texttt{post}$) and $\beta = \beta' \cdot \sigma$ (resp. $\beta' = \sigma \cdot \beta'$), while transitioning from configuration β to configuration β'. A *run* $\rho = \beta_{\text{init}} \xrightarrow{o_1,\sigma_1} \beta_1 \xrightarrow{o_2,\sigma_2} \ldots \beta_n$ of MB is a finite sequence of transitions starting from the initial configuration β_{init}.

Configuration of ED-Programs. We use $h, g, \ldots$ for handlers, m for messages, x,y,z for shared variables, and a,b,c for local registers. Members of D will be denoted by v. Configurations of programs and mailboxes will be denoted by α and β respectively. The local state $s_h = \langle \texttt{val}, \beta, \texttt{line}, mid, mcount \rangle$ of a handler h is a tuple containing the valuation $\texttt{val} \colon R_h \mapsto D$ of its local registers, the configuration of its mailbox β, $\texttt{line}$ which is the label of the next instruction that will be executed by the handler, the message id mid of its currently active message and a counter $mcount$. The valuation function $\texttt{val}$ is extended to expressions in the standard way. When a message m is to be posted by handler h to the mailbox of handler h', the local counter $mcount$ is incremented by 1. A unique mid $(h, mcount)$ is generated and associated with the message instance. We will write $s_h.\texttt{val}, s_h.\beta$ etc. to denote the components of s_h. Given a particular message name m, let $m.\text{init}$ denote the label of the first instruction in the code of m.

A configuration $\alpha = (\{s_h \mid h \in H\}, \nu)$ of a program consists of the local state of each handler h along with a valuation $\nu \colon X \mapsto D$ of the shared variables. We sometimes write $\alpha.\nu$, $\alpha.s_h$ etc. to denote the valuation of global variables and the local state of handler h respectively, in configuration α. A program $\mathcal{P}$ starts in some initial configuration[2] $\alpha_0 = (\{s_h^0 \mid h \in H\}, \nu)$ which satisfies the condition that for each handler h, we have $s_h^0.\texttt{line} = m.\text{init}$ for some $m \in M_h$ i.e. the execution of some message is initialised in each handler. Note that there is no post event associated with this initialization. Furthermore, the mailboxes are all empty i.e. $s_h^0.\beta = \beta_{\text{init}}$ for all h, $s_h^0.mid = (h, 0)$ and $s_h^0.mcount = 1$.

We have four kinds of transitions:

- $\alpha \xrightarrow{\langle h, write, x, v \rangle} \alpha'$ iff $\texttt{inst}(\alpha.s_h.\texttt{line}) = l_i \colon x = a \wedge \alpha.s_h.\texttt{val}(a) = v$ and α' is s.t. $\nu \leftarrow \nu(x \leftarrow v), s_h.\texttt{line} \leftarrow \texttt{succ}(s_h.\texttt{line})$.

---

[2] Note that we intentionally do not specify the initial values of local registers and shared variables, or the initial message each handler should execute, as the event-driven consistency problem treats the program code as a black box. However, our framework can be easily extended to take into account such initial conditions.

- $\alpha \xrightarrow{\langle h, read, x \rangle} \alpha'$ iff $\mathtt{inst}(\alpha.s_h.\mathtt{line}) = l : a = x$ and α' is s.t. $s_h.\mathtt{val} \leftarrow s_h.\mathtt{val}(a \leftarrow \nu(x)), s_h.\mathtt{line} \leftarrow \mathtt{succ}(s_h.\mathtt{line})$.
- $\alpha \xrightarrow{\langle h, post, h', newmid \rangle} \alpha'$ iff $\alpha.s_h.\mathtt{line} = l : post(h', m), \alpha.s_{h'}.\beta \xrightarrow{post,(m, newmid)} \beta'$, $newmid = (h, \alpha.s_h.mcount)$ and α' is s.t. $s_{h'}.\beta \leftarrow \beta', s_h.mcount \leftarrow s_h.mcount + 1, s_h.\mathtt{line} \leftarrow \mathtt{succ}(s_h.\mathtt{line})$.
- $\alpha \xrightarrow{\langle h, get, mid \rangle} \alpha'$ iff $\alpha.s_h.\mathtt{line} = l : last, \alpha.s_h.\beta_h \xrightarrow{get,(m,mid)}_{\mathrm{MB}} \beta'$ and α' is s.t. $s_h.\beta \leftarrow \beta', s_h.mid \leftarrow mid, s_h.\mathtt{line} \leftarrow m.\mathtt{init}$.

Given a tuple/mapping f, we use $f(x \leftarrow d)$ to denote the tuple/mapping f' which agrees with f on all parameters except x, on which it takes the value d. We write $f(x \leftarrow d)$ (resp. $f(x_1 \leftarrow d_1, \ldots, x_n \leftarrow d_n)$) instead of $f(g \leftarrow g(x \leftarrow d))$ (resp. $f(x_1 \leftarrow d_1) \cdots (x_n \leftarrow d_n)$) when it is clear from the context.

An *execution sequence* or run ρ of program $\mathcal{P}$ is a finite sequence of transitions $\alpha_0 \xrightarrow{a_1} \alpha_1 \xrightarrow{a_2} \ldots \xrightarrow{a_n} \alpha_n$ starting with an initial configuration α_0.

2.3 Events, Traces and Axiomatic Consistency

In this subsection, we introduce an axiomatic semantics for ED programs. We first define the relevant types of events and then formalize the notion of a trace.

Events. An event is a collection of information about a transition that is meant to be made visible. Transitions which contain such information are called event-transitions (observe that local-transitions do not have corresponding events). There are four types of event-transitions: reads, writes, posts and gets. The event is obtained from the event-transition by dropping the mid and newmid information. Note that newmid is basically a newly created mid written this way for clarity. Formally,

- A write event is a tuple $e = \langle h, write, x, v \rangle$ which denotes the writing of the value v by handler h into global variable x. We say $e.var = x$ and $e.val = v$. We denote by $\mathscr{W}_x$ the set of all write events on x.
- A read event is a tuple $e = \langle h, read, x \rangle$ which denotes the reading of the value stored in global variable x by handler h. We say $e.var = x$. We denote by $\mathscr{R}_x$ the set of all read events on x.
- A post event is a tuple $e = \langle h, post, h' \rangle$ which denotes the posting of a message by handler h to the mailbox of the handler h'. We write $e.sender$ to denote h and $e.receiver$ to denote h'.
- A get event is a tuple $e = \langle h, \mathtt{get} \rangle$ which denotes the downloading of a message by handler h.

In general, we write $e.h$ to denote the handler on which a message is being executed. In particular, $e.h$ is the same as $e.sender$ for a post event. Given a transition $\alpha \xrightarrow{a} \alpha'$ we write $e(a)$ for the event corresponding to a if a is an event-transition. In case the transitions are indexed e.g. a_i then we just write e_i instead of $e(a_i)$. For an event e, we denote by $e.type$ the *type* of the event i.e. whether it is a read, write, post or get. Note that unless necessary, we omit handler identifiers from events for readability.

Traces. Let rels = $\{\mathsf{rf}, \mathsf{co}, \mathsf{po}, \mathsf{eo}, \mathsf{pb}, \mathsf{mo}\}$ be a set of relation names. A trace is a directed graph $\tau = (E, \Delta)$ where E is a finite set of events, $\Delta \subseteq E \times \mathsf{rels} \times E$ is a set of edges on E with labels from rels. Let $E_h = \{e \mid e.h = h\}$ be the set of events occurring on handler h. Let $G_h = \{e \mid e.type = get\} \cap E_h$ and $P_h = \{e \mid e.type = post \wedge e.receiver = h\}$ be respectively the get events of handler h and the post events to h. The following conditions are satisfied by Δ:

- rf: (reads-from) maps each read instruction to a write instruction. For each $x \in X$ and each $e \in \mathscr{R}_\mathsf{x}$, there exists exactly one $e' \in \mathscr{W}_\mathsf{x}$ such that e' rf e.
- po: (program order) is a union of total orders on the set of events E_h which occur on a particular handler. This is a total ordering on all events which happen as part of the execution of a particular message instance. Formally, we have
  - For any $e \in E_h \setminus G_h$, there exists at most one event $e' \in G_h$ s.t. e' po e.
  - For every $e, e'' \in E_h \setminus G_h$ s.t. e' po e and e' po e'' for some $e' \in G_h$, it is the case that either e po e'' or e'' po e.
  - Let E'_h be the set of events $e \in E_h \setminus G_h$ s.t. there is no event $e' \in G_h$ with e' po e. Then, po is a total order over E'_h. Furthermore, for every $e \in E'_h$ and $e' \in G_h$, we have e po e'. This means that all events of the initial message are ordered before the events of any other message.
- co: (coherence order) For each pair of writes $e, e' \in \mathscr{W}_\mathsf{x}$, either e co e' or e' co e. Note that co is a total order on the set $\mathscr{W}_\mathsf{x}$ for each $x \in X$.
- eo: (execution order) is a total order on the set of get events occurring on a handler. Let $e, e' \in G_h$ for some h. Then either e eo e' or e' eo e.
- pb: (posted by) is a relation which relates each get event on a handler to the corresponding post event. In other words, it is a bijection between the sets P_h and G_h: for each $e \in G_h$ there is exactly one $e' \in P_h$ s.t. e' pb e.
- mo: (message order) orders the events that posts messages to the mailbox of a particular handler. For every $e, e' \in P_h$ either e mo e' or e' mo e.

A partial trace is a subgraph of a trace. A partial trace $\tau' = (E', \Delta')$ is said to *extend* a partial trace $\tau = (E, \Delta)$ if $E \subseteq E', \Delta \subseteq \Delta'$. A linearization $\pi = (E, \leq_\pi)$ of a partial trace $\tau = (E, \Delta)$ is a total ordering $\leq_\pi$ satisfying $\delta \in \Delta \Rightarrow \delta \in \leq_\pi$.

Traces of Programs. Given a program $\mathcal{P}$ and its execution $\rho = \alpha_0 \xrightarrow{a_1} \alpha_1 \xrightarrow{a_2} \ldots \xrightarrow{a_n} \alpha_n$, we define the set $E(\rho) = \{e_i \mid a_i \text{ is an event-transition}\}$ to be the *event set of* ρ. Clearly ρ induces a total order $\leq_\rho$ on $E(\rho)$ defined in the natural way: $e_i \leq_\rho e_j$ iff $i \leq j$. Each get event-transition specifies an mid for the message instance which is obtained from the mailbox. The execution of this message instance may contain more event-transitions later in ρ. Hence we extend the notion of mid to all non-get event-transitions in the following way. For each event e_i which is a not a get event, let e_j be the first preceding get event e_j in the order ρ such that $e_i.h = e_j.h$, if such an event exists. We assign the message id $a_j.mid$ to the transition a_i, since by the event-driven semantics, only one message can be executed by a handler at any point in time. If no such get event exists, then we assign message id $(h, 0)$ to a_i. Note that a post event has both an mid from the message it is part of as well as a newmid for the message it is creating.

Recall that for $x \in X$, we have $\mathscr{R}_x = \{e \in E \mid e.type = read, e.var = x\}$, $\mathscr{W}_x = \{e \in E \mid e.type = write, e.var = x\}$. The event set E together with the total order $\leq_\rho$ derived from a run *induces* a trace $\tau(\rho)$ in the following way:

rf: If $e_i \leq_\rho e_j$ where $e_i \in \mathscr{W}_x, e_j \in \mathscr{R}_x$, and for all $e_i \leq_\rho e_k \leq_\rho e_j$ we have $e_k \notin \mathscr{W}_x$, then e_i rf e_j.

co: If $e_i, e_j \in \mathscr{W}_x$ for some x and $e_i \leq_\rho e_j$ then e_i co e_j.

po: If e_i, e_j are s.t. $a_i.mid = a_j.mid$ and $e_i \leq_\rho e_j$ then e_i po e_j. Further, if e_i, e_j are s.t. $e_i.h = e_j.h$, $a_i.mid = (h, 0)$ and $a_j.mid \neq a_i.mid$ then e_i po e_j.

eo: If $e_i \leq_\rho e_j$ satisfies $e_i.type = e_j.type =$ get and $e_i.h = e_j.h, a_i.mid \neq a_j.mid$ then e_i eo e_j.

pb: If $e_i \leq_\rho e_j$ satisfies $e_i.type = post, e_j.type =$ get and $a_i.newmid = a_j.mid$ then e_i pb e_j.

mo: If e_i, e_j are both post events s.t. $e_i.receiver = e_j.receiver$ and $e_i \leq_\rho e_j$ then e_i mo e_j.

The definition of rf ensures that every read on a variable reads from the latest write on that variable. The coherence order co is just the sequence of writes on a variable. The mid information tells us which set of instructions belong to the same message from which we can infer po. Similarly the mid information also tells us which get is posted-by which post. The sequence of message executions on a handler (eo) and the order in which messages were posted to a handler (mo) can be inferred from $\leq_\rho$. This gives us the following lemma:

Lemma 1. *For any program $\mathcal{P}$ and its execution ρ, $\tau(\rho)$ is a trace.*

Remark 1. Since the mailbox is a FIFO queue, the restriction here is that the order in which messages are extracted should be according to the mo between the events that posts the messages to the same mailbox.

Axiomatic Consistency. We introduce conditions under which a trace τ is said to be *axiomatically consistent* and show that this happens iff τ can be derived from the run of some event driven program. The conditions are given as is standard by means of acyclicity of the union of relations. To this end, we introduce new relations: The *queue order* qo is defined as qo = pb^{-1}.mo.pb. The from-reads relation be defined as fr = rf^{-1}.co. Let eo† = $(\text{po}^{-1})^*$.eo.po*.

Definition 1. *A trace τ is said to be axiomatically consistent if the happens-before relation* hb = (po $\cup$ rf $\cup$ fr $\cup$ co $\cup$ pb $\cup$ mo $\cup$ eo† $\cup$ qo) *is acyclic.*

Theorem 1. *A trace τ is axiomatically consistent iff there exists an event-driven program $\mathcal{P}$ and a run ρ such that $\tau = \tau(\rho)$.*

2.4 Event-Driven Consistency Problem

Having defined both operational and axiomatic semantics, we now introduce the event-driven consistency problem, which asks whether a partial trace can be extended to an axiomatically consistent trace.

We first recall a related problem in the non-event-driven setting, where only the relations po (program order), rf (reads from) and co (coherence order) are relevant. When all three are given, consistency checking is tractable. However, if only po and rf are provided (aka rf-consistency), is known to be NP-complete [21]. In ED programs, we additionally deal with pb, mo and eo. Given the NP-completeness of the rf-consistency problem, it is natural to ask about the complexity of ED-consistency where mo and eo are not provided[3]. As in the nonED case, our proof of equivalence in Theorem 1 implies that consistency is in polynomial time if all the relations are given. This leads to the well-motivated consistency problem for event-driven programs. Let $\text{rels}' = \{\text{po} \cup \text{rf} \cup \text{co} \cup \text{pb}\}$.

Definition 2 (ED-Consistency Problem). *Given a partial trace $\tau' = (E', \Delta')$ with $\Delta' \subseteq E \times \text{rels}' \times E$, decide whether there exists an axiomatically consistent extension trace $\tau = (E, \Delta)$ of τ' such that $\Delta' \cap (E \times \text{rels}' \times E) = \Delta \cap (E \times \text{rels}' \times E)$.*

3 Complexity of Event-Driven Consistency

In this section, we study the complexity of the event-driven consistency problem. We show that the problem is NP-hard. Further, since our reduction uses only 12 handlers, this also implies the hardness for the more restricted version of the problem, with only a bounded number of handler threads.

The proof will follow from a reduction from *3-Bounded Instance 3SAT* (3-BI-3SAT in short), a problem known to be NP-complete [46]. Further details and a proof of correctness are given in [4].

Definition 3 (3-BI-3SAT). *A 3-BI-3SAT problem is the Boolean satisfiability problem restricted to conjunctive normal form formulas such that: (1) each clause contain two or three literals, (2) each variable occurs in at most 3 clauses, and (3) each variable appears at most once per clause.*

Theorem 2. *The ED-consistency problem is NP-complete for traces with at most 12 handlers.*

The proof is done by reduction from the 3-BI-3SAT. Let ϕ be a 3-BI-3SAT instance with variables $x_1, x_2, \ldots, x_n$ and clauses $C_1, C_2, \ldots, C_m$. We will construct a partial ED trace $\tau = (E, \Delta)$, with $\Delta \subseteq E \times \text{rels}' \times E$, such that τ can be extended to a axiomatically consistent trace $\tau' = (E, \Delta')$, with $\Delta' \cap (E \times \text{rels}' \times E) = \Delta \cap (E \times \text{rels}' \times E)$, iff ϕ is satisfiable.

---
[3] Note that the eo order should respect the mo order, since the mailbox is a FIFO queue. When we talk about partial traces, we do not explicitly mention the relations present. The understanding is that both mo and eo are missing.

High Level Structure. The construction of the trace τ is divided into two stages, which we call Stage 1 and Stage 2 respectively. There are 8 handlers in Stage 1 and 5 handlers in Stage 2. One handler, namely h_W is common to both stages, hence totally there are 12 handlers. If a satisfying assignment exists for ϕ, then there is a program which can execute the events in Stage 1 followed by those in Stage 2, i.e., τ is consistent. If ϕ is unsatisfiable then there is no witnessing execution possible which executes both stages and τ is inconsistent.

Stage 1 corresponds to the selection of a satisfying assignment f for ϕ. We can encode the information of whether a variable x_i is assigned true or false using the order of execution of two messages $m_{i,1}$ and $m_{i,0}$ on the same handler, where x_i is assigned true (resp. false) if $m_{i,1}$ (resp. $m_{i,0}$) is executed later. Unfortunately, this will not work due to technical difficulties faced in clause verification (see Remark 3 in Subsect. 3.2). This necessitates our extremely technical reduction which makes use of the structure of the 3-BI-3SAT instance where each variable occurs in *at most* three clauses and the variables occurring in a clause are all different. We have to create (at most) 3 copies of the messages, one for each clause in which x_i occurs and find a way to synchronise the assignment between these three copies.

Hence the messages for x_i are actually of the form $m_{i,j,b}$ where j refers to clause C_j and $b \in 0,1$. Using the technique of *post sequences* which use nested posting (explained using example in Subsect. 3.2), we post the set M of $m_{i,j,b}$ messages in the queue of h_W in some order σ. The remaining 7 handlers of Stage 1 are used to shuffle the messages in M with certain restrictions on the order σ of messages. The set S of all the possible orders σ is such that, every σ is constrained to be *consistent* (see Challenge 2 of Subsect. 3.1) with some particular assignment f of variables of ϕ. There are no other constraints on the order σ. At the end of Stage 1, the queues of all other Stage 1 handlers is empty and the queue of h_W is populated in some order $\sigma \in S$ consistent with some assignment f. Note that there are multiple σ which are consistent with a particular f, this fact will be important later.

Stage 2 Let us fix σ and f from Stage 1. Then Stage 2 verifies that f indeed satisfies all the clauses of ϕ. For this, we build a clause gadget G_j corresponding to each clause C_j. The set E_G of events of these clause gadgets occupy the 4 non-h_W handlers of Stage 2. The E_G events belong to an initial message of each of the 4 handlers, and consist purely of read and write events. Recall that the queue of h_W is populated at this point with message set M. The information regarding the assignment is encoded in the order of the messages in h_W. This information is transferred to the other 4 non-h_W handlers via a technique we call *sandwiching* (explained using example in Subsect. 3.1). There are now two possibilities:

(1) If f is not a satisfying assignment, then some clause C_j is not satisfied by f. In this case, any order σ of messages consistent with f will induce a hb (happens before) cycle in the corresponding gadget G_j via the sandwiching. Therefore Stage 2 cannot be executed by any witnessing execution. If there are no satisfying assignments, then ϕ is unsatisfiable and hence τ is not consistent.

(2) If f is a satisfying assignment then there is some order σ of the messages in M which is consistent with f such that there is a witnessing execution. The clause gadgets are executed interleaved with the messages in M due to the sandwiching. The execution happens sequentially i.e. G_1 is executed, then G_2 etc. This implies τ is consistent.

Remark 2. When we say that message m is posted to handler h before message m' is posted to h, we refer to the order of post operations as executed in the witnessing execution.

Through the use of examples, we now give intuition on how the two Stages work, beginning with Stage 2.

3.1 Stage 2: Checking Satisfaction of Clauses

We assume that h_W has been populated with messages in accordance with a variable assignment function f in Stage 1. Each clause C_j is associated with a *clause gadget* G_j implemented using handlers $h_{C_a}, h_{C_b}, h_{C_c}, h_{C_d}$ (the non-h_W handlers of Stage 2). For example, for $C_2 = x_1 \vee x_2 \vee \overline{x_n}$, Fig. 2 shows the corresponding gadget G_2 and two messages posted to h_W in Stage 1. For reasons of space we use W and R for *write* and *read* to describe events.

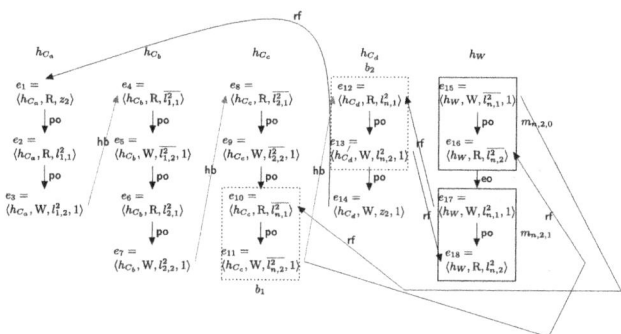

Fig. 2. The structure of clause gadget G_2 of C_2 for the example in Fig. 3.

Within each gadget, there are *boxes* that contain a read followed by a write event in po. Each box is linked to messages in h_W through rf relations. Consider the box b_1 in Fig. 2. Here, the variable $l_{n,1}^2$ in e_{10} has the information: superscript 2 for clause C_2, subscript $n, 1$ indicating the literal $\overline{x_n}$ and 1 indicating it is the first event in the box. The events in b_1 are linked to the read and write events in the message $m_{n,2,0}$ via rf arrows. The direction of the arrows implies that the events in box b_1 have to be executed after event e_{15} and before e_{16} which are both in message $m_{n,2,0}$. This is the technique we call *sandwiching*. Similarly b_2 has to be executed during the execution of $m_{n,2,1}$. Suppose $m_{n,2,0}$ is executed before $m_{n,2,1}$ as indicated by the eo, this means that x_n is assigned the value **true**. This sandwiching induces the red hb relation shown between e_{11} and e_{12}.

Clause Satisfaction. Notice that similar boxes can be drawn around events e_2, e_3 and e_4, e_5 corresponding to copying the assignment to variable x_1 and for e_6, e_7 and e_8, e_9 for variable x_2. Each of these boxes has similar sandwiching rf relations to messages in h_W which are not shown in the figure. The three red hb arrows correspond to setting each of the three variables in C_2 to a value that falsifies the corresponding literal in C_2. The events e_1 and e_{14} use a variable z_2 (where the subscript refers to the clause C_2) and are connected by an rf. Under these conditions, a cycle is formed and thus the clause gadget cannot be executed. On the other hand, if even one of the red arrows is flipped (indicating that a literal of C_2 is set to true), then the arrows form a partial order allowing execution of the clause gadget G_2.

Note that the clause gadgets $G_1, G_1, \ldots, G_m$ are placed in that order in the handlers $h_{C_a}, h_{C_b}, h_{C_c}, h_{C_d}$ and connected by po arrows. For example, $G_j.e_3$ will be po before $G_{j+1}.e_1$ in h_{C_a}, $G_j.e_7$ will be po before $G_{j+1}.e_4$ in h_{C_b}, etc. In other words, the events of each of these four handlers can be assumed to be in an initial message in the respective handlers. There is no posting of events either from or to these 4 handlers.

3.2 Stage 1: Encoding Variable Assignments

In this Stage, we use the handlers $h_V, h_{t_1}, h_{t_2}, h_{t_3}, h_{t_4}, h_{t_5}, h_{t_6}$ in order to post messages to h_W. We stated that an assignment to variable x_i can be encoded as the order between $m_{i,j,0}, m_{i,j,1}$.

Challenge 1: How can we ensure that the messages $m_{i,j,0}, m_{i,j,1}$ can be posted in any order to h_W?
In order to solve this, we use *nested posting*. h_V posts $m'_{i,j,0}$ to h_1 and $m'_{i,j,1}$ to h_2, which in turn post $m_{i,j,0}$ and $m_{i,j,1}$ to h_W. Since $m'_{i,j,0}$ and $m'_{i,j,1}$ are on different handlers, they can be executed in any order, thus ensuring that $m_{i,j,0}, m_{i,j,1}$ can posted in any order to h_W. Next we take up the reason for using multiple messages for each variable.

Remark 3. Consider the sandwiching technique that we presented in Stage 2 in order to copy the assignment of a variable to the clause gadget. Suppose we were to use a single pair of messages $m_{i,0}, m_{i,1}$ in h_W for a variable x_i from which this value was copied to the different clauses in which x_i occurs. This means that any handler in which a clause gadget is being executed would be blocked from running till all of the clauses containing x_i are able to finish executing the boxes corresponding to x_i. This leads to a cascading set of blocked handlers, requiring an unbounded number of handlers to execute the clause gadgets. In order to overcome this difficulty, we have to use upto three copies of the two messages $m_{i,0}, m_{i,1}$ as mentioned before. But this leads to a different challenge.

Challenge 2: How can we ensure that the different copies of the messages corresponding to the same variable exhibit the same value?
To solve this, we rely on the structure of the 3-BI-3SAT formula. Figure 3 depicts a grid with variables as rows and clauses as columns. Marked cells indicate

variable occurrences. For each literal l, we define a *post sequence* p^l composed of segments $p_1^l, \ldots, p_7^l$ corresponding to marked and unmarked cells. To address this, we further extend the nesting of posts, relying on the structure of the 3-BI-3SAT formula ϕ. Figure 3 depicts a grid with variables as rows and clauses as columns. Marked cells indicate variable occurrences. Each row contains 2 or 3 marked cells and each column contains 4 or 6 marked cells as per the restriction on 3-BI-3SAT. For each literal l, we define a *post sequence* p^l composed of segments $p_1^l, \ldots, p_7^l$ corresponding to marked and unmarked cells. Marked cells trigger the posting of messages to h_W, while unmarked ones simply post to h_V and defer execution. The post sequence of each marked cell is designed to enforce consistent ordering of the associated messages. We will now describe the post sequences in detail.

A post sequence is a partial trace of the form

$$\langle h_0, \text{post}, h_1\rangle \xrightarrow{\text{pb}} \langle h_1, \text{get}\rangle \xrightarrow{\text{po}} \langle h_1, \text{post}, h_2\rangle \xrightarrow{\text{pb}} \xrightarrow{\text{po}} \cdots \langle h_{n-1}, \text{post}, h_n\rangle$$

We will simply write this as $p = \langle h_1, \text{post}, h_2, \text{post}, \ldots, \text{post}, h_n\rangle$. In case $h_i = h_{i+1} = \ldots = h_j$ we will further shorten this to $\langle h_1, \text{post}, h_2, \text{post}, \ldots, h_i, \text{post}^{j-i-1}, h_j, \text{post}, h_{j+1}, \text{post}, \ldots, \text{post}, h_n\rangle$.

Consider the row labelled by $\overline{x_1}$ in the Fig. 3. The post sequence is the concatenation of 7 post sequences $p^{\overline{x_1}} = p_1^{\overline{x_1}} p_2^{\overline{x_1}} p_3^{\overline{x_1}} p_4^{\overline{x_1}} p_5^{\overline{x_1}} p_6^{\overline{x_1}} p_7^{\overline{x_1}}$ where $p_2^{\overline{x_1}}, p_4^{\overline{x_1}}, p_6^{\overline{x_1}}$ correspond to the cells marked $\overline{1,1}$, $1,2$ and $\overline{1,3}$ respectively, while the others correspond to the part of the row consisting of unmarked cells, with $p_1^{\overline{x_1}}$ for the part from the beginning till the first marked cell, etc. Each of the post sequences $p_1^{\overline{x_1}}, p_3^{\overline{x_1}}, p_5^{\overline{x_1}}, p_7^{\overline{x_1}}$ consists of a long sequence of posts to h_V of length the number of unmarked cells in the segment they correspond to.

For example $p_1^{\overline{x_1}} = p_3^{\overline{x_1}} = \langle h_V, \text{post}, h_V\rangle$ while $p_5^{\overline{x_1}} = \langle h_V, \text{post}^3, h_V\rangle$ since there are 3 empty cells in between (in the figure they are not explicitly shown, but rather by $\ldots$, but once can infer that the boxes corresponding to C_5, C_6, C_7 are empty along this row). The idea is that the post sequences are executed column by column. The empty cell post sequences simply 'send to back of queue' while the marked cells are responsible for populating h_W with an appropriate sequence of messages as explained below.

We now describe the post sequences made in the marked cells. Consider the 6 marked cells corresponding to column C_2. Top to bottom, these are $p_2^{x_1}, p_2^{\overline{x_1}}, p_4^{x_2}, p_4^{\overline{x_2}}, p_2^{x_n}, p_2^{\overline{x_n}}$.

Fig. 3. Relationship between variables and clauses dictating the nesting of posts. Empty cell means variable does not occur in clause (not all nonempty cells are shown). A cell marked (u, v) or $\overline{(u, v)}$ indicates that it is the u-th occurrence of the variable in a clause and is the v-th variable of the clause. The bars on the tuple indicate the polarity of the variable occurrence. $C_2 = x_1 \vee x_2 \vee \overline{x_n}$, x_1 occurs in C_2, C_8 and $\overline{x_1}$ occurs in C_4.

Let us consider the post sequence for a cell labelled (u,v) (resp. $\overline{(u,v)}$), indicating that it is the u-th occurrence of the variable in a clause and is the v-th variable of the clause, with the bar indicating whether the variable or its negation occurs in the clause. Suppose $u \neq 1$, then the post sequence is $\langle h_V, \text{post}, h_{t_v}, \text{post}, h_V \rangle$ for both (u,v) as well as $\overline{(u,v)}$. If $u = 1$ then the post sequence is $\langle h_V, \text{post}^2, h_{t_v}, \text{post}, h_V \rangle$ for (u,v) but it is $\langle h_V, \text{post}, h_{t_{v+3}}, \text{post}, h_{t_v}, \text{post}, h_V \rangle$ for $\overline{(u,v)}$. For example, $p_2^{x_n}$ which is marked $\overline{(1,3)}$ has the post sequence $\langle h_V, \text{post}, h_{t_6}, \text{post}, h_{t_3}, \text{post}, h_V \rangle$. Intuitively, the post sequences of the variable and its negation move to different handlers h_{t_k} before coming back to the same handler iff a variable is occurring for the first time in a clause i.e., if $u = 1$. We modify each post sequence of a marked cell to post a message $m_{i,j,b}$ (corresponding to the occurrence of x_i in C_j in positive or negative form based on the value of the bit b) to h_W just before its return to h_V. For example, in $p_2^{x_n}$ we insert the events e_2, e_3, e_4, e_5 between the events e_1 and e_6 which are part of $p_2^{x_n}$ as follows:

$$e_1 = \langle h_{t_3}, \text{get} \rangle \xrightarrow{\text{po}} e_2 = \langle h_{t_3}, \text{post}, h_W \rangle \xrightarrow{\text{pb}} e_3 = \langle h_W, \text{get} \rangle \xrightarrow{\text{po}} e_4 = \langle h_W, W, l_{n,1}^2, 1 \rangle$$

$$\downarrow \text{po} \qquad\qquad\qquad\qquad\qquad \text{rf} \qquad \downarrow \text{po}$$

$$e_6 = \langle h_{t_3}, \text{post}, h_V \rangle \qquad \boxed{\text{Stage 2}} \xleftarrow{\text{rf}} e_5 = \langle h_W, R, l_{n,2}^2 \rangle$$

This means that six messages are posted to h_W corresponding to C_2. The assignment to x_1 and x_n are chosen by using different handlers h_{t_i} for them, but the assignment to x_2 was already chosen when executing the post sequence for C_1 corresponding to x_2. Hence $p_4^{x_2}, p_4^{\overline{x_2}}$ will both contain h_{t_2} and the corresponding messages will be posted to h_W in the order already chosen. Crucially, we prevent orderings in h_W which do not correspond to consistent assignment of variables. However we allow all other possible reorderings of messages and this is essential for the verification in Stage 2, where only some of these reorderings may be allowed based on the partial order of events in a satisfiable clause i.e. one where not all red hb arrows are present (see Fig. 2).

In this way, the post sequences ensure that (1) all copies of the same variable agree on the assignment, (2) messages are posted in an order reflecting this assignment, and (3) the clause gadgets can detect satisfiability by checking the consistency of the induced trace τ.

4 Event-Driven Programs Without Nested Posting

We have shown that the event-driven consistency problem is NP-hard, even when the number of handlers is bounded. However, a closer examination of our reductions reveals that they rely critically on the ability of a message to post another message to a handler—a feature we refer to as *nested posting*. This observation motivates the study of a restricted setting in which nested posting is disallowed: does the problem become easier in this case? We answer this question affirmatively in Theorem 3,which shows that the event-driven consistency problem becomes tractable under this restriction. Specifically, we present a polynomial-time procedure for checking consistency when the number of handlers is bounded and nested posting is not allowed.

Theorem 3. *Given a trace $\tau = (E, \Delta')$ containing k handlers and no nesting of posts, the ED-Consistency problem for τ can be solved in time polynomial in $|E| = n$ and exponential in the number k of handlers.*

Proof Sketch. Since there is no nesting of posts, all post events occur in the initial message of each handler. The po order within the initial message therefore implies an mo order on all posts made by a given handler h. Due to queue semantics, this also implies the corresponding eo order on the corresponding get events and also the eo† relation between all pairs of events occurring in two messages ordered by eo. This implies that for the messages posted to a handler h', we obtain k different total orders of based on the handler h making the post. We can now express the consistency problem in terms of program termination as follows. We define the notion of a configuration C which consists of

(P1) k pointers for each handler h' which indicates the messages which have been executed so far in each of the k total orders (for a total of k^2 pointers), and
(P2) k additional pointers which indicate the event to be executed next in the message currently being executed in each handler.

This information requires $O(k^2 \log(n))$ space and thus the total number of configurations is exponential in k and polynomial in n.

We can now construct the configuration graph G which consists of nodes representing the configurations and edges which indicate when a transition is possible (e.g. when the a pointer in P1 is moved to the successor event inside a message, all other pointers remaining the same). Thus, the trace is consistent iff there is a path from the initial configuration to the final configuration in G.

5 Consistency Checking: Procedure and Optimisations

In this section, we propose two concrete procedures for checking event-driven consistency. Both the procedures take as input the trace as a graph G whose nodes are events and whose edges are the program relations rf, co, message relation po, and posted-by relation pb. The first procedure is based on some *saturation rules*, designed to accelerate consistency checking. The second procedure involves encoding the consistency problem as a constraint satisfaction problem and uses the Z3 SMT solver to solve it. Observe that the ED-consistency problem is in NP. Since checking consistency is in polynomial time if all the relations are given, it suffices to guess the missing relations.

5.1 Procedure Using Saturation Rules

The CheckQconsistency(G) procedure iterates over all possible assignments of eo and mo edges for G, and for each of these assignments, adds the fr, qo and eo† edges that are defined in Sect. 2.3, and checks whether there is one for which G is acyclic after the addition of these edges. If there is an assignment for which the graph G is acyclic, the procedure returns true, otherwise, it returns false.

Algorithm 1: Consistency checking

Input: A partial trace $G = (E, \Delta)$ where $\Delta \subseteq E \times \text{rels}' \times E$.

1 **if** G contains a cycle **then**
2   **return** Inconsistent
3 **else**
4   Apply saturation rules (1) - (3) to G;
5   CheckQconsistency(G);

Saturation Rules. To reduce the search space and speed up the consistency check, we define the following saturation rules, depicted in Fig. 4:

Rule 1: If there is a hb edge between two events in two different messages of the same handler, the eo edge between these messages have to respect this order.

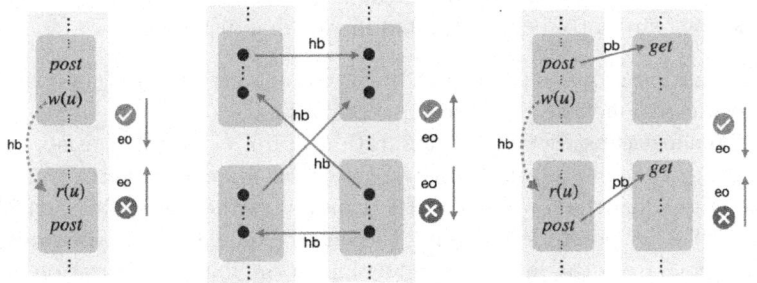

Fig. 4. Patterns corresponding to saturation rules.

Rule 2: Consider the sequence of hb edges between events as depicted in the second figure. It can be seen that this pattern forces the eo edge to be as shown in the figure - the inverse eo edge immediately creates a cycle in the trace.

Rule 3: This rule checks that the order in which messages are processed follows the queue semantics. Consider the sequence of hb edges between events as depicted in the third figure. It can be seen that this pattern forces the eo edge to be as shown in the figure - the inverse eo edge immediately creates a cycle in the trace.

5.2 Procedure Using SMT Encoding

Here, we present an algorithm to check consistency of a partial event-driven trace using the Z3 solver [40]. Note that each event e is part of one message, and each message is part of one handler. The algorithm uses the *Special Relations* theory in Z3. The algorithm takes the input trace G and the set of events E. An enum datatype T is created, where each value corresponds to an event. Then, a partial order O is declared over the events in T using Z3's Special Relations theory - this order will represent the orderings that must be satisfied for the trace to be consistent. Then, a Z3 solver instance I is created to solve the logical constraints defined over the events and their orderings. Then, in lines 4-5, we enforces that each known relation is a subrelation of the partial order O, meaning that O must respect all the orders that are already known from the event-driven semantics. Then, for each handler, and for every pair of messages m_1, m_2 on this handler, we require (m_1.last $<_O$ m_2.first $\lor$ m_2.last $<_O$ m_1.first) where m.first and m.last denote the first (respectively last) instruction of a message m. This constraint enforces that the event order (eo) is total within each handler, i.e., the execution of messages is serial. Similarly, we let m.post denote the posting event of message m, and require (m_1.post $<_O$ m_2.post $\lor$ m_2.post $<_O$ m_1.post) which corresponds to the requirement of mo being total for the posts to a given handler. Finally, the Z3 solver is called to check if the given set of constraints are satisfiable. If the solver returns Yes, then there exists a global partial order O that extends the known relations and satisfies all handler-level ordering constraints and therefore, the trace is consistent. Otherwise, no such order exists, which implies that the trace is inconsistent.

Algorithm 2: Consistency checking

Input: A partial trace $G = (E, \Delta)$ where $\Delta \subseteq E \times \text{rels}' \times E$.

1 $T \leftarrow Enum(E)$;
2 $O \leftarrow PartialOrder(T)$;
3 $I \leftarrow Z3instance$;
4 **for** $(a, b) \in \Delta$ **do**
5 $\quad I.assert(O(a, b))$;
6 **for** $h \in handlers$ **do**
7 $\quad$ **for** $m_1, m_2 \in h.messages$ **do**
8 $\quad\quad I.assert(O(m_1.last, m_2.first) \lor O(m_2.last, m_1.first))$;
9 $\quad\quad I.assert(O(m_1.post, m_2.post) \lor O(m_2.post, m_1.post))$;
10 **return** $I.check()$;

6 Implementation and Experimental Evaluation

We have implemented a prototype tool for consistency checking of event-driven traces, based on the algorithms described in Sect. 5. The prototype verifies whether a given partial trace admits a consistent extension, and, when successful, produces a witness: a concrete assignment to the missing relations (i.e., *mo* and *eo*). From this witness, a valid execution can be reconstructed. All experiments were conducted on a machine running Debian 12.4 with an Intel(R) Xeon(R) Platinum 8168 CPU @ 2.70GHz and 192 GB of RAM. Selected results are presented in Table 1.

Additional experimental results are available in the extended version of the paper [4].

Experiment Setting. To evaluate our approach, we used traces generated from Android applications via DROIDRACER [37]. DROIDRACER's Trace Generator executes Android binaries on an emulator and exhaustively generates event sequences up to a bound k using depth-first search. We developed a custom parser to transform these sequences into partial traces suitable for our tool. These traces extracted from Android apps available at [36], originally used by Maiya et al. [37]. Static edges (e.g., program order, reads-from, and posted-by) are added during parsing, while the other relations are left unspecified. The tool then checks whether a consistent extension exists. Since Android's semantics closely follow queue-based message handling, we expect all DROIDRACER traces to be consistent.

Experimental Results. We compared the performance of our two algorithms described in Sect. 5 for event-driven consistency.

The results, shown in Table 1, clearly demonstrate the advantage of Algorithm 2 in both performance and scalability. While Algorithm 1 performs accept-

Table 1. Experimental results for benchmark programs collected from droidracer. The field # T denotes the number of traces. The traces can differ in size (events # E), messages # M, handlers # H), and the field contains the maximum of its traces. The field # Consistent traces denotes the number of these traces for which the implementation reports the existence of a satisfying execution. The field # T/O traces denotes the number of traces for which our tool timed out (with a timeout of 120 s). For any remaining traces, the tool concludes inconsistency. The time fields represent the average runtime for the traces that did not time out. A value of - indicates that the corresponding algorithm timed out on every trace.

Benchmark	Max # E	Max # M	Max # H	# T	Algorithm 1			Algorithm 2		
					# Consistent traces	# T/O traces	Time in sec.	# Consistent traces	# T/O traces	Time in sec.
SampleApp	4776	13	5	1	0	1	-	1	0	2.9816
Tomdroid	4776	13	5	2	0	2	-	2	0	1.8621
Opensudoku	11292	14	5	1	0	1	-	1	0	22.0052
Sgtpuzzles	18406	18	5	2	0	2	-	2	0	34.6982
Remindme	6870	23	5	1	0	1	-	1	0	16.7987
Modelcheckingserver	4057	26	4	1	0	1	-	1	0	3.6556
Messenger	5034	26	7	2	0	2	-	2	0	5.4606
Music	4253	33	5	3	0	3	-	3	0	4.3871
Fbreader	6159	35	8	6	0	6	-	6	0	9.4964
K9Mail	5309	46	9	2	0	2	-	2	0	13.2162
Aarddict	1220	12	5	2	1	1	2.0932	2	0	0.0982
AdobeReader	15717	140	7	1	0	1	-	0	1	-
Facebook	5319	14	12	1	0	1	-	1	0	1.9775
Twitter	9889	30	12	1	0	1	-	1	0	18.7847
Browser	9762	34	15	6	0	6	-	3	3	46.9663
Flipkart	116945	61	15	1	0	1	-	0	1	-
Mytracks	3671	32	16	3	1	2	27.7057	3	0	2.2841

ably on small traces (e.g. Aardict), it fails to scale to complex instances due to the combinatorial explosion in possible execution orderings. In contrast, Algorithm 2 benefits from Z3n's efficient constraint-solving capabilities, enabling fast detection of consistency or inconsistency even in challenging benchmarks.

To summarise, our experiments indicate that SMT-based techniques can be effectively leveraged for consistency checking in event-driven programs. The integration of SMT solvers, which are already widely adopted in verification tools, provides a scalable and precise foundation for reasoning about partial traces.

7 Conclusion and Future Work

In this paper, we investigate the problem of ED consistency under the sequential consistency memory model. We propose axiomatic semantics for event-driven programs and show equivalence of axiomatic and operational semantics. Furthermore, we establish that checking event-driven consistency is NP-hard, even when the number of handler threads is bounded. Further, when there is no nested posting in the trace, we show that checking consistency can be done in polynomial time. Finally, we also implement our event-driven consistency checking in a prototype tool, and provide promising experimental results on standard event-driven examples.

In the future, we plan to extend this work to the setting of other memory models such as Release-Acquire, Total Store Ordering etc. We also plan to integrate our implementation in procedures for Dynamic partial order reduction for event-driven programs, race detection and predictive analysis. Finally, we also plan to evaluate our implementation on a wider range of examples, for instance the traces generated from android applications.

References

1. Abdulla, P.A., Aronis, S., Atig, M.F., Jonsson, B., Leonardsson, C., Sagonas, K.: Stateless model checking for TSO and PSO. Acta Inf. **54**(8), 789–818 (2017)
2. Abdulla, P.A., Aronis, S., Jonsson, B., Sagonas, K.: Optimal dynamic partial order reduction. In: POPL, pp. 373–384. ACM (2014)
3. Abdulla, P.A., et al.: Tailoring stateless model checking for event-driven multithreaded programs. In: Automated Technology for Verification and Analysis - 21st International Symposium, ATVA 2023, Proceedings. Lecture Notes in Computer Science, vol. 14216. Springer, Heidelberg (2023). https://doi.org/10.1007/978-3-031-45332-8_9
4. Abdulla, P.A., Atig, M.F., Govind, R., Grahn, S., Thinniyam, R.S.: Checking consistency of event-driven traces. CoRR arxiv:2508.07855 (2025)
5. Abdulla, P.A., Atig, M.F., Jonsson, B., Lång, M., Ngo, T.P., Sagonas, K.: Optimal stateless model checking for reads-from equivalence under sequential consistency. Proc. ACM Program. Lang. **3**(OOPSLA), 150:1–150:29 (2019)
6. Abdulla, P.A., Atig, M.F., Jonsson, B., Leonardsson, C.: Stateless Model Checking for POWER. In: Chaudhuri, S., Farzan, A. (eds.) CAV 2016. LNCS, vol. 9780, pp. 134–156. Springer, Cham (2016). https://doi.org/10.1007/978-3-319-41540-6_8

7. Abdulla, P.A., Atig, M.F., Jonsson, B., Ngo, T.P.: Optimal stateless model checking under the release-acquire semantics. PACMPL **2**(OOPSLA), 135:1–135:29 (2018)
8. kernel-mode driver architecture., M.I.W.: http://msdn.microsoft.com/en-us/library/windows/hardware/ff557560(v=vs.85).aspx
9. Bouajjani, A., Emmi, M., Enea, C., Ozkan, B.K., Tasiran, S.: Verifying robustness of event-driven asynchronous programs against concurrency. In: Yang, H. (ed.) ESOP 2017. LNCS, vol. 10201, pp. 170–200. Springer, Heidelberg (2017). https://doi.org/10.1007/978-3-662-54434-1_7
10. Bouajjani, A., Enea, C., Guerraoui, R., Hamza, J.: On verifying causal consistency. In: POPL, pp. 626–638. ACM (2017)
11. Chakraborty, S., Krishna, S.N., Mathur, U., Pavlogiannis, A.: How hard is weak-memory testing? Proc. ACM Program. Lang. **8**(POPL), 1978–2009 (2024)
12. Christakis, M., Gotovos, A., Sagonas, K.: Systematic testing for detecting concurrency errors in erlang programs. In: ICST, pp. 154–163. IEEE Computer Society (2013)
13. Clarke, E.M., Grumberg, O., Minea, M., Peled, D.A.: State space reduction using partial order techniques. Int. J. Softw. Tools Technol. Transf. **2**(3), 279–287 (1999)
14. Cunningham, R., Kohler, E.: Making events less slippery with eel. In: HotOS. USENIX Association (2005)
15. Dabek, F., Zeldovich, N., Kaashoek, M.F., Mazières, D., Morris, R.: Event-driven programming for robust software. In: ACM SIGOPS European Workshop, pp. 186–189. ACM (2002)
16. Desai, A., Gupta, V., Jackson, E.K., Qadeer, S., Rajamani, S.K., Zufferey, D.: P: safe asynchronous event-driven programming. In: PLDI, pp. 321–332. ACM (2013)
17. Fischer, J., Majumdar, R., Millstein, T.D.: Tasks: language support for event-driven programming. In: PEPM, pp. 134–143. ACM (2007)
18. Ganty, P., Majumdar, R.: Analyzing real-time event-driven programs. In: Ouaknine, J., Vaandrager, F.W. (eds.) FORMATS 2009. LNCS, vol. 5813, pp. 164–178. Springer, Heidelberg (2009). https://doi.org/10.1007/978-3-642-04368-0_14
19. Gay, D., Levis, P., von Behren, J.R., Welsh, M., Brewer, E.A., Culler, D.E.: The nesc language: a holistic approach to networked embedded systems. In: Cytron, R., Gupta, R. (eds.) PLDI, pp. 1–11. ACM (2003)
20. central dispatch (GCD) reference., A.C.I.G. http://developer.apple.com/library/mac/#documentation/performance/reference/gcd_libdispatch_ref/reference/reference.html
21. Gibbons, P.B., Korach, E.: Testing shared memories. SIAM J. Comput. **26**(4), 1208–1244 (1997)
22. Godefroid, P.: Partial-Order Methods for the Verification of Concurrent Systems: An Approach to the State-Explosion Problem. Ph.D. thesis, University of Liège (1996). https://doi.org/10.1007/3-540-60761-7. http://www.springer.com/gp/book/9783540607618
23. Godefroid, P.: Model checking for programming languages using verisoft. In: POPL, pp. 174–186. ACM Press (1997)
24. Godefroid, P.: Software model checking: the verisoft approach. Formal Methods Syst. Des. **26**(2), 77–101 (2005)
25. Godefroid, P., Hanmer, R.S., Jagadeesan, L.J.: Model checking without a model: an analysis of the heart-beat monitor of a telephone switch using verisoft. In: ISSTA, pp. 124–133. ACM (1998)
26. Hill, J.L., Szewczyk, R., Woo, A., Hollar, S., Culler, D.E., Pister, K.S.J.: System architecture directions for networked sensors. In: ASPLOS, pp. 93–104. ACM Press (2000)

27. Jensen, C.S., Møller, A., Raychev, V., Dimitrov, D., Vechev, M.T.: Stateless model checking of event-driven applications. In: OOPSLA, pp. 57–73. ACM (2015)
28. Kokologiannakis, M., Lahav, O., Sagonas, K., Vafeiadis, V.: Effective stateless model checking for C/C++ concurrency. Proc. ACM Program. Lang. 2(POPL), 17:1–17:32 (2018)
29. Kokologiannakis, M., Marmanis, I., Gladstein, V., Vafeiadis, V.: Truly stateless, optimal dynamic partial order reduction. Proc. ACM Program. Lang. 6(POPL), 1–28 (2022)
30. Kokologiannakis, M., Sagonas, K.: Stateless model checking of the linux kernel's hierarchical read-copy-update (tree RCU). In: SPIN, pp. 172–181. ACM (2017)
31. Kokologiannakis, M., Vafeiadis, V.: GenMC: a model checker for weak memory models. In: Silva, A., Leino, K.R.M. (eds.) CAV 2021. LNCS, vol. 12759, pp. 427–440. Springer, Cham (2021). https://doi.org/10.1007/978-3-030-81685-8_20
32. LIBASYNC. http://pdos.csail.mit.edu/6.824-2004/async/
33. LIBEVENT. http://monkey.org/~provos/libevent/
34. Lukkarinen, A., Malmi, L., Haaranen, L.: Event-driven programming in programming education: a mapping review. ACM Trans. Comput. Educ. **21**(1), 1:1–1:31 (2021)
35. Maiya, P., Gupta, R., Kanade, A., Majumdar, R.: Partial order reduction for event-driven multi-threaded programs. In: Chechik, M., Raskin, J.-F. (eds.) TACAS 2016. LNCS, vol. 9636, pp. 680–697. Springer, Heidelberg (2016). https://doi.org/10.1007/978-3-662-49674-9_44
36. Maiya, P., Kanade, A., Majumdar, R.: Droidracer tested apps repository (2014). https://bitbucket.org/iiscseal/droidracer-related-files/src/master/pldi-2014-tested-apps/
37. Maiya, P., Kanade, A., Majumdar, R.: Race detection for android applications. In: PLDI, pp. 316–325. ACM (2014)
38. Mazières, D.: A toolkit for user-level file systems. In: Park, Y. (ed.) Proceedings of the General Track: 2001 USENIX Annual Technical Conference, pp. 261–274. USENIX (2001). http://www.usenix.org/publications/library/proceedings/usenix01/mazieres.html
39. Mednieks, Z., Dornin, L., Meike, G.B., Nakamura, M.: Programming Android. O'Reilly Media, Inc., Boston (2012)
40. de Moura, L., Bjørner, N.: Z3: An efficient SMT solver. In: Ramakrishnan, C.R., Rehof, J. (eds.) TACAS 2008. LNCS, vol. 4963, pp. 337–340. Springer, Heidelberg (2008). https://doi.org/10.1007/978-3-540-78800-3_24
41. Musuvathi, M., Qadeer, S., Ball, T., Basler, G., Nainar, P.A., Neamtiu, I.: Finding and reproducing heisenbugs in concurrent programs. In: OSDI, pp. 267–280. USENIX Association (2008)
42. Norris, B., Demsky, B.: A practical approach for model checking C/C++11 code. ACM Trans. Program. Lang. Syst. **38**(3), 10:1–10:51 (2016)
43. Peled, D.: All from one, one for all: on model checking using representatives. In: Courcoubetis, C. (ed.) CAV 1993. LNCS, vol. 697, pp. 409–423. Springer, Heidelberg (1993). https://doi.org/10.1007/3-540-56922-7_34
44. Project, T.M.: http://mace.ucsd.edu
45. Raychev, V., Vechev, M.T., Sridharan, M.: Effective race detection for event-driven programs. In: OOPSLA, pp. 151–166. ACM (2013)
46. Tovey, C.A.: A simplified np-complete satisfiability problem. Disc. Appl. Math. **8**(1), 85–89 (1984)

47. Tunç, H.C., Abdulla, P.A., Chakraborty, S., Krishna, S., Mathur, U., Pavlogiannis, A.: Optimal reads-from consistency checking for c11-style memory models. Proc. ACM Program. Lang. **7**(PLDI), 761–785 (2023)
48. Valmari, A.: Stubborn sets for reduced state space generation. In: Rozenberg, G. (ed.) ICATPN 1989. LNCS, vol. 483, pp. 491–515. Springer, Heidelberg (1991). htttps://doi.org/10.1007/3-540-53863-1_36
49. Zhang, N., Kusano, M., Wang, C.: Dynamic partial order reduction for relaxed memory models. In: PLDI, pp. 250–259. ACM (2015)

Specification Inference Modulo Oracles for Database-Backed Web Applications

Nitesh Trivedi[✉] and Subhajit Roy

Indian Institute of Technology, Kanpur, India
{nitesht,subhajit}@iitk.ac.in

Abstract. In logical reasoning, specification inference attempts to synthesize an explanatory hypothesis from a given conclusion. We consider the specification synthesis problem for database-backed web-applications where only an *oracle* access to the application is available. Such is a real case for test teams where they are not provided access to the application. Our algorithm begins with an initial hypothesis constructed from responses of the web-application on a sampled dataset, and then improves this hypothesis iteratively via carefully constructed queries to the application (via an SMT solver). Finally, statistical tests are used to validate the *soundness* and *maximality* of the constructed hypothesis. We implement our algorithm in a tool, VIVARAN, and demonstrate its capabilities on a large web-based enterprise resource planning (ERP) software. VIVARAN infers *semantically equivalent* specifications as the ground-truth in all cases.

Keywords: Specification Inference · Oracle · SMT Solvers

1 Introduction

Synthetic datasets have an important place in testing of database-backed applications—the backing database must be reasonably well-populated with relevant data for reliable functioning of the test engines. Due to privacy concerns, such applications are not tested with real customer data, thereby necessitating synthetic data. However, generation of *semantically consistent* datasets is challenging; for example, the *date of joining* of an employee must be later than their *date of birth*. If the datasets are generated randomly without enforcing such semantic relations *amongst* the database fields, testing engines would report a large number of *false positives*. For example, for the above case, if the date of birth appears later than the date of joining, the age of the candidate at joining would be computed as a negative number that may lead to test failures or even crashing of the application. As many applications enforce these semantic relations within the data-entry and update modules, such relations can be extracted by examinig the application code. However, in most modern web-applications, these checks are sprawled across the frontend and the backend code, making code

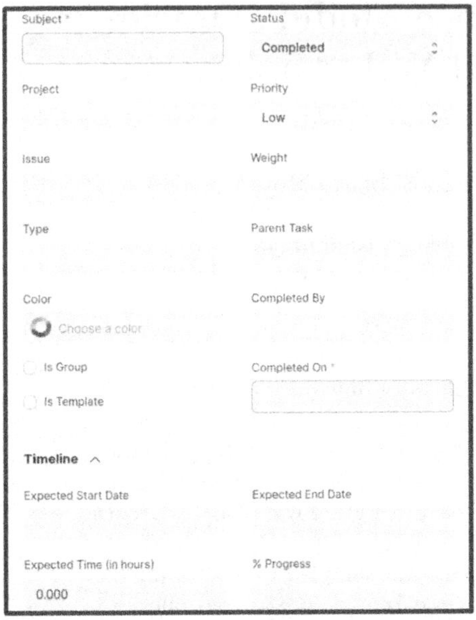

```
...
def validate_dates(self):
    self.validate_from_to_dates(
        "exp_start_date", "exp_end_date")
...
def validate_completed_on(self):
    if self.completed_on and
        getdate(self.Completed On) > getdate():
        frappe.throw(_(
        "Completed On cannot be greater
        than Today"))
...
def validate_progress(self):
    if flt(self.progress or 0) > 100:
        frappe.throw(_(
        "Progress % for a task cannot be
        more than 100."))
...
```

Fig. 1. Task web application from the ERPNext software

Fig. 2. Back-end constraints of Task web application of ERPNext

analysis challenging. Moreover, many organizations do not share their application code with the testing team for confidentiality concerns. Often the testing of such applications are outsourced to third-party vendors making the confidentiality bridge till harder to cross.

In this work, we attempt to infer such semantic relations by setting it up as a *specification inference* problem. Further, we assume only an *oracle access* to the application—that is, we only assume an interface that allows us to execute the application with an input set and get a response on whether the application executed successfully with the provided input.

In logical reasoning, while *deduction* follows forward reasoning to infer a valid conclusion from premises, *specification inference* attempts backward reasoning to construct an *explanatory hypothesis* from a given conclusion. Specification inference has applications in automated planning [9,53], fault diagnosis [22,46], belief revision [10], inference of loop invariants [13], learning specifications of unspecified harnesses [11] and synthesis of programs [14]. In such prior works, it was assumed that the conclusion is available, mostly as a logic formula. In this work, we assume that only an *oracle* access to the application is available, and hence, the above approaches are not available.

For example, Fig. 1 shows a web-application from a remotely hosted ERP software [20] that allows creating new tasks within existing projects. The web-application imposes multiple frontend and backend constraints on inputs, e.g., the frontend (implemented in JavaScript) enforces following checks:

- Text field **Subject** is mandatory (i.e. it cannot be left empty).
- If **Status** is **Completed**, then the date field **Completed On** is mandatory.

On the other hand, the following checks are enforced in the application backend that is implemented in Python (see Fig. 2):

- If the Expected Start Date and Expected End Date are both filled, then the start date must be *before* the end date. However, this form allows any of these fields to be empty, in which case, no constraint is imposed;
- The date in Completed On field cannot be later than the date when the form is filled. However this date field can remain empty if Status is not Completed (see frontend constraints above) and no constraint is imposed if the field is left empty;
- The % Progress must be less than equal to 100;

The web-application (webapp) rejects a submitted form if it violates any of the constraints. These constraints often conceal important business rules implemented by the application; inferring these constraints has important applications for synthetic data generation and testing of such web-applications [1,36,54].

Our approach to inferring these constraints with only an *oracle access* to the application invokes the application on different inputs $\mathcal{I}$, and *observes* if the submitted form is accepted or not. These observations are used to construct relevant *hypotheses* on the constraints, which are refined by more carefully crafted inputs via an SMT solver, and validated via statistical tests. Inferring constraints, or the *input semantics*, for such a web-application is an specification inference task: given the domain of inputs (say γ) and an oracle access to the web-application (say ψ), we are required to infer an *input specification* (say φ) such that $\gamma \wedge \varphi \models \psi$. As symbolic verification is impossible due to unavailability of the application code, we solve this *specification inference* tasks with high statistical guarantees.

We build our algorithm into a tool, VIVARAN, that is capable of learning *semantic relations* as specifications with high statistical guarantees. We undertake a non-trivial use-case on a large enterprise resource planning (ERP) software. VIVARAN was able to learn hypotheses that were *semantically equivalent* to the ground-truths, showcasing the effectiveness of our algorithm. The ground-truths were manually-constructed by careful examination the frontend and backend source-code of the web-applications within the ERP framework.

We make the following contributions in this work:

- We design an algorithm for specification inference on web-applications with only an oracle access to them;
- We implement our algorithm in a tool, VIVARAN;
- We demonstrate the utility of VIVARAN to successfully infer *input specifications* for remotely hosted web-based frameworks.

2 Preliminaries

We represent logical formulas in a fragment of first-order logic consisting of linear real arithmetic (LRA) and uninterpreted functions (UF). Our formula is built

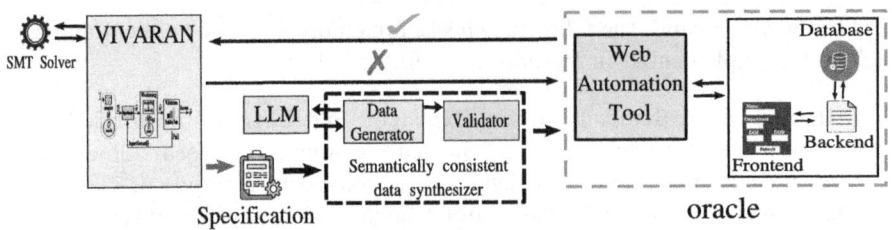

Fig. 3. System Architecture

over predicates involving expressions over first-order variables with relational operators; the predicates can be composed with conjunction (∧), disjunction (∨), negation (¬), implication (→), bi-implication (↔), and can be quantified by universal (∀) and existential (∃) quantification, to create a logical formula. We use the resolution proof system for proofs. Variables occurring in a logical formula is said to be the *support* of the formula. We denote True as ⊤ and False as ⊥. A formula, α is said to be *stronger* than a formula β (or β is *weaker* than α) if and only if $\alpha \implies \beta$. Extending this to a set of formula, α_i is the *strongest* (resp. *weakest*) formula in a set $\{\alpha_1, \ldots, \alpha_n\}$ if $\forall_{k \in [1,\ldots,n]} \alpha_i \implies \alpha_k$ (resp. $\forall_{k \in [1,\ldots,n]} \alpha_k \implies \alpha_i$).

The inference of mathematical artifacts, like *specifications* (in this paper), are often constrained to a *syntactic space*, defined by a formal *language*. A language is, essentially, a set of strings, and commonly described by a *grammar*. A grammar consists of a set of terminals (T), a set of non-terminals (N) and a set of production rules (R); a production rule $X \to \alpha$ in a *context-free grammar* derives a sentential form $\alpha \in (N \cup T)^* \cup \{\epsilon\}$ from a non-terminal symbol $X \in N$. One of the non-terminals is charatererized as the start-symbol that captures the whole language. A language L_1 is more *expressive* than L_2 if $L_2 \subset L_1$.

Given a premise γ and a desired conclusion ψ, specification inference attempts to synthesize a explanatory hypothesis φ, such that:

- premise and explanatory hypothesis *explain* conclusion: $\gamma \wedge \varphi \models \psi$ (1)
- premise and explanatory hypothesis are *not contradictory* (i.e., the explanation is not vacuous): $\gamma \wedge \varphi \not\models \bot$ (2)

3 Overview

3.1 Architecture of VIVARAN

Figure 3 shows a high-level schematic of VIVARAN. Given a web-application, VIVARAN synthesizes a specification that captures the semantic relations between the inputs of the application. VIVARAN uses a web-automation tool to automatically invoke the application with diverse set of inputs, and observes if the respective inputs execute successfully (✓) or cause an exception (✗) on the application. VIVARAN learns a set of candidate hypotheses based on this generated data, and refines them via an active learning algorithm, by generating new *interesting* datapoints using an SMT solver. This specification provides a formal representation of semantic relationships between the inputs, and is used to create semantically consistent data: our data-generator creates a prompt for the LLM that instructs the LLM to generate synthetic data-points that satisfies this inferred specification. Further, as LLMs are prone to hallucinations, the generated data-points are validated against the inferred specifications. Finally, the application is invoked by the web-automation tool to populate the database with semantically consistent data that satisfy the inferred specification.

The web-automation tool and the application form an *oracle* that can provide ✓ or ✗ responses for a provided input. This work focusses on automatically synthesizing such specifications with only an oracle access to the system.

3.2 Problem Statement: Specification Inference Modulo Oracles

We handle the task of specification inference when only an *oracle* access to the conclusion is provided; we assume a *decision* oracle ψ such that $\psi(\boldsymbol{x})$ returns $\top$ (true) or $\bot$ (false) depending on if the conclusion holds on the input (vector) $\boldsymbol{x}$. Given a premise γ and oracle access to a conclusion ψ, we attempt to synthesize an explanatory hypothesis φ such that Eqs. 1 and (2) are satisfied. It is desirable that the explanatory hypothesis φ satsifies *soundness* and *maximality*.

Soundness: For all inputs that satisfy the premise, whenever the explanatory hypothesis holds, the conclusion must also hold. Intuitively, it summarizes the set of inputs that satisfy the conclusion. As a symbolic test is ruled out due to only an oracle access to the conclusion, we would rely on a statistical test that ensures that the probability of violating the above soundness check is small:

$$\mathcal{P}(\{\boldsymbol{x} \mid \gamma(\boldsymbol{x}) \wedge \varphi(\boldsymbol{x}) \wedge \neg\psi(\boldsymbol{x})\}) \leq \epsilon_1 \qquad (3)$$

Maximality: As the soundness check can be satisfied trivially if φ is $\bot$, it is necessary to ensure *coverage* on the input set, via the condition of *maximality*, i.e. the specification must capture all inputs where the conclusion holds. Due to our inability to do a symbolic check, we rely on a statistical test that ensures that the probability of "missing" out a valid input is low.

$$\mathcal{P}(\{\boldsymbol{x} \mid \psi(\boldsymbol{x}) \wedge \gamma(\boldsymbol{x}) \wedge \neg\varphi(\boldsymbol{x})\}) \leq \epsilon_2 \qquad (4)$$

In the above equations, ϵ_1 and ϵ_2 are small probabilities that a user can provide, depending on the strictness of the guarantees desired.

4 Algorithm: Specification Inference Modulo Oracles

In this section, we describe our generic algorithm that solves the abstract problem of inferring maximal specifications (with high statistical guarantees) with

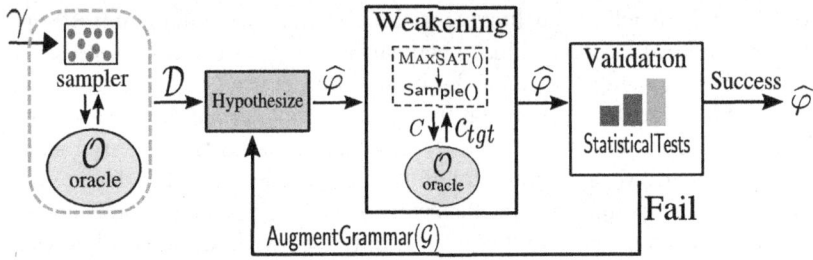

Fig. 4. Solving specification inference modulo Oracles

only an oracle access to the system under study. In Sect. 5, we describe how this algorithm is instantiated for specification inference on web-applications.

Our algorithm (Algorithm 1) accepts a premise γ, and an oracle $\mathcal{O}$, to return a learned explanatory hypothesis, $\widehat{\varphi}$. The user is also required to provide a grammar $\mathcal{G}$ to define the syntactic space for representing inferred hypothesis. We assume the availability of a constrained sampler: given a logical formula β, Sample(β) performs random sampling from the space of satisfiable solutions of β. We use a procedure, MaxSAT(β_1, β_2); to compute the *partial* maximum satisfiable solution [55] (maxsat): given a set (conjunction) of *hard* constraints as a formula β_1 and a set (conjunction) of *soft* constraints β_2, it returns a result SAT if β_1 is satisfiable, else it returns UNSAT. If satisfiable, MaxSAT(β_1, β_2) also returns a largest subset of the constraints in β_2 that could be satisfied.

Figure 4 summarizes our complete algorithm. The *sampler* generates satisfiable solutions of the premise (γ) as datapoints and prepares the dataset ($\mathcal{D}$) by verifying satisfiability of each datapoint against the oracle ($\mathcal{O}$). This dataset is passed to Hypothesize, which produces a candidate hypothesis ($\widehat{\varphi}$). The candidate hypothesis undergoes a counterexample-guided weakening phase to generate a maximal hypothesis. This hypothesis is validated using statistical tests. If the tests fail, Hypothesize is again executed on an updated dataset with an augmented grammar; the loop continues until a maximal hypothesis with strong statistical guarantees is learned or the grammar's total order is fully exploited.

Learning a Candidate Hypothesis. Our algorithm starts off by creating an initial dataset, $\mathcal{D}$ via constrained sampling from the satisfiable solutions of the premise γ (Line 1). It uses an oracle, $\mathcal{O}$, to find the satisfiability status of the datapoints in $\mathcal{D}$ (Line 2), and then, enters a loop to learn a high-confidence explanatory hypothesis (Lines 3 to 30).

Hypothesize uses the satisfiability status from the oracle responses to construct a candidate hypothesis $\widehat{\varphi}$ (Line 4). The hypothesis, $\widehat{\varphi}$, is essentially a *binary classifier* that discriminates between the instances when the oracle $\mathcal{O}$ returns $\top$ and others, where it returns $\bot$. Our Hypothesize procedure is an enumerative synthesis engine: it enumerates boolean expressions h_i within the specified grammar $\mathcal{G}$ over the support variables, to create a conjunctive set, i.e. $\widehat{\varphi} \equiv \{h_1, h_2, \ldots, h_n\}, h_i \in \mathcal{L}(\mathcal{G})$; we will refer to such h_i as *sub-hypothesis*. Then,

Algorithm 1. SpecificationInferenceModuloOracles($\gamma, \mathcal{G}, \mathcal{O}$)

1:   $\mathcal{D} \leftarrow$ Sample(γ)
2:   $\mathcal{D}_{tgt} \leftarrow \mathcal{O}(\mathcal{D})$
3:   **repeat**
4:       $\widehat{\varphi} \leftarrow$ Hypothesize($\mathcal{G}, \gamma, \mathcal{D}, \mathcal{D}_{tgt}$)
5:       $done \leftarrow \bot$
6:       **for** $h_i \in \widehat{\varphi}$ **do**
7:          **if** $\gamma \wedge \neg h_i$ is Unsatisfiable **then**
8:             $\widehat{\varphi} \leftarrow \widehat{\varphi} \setminus \{h_i\}$
9:       **while** $\neg done$ **do**
10:          $done \leftarrow \top$
11:          **for** $h_i \in \widehat{\varphi}$ **do**
12:             $\zeta \leftarrow \text{MaxSAT}(\{\neg h_i\} \cup \gamma, (\widehat{\varphi} \setminus \{h_i\}))$
13:             $C \leftarrow$ Sample($\gamma \wedge \neg h_i \wedge \zeta$)
14:             $C_{tgt} \leftarrow \mathcal{O}(C)$
15:             $\mathcal{D}, \mathcal{D}_{tgt} \leftarrow \mathcal{D} \cup C, \mathcal{D}_{tgt} \cup C_{tgt}$
16:             **if** C_{tgt} is all $\top$ **then**
17:                 $\widehat{\varphi} \leftarrow \widehat{\varphi} \setminus \{h_i\}$
18:                 $done \leftarrow \bot$
19:       $st_1, ci_1, \mathcal{W}1, \mathcal{W}1_{tgt} \leftarrow$ Validate($\gamma, \widehat{\varphi}, \gamma \wedge \widehat{\varphi}, \mathcal{O}$)
20:       $st_2, ci_2, \mathcal{W}2, \mathcal{W}2_{tgt} \leftarrow$ Validate($\gamma, \widehat{\varphi}, \gamma \wedge \neg\widehat{\varphi}, \neg\mathcal{O}$)
21:       **if** st_1 and st_2 are Success **then**
22:          **return** $\widehat{\varphi}, ci_1, ci_2$
23:       **else if** st_1 or st_2 is FailTest **then**
24:          $\mathcal{D} \leftarrow \mathcal{D} \cup \mathcal{W}1 \cup \mathcal{W}2$
25:          $\mathcal{D}_{tgt} \leftarrow \mathcal{D}_{tgt} \cup \mathcal{W}1_{tgt} \cup \mathcal{W}2_{tgt}$
26:          $\mathcal{G} \leftarrow$ AugmentGrammar($\mathcal{G}$)
27:       **else**
28:          $\mathcal{D} \leftarrow \mathcal{D} \cup$ Sample(γ)
29:          $\mathcal{G} \leftarrow$ AugmentGrammar($\mathcal{G}$)
30:   **until** $\top$

the algorithm checks the validity of each sub-hypothesis against the dataset $\mathcal{D}$; all sub-hypotheses that are satisfied on all instances in $\mathcal{D}$ are included in the *candidate hypothesis* ($\widehat{\varphi}$), that is,

$$\widehat{\varphi} = \{h_i \mid \forall d \in \mathcal{D}.\ (\gamma(d) \wedge h_i(d) \implies \mathcal{O}(d)), h_i \in \mathcal{L}(\mathcal{G})\}$$

By construction, the candidate hypothesis $\widehat{\varphi}$ is sound on the dataset $\mathcal{D}$ as it only keeps the sub-hypotheses h_i that satisfy the soundness check. Additionally, we disallow contradictory sub-hypotheses that would make the candidate hypothesis vacuous. Hence, $\widehat{\varphi}$, has the following property:

$$(\forall d \in \mathcal{D}.\ \gamma(d) \wedge \widehat{\varphi}(d) \implies \mathcal{O}(d)) \wedge (\exists d.\gamma(d) \wedge \widehat{\varphi}(d))$$

At this point, $\widehat{\varphi}$ is the *strongest* hypothesis, with the above property, that can be constructed in the grammar $\mathcal{G}$ on the dataset $\mathcal{D}$. Lines 6 to 8 removes all sub-hypotheses that are implied by the precondition γ to reduce redundancy.

Counterexample-Guided Weakening. Next, we enter a counterexample-guided hypothesis weakening loop (Lines 9 to 18) to iteratively *weaken* the candidate

Algorithm 2. Validate($\gamma, \widehat{\varphi}, \sigma, \mathcal{O}$)

1: $\mathcal{W} \leftarrow \mathsf{Sample}(\sigma)$
2: $\mathcal{W}_{tgt} \leftarrow \mathcal{O}(\mathcal{W})$
3: **if** $\mathcal{W}_{tgt}$ are all $\top$ **then**
4:     $ci \leftarrow \mathsf{StatisticalTests}(\gamma, \widehat{\varphi}, \mathcal{O})$
5:     **if** ci is acceptable **then**
6:         **return** Success, ci, $\emptyset$, $\emptyset$
7:     **else**
8:         **return** FailStat, ci, $\emptyset$, $\emptyset$
9: **else**
10:     **return** FailTest, N$_{\text{IL}}$, $\mathcal{W}, \mathcal{W}_{tgt}$

hypothesis, while maintaining soundness. This loop attempts to create *interesting* queries on datapoints outside $\mathcal{D}$, in an attempt to drop sub-hypotheses in search for *maximality*. Our weakening step uses a *data-driven* resolution rule: for each sub-hypothesis, h_i, we generate new samples to check if the other sub-hypotheses continue to hold even if h_i is negated (Line 16). If it is indeed the case for all of these new datapoints, h_i can be dropped (Line 17). The weakening step uses the following *sub-hypothesis elimination* rule, which is essentially a rewrite of resolution rule.

$$\frac{\gamma \wedge \widehat{\varphi} \implies \psi \quad \gamma \wedge (\widehat{\varphi} \setminus h_i) \wedge \neg h_i \implies \psi}{\gamma \wedge (\widehat{\varphi} \setminus h_i) \implies \psi} \qquad (5)$$

Handling Conflicts. It is possible that the sub-hypothesis that is negated is *related* to certain other sub-hypotheses; for example, consider a set of sub-hypotheses,

$$\{s \implies \neg a, a \implies b, s \implies \neg b\}$$

Negating the first hypothesis makes the set unsatisfiable as the other two sub-hypothesis are *related* to the first; so, the first sub-hypothesis cannot be negated in isolation.

As in the above case, when negating the selected sub-hypothesis h_i makes $\gamma \wedge (\widehat{\varphi} \setminus \{h_i\})$ unsatisfiable, we identify the largest set of sub-hypotheses that are still feasible even if h_i is negated, by computing the *maximum satisfiability* (*maxsat*) of the given constraints. To ensure that the solution is consistent with $\neg h_i$ and γ, we add them as *hard* constraints while the remaining sub-hypotheses appear as soft constraints; the procedure returns all the soft constraints it could satisfy as ζ (Line 12).

Validation. The Validate routine (Algorithm 2) accepts a logical formula σ and an oracle $\mathcal{O}$, and checks whether $\sigma \models \mathcal{O}$. This routine is invoked in Algorithm 1 on lines Lines 19 to 20. Here, the algorithm samples a set of datapoints ($\mathcal{W}$) and queries the oracle $\mathcal{O}$ to construct a response set $\mathcal{W}_{tgt}$ (Lines 1 to 2). If all responses are $\top$, then the validation check passes on $\mathcal{W}$ and the algorithm proceeds to perform a statistical check (Lines 3 and 4). If the confidence interval ci is found acceptable, it declares Success (Line 6), else it returns FailStat to indicate statistical check failure (Line 8). Otherwise, if some responses in the set $\mathcal{W}_{tgt}$ are $\bot$ then it returns FailTest along with sampled examples $\langle \mathcal{W}, \mathcal{W}_{tgt} \rangle$ that can be used to enrich the original dataset $\mathcal{D}$ (Line 10).

On the other hand, if any of the elements in $\mathcal{W}_{tgt}$ violates the condition (i.e., $\exists d \in \mathcal{W}.\ \sigma(d) \wedge \neg \mathcal{O}(d)$ is non-empty), then the algorithm indicates the existence of such a failing test and also returns the dataset containing this test (10).

Our primary algorithm (Algorithm 1) uses the Validate subroutine for both the soundness and maximality tests:

- for soundness validation, the algorithm calls the Validate subroutine with $\gamma \wedge \widehat{\varphi}$ and the oracle $\mathcal{O}$ (Line 19);
- for maximality validation, the algorithm calls the Validate subroutine with $\gamma \wedge \neg \widehat{\varphi}$ and a *negated* oracle $\neg \mathcal{O}$ that returns polarity opposite to that of $\mathcal{O}$ (Line 20);

If both the tests are successful, the algorithm returns the candidate hypothesis $\widehat{\varphi}$ along with the confidence interval ci. If any of the tests fail, i.e. soundness or maximality counterexamples are found, the algorithm augments the dataset $\mathcal{D}$ with the newly sampled examples $\mathcal{W}1 \cup \mathcal{W}2$ (Lines 21 to 25), and goes back in the loop with an augmented grammar (Line 26) to learn more expressive hypotheses.

If all the oracle tests pass but the statistical test fails for at least one of soundness or maximality, the dataset $\mathcal{D}$ is augmented with newly sampled examples (Line 28), and the grammar is augmented to enable learning more expressive hypotheses (Line 29). This procedure is run till a high-confidence explanatory hypothesis is found, or the time/resource budgets are exceeded.

Statistical Test. The StatisticalTests routine (in Algorithm 2) attempts to find the probability that the candidate hypothesis is indeed a valid explanatory hypothesis for the conclusion: given the input space (or sample space) σ, let p be the probability of drawing an input $x \in \sigma$ such that it is inconsistent with the oracle, i.e., $\sigma(x) \wedge \neg \mathcal{O}(x)$. As drawing a sample is essentially a Bernoulli trial, drawing, say n, samples ($n = |\mathcal{W}|$ in Algorithm 2) is a Binomial distribution with parameters n and p.

We use Wilson score interval [52] to calculate binomial proportion confidence interval. This test improves over Wald interval [31] normal approximation of the Binomial distribution. It does not have problems with overshoot and zero-width intervals that afflict the Wald interval and can be employed with small samples and skewed observations [15]. The Wilson score interval is given by Eq. (6), where $\hat{p}$ is the observed proportion or success rate in the sample, n is the sample size, and z is the Z-score corresponding to the desired confidence level.

$$\frac{\hat{p} + \frac{z^2}{2n} \pm z\sqrt{\frac{\hat{p}(1-\hat{p})}{n} + \frac{z^2}{4n^2}}}{1 + \frac{z^2}{n}} \quad \text{[Wilson Score]} \quad (6)$$

Grammar Augmentation and Termination. We maintain a total order on the grammars (languages) that express the sub-hypotheses; we augment the grammar (Line 25 and 28 in Algorithm 1) along this total order. If the set of these grammars is bounded, our algorithm will surely terminate, as the grammar can then only be augmented a bounded number of times. Otherwise, we run the system with a finite resource bound, like a time budget or a bound on the number of iterations of the outermost loop.

Lemma 1. *Given a premise γ, and an hypothesis $\mathcal{H}$ as $h_1 \wedge h_2 \wedge \cdots h_n$, the following inference rule is valid:*

$$\frac{\gamma \wedge \widehat{\varphi} \implies \psi \quad \gamma \wedge (\widehat{\varphi} \setminus h_i) \wedge \neg h_i \implies \psi}{\gamma \wedge (\widehat{\varphi} \setminus h_i) \implies \psi}$$

1. $\gamma \wedge \widehat{\varphi} \implies \psi$ *(Premise #1)*
2. $\gamma \wedge (\widehat{\varphi} \setminus h_i) \wedge h_i \implies \psi$ *(Extracting h_i from $\widehat{\varphi}$)*
3. $\gamma \wedge (\widehat{\varphi} \setminus h_i) \wedge \neg h_i \implies \psi$ *(Premise #2)*
4. $\neg\gamma \vee \neg(\widehat{\varphi} \setminus h_i) \vee \neg h_i \vee \psi$ *(Logical equivalence, from (2))*
5. $\neg\gamma \vee \neg(\widehat{\varphi} \setminus h_i) \vee h_i \vee \psi$ *(Logical equivalence, from (3))*
6. $\neg\gamma \vee \neg(\widehat{\varphi} \setminus h_i) \vee \psi$ *(Resolution, (4) & (5))*
7. $\gamma \wedge (\widehat{\varphi} \setminus h_i) \implies \psi$ *(Logical equivalence, from (6))*

Theorem 1. *The learned hypothesis from Algorithm 1 will be sound and maximal on the set $\mathcal{D}$ and the grammar $\mathcal{G}$. Further, they possess these properties on the whole input space with high statistical confidence.*

Proof of the above theorem is based on the argument that Algorithm 1 maintains soundness of $\widehat{\varphi}$ as an inductive invariant throughout its run, and by validity of Eq. (5). Maximality is achieved as the algorithm runs a fixpoint loop that removes sub-hypotheses till no more can be removed. The final statistical check ensures high confidence on the hypothesis.

The algorithm is complete *modulo the provided grammar*, i.e., if a solution exists that is expressible in the provided domain-specific language, then the algorithm would find it. This can be argued based on two facts: firstly, the Hypothesize function (Line 4) constructs all sub-hypotheses that are expressible in the grammar. Secondly, a sub-hypotheses is dropped only at Line 17: this operation is sound (see Lemma 1).

5 Specification Learning on Web Applications

We, now, discuss our instantiation of *specification inference modulo oracles* on web applications.

5.1 Oracle

To build an oracle for remotely hosted web applications, we need the ability to automatically fill web-pages on web-browsers, submit them to the web-server, and observe the response (that is, *success* or *error*) from the web-server. To that end, we use Playwright [38], a test-automation software for web-browsers. Our driver for the oracle parses the DOM (document object model) [33] of the presented web application form to create a test harness. We check the response of the oracle on a provided input vector, our driver uses Playwright to automatically fill the form based on the values from the provided input vector, and the mapping of form elements extracted from the DOM. Playwright submits the filled form to the web application and collects the response from the web-server. In case the web-application proceeds successfully, we return ACCEPT; on the other hand, if the web-application throws an exception, we return REJECT. To render automation in headed/headless mode, Playwright supports engines like Chromium, WebKit and Firefox and its API is available for multiple languages. We use Firefox in headless mode, and our automation script is in Python.

5.2 Hypothesis Learning

Our hypothesis learning algorithm uses the inference engine of the Daikon [19] invariant inference engine. Daikon packages a large library of expression templates, enabling it to learn non-trivial expressions. As Daikon performs a data-driven learning over these template expressions, it was ideal for our purpose. Our hypothesis grammar ($\mathcal{G}$) comprises of the template library of Daikon instantiated on the support, i.e. the input fields of the web-application form under study. Daikon uses the positive examples (form inputs that the application accepted successfully), to learn invariants as a conjunction of expressions instantiated from its template library—that serve our purpose of learning the strongest explanatory hypotheses. However, as Daikon does not use negative examples (form inputs that get rejected by the application), to maintain soundness on our dataset, we extend Daikon to drop sub-hypotheses based on the negative examples. As Daikon infers a large number of expressions, we postprocess inferred rules to remove trivial, repetitive, and semantically equivalent rules.

5.3 Hypothesis Grammar ($\mathcal{G}$)

Daikon has a huge list of invariant templates, comprising, but not limited to *arithmetic* (e.g., x + y = z), *equality and inequality* (e.g., x == y, x $\neq$ z), *ordering* (e.g., x $\leq$ y), *lower/upper bounds* (e.g., x $\geq$ 0, x $\leq$ 15), *array and list Invariants* (e.g., x[] elements $\leq$ c), *implications* (e.g., x $\implies$ y), etc.

The hypothesis grammar ($\mathcal{G}$) comprises of Daikon's expression template library. Further, our language is *typed*: we assign types based on the class of form's input fields: for example, textfields have a type string, integers as int, choices and links as bool, selections as enum etc.

Other than predicates formed by Daikon, we create certain additional predicates: for example, we add non-emptiness predicates (e.g. a textfield remains blank, or no selection was selected, etc.) for input fields. Further, Daikon allows the user to provide *split points* to generate predicates for implication invariants: adding more split points is our mechanism for augmenting the grammar $\mathcal{G}$. We initially start with split points that only comprise of list elements, non-emptiness predicates, bool and enum type elements. To augment the grammar, we add more complex splits comprising of combination of multiple input elements. We also discover predicates by performing binary search on the *bound*-type expressions to discover tighter upper/lower bounds. Users can also provide their own split points to have better control on the shape of the hypotheses.

5.4 High-Coverage Sampling

We build a test-driven strategy to constrained sampling that is inspired by similar work for fast sampling of propositional and bitvector formulas [16,17], and approximation of model counting in first-order logic [45]. We use a Satisfiability Modulo Theories (SMT) solver to perform constrained sampling over the premise and candidate hypothesis. SMT solver heuristics are tuned to perform local searching on "promising" search spaces, and hence, in general, using an SMT solver for building a sampler by enumerating models does not provide a good coverage. Our approach employs random input-space partitioning for constrained sampling over the input constraints. Let us assume that the form of a web-application has n input fields and we desire to constrained sample on logic formula σ. Considering the form inputs as points in an n-dimensional hyperspace, we use an SMT solver to sample n points. As n points uniquely determine an n-dimensional hyperplane, we attempt to construct the desired hyperplane, say, $a_n \cdot x_n + a_{n-1} \cdot x_{n-1} + \cdots + a_1 \cdot x_1 + a_0 = 0$. To that end, we solve the set of n simultaneous linear equations (corresponding to the n sampled points) to compute the coefficients $a_n, \ldots, a_1, a_0$.

For better distribution of the samples, we create two queries, $(\sigma \wedge a_n \cdot x_n + a_{n-1} \cdot x_{n-1} + \cdots + a_1 \cdot x_1 + a_0 > \delta)$ and $(\sigma \wedge a_n \cdot x_n + a_{n-1} \cdot x_{n-1} + \cdots + a_1 \cdot x_1 + a_0 < \delta)$, for user-selected values of δ, to compute two new inputs (points) in the input space. Now, with $n+2$ points, we again randomly select n points and repeat the above procedure till we obtain the desired number of samples.

5.5 Running Example

Figure 1 shows a web-application from the ERPNext software that creates tasks for a project. As a first step, we run Daikon to infer a candidate hypothesis as a conjunction of multiple sub-hypotheses. In this case, Daikon returns 472 sub-hypotheses: we show 10 of them in Table 1; the text highlighted in blue are the form fields and comparison with $\emptyset$ shows the non-emptiness predicate.

In the iterative weakening phase, we check if sub-hypothesis h_i can be dropped by querying the validity of the conclusion on dropping h_i from $\mathcal{H}$.

Table 1. Some example sub-hypotheses inferred by Vivaran

Tag	Hypothesis	Retained
h_1	(Status == 'Completed') $\implies$ (Completed On $\neq \emptyset$)	✓
h_2	(Status == 'Overdue') $\implies$ (Completed By == $\emptyset$)	✗
h_3	(Status == 'Overdue') $\implies$ (Completed On == $\emptyset$)	✗
h_4	(Status == 'Completed') $\implies$ (Completed On $\leq$ Today)	✓
h_5	(Expected Start Date $\neq \emptyset$) $\wedge$ (Expected End Date $\neq \emptyset$) $\implies$ (Expected Start Date $\leq$ Expected End Date)	✓
h_6	(Completed By $\neq \emptyset$) $\implies$ (Completed On $\neq \emptyset$)	✗
h_7	(Subject $\neq \emptyset$)	✓
h_8	%Progress $\leq$ 100	✓
h_9	%Progress $\geq$ Weight	✗
h_{10}	Weight $\leq$ 60	✗

On testing with sub-hypotheses h_1, h_4, h_5, h_7, and h_8, the oracle responds with ACCEPT for all samples in C, and hence, all are retained.

However, for h_2, the query $\neg h_2 \wedge (\mathcal{H} \setminus h_2)$ becomes *unsat*: if the Status is 'Overdue', then Completed On has to be $\emptyset$ because of h_3, but Completed On cannot be $\emptyset$ because of h_6. Therefore, we perform MaxSAT with $\neg h_2$ as the hard constraint and all other sub-hypotheses as soft constraints. MaxSAT is able to satisfy all sub-hypotheses except h_6. After sampling data points based on the returned sub-hypotheses, we find that all data-points are accepted, and hence, h_2 can be dropped (by Eq. (5)).

Overall, in the first iteration, sub-hypotheses h_2, h_3, and h_6 get dropped, while we learn improved bounds for h_{10} with binary search. In the second iteration, sub-hypotheses h_9 and h_{10} get dropped. In Table 1, column Retained shows green ticks for sub-hypotheses that survive the iterative weakening phase, and a red cross otherwise.

For statistical validation, we collect 100 assignments that satisfy input types of the data-fields. High-coverage sampling does not yield any (soundness or maximality) counterexamples. Finally, Wilson score gives a confidence interval that falls in the range [0.96, 1] with 95% probability.

Table 1 lists 10 sub-hypotheses generated by Daikon for the web application form shown in Fig. 1. All the retained sub-hypotheses correspond to manually constructed ground-truth hypotheses embedded in the web-application.

Discussion on the Inferred Constraints. The sub-hypotheses h_1, h_4 together impose an interesting *data-sanity* constraint that Completed On cannot be empty if the Status is 'Completed'; further, if the Status is 'Completed', then the Completed On date cannot be later than today. Again, h_5 imposes an interesting *semantic constraint* constraint over two, seemingly independent, data-fields to impose that the Expected Start Date cannot be later than the Expected End

Table 2. Experimental Evaluation of VIVARAN on ERPNext web applications

Name	Web Application Details (T,L,C,S,D,Cu,F,I,P,Dl,Co)	Number of Rules			Reduction		MaxSat	
		#IH	#AW	#FH	%AW	%FH	#Q	ST (secs)
Task	(2,7,3,2,5,0,2,2,1,0,1)	472	289	6	39	98	6333±9	2596±6
Project	(3,8,1,7,2,1,0,0,0,0,0)	197	101	2	48	98	2807±19	822±7
AMLog	(1,2,1,2,1,0,0,0,0,0,0)	29	15	7	48	53	301±7	90±1
SComp	(3,0,15,2,0,2,0,0,0,0,0)	7	2	2	71	0	73±0	24±0
Customer	(4,19,5,1,0,0,1,0,0,0,0)	16	4	4	75	0	298±1	63±5
SPlan	(1,3,0,0,2,1,0,1,0,0,0)	26	23	7	11	70	316±0	69±1
EClaim	(2,10,1,2,3,2,0,0,0,0,0)	146	109	8	25	93	2423±3	643±3
MRequest	(2,10,0,2,2,0,1,0,0,0,0)	80	63	10	21	84	1634±0	377±2
POrder	(6,26,5,2,5,2,4,0,0,0,0)	113	98	9	13	90	2949±1	858±3
LoanType	(2,7,2,2,0,2,0,1,2,0,0)	171	137	10	20	93	2134±13	434±3
PProfile	(1,20,11,1,0,1,0,0,0,0,0)	12	10	8	17	20	225±0	70±1
Grievance	(4,6,0,1,2,0,0,0,0,2,0)	41	29	12	29	59	740±3	162±1
IPrice	(2,6,0,0,2,1,0,2,0,0,0)	33	25	4	24	84	339±0	69±1
ECategory	(1,1,1,0,0,1,0,0,0,0,0)	5	4	2	20	50	36±0	16±0
CCenter	(1,2,2,0,0,0,0,0,0,0,0)	3	3	3	0	0	4±0	0.1±0
ACategory	(1,5,1,0,0,0,0,0,0,0,0)	4	4	4	0	0	13±0	0.2±0
Voucher	(1,3,0,0,2,0,0,0,0,0,0)	16	13	7	19	46	225±0	51±1
Contract	(2,2,2,2,3,0,0,0,0,2,0)	128	85	3	34	96	1773±9	432±2
Attendance	(0,4,2,2,1,0,0,0,0,0,0)	47	38	7	19	82	647±62	115±12
AssetMain	(1,4,0,2,1,0,0,0,0,0,0)	27	23	6	18	74	290±0	64±1

Date; however, any of these fields are allowed to be empty and the constraint holds only if both are filled. It is quite impressive that VIVARAN can infer such deep constraints with only an oracle access to the application.

6 Case Study

We conduct a study on a large Enterprise Resource Planning (ERP) software, ERPNext [20], consisting of many different web-applications serving a variety of business needs. ERP softwares are complex systems that manage and automate core business processes of entire organizations. We conducted our studies on 20 web-applications of ERPNext across the diverse set of functionalities it offers. Below we discuss some of the web-applications within ERPNext that we included in this case-study.

Task: This web-application allows employees to create and update the status of the tasks within existing projects. If the created task is in progress, an expected time frame for its completion must be specified, in which case, the expected start date must be earlier than the expected end date, or a task may be created without any deadline. When a task is marked completed, it is mandatory to provide its completion date. The form is dynamic: the completion date only appears if task status is completed. The application also allows other functionalities like setting task priority, adding a task description, allocating estimated working hours, etc.

LoanType: Defines the structure and repayment terms for loan requests raised by companies within the organization. It requires the user to specify the annual interest rate, grace period, repayment schedule, and related conditions. If the loan is categorized as a term loan, it is mandatory to specify how the loan repayment will be scheduled—either monthly or based on a fixed number of days. In cases where the schedule is based on calendar days, the user must also specify whether repayments should begin at the start of the next month or at the end of the current month. Both repayment schedule and the repayment start timing are dynamic fields: they appear only when the relevant schemes are selected.

Attendance: It records an employee's current status—such as present, absent, on leave, working from home, or on half-day leave. If the employee is on full-day or half-day leave, it is mandatory to specify the type of leave, such as, casual leave, leave without pay, or others; these option appears dynamically only when half-day or full-day leave type is selected. If the status is marked as on leave, the attendance date must not be later than the current date.

EClaim (expense claim): This web-application allows employees to draft, submit, and track their claims, while also enabling managers to approve or reject them. The claim amount raised by the employee should always be greater or equal to the sanctioned amount. If the claimed amount was already paid by the employee, it is mandatory to specify the mode of payment. A table lists out all the claims raised by a particular employee.

We ran our tool VIVARAN on a machine with an Intel(R) Xeon(R) Silver 4108 CPU @ 1.80GHz machine with 48 GB RAM. We use Playright [38] for automating our oracle queries on the web-application and the SMT solver Z3 [12] for constrained sampling.

The column *Web Application Details* in Table 2 shows (**T, L, C, S, D, Cu, F, I, P, Dl, Co**) to represent the counts of different types of elements in the form of the web-application (in respective order): text, link, checkbox, selections, date, currency, floats, integers, percent, dynamic link and color. To understand the quality of our inference routine, for each of these, we manually examine the source code of both the frontend (in JavaScript) and backend scripts (in Python) to also construct the ground truths as first-order logical constraints.

Quality of The Inferred Specification. We test our inferred hypothesis with 100 samples where all our tests pass, i.e., the hypothesis is consistent with the oracle responses, both for soundness and maximality. On the Wilson score interval statistical test, the confidence interval lies in [0.96, 1] with 95% probability.

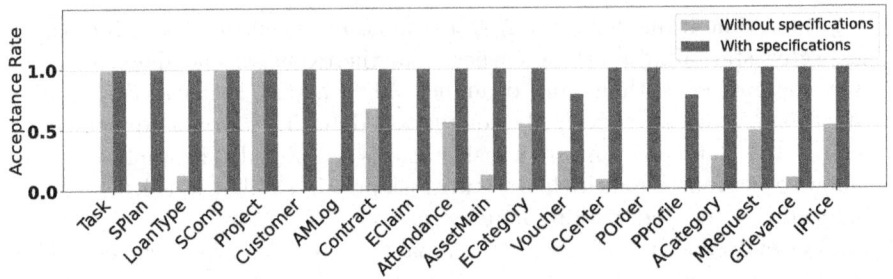

Fig. 5. Comparison of acceptance rate between the datasets generated using LLM

We, also, perform exact checks (Eqs. 1 and 2) with manually constructed ground-truth hypothesis. We found that the hypothesis inferred by VIVARAN was *semantically equivalent* to the ground-truths for all of our benchmarks.

Effectiveness of Weakening and Postprocessing. In Table 2, column #**IH** shows the initial number of sub-hypotheses, #**AW** shows number of sub-hypotheses after the counterexample-guided iterative weakening phase terminates, #**FH** shows final number of sub-hypotheses obtained after post-processing, %**AW** shows the percentage drop in number of sub-hypotheses after weakening phase, and %**FH** shows the percentage drop in number of sub-hypotheses from weakening phase to rules after post-processing phase. Iterative weakening is quite effective at improving the *coverage* of the hypothesis by dropping many sub-hypotheses via the elimination rule: on an average, 28% sub-hypotheses were dropped by this phase. The post-processing phase is semantics preserving; it only removes trivial and semantically equivalent sub-hypotheses, generating a hypothesis that is better for human consumption. This phase removes about 59% sub-hypotheses on an average.

Cost of VIVARAN. In Table 2, column #**Q** shows the number of oracle queries, and **ST** shows the time taken by the SMT solver (in seconds) in constrained sampling. For both time and number of queries, we show average and standard deviation over three runs for each benchmark instance. VIVARAN takes between 0.1s for simpler forms to about 43 mins for complex forms where Diakon infers a large number of invariants. VIVARAN takes an average time of 347.8 s for an instance, and makes (on an average) 1178 queries to the oracle for inferring explanatory hypothesis for a benchmark instance.

Synthetic Data Generation. While the focus of our work is specification inference modulo oracles, we did some preliminary experiments to show the utility of the same in synthetic data-generation. We used the GPT-4o-mini model to generate synthetic data for our web-applications.

For each benchmark, we created two datasets: one where inferred specifications from our tool were included in the prompt (*with specifications*), and another where they were not included (*without specifications*). We generated 25 samples per benchmark, resulting in a total of 500 samples. We chose to use an LLM for this task because there is evidence that LLMs can produce synthetic data that closely resembles real-world data in both structure and meaning across different domains [51,56]. For each web-application, we provide the purpose of the form, the domain of values for each field and the label corresponding to each field within the prompt. For the case of *with specifications*, we also include the inferred specifications while instructing the LLM to only generate data that adhere to these specifications.

Figure 5 shows a grouped histogram comparing the *acceptance rate* (y-axis) of each benchmark web application (x-axis): the *acceptance rate* provides the percentage of the data-points that were accepted by the respective web-application; in other words, these data-points passed all the semantic checks sprawled across the frontend and backend of the web-application.

We can make the following observations:

- In some cases, like TASK, SCOMP, and PROJECT, the LLM could generate semantically consistent data even without the inferred specifications. In these cases, the LLM could decipher meaningful field names in these applications to understand the underlying semantics of these data-fields.
- In most cases, the *acceptance rate* is quite low when the specifications were not included. This shows that only the field names are not enough for the LLM to generate semantically consistent data-points.
- When the specifications were included, semantically consistent data was genarated with a cent-percent acceptance rate in most cases. This shows the value of specification inference.
- There exist a couple of web-applications (VOUCHER and PPROFILE), where the acceptance rate did not reach 100%. The reason for this is that like any other machine-learning model, the LLMs are not guaranteed to follow all the provided instructions; in these cases, some of the provided specifications were violated in the synthetic data generated by the LLM. However, even in these cases, the acceptance rate is close to 80%. Of course, our synthetic data-generation module employs a static checker to checks if the data generated by LLM indeed satisfies all the inferred specifications, allowing only semantically consistent data to included in the dataset (Fig. 3).

On an average, only 36% of the samples were accepted when specifications were not provided versus 98% when specifications were included in the prompt. Hence, specification inference can significantly improve semantic consistency of the synthesized data-points. Note that specification inference is an offline and one-time activity. Once these specifications are generated, large volumes of semantically consistent databases can be generated.

7 Related Works

Specification Inference. Previous work assume availability of the logical description of conclusion ϕ, while VIVARAN only requires an oracle access to

ϕ. To the best of our knowledge, ours is the first work that proposes and solves the problem of specification inference modulo oracles. Albarghouthi et al. [2] infer logical specifications of unknown procedures in a program by casting it into a multi-abduction problem and solve it using counterexample guided inductive synthesis (CEGIS). Farzan et al. [21] synthesize specifications for divide and conquer programs where individual maximal specification for components do not exist. Prabhu et al. [40] proposed a CEGIS based framework to synthesize specification/invariants for programs with complex-control flow. Reynolds et al. [42] propose a syntax-guided technique for abduction problems in quantifier-free logic by recursively generating first-order logic formulae ϕ based on a grammar, checking if ϕ is consistent with axioms and goals, and refining it with counterexamples, if any. Echenim et al. [18] propose an algorithm to synthesize implicates of a formula ϕ module theory $\mathcal{T}$ that iterates over the subsets of user-defined abducibles and checks if the subset-abducibles with ϕ is $\mathcal{T}$-unsatisfiable. All these approaches need the complete description of the conclusion (i.e., the program) so that they can use techniques like quantifier elimination and CEGIS.

Program Synthesis. Our work is closely related to program synthesis. SyGuS [3] synthesizes programs from input-output specifications using a predefined context-free grammar to constrain the function body. Synthesis has seen applications in learning heap-manipulations [23,41,43,49,50], parsers [32,47], puzzles [29], generating buggy corpus [45], debugging [7,8], abstract transformers [26–28], learning differentially private mechanisms [44], and repairing faulty programs [48–50]. However, in contrast to learning programs, our approach focuses on learning hypotheses or specifications.

Logic Modulo Oracles. It increasingly becoming important to handle logic problems modulo oracles. Sādhak [35], and Delphi [39] propose SMT solvers that are capable of answering satisfiability queries modulo oracles. While Sādhak uses a synergistic combination of fuzzer and SMT engine in a conflict-driven fuzz loop (CDFL), Delphi attempts to construct a satisfiable assignment by using an SMT solver to query the oracle. Starfuzz [34] builds upon Sādhak to improve the reliability of proofs on interactive theorem provers that use lemmas from external sources. Achar [30] proposed an algorithm to synthesize inductive invariants for programs with concealed components by dividing the task between and SMT solver and a fuzzer. Colossus [37] is a symbolic execution engine that uses fuzzer to solve path conditions, allowing symbolic execution to be used when only an oracle access to some functions are available.

Data-Driven Learning. Data-driven techniques have been used to learn invariants for probabilistic programs [4–6], boolean functions [24] and maximal specifications [57]. Ignatiev et al. [25] perform rule mining via formal methods.

Testing Database-Backed Applications. Yan et al. [54] tackle the problem of creating synthetic databases for database-backed applications by ensuring that the generated data is consistent with the application semantics via static analysis on the application code. In contrast, we propose a *black-box* technique of inferring input specifications of the application directly from its behavior.

These inferred specifications can then be used to generate application-consistent synthetic inputs (database).

8 Conclusions

We apply *specification inference modulo oracles* in extracting validation rules for webapps, that has applications in testing database-backed applications [54]. The specifications inferred by VIVARAN also reveals interesting semantic relations between the inputs rules required by the applications.

Acknowledgements. We thank the annonymous reviewers for their valuable feedback. This research is supported, in part, by Qualcomm Faculty Award.

References

1. Agrawal, P., Chandra, B., Emani, K.V., Garg, N., Sudarshan, S.: Test data generation for database applications. In: 2018 IEEE 34th International Conference on Data Engineering (ICDE), pp. 1621–1624. IEEE (2018)
2. Albarghouthi, A., Dillig, I., Gurfinkel, A.: Maximal specification synthesis. ACM SIGPLAN Notices **51**(1), 789–801 (2016)
3. Alur, R., et al.: Syntax-guided synthesis. IEEE (2013)
4. Bao, J., Trivedi, N., Pathak, D., Hsu, J., Roy, S.: Data-driven invariant learning for probabilistic programs. In: Shoham, S., Vizel, Y. (eds.) CAV 2022. LNCS, vol. 13371. Springer, Cham (2022). https://doi.org/10.1007/978-3-031-13185-1_3
5. Bao, J., Trivedi, N., Pathak, D., Hsu, J., Roy, S.: Data-driven invariant learning for probabilistic programs (extended abstract). In: Elkind, E. (ed.) Proceedings of the Thirty-Second International Joint Conference on Artificial Intelligence, IJCAI 2023, pp. 6415–6419. International Joint Conferences on Artificial Intelligence Organization (Aug 2023). https://doi.org/10.24963/ijcai.2023/712, sister Conferences Best Papers
6. Bao, J., Trivedi, N., Pathak, D., Hsu, J., Roy, S.: Data-driven invariant learning for probabilistic programs. Formal Methods Syst. Design, 1–29 (2024)
7. Bavishi, R., Pandey, A., Roy, S.: Regression aware debugging for mobile applications. In: Proceedings of the 1st International Workshop on Mobile Development, pp. 21–22 (2016)
8. Bavishi, R., Pandey, A., Roy, S.: To be precise: regression aware debugging. ACM SIGPLAN Not. **51**(10), 897–915 (2016)
9. Beyene, T., Chaudhuri, S., Popeea, C., Rybalchenko, A.: A constraint-based approach to solving games on infinite graphs. In: Proceedings of the 41st ACM SIGPLAN-SIGACT Symposium on Principles of Programming Languages, pp. 221–233 (2014)
10. Boutilier, C., Beche, V.: Abduction as belief revision. Artifi. Intell. **77**(1), 43–94 (1995)
11. Das, A., Lahiri, S.K., Lal, A., Li, Y.: Angelic verification: precise verification modulo unknowns. In: Kroening, D., Păsăreanu, C.S. (eds.) CAV 2015. LNCS, vol. 9206, pp. 324–342. Springer, Cham (2015). https://doi.org/10.1007/978-3-319-21690-4_19

12. Moura, L., Bjørner, N.: Z3: an efficient SMT solver. In: Ramakrishnan, C.R., Rehof, J. (eds.) TACAS 2008. LNCS, vol. 4963, pp. 337–340. Springer, Heidelberg (2008). https://doi.org/10.1007/978-3-540-78800-3_24
13. Dillig, I., Dillig, T., Li, B., McMillan, K.: Inductive invariant generation via abductive inference. Acm Sigplan Notices **48**(10), 443–456 (2013)
14. Dimovski, A.S.: Generalized program sketching by abstract interpretation and logical abduction. In: International Static Analysis Symposium. pp. 212–230. Springer (2023)
15. Doane, D.P., Seward, L.E.: Measuring skewness: a forgotten statistic? J. Statist. Educ. **19**(2) (2011)
16. Dutra, R., Bachrach, J., Sen, K.: Guidedsampler: coverage-guided sampling of smt solutions. In: 2019 Formal Methods in Computer Aided Design (FMCAD), pp. 203–211. IEEE (2019)
17. Dutra, R., Laeufer, K., Bachrach, J., Sen, K.: Efficient sampling of sat solutions for testing. In: Proceedings of the 40th International Conference on Software Engineering, pp. 549–559 (2018)
18. Echenim, M., Peltier, N., Sellami, Y.: A generic framework for implicate generation modulo theories. In: Galmiche, D., Schulz, S., Sebastiani, R. (eds.) IJCAR 2018. LNCS (LNAI), vol. 10900, pp. 279–294. Springer, Cham (2018). https://doi.org/10.1007/978-3-319-94205-6_19
19. Ernst, M.D., et al.: The daikon system for dynamic detection of likely invariants. Sci. Comput. Program. **69**(1–3), 35–45 (2007)
20. ERPNext: Free and open source enterprise resource planning (erp). https://github.com/frappe/erpnext (Aug 2023)
21. Farzan, A., Nicolet, V.: Phased synthesis of divide and conquer programs. In: Proceedings of the 42nd ACM SIGPLAN International Conference on Programming Language Design and Implementation, pp. 974–986 (2021)
22. Finin, T., Morris, G.: Abductive reasoning in multiple fault diagnosis. Artif. Intell. Rev. **3**(2–3), 129–158 (1989)
23. Garg, A., Roy, S.: Synthesizing heap manipulations via integer linear programming. In: Blazy, S., Jensen, T. (eds.) SAS 2015. LNCS, vol. 9291, pp. 109–127. Springer, Heidelberg (2015). https://doi.org/10.1007/978-3-662-48288-9_7
24. Golia, P., Roy, S., Meel, K.S.: Manthan: a data-driven approach for boolean function synthesis. In: Lahiri, S.K., Wang, C. (eds.) CAV 2020. LNCS, vol. 12225, pp. 611–633. Springer, Cham (2020). https://doi.org/10.1007/978-3-030-53291-8_31
25. Ignatiev, A., Lam, E., Stuckey, P.J., Marques-Silva, J.: A scalable two stage approach to computing optimal decision sets. In: Proceedings of the AAAI Conference on Artificial Intelligence, vol. 35, pp. 3806–3814 (2021)
26. Kalita, P.K., Muduli, S.K., D'Antoni, L., Reps, T., Roy, S.: Synthesizing abstract transformers. Proc. ACM Programming Lang. **6**(OOPSLA2), 1291–1319 (2022)
27. Kalita, P.K., Reps, T., Roy, S.: Synthesizing abstract transformers for reduced-product domains. In: Giacobazzi, R., Gorla, A. (eds.) SAS 2024. LNCS, vol. 14995. Springer, Cham (2025). https://doi.org/10.1007/978-3-031-74776-2_6
28. Kalita, P.K., Reps, T., Roy, S.: Automated abstract transformer synthesis for reduced product domains. ACM Trans. Softw. Eng. Methodol. (2025)
29. Lahiri, S., Kalita, P.K., Chittora, A.K., Vankudre, V., Roy, S.: Program synthesis meets visual what-comes-next puzzles. In: Proceedings of the 39th IEEE/ACM International Conference on Automated Software Engineering, pp. 418–429 (2024)
30. Lahiri, S., Roy, S.: Almost correct invariants: synthesizing inductive invariants by fuzzing proofs. In: Proceedings of the 31st ACM SIGSOFT International Symposium on Software Testing and Analysis, pp. 352–364 (2022)

31. de Laplace, P.S.: Théorie analytique des probabilités, vol. 7. Courcier (1820)
32. Leung, A., Sarracino, J., Lerner, S.: Interactive parser synthesis by example. ACM SIGPLAN Notices **50**(6), 565–574 (2015)
33. Marini, J.: Document object model. McGraw-Hill, Inc (2002)
34. Muduli, S.K., Padulkar, R.R., Roy, S:. Interactive theorem proving modulo fuzzing. In: Gurfinkel, A., Ganesh, V. (eds.) CAV 2024. LNCS, vol. 14681. Springer, Cham (2024).https://doi.org/10.1007/978-3-031-65627-9_24
35. Muduli, S.K., Roy, S.: Satisfiability modulo fuzzing: a synergistic combination of SMT solving and fuzzing. Proc. ACM Program. Lang. **6**(OOPSLA2), 1236–1263 (2022)
36. Pan, K., Wu, X., Xie, T.: Guided test generation for database applications via synthesized database interactions. ACM Trans. Softw. Eng. Methodol. (TOSEM) **23**(2), 1–27 (2014)
37. Pandey, A., Kotcharlakota, P.R.G., Roy, S.: Deferred concretization in symbolic execution via fuzzing. In: Proceedings of the 28th ACM SIGSOFT International Symposium on Software Testing and Analysis, pp. 228–238 (2019)
38. playwright: Framework for web testing and automation. https://github.com/microsoft/playwright (Aug 2023)
39. Polgreen, E., Reynolds, A., Seshia, S.A.: Satisfiability and synthesis modulo oracles. In: Finkbeiner, B., Wies, T. (eds.) VMCAI 2022. LNCS, vol. 13182, pp. 263–284. Springer, Cham (2022). https://doi.org/10.1007/978-3-030-94583-1_13
40. Prabhu, S., Fedyukovich, G., Madhukar, K., D'Souza, D.: Specification synthesis with constrained horn clauses. In: Proceedings of the 42nd ACM SIGPLAN International Conference on Programming Language Design and Implementation, pp. 1203–1217 (2021)
41. Qiu, X., Solar-Lezama, A.: Natural synthesis of provably-correct data-structure manipulations. Proc. ACM Program. Lang. **1**(OOPSLA), 1–28 (2017)
42. Reynolds, A., Barbosa, H., Larraz, D., Tinelli, C.: Scalable algorithms for abduction via enumerative syntax-guided synthesis. In: Peltier, N., Sofronie-Stokkermans, V. (eds.) IJCAR 2020. LNCS (LNAI), vol. 12166, pp. 141–160. Springer, Cham (2020). https://doi.org/10.1007/978-3-030-51074-9_9
43. Roy, S.: From concrete examples to heap manipulating programs. In: Logozzo, F., Fähndrich, M. (eds.) SAS 2013. LNCS, vol. 7935, pp. 126–149. Springer, Heidelberg (2013). https://doi.org/10.1007/978-3-642-38856-9_9
44. Roy, S., Hsu, J., Albarghouthi, A.: Learning differentially private mechanisms. In: 2021 IEEE Symposium on Security and Privacy (SP), pp. 852–865. IEEE (2021)
45. Roy, S., Pandey, A., Dolan-Gavitt, B., Hu, Y.: Bug synthesis: challenging bug-finding tools with deep faults. In: Proceedings of the 2018 26th ACM Joint Meeting on European Software Engineering Conference and Symposium on the Foundations of Software Engineering, pp. 224–234 (2018)
46. Sidhu, T., Cruder, O., Huff, G.: An abductive inference technique for fault diagnosis in electrical power transmission networks. IEEE Trans. Power Delivery **12**(1), 515–522 (1997)
47. Singal, D., et al.: Parse condition: symbolic encoding of ll (1) parsing. In: LPAR, pp. 637–655 (2018)
48. Verma, A., Kalita, P.K., Pandey, A., Roy, S.: Interactive debugging of concurrent programs under relaxed memory models. In: Proceedings of the 18th ACM/IEEE International Symposium on Code Generation and Optimization, pp. 68–80 (2020)
49. Verma, S., Roy, S.: Synergistic debug-repair of heap manipulations. In: Proceedings of the 2017 11th Joint Meeting on Foundations of Software Engineering, pp. 163–173 (2017)

50. Verma, S., Roy, S.: Debug-localize-repair: a symbiotic construction for heap manipulations. Formal Methods Syst. Design **58**(3), 399–439 (2021)
51. Veselovsky, V., Ribeiro, M.H., Arora, A., Josifoski, M., Anderson, A., West, R.: Generating faithful synthetic data with large language models: a case study in computational social science. arXiv preprint arXiv:2305.15041 (2023)
52. Wilson, E.B.: Probable inference, the law of succession, and statistical inference. J. Am. Stat. Assoc. **22**(158), 209–212 (1927)
53. Wu, K., et al.: Automatic synthesis of generalized winning strategies of impartial combinatorial games using smt solvers. In: IJCAI, pp. 1703–1711 (2020)
54. Yan, C., Nath, S., Lu, S.: Generating test databases for database-backed applications. In: 2023 IEEE/ACM 45th International Conference on Software Engineering (ICSE), pp. 2048–2059. IEEE (2023)
55. Zhang, H., Shen, H., Manyà, F.: Exact algorithms for max-sat. Electr. Notes Theoret. Comput. Sci. **86**(1), 190–203 (2003)
56. Zhang, X., Chowdhury, R.R., Gupta, R.K., Shang, J.: Large language models for time series: A survey. arXiv preprint arXiv:2402.01801 (2024)
57. Zhou, Z., Dickerson, R., Delaware, B., Jagannathan, S.: Data-driven abductive inference of library specifications. Proc. ACM Program. Lang. **5**(OOPSLA), 1–29 (2021)

Decision Procedure for a Theory of String Sequences

Denghang Hu[1,2(✉)], Taolue Chen[3], Philipp Rümmer[4], Fu Song[1,2,5], and Zhilin Wu[1,2]

[1] Key Laboratory of System Software and State Key Laboratory of Computer Science, Institute of Software, Chinese Academy of Sciences, Beijing, China
[2] University of Chinese Academy of Sciences, Beijing, China
hudh@ios.ac.cn
[3] Birkbeck, University of London, London, UK
[4] University of Regensburg, Regensburg, Germany
[5] Nanjing Institute of Software Technology, Nanjing, China

Abstract. The theory of sequences, supported by many SMT solvers, can model program data types including bounded arrays and lists. Sequences are parameterized by the element data type and provide operations such as accessing elements, concatenation, forming sub-sequences and updating elements. Strings and sequences are intimately related; many operations, e.g., matching a string according to a regular expression, splitting strings, or joining strings in a sequence, are frequently used in string-manipulating programs. Nevertheless, these operations are typically not directly supported by existing SMT solvers, which instead only consider the generic theory of sequences. In this paper, we propose a theory of string sequences and study its satisfiability. We show that, while it is undecidable in general, the decidability can be recovered by restricting to the straight-line fragment. This is shown by encoding each string sequence as a string, and each string sequence operation as a corresponding string operation. We provide pre-image computation for the resulting string operations with respect to automata, effectively casting it into the generic OSTRICH string constraint solving framework. We implement the new decision procedure as a tool OSTRICH^{SEQ}, and carry out experiments on benchmark constraints generated from real-world JavaScript programs, hand-crafted templates and unit tests. The experiments confirm the efficacy of our approach.

1 Introduction

Many real-world applications, such as web applications and programs processing data of type string, involve a multitude of complex operations that convert between strings and string sequences. Typical examples include join and split, which are present in almost all built-in libraries of modern programming languages. Reasoning about string sequences, also known as extendable string arrays [33], is therefore a crucial aspect of program analysis.

Satisfiability Modulo Theory (SMT [9]) solving provides an automatic way to verify software systems. At the moment, there is no standardized sequence theory in SMT-LIB [8]. Instead, in verification tools, often the theory of arrays is used, which is limited and does not provide even basic operations like sequence length. Fortunately, [14] proposed a basic format for a sequence theory, which has been implemented and extended by SMT solvers such as Z3 [25] and cvc5 [7] with practical operations. In particular, [43] presents a calculus in cvc5 for reasoning about string sequences, which extends the proposal [14] with update (aka write) operations. The implementation of sequences in Z3 has been documented in the Z3 guide [49] and includes operations such as map and foldleft (but no update).

Although existing SMT solvers are effective at reasoning about sequences in general, to the best of our knowledge, none of them directly support functions that convert between strings and string sequences such as join and split. While it is possible to implement these functions using existing ones for some SMT solvers (e.g., Z3 can use map and foldleft to implement the join function), usually the solvers do not provide decision procedures for those theories and fail to solve many instances. This limitation poses a significant challenge for program analysis that involves such operations. The purpose of our work is to fill this gap.

Contributions. We propose a logic (aka constraint language) SeqStr of string sequences, which extends the existing sequence theory in SMT solvers with dedicated operations of string sequences and strings. In addition to the standard string operations (replace/replaceAll, reverse, finite transducers, regular constraints, length, indexOf, substring, etc.), our logic emphasizes the interaction between strings and string sequences through operations such as split, join, filter, and matchAll. For instance, split splits a string into a sequence of substrings according to a regular expression; join concatenates all the strings in a sequence to obtain a single string. More details can be found in Sect. 4. Typically, when string sequences are considered, it is natural to consider the integer data type as well; for instance, one usually needs to refer to the length of a sequence or the index of a specific sequence element. As a result, SeqStr features three data types: integers, strings, and string sequences. In terms of operations, the logic subsumes, to our best knowledge, most string constraint languages that have been proposed in the literature.

Our main focus is the decision procedure for the satisfiability problem of SeqStr. Because of its expressiveness, it is perhaps not surprising that SeqStr is undecidable in general. To reinstate decidability, we consider the straight-line fragment, which imposes a syntactic restriction on the constraints written in the logic. Straight-line formulas naturally arise when verifying programs using bounded model checking or symbolic execution, which unroll loops in the programs up to a given depth and convert programs to static single assignment form (i.e. each variable is defined at most once). For example, a majority of the constraints in the standard Kaluza benchmarks [41] satisfy this condition. (Cf. Sect. 3 for a concrete example.)

The general strategy of our decision procedure is to encode each string sequence as a string in such a way that all operations for string sequences considered in SeqStr can be transformed into string operations, possibly involving integers. As such, the decidability of (straight-line) SeqStr is reduced to string constraints with the integer data type, which was shown to be decidable [19]. Needless to say, this strategy requires overcoming certain technical challenges, as the string constraints resulting from the reduction typically encompass complex (and sometimes non-standard) string operations, which go well beyond the capacity of state-of-the-art string constraint solvers. Recall that for the decidability of string constraints with integers, cost-enriched finite automata (CEFA), a variant of cost-register automata, were utilized [19]. The crux of our technical contributions is thus to compute the backward images of CEFAs under the fairly complex string operations (cf. Section 5.2), so the powerful string constraint solving framework OSTRICH [17,20] can be harnessed.

We implement the decision procedure as a new solver OSTRICH[SEQ] on top of OSTRICH [20] and Princess [39]. To evaluate the effectiveness of OSTRICH[SEQ], we curate two benchmark suites of constraints that are randomly generated from templates (only using the operations directly supported by some existing SMT solvers) and extracted from real-world JavaScript programs and unit tests (involving string sequence operations that existing SMT solvers do not natively support), respectively. On both benchmark suites, the experimental results show that OSTRICH[SEQ] can solve considerably more constraints than SOTA string solvers including cvc5, Z3, Z3-noodler [22], OSTRICH and Princess[ARR] [40], while being largely as efficient as most of them.

Organization. Section 2 gives the preliminaries. Section 3 presents a motivating example. Section 4 defines the logic SeqStr of string sequences. Section 5 presents the decision procedure. Section 6 presents the benchmarks and experiments. Section 7 discusses the related work. The paper is concluded in Sect. 8.

2 Preliminaries

Let $\mathbb{N}$ denote the set of natural numbers. For $1 \leq n \in \mathbb{N}$, let $[n] := \{1, \ldots, n\}$, and for $m < n \in \mathbb{N}$, let $[m, n] := \{j \mid m \leq j \leq n\}$. We also use standard quantifier-free/existential *linear integer arithmetic* (LIA) formulas, which are typically ranged over by ϕ, φ, etc. For an integer term t, we use $t[t_1/t_2]$ to denote the term obtained by replacing t_2 with t_1 in t, where t_1 and t_2 are integer terms.

Strings, Languages, and Transductions. We fix an alphabet Σ, i.e., a finite set of letters. A *string* over Σ is a finite sequence of letters from Σ. We use Σ^* to denote the set of strings over Σ and ε to denote the empty string. A *language* over Σ is a subset of Σ^*. We will use $L_1, L_2, \ldots$ to denote languages. For two languages $L_1, L_2 \subseteq \Sigma^*$, $L_1 \cup L_2$ denotes the union of L_1 and L_2, and $L_1 \cdot L_2$ denotes the concatenation of L_1 and L_2, that is, $\{u_1 \cdot u_2 \mid u_1 \in L_1, u_2 \in L_2\}$. For a language $L \subseteq \Sigma^*$, we define the complement of L as $\bar{L} = \{w \in \Sigma^* \mid w \notin L\}$, moreover, we define L^n for $n \in \mathbb{N}$, the *iteration* of L for n times, inductively as: $L^0 = \{\varepsilon\}$ and $L^n = L \cdot L^{n-1}$ for $n > 0$. We also use L^* to denote the iteration of L for arbitrarily many times, that is, $L^* = \bigcup_{n \in \mathbb{N}} L^n$, and let $L^+ = \bigcup_{n>0} L^n$. A *transduction* over Σ is a binary relation over Σ^*, namely, a subset of $\Sigma^* \times \Sigma^*$.

Regular expressions over Σ are defined in a standard way, i.e.,

$$e \stackrel{\text{def}}{=} \emptyset \mid \varepsilon \mid a \mid e + e \mid e \cdot e \mid e^* \text{where } a \in \Sigma.$$

The language $\mathcal{L}(e) \subseteq \Sigma^*$ of a regular expression e is defined inductively as: $\mathcal{L}(\emptyset) = \emptyset$, $\mathcal{L}(\varepsilon) = \{\varepsilon\}$, $\mathcal{L}(a) = \{a\}$, $\mathcal{L}(e_1 + e_2) = \mathcal{L}(e_1) \cup \mathcal{L}(e_2)$, $\mathcal{L}(e_1 \cdot e_2) = \mathcal{L}(e_1) \cdot \mathcal{L}(e_2)$, $\mathcal{L}(e_1^*) = (\mathcal{L}(e_1))^*$. A *regular language* is a language that can be defined by a regular expression.

Automata. A *(nondeterministic) Finite Automaton* (NFA) $\mathcal{A}$ is a 5-tuple $(Q, \Sigma, \delta, I, F)$, where Q is a finite set of states, Σ is a finite alphabet, $\delta \subseteq Q \times \Sigma \times Q$ is the transition relation, $I, F \subseteq Q$ are the sets of initial and final states respectively. For readability, we write a transition $(q, a, q') \in \delta$ as $q \xrightarrow[\delta]{a} q'$ (or simply $q \xrightarrow{a} q'$). A *run* of $\mathcal{A}$ on a string $w = a_1 \cdots a_n$ is a sequence of transitions $q_0 \xrightarrow{a_1} q_1 \cdots q_{n-1} \xrightarrow{a_n} q_n$ with $q_0 \in I$. The run is *accepting* if $q_n \in F$. A string w is accepted by an NFA $\mathcal{A}$ if there is an accepting run of $\mathcal{A}$ on w. In particular, the empty string ε is accepted by $\mathcal{A}$ if $I \cap F \neq \emptyset$. The language of $\mathcal{A}$, denoted by $\mathcal{L}(\mathcal{A})$, is the set of strings accepted by $\mathcal{A}$. In addition, an NFA can be built to recognize the language of each given regular expression, and vice versa.

A *(nondeterministic) finite transducer (*NFT*)* $\mathfrak{T}$ is an extension of NFA with outputs. Formally, an NFT $\mathfrak{T}$ is a 5-tuple $(Q, \Sigma, \delta, I, F)$, where Q, Σ, I, F are the same as in NFA and the transition relation δ is a finite subset of $Q \times \Sigma \times Q \times \Sigma^*$. For readability, we write a transition $(q, a, q', u) \in \delta$ as $q \xrightarrow[\delta]{a,u} q'$ or $q \xrightarrow{a,u} q'$. A run of $\mathfrak{T}$ over a string $w = a_1 \cdots a_n$ is a sequence of transitions $q_0 \xrightarrow{a_1, u_1} q_1 \xrightarrow{a_2, u_2} q_2 \cdots q_{n-1} \xrightarrow{a_n, u_n} q_n$ where $q_0 \in I$. Similar to NFA, the run is *accepting* if $q_n \in F$. The string $u_1 \cdots u_n$ is called the *output* of the run. The transduction $\mathcal{T}(\mathfrak{T}) \subseteq \Sigma^* \times \Sigma^*$ defined by $\mathfrak{T}$ is the set of string pairs (w, u) such that there is an accepting run of $\mathfrak{T}$ on w, with the output u.

Definition 1 (Cost-enriched finite automata). *A cost-enriched finite automaton (CEFA for short) $\mathcal{A}$ is a 6-tuple $(R, Q, \Sigma, \delta, I, F)$ where*

- *$R = \{r_1, \cdots, r_k\}$ is a finite set of registers,*
- *Q, I, F are the same as in NFA, i.e., the set of states, the set of initial states, and the set of final states, respectively,*
- *$\delta \subseteq Q \times \Sigma \times Q \times \mathbb{Z}^k$ is a transition relation, where $\mathbb{Z}^k$ represents the values to update the registers in R.*

We write $R_\mathcal{A}$ for the set of registers of $\mathcal{A}$ and represent it as a vector $(r_1, \cdots, r_k)$. Accordingly, updates $r_i := r_i + v_i$ for all $i \in [k]$ are simply identified as the vector $\vec{v} = (v_1, \cdots, v_k)$, i.e., r_i is incremented by v_i for each $i \in [k]$. Typically, we write a transition $(q, a, q', \vec{v}) \in \delta$ as $q \xrightarrow[\vec{v}]{a} q'$.

Intuitively, CEFAs add write-only cost registers to finite automata, where "write-only" means that the cost registers can only be written/updated but cannot be read, i.e., they cannot be used in the guards of the transitions.

A *run* of the CEFA $\mathcal{A}$ on a string $w = a_1 \cdots a_n$ is a sequence of transitions $q_0 \xrightarrow[\vec{v}_1]{a_1} q_1 \cdots q_{n-1} \xrightarrow[\vec{v}_n]{a_n} q_n$ such that $q_0 \in I$ and $q_{i-1} \xrightarrow[\vec{v}_i]{a_i} q_i$ for each $i \in [n]$. It is *accepting* if $q_n \in F$, and the vector $\vec{c} = \sum_{i \in [n]} \vec{v}_i$ is defined as the *cost* of the run. (Note that all registers are initialized to zero.) We write $\vec{c} \in \mathcal{A}(w)$ if there is an accepting run of $\mathcal{A}$ on w whose cost is $\vec{c}$. The language of a CEFA $\mathcal{A}$, denoted by $\mathcal{L}(\mathcal{A})$, is defined as the set of pairs $\{(w, \vec{c}) \in \Sigma^* \times \mathbb{Z}^{|R|} \mid \vec{c} \in \mathcal{A}(w)\}$. In particular, if $I \cap F \neq \emptyset$, then $(\varepsilon, \vec{0}) \in \mathcal{L}(\mathcal{A})$. We denote by $\mathcal{L}_1(\mathcal{A})$ the language $\{w \in \Sigma^* \mid \exists \vec{c} \in \mathbb{Z}^{|R|}. (w, \vec{c}) \in \mathcal{L}(\mathcal{A})\}$.

Pre-images Under String Functions. Consider a language $L \subseteq \Sigma^* \times \mathbb{Z}^{k_0}$ defined by a CEFA $\mathcal{A} = (R, Q, \Sigma, \delta, I, F)$ with the registers $R = (r_1, \cdots, r_{k_0})$ and a function $f : (\Sigma^* \times \mathbb{Z}^{k_1}) \times \cdots \times (\Sigma^* \times \mathbb{Z}^{k_l}) \to \Sigma^*$. For each $i \in [k_0]$, let $r_1^i, \cdots, r_l^i$ be the freshly introduced registers, and $\vec{t} = (t_1, \cdots, t_{k_0})$ be a vector of LIA formulas such that t_i is a linear combination of $r_1^i, \cdots, r_l^i$ for each $i \in [k_0]$.

The pre-image of L under f with respect to $\vec{t}$, denoted by $f_{\vec{t}}^{-1}(L)$, is a relation

$$\mathcal{R} \subseteq (\Sigma^* \times \mathbb{Z}^{k_1+k_0}) \times \cdots \times (\Sigma^* \times \mathbb{Z}^{k_l+k_0})$$

that comprises tuples of the form $((w_1, (\vec{c_1}, \vec{d_1})), \cdots, (w_l, (\vec{c_l}, \vec{d_l})))$ such that

- for every $j \in [l]$, $\vec{c_j} \in \mathbb{Z}^{k_j}$ and $\vec{d_j} = (d_j^1, \cdots, d_j^{k_0}) \in \mathbb{Z}^{k_0}$,
- let $w_0 = f((w_1, (\vec{c_1}, \vec{d_1})), \cdots, (w_l, (\vec{c_l}, \vec{d_l})))$ and

$$\vec{d'} = \left(t_1 \left[d_1^1/r_1^1, \cdots, d_l^1/r_l^1 \right], \cdots, t_{k_0} \left[d_1^{k_0}/r_1^{k_0}, \cdots, d_l^{k_0}/r_l^{k_0} \right] \right),$$

it holds that $(w_0, \vec{d'}) \in L$.

The pre-image $f_{\vec{t}}^{-1}(L)$ is *CEFA-definable* if $f_{\vec{t}}^{-1}(L) = \bigcup_{i=1}^{n} \mathcal{L}(\mathcal{A}_{i,1}) \times \cdots \times \mathcal{L}(\mathcal{A}_{i,l})$ for some $n \geq 1$, where for all $i \in [n]$ and $j \in [l]$, $\mathcal{A}_{i,j}$ is a CEFA such that $\mathcal{L}(\mathcal{A}_{i,j}) \subseteq \Sigma^* \times \mathbb{Z}^{k_j}$. Finally, the pre-image of L under f, denoted by $f^{-1}(L)$, is a pair $(\mathcal{R}, \vec{t})$ such that $\mathcal{R} = f_{\vec{t}}^{-1}(L)$.

The core concept of *pre-image computation* for the function f involves determining the vector $\vec{t}$ of LIA formulas and, for each CEFA $\mathcal{A}$, computing $f_{\vec{t}}^{-1}(\mathcal{L}(\mathcal{A}))$ represented as a finite set of CEFAs. Intuitively, we remove the string equalities of the form $y = f(x_1, \vec{it_1}, \cdots, x_l, \vec{it_l})$ (where $\vec{it_1}, \cdots, \vec{it_l}$ are vectors of integer terms) one by one by computing the pre-images and adding the resulting CEFA membership constraints for $x_1, \cdots, x_l$. In the end, the original string constraint is transformed into a conjunction of CEFA membership constraints and LIA formulas, whose satisfiability checking is known to be PSPACE-complete [19].

3 Motivating Example

To motivate and illustrate our approach, we consider a JavaScript snippet shown in Listing 1.1, which is extracted, with a slight adaptation, from a real-world example.[1] Here, the function prepareVersionNo extracts from the input string version a version number in the floating-point number format. Specifically, it splits version into a sequence/array numbers according to the non-numeric

---
[1] https://github.com/hgoebl/mobile-detect.js/blob/master/mobile-detect.js

```
function prepareVersionNo(version) {
  // precondition: version in [0-9]+([0-9a-zA-Z._ /-])*
  numbers = version.split(/[a-z._ \/\-]/i);
  if (numbers.length === 1) { // path-1
    result = numbers[0];        }
  if (numbers.length > 1) { // path-2
    temp = numbers[0] + ".";
    numbers1 = numbers.slice(1, numbers.length);
    result = temp + numbers1.join("");         }
  return Number(result);
  // postcondition: result in [0-9]+(\.[0-9]*)?
}
```

Listing 1.1. JavaScript code snippet: The motivating example

```
; precondition
(assert (str.in_re version preReg))
(assert (= numbers (str.splitre version splitReg)))
(assert (< 1 (seq.len numbers)))
(assert (= temp (str.++ (seq.nth numbers 0) ".")))
(assert (= numbers1
           (seq.extract numbers 1 (- (seq.len numbers) 1))))
(assert (= result (str.++ temp (seq.join numbers1 ""))))
; postcondition
(assert (not (str.in_re result postReg)))
```

Listing 1.2. SMT formula for path-2 in prepareVersionNo

characters. If numbers contains exactly one element, numbers[0] is returned; otherwise, the function returns the concatenation of numbers[0], the dot, and the string obtained by concatenating the other elements of numbers. For instance, if version = 12a56b23, the output is 12.5623.

To verify the functional correctness of prepareVersionNo, we specify the following precondition and postcondition.

- The precondition version ∈ [0-9]+([0-9a-zA-Z._ /-])* requires that the input string starts with a decimal number, followed by a string of digits, letters, dot ., underline _, blank symbol, slash /, or hyphen -.
- The postcondition result ∈ [0-9]+(\.[0-9]*)? ensures that the output string starts with a decimal number, possibly followed by a dot . and a decimal number.

We apply symbolic execution to verify prepareVersionNo. We enumerate its execution paths and check for each path that, provided the input string satisfies the precondition, the output string satisfies the postcondition after the executing the path. There are three execution paths: path-1 taking numbers.length===1, path-2 taking numbers.length>1, and path-3 where both conditions are false. As an example, we consider path-2, and the symbolic execution reduces to deciding the satisfiability of the SMT formula in Listing 1.2, where preReg and postReg denote the regular expressions in the precondition and postcondition, i.e., ([0-9]+([0-9a-zA-Z._/-])*) and ([0-9]+(\.[0-9]*)?), respectively, and splitReg represents the regular expression [a-zA-Z._/-].

This SMT formula involves various operations of string sequences and strings, including sequence length seq.len, string split str.splitre, sequence read seq.nth, string concatenation str.++, sequence extract seq.extract, sequence join seq.join, as well as regular constraints str.in_re. While state-of-the-art SMT solvers such as Z3 and cvc5 can solve constraints in the generic sequence theory, they do not directly support complex operations that feature mutual transformations between strings and string sequences, such as str.splitre and seq.join. This motivates us to define an SMT theory of string sequences (SeqStr, cf. Sect. 4) and investigate its decision procedure (Sect. 5).

Due to the undecidability of SeqStr, we focus on its straight-line fragment (cf. Definition 2), into which the formula in Listing 1.2 falls. We encode string sequences as strings, and, accordingly, string sequence operations become string operations (Sect. 5.1). Then we transform the formula in Listing 1.2 into the following string constraint:

$$\text{version} \in \text{preReg} \wedge \text{snumbers} = \text{splitstr}_{\text{splitReg}}(\text{version}) \wedge$$
$$1 < \text{seqlen}(\text{snumbers}) - 1 \wedge \text{temp} = \text{elem}(\text{snumbers}, 0) \cdot \text{'.'} \wedge$$
$$\text{snumbers1} = \text{subseq}[\text{snumbers}, 2, \text{seqlen}(\text{snumbers}) - 2] \wedge \qquad (1)$$
$$\text{result} = \text{temp} \cdot \text{join}_\epsilon(\text{snumbers1}) \wedge \text{result} \notin \text{posReg}.$$

where snumbers, snumbers1 are string variables that encode the string sequences numbers, numbers1 in Listing 1.2. Note that the resulting string constraint contains new string operations splitstr, seqlen, elem, ⋯ introduced in this paper (cf. Sect. 5.1). Subsequently, we employ the decision procedure outlined in [19], which *back propagates* the CEFA membership constraints by computing the pre-images under string functions (see Sect. 5.2).

In the sequel, we show how to solve the formula in (1).

1. We back propagate the regular membership constraint $\text{result} \in \overline{\text{posReg}}$ (where $\overline{\text{posReg}}$ denotes the complement of posReg) by computing the pre-images under the concatenation · and join_ϵ, and adding the CEFA constraints for temp and snumbers1, say, $\text{temp} \in \mathcal{A}_1 \wedge \text{snumbers1} \in \mathcal{A}_2$ (where $\text{temp} \in \mathcal{A}_1$ means that the value of temp belongs to $\mathcal{L}_1(\mathcal{A}_1)$, similarly for $\text{snumbers1} \in \mathcal{A}_2$). Note that nondeterministic choices may be made here since the pre-images of $\mathcal{L}(\overline{\text{posReg}})$ under · may be a union of products of CEFAs. After the propagation, the string equality $\text{result} = \text{temp} \cdot \text{join}_\epsilon(\text{snumbers1})$ is removed.

2. Then we back propagate the CEFA membership constraint $\text{temp} \in \mathcal{A}_1$ for the equality $\text{temp} = \text{elem}(\text{snumbers}, 0) \cdot \text{'.'}$ by computing the pre-image of $\mathcal{L}(\mathcal{A}_1)$ under · as well as elem and adding some CEFA membership constraint for snumbers, say, $\text{snumbers} \in \mathcal{A}_3$. Similarly, we back propagate the CEFA membership constraint $\text{snumbers1} \in \mathcal{L}(\mathcal{A}_2)$ for the equality $\text{snumbers1} = \text{subseq}[\text{snumbers}, 2, \text{seqlen}(\text{snumbers}) - 1]$ by computing the

pre-image of $\mathcal{L}(\mathcal{A}_2)$ under subseq and adding some CEFA membership constraint for snumbers, say, snumbers $\in \mathcal{A}_4$. After these back-propagation operations, the two string equalities are removed.
3. Finally, we back propagate the CEFA membership constraint snumbers $\in \mathcal{A}_3 \cap \mathcal{A}_4$ for snumbers = splitstr$_{\text{splitReg}}$(version) by computing the pre-image of $\mathcal{L}(\mathcal{A}_3 \cap \mathcal{A}_4)$ under the function splitstr$_{\text{splitReg}}$ and adding a CEFA membership constraint version $\in \mathcal{A}_5$. Moreover, the equality snumbers = splitstr$_{\text{splitReg}}$(version) is removed.
4. In the end, we obtain a string constraint that contains no string equalities, namely, a Boolean combination of CEFA membership constraints and LIA formulas, which are solvable using existing methods.

Note that here we prioritize the illustration of the main idea over the precision of the description; the technical details of the decision procedure are deferred to later sections.

Overall, the formula in Listing 1.2 can be transformed into a string constraint containing a complex combination of str.replace_re_all, str.substr and str.len, which cannot be solved by Z3 or cvc5 in a reasonable time limit (Z3 returns unknown as it does not support the str.replace_re_all function; cvc5 fails to solve the stirng constraint in 20 h). In contrast, our new solver OSTRICH^{SEQ} solves it in less than 1 s.

4   A Theory of String Sequences (SeqStr)

A *sequence* over the set X is $(a_0, \ldots, a_{n-1})$, where $a_i \in X$ for each $i \in [0, n-1]$, and n is the *length* of the sequence. We shall focus on *string sequences*, namely, sequences over Σ^*. We use () to denote the empty sequence.

Operations on string sequences and strings. We assume two string sequences $s_1 = (u_0, \ldots, u_{m-1})$ and $s_2 = (v_0, \ldots, v_{n-1})$.

- $s_1 \cdot s_2$ is the concatenation of s_1 and s_2, i.e., $(u_0, \ldots, u_{m-1}, v_0, \ldots, v_{n-1})$.
- nth(s_1, i) is u_i if $i \in [0, m-1]$, and undefined otherwise.
- join$_v(s_1)$ joins the elements in s_1 with v as the intermediate string, i.e., join$_v(s_1) = u_0 v u_1 v u_2 v \cdots v u_{m-1}$.
- $s_1[i \to u]$ replaces u_i in s_1 by u if $i \in [0, m-1]$, and is s_1 otherwise, i.e.

$$[s_1[i \to u]] = \begin{cases} (u_0, \ldots, u_{i-1}, u, u_{i+1}, \ldots, u_{m-1}), & \text{if } i \in [0, m-1]; \\ s_1, & \text{otherwise.} \end{cases}$$

- filter$_e(s_1)$ filters out all elements in s_1 that do not match the regular expression e, i.e., filter$_e(s_1) = (u_{i_1}, \ldots, u_{i_k})$ such that $0 \le i_1 < \cdots < i_k \le m-1$ and for all $j \in [0, m-1]$, $u_j \in \mathcal{L}(e)$ iff $j \in \{i_1, \ldots, i_k\}$. In particular, if none of $u_0, \ldots, u_{m-1}$ are in $\mathcal{L}(e)$, then filter$_e(s_1) = ()$.
- split$_e(u)$ splits a string u into a sequence of substrings according to the regular expression e, i.e., split$_e(u) = (u'_1, \ldots, u'_k)$, where $u = u'_1 v_1 u'_2 v_2 \cdots u'_{k-1} v_{k-1} u'_k$ such that (1) for each $i \in [k-1]$, v_i is the leftmost and longest substring of

$u'_i v_i u'_{i+1} \cdots v_{k-1} u'_k$ that matches e, and (2) u'_k does not contain any substring that matches e. In particular, if u does not contain any substring that matches e, then $\mathsf{split}_e(u) = (u)$.
- $s_1[i,j]$ is defined as follows: if $i \in [0, m-1]$ and $j \geq 1$, then $s_1[i,j]$ is the subsequence $(u_i, \ldots, u_{\min(i+j-1, m-1)})$; if $i \in [0, m-1]$ and $j = 0$, then $s_1[i,j]$ is the empty sequence (); if $i \notin [0, m-1]$ or $j < 0$, then $s_1[i,j]$ is undefined.
- $\mathsf{matchAll}_e(u)$ extracts the substrings of u that match the regular expression e, i.e., $\mathsf{matchAll}_e(u) = (v_1, \ldots, v_{k-1})$ such that $u = u'_1 v_1 u'_2 v_2 \cdots u'_{k-1} v_{k-1} u'_k$ and (1) for each $i \in [k-1]$, v_i is the leftmost and longest substring of $u'_i v_i u'_{i+1} \cdots v_{k-1} u'_k$, and (2) u'_k has no substring that matches e.

Note that we choose the longest match semantics in $\mathsf{split}_e(u)$ and $\mathsf{matchAll}_e(u)$ just for illustrating our approach, where the shortest match semantics can be captured by adapting the automata construction in the pre-image computation.

The logic SeqStr *of string sequences.* SeqStr has three data types: Int (integer), Str (strings), and Seq (sequences). We use $u, v, \ldots$ (resp. $\mathfrak{u}, \mathfrak{v}, \ldots$) to denote string constants (resp. variables); $m, n, \ldots$ (resp. $\mathfrak{m}, \mathfrak{n}, \ldots$) to denote integer constants (resp. variables); $s, t, \ldots$ (resp. $\mathfrak{s}, \mathfrak{t}, \ldots$) to denote sequence constants (resp. variables); and e to denote regular expressions.

The syntax of SeqStr is defined as follows:

$$
\begin{aligned}
it &\stackrel{\text{def}}{=} m \mid \mathfrak{m} \mid it + it \mid it - it \mid \mathsf{strlen}(strt) \mid \mathsf{seqlen}(seqt) & \text{integer terms} \\
strt &\stackrel{\text{def}}{=} u \mid \mathfrak{u} \mid strt \cdot strt \mid \mathsf{nth}(seqt, it) \mid \mathsf{join}_u(seqt) & \text{string terms} \\
seqt &\stackrel{\text{def}}{=} (strt) \mid s \mid \mathfrak{s} \mid seqt \cdot seqt \mid seqt[it \to strt] \mid \mathsf{filter}_e(seqt) \mid \\
& \quad seqt[it, it] \mid \mathsf{split}_e(strt) \mid \mathsf{matchAll}_e(strt) & \text{sequence terms} \\
\varphi &\stackrel{\text{def}}{=} it \bowtie it \mid seqt = seqt \mid strt = strt \mid strt \in e \mid \varphi \wedge \varphi & \text{formulas}
\end{aligned}
$$

where $\bowtie \in \{=, \neq, <, \leq, >, \geq\}$.

Here, it, $seqt$ and $strt$ denote integer, sequence and string terms, respectively. In particular, the integer terms are linear arithmetic expressions where $\mathsf{seqlen}(\mathfrak{s})$ (resp. $\mathsf{strlen}(\mathfrak{u})$) denotes the length of a sequence $\mathfrak{s}$ (resp. string $\mathfrak{u}$); the sequence terms are constructed from a singleton sequence, sequence constants and sequence variables by applying the aforementioned sequence/string operations. A SeqStr formula is a conjunction of atomic formulas, each of which is of the form $it_1 \bowtie it_2$ where $\bowtie \in \{=, \neq, <, \leq, >, \geq\}$, a sequence equality $seqt_1 = seqt_2$, or a string equality $strt_1 = strt_2$. Note that sequence and string inequalities can be expressed as well. For instance (using disjunctions and quantifiers for the sake of presentation):

$$\mathfrak{x} \neq \mathfrak{y} \equiv \exists \mathfrak{x}_1, \mathfrak{x}_2, \mathfrak{y}_2. \bigvee_{a,b \in \Sigma, a \neq b} (\mathfrak{x} = \mathfrak{x}_1 a \mathfrak{x}_2 \wedge \mathfrak{y} = \mathfrak{x}_1 b \mathfrak{y}_2) \vee \exists \mathfrak{z}. \bigvee_{a \in \Sigma} (\mathfrak{x} = \mathfrak{y} a \mathfrak{z} \vee \mathfrak{y} = \mathfrak{x} a \mathfrak{z})$$

$$\alpha \neq \beta \equiv (\exists \alpha_1, \alpha_2, \beta_2, \mathfrak{z}_1, \mathfrak{z}_2. \, \alpha = \alpha_1 \cdot (\mathfrak{z}_1) \cdot \alpha_2 \wedge \beta = \alpha_1 \cdot (\mathfrak{z}_2) \cdot \beta_2 \wedge \mathfrak{z}_1 \neq \mathfrak{z}_2) \vee$$
$$\exists \gamma, \mathfrak{z}. \, \alpha = \beta \cdot (\mathfrak{z}) \cdot \gamma \vee \beta = \alpha \cdot (\mathfrak{z}) \cdot \gamma.$$

Though rewriting inequalities produces disjunctions, they can still be handled in the DPLL(T) framework [29]. Hence, we focus on the disjunction-free fragment.

Proposition 1. *The satisfiability of* SeqStr *is undecidable.*

We define the *straight-line fragment* SeqStr$_{SL}$ of SeqStr. It is easy to see that by introducing fresh variables, we can rewrite a SeqStr formula to a form in which the left-hand side of each equality $seqt_1 = seqt_2$ (resp. $strt_1 = strt_2$) is a sequence (resp. string) variable. Note that the original and rewritten formulas are equisatisfiable. Henceforth, we assume that all sequence/string equalities satisfy this constraint unless otherwise stated.

Definition 2 (Straight-line fragment). *Given a* SeqStr *formula φ, the dependency graph G_φ of φ is a directed graph (V, E) such that V is the set of string and sequence variables in φ, and $(v_1, v_2) \in E$ iff $v_1 = $ rhs is a sequence or string equality in φ and v_2 occurs in rhs except for integer terms.*

φ is straight-line if φ is disjunction-free, and each string/sequence variable occurs as the left-hand side of equalities at most once; moreover, G_φ is acyclic.

Example 1. $\mathfrak{s} = \mathsf{split}_e(\mathfrak{u}) \wedge \mathfrak{t} = \mathfrak{s}[1, \mathsf{seqlen}(\mathfrak{s}) - 1]$ *is straight-line, while* $\mathfrak{s} = \mathfrak{s}[1, \mathsf{seqlen}(\mathfrak{s}) - 1]$ *is not, since there is a self-dependency on* $\mathfrak{s}$.

5 The Decision Procedure

Theorem 1. *The satisfiability of* SeqStr$_{SL}$ *is decidable.*

The general idea of the decision procedure is to encode each string sequence as a string, based on which all string sequence operations in SeqStr$_{SL}$ can be transformed into string operations. It utilizes the framework [19] for solving straight-line string constraints with integer data type, as illustrated in Sect. 3. There are, however, certain technical challenges. For instance, $seqt[it \rightarrow strt]$ and $seqt[it, it]$ cannot be captured directly by standard string operations, so new ones have to be provided whose pre-images need to be computed.

5.1 From String Sequences to Strings

We fix a symbol $\dagger \notin \Sigma$ and let $\Sigma_\dagger := \Sigma \cup \{\dagger\}$. Each string sequence $s = (u_1, \cdots, u_m)$ over Σ is encoded as a string $\mathsf{enc}(s) := \dagger u_1 \dagger u_2 \dagger \cdots \dagger u_m \dagger$ over $\Sigma_\dagger$. Note that the strings resulted from the encoding should match the regular expression $\dagger(\Sigma^*\dagger)^*$ and the string $\dagger$ encodes the empty sequence.

With this encoding of string sequences as strings, each string sequence operation is also transformed into the corresponding *string operation*.

sequence concatenation $s_1 \cdot s_2$: string concatenation $\mathsf{enc}(s_1) \cdot \mathsf{enc}(s_2)$.
sequence write $s[i \rightarrow u]$: $\mathsf{write}(\mathsf{enc}(s), i+1, u)$, which replaces the substring of $\mathsf{enc}(s)$ between the $(i+1)$-th occurrence of $\dagger$ and the $(i+2)$-th occurrence of $\dagger$, by u, if $i \in [0, n-2]$, where n is the number of occurrences of $\dagger$ in $\mathsf{enc}(s)$, and is undefined otherwise (i.e. $i \notin [0, n-2]$).
sequence filter operation $\mathsf{filter}_e(s)$: $\mathsf{filter}_e(\mathsf{enc}(s))$, which removes every substring of $\mathsf{enc}(s)$ between two consecutive occurrences of $\dagger$ that does not match the regular expression e. (For instance, if $e = a^*b$ and $s = (ab, ac, aab)$, then $\mathsf{filter}_e(\mathsf{enc}(s)) = \dagger ab \dagger aab \dagger$.)

subsequence operation $s[i,j]$: subseq(enc(s), $i+1, j$), which keeps only the substring of enc(s) between the $(i+1)$-th occurrence and the $\min(i+j, n-1)$-th occurrence of †, if $i \in [0, n-2]$, where n is the number of occurrences of † in enc(s), and is undefined otherwise (i.e. $i \notin [0, n-2]$).

split$_e(u)$: string operation splitstr$_e(u)$ that transforms $u = u'_1 v_1 u'_2 \cdots u'_{k-1} v_{k-1} u'_k$ into $\dagger u'_1 \dagger u'_2 \cdots u'_{k-1} \dagger u'_k \dagger$, where for each $i \in [k-1]$, v_i is the leftmost and longest matching of e in $u'_i v_i u'_{i+1} \cdots v_{k-1} u'_k$, and u'_k does not contain any substring that matches e.

matchAll$_e(u)$: matchAllstr$_e(u)$ that transforms $u = u'_1 v_1 u'_2 v_2 \cdots u'_{k-1} v_{k-1} u'_k$ into $\dagger v_1 \dagger \cdots \dagger v_{k-1} \dagger$, where for each $i \in [k-1]$, v_i is the leftmost and longest occurrence of e in $u'_i v_i u'_{i+1} \cdots v_{k-1} u'_k$, moreover, u'_k does not contain any substring that matches e.

sequence read operation nth($s, i+1$): elem(enc(s), $i+1$) that keeps only the substring between the $(i+1)$-th occurrence and the $(i+2)$-th occurrence of †, if $i \in [0, n-2]$, where n is the number of occurrences of † in enc(s), and is undefined otherwise (i.e. $i \notin [0, n-2]$). (For instance, if $s = (ab, ac)$ and $i = 0$, then elem(enc(s), 1) = elem($\dagger ab \dagger ac \dagger, 1$) = ab.)

sequence join operation join$_u(s)$: join$_u$(enc(s)) that removes the first and the last occurrences of † and replaces all the remaining occurrences of † by u.

sequence length operation seqlen(s): seqlen(enc(s)) - 1 where seqlen(enc(s)) counts the number of occurrences of † in enc(s).

Hence, we obtain atomic string constraints of the following forms:

$$\mathfrak{x} = u \mid \mathfrak{x} = \mathfrak{y} \mid \mathfrak{x} = \mathfrak{y} \cdot \mathfrak{z} \mid \mathfrak{x} = \mathfrak{T}(\mathfrak{y}) \mid \mathfrak{z} = \text{write}(\mathfrak{x}, it, \mathfrak{y}) \mid \mathfrak{y} = \text{filter}_e(\mathfrak{x}) \mid$$
$$\mathfrak{y} = \text{splitstr}_e(\mathfrak{x}) \mid \mathfrak{y} = \text{subseq}(\mathfrak{x}, it_1, it_2) \mid \mathfrak{y} = \text{matchAllstr}_e(\mathfrak{x}) \mid \mathfrak{y} = \text{elem}(\mathfrak{x}, it) \mid$$
$$\mathfrak{y} = \text{join}_u(\mathfrak{x}) \mid it = \text{strlen}(\mathfrak{x}) \mid it = \text{seqlen}(\mathfrak{x}),$$

where $\mathfrak{T}$ is a finite-state transducer.

We denote by XStr the class of string constraints which are positive Boolean combinations (no negation) of the atomic string constraints, and XStr$_{\mathsf{SL}}$ denotes its straight-line fragment. For each formula φ in SeqStr$_{\mathsf{SL}}$, enc(φ) is the resulting formula in XStr. We have the following result.

Proposition 2. *For each constraint φ in SeqStr, φ and enc(φ) are equisatisfiable. Moreover, if φ is in SeqStr$_{\mathsf{SL}}$, then enc(φ) is in XStr$_{\mathsf{SL}}$.*

Example 2. Consider the constraint $\varphi := (\mathfrak{s}_1 = \mathfrak{s}_0 \cdot (u, v) \wedge \text{seqlen}(\mathfrak{s}_1) < 2)$ in SeqStr$_{\mathsf{SL}}$ where $\mathfrak{s}_0$ is a string variable and u, v are string constants. Then, its string encoding is enc(φ) := (enc($\mathfrak{s}_1$) = enc($\mathfrak{s}_0$) $\cdot \dagger u \dagger v \dagger \wedge$ seqlen(enc($\mathfrak{s}_1$)) $- 1 < 2$), which is unsatisfiable, as there are at least three occurrences of † in enc($\mathfrak{s}_1$). □

The satisfiability of SeqStr$_{\mathsf{SL}}$ is now reduced to that of XStr$_{\mathsf{SL}}$. The operations filter$_e$, splitstr$_e$, matchAllstr$_e$ and join$_u$ can all be represented by a finite-state transducer (see the full version of the paper), so the results in [19] are directly applicable. In the next section, we show that the pre-images under the remaining string operations, i.e., write, subseq, elem and seqlen, can be effectively computed.

5.2 Computing the Pre-images Under write, subseq, elem and seqlen

We now show how to compute the pre-images under write, subseq, elem and seqlen. Note that the pre-image computation utilizes an NFA $\mathcal{A}_0$ (resp. $\mathcal{A}_1$) to format the strings that represent the string sequences (resp. strings), namely, $\mathcal{A}_0$ (resp. $\mathcal{A}_1$) recognizes the language $\dagger(\Sigma\dagger)^*$ (resp. Σ^*).

Pre-image under write. Let $\mathcal{A} = (R, Q, \Sigma_\dagger, \delta, I, F)$ be a CEFA. write$^{-1}(\mathcal{L}(\mathcal{A}))$ is computed as the collection $((\mathcal{B}_{(p,q)} \cap \mathcal{A}_0, \mathcal{A}_{R_2/R}[p,q] \cap \mathcal{A}_1), t_{(p,q)})_{(p,q) \in Q \times Q}$, where $\mathcal{B}_{(p,q)}$, $\mathcal{A}_{R_2/R}[p,q]$ and $t_{(p,q)}$ are constructed as follows:

- $\mathcal{B}_{(p,q)}$ is constructed by the following procedure:
  - We create two copies of R, say R_1, R_2. Moreover, we introduce a fresh cost register, say r', to count the number of occurrences of $\dagger$.
  - We run $\mathcal{A}$ on the input string and increase the cost register r' each time when $\dagger$ is read. Moreover, the registers in R_1, instead of R, are updated in the transitions.
  - When the current symbol is $\dagger$, we nondeterministically choose to stop increasing r' and pause the running of $\mathcal{A}$ at the state p. Let us call this position as the pause position.
  - Finally, when reading the first $\dagger$ after the pause position, we resume the run of $\mathcal{A}$ at q, where the registers in R_1 (but not r') are updated.
- $\mathcal{A}_{R_2/R}[p,q]$ is obtained from $\mathcal{A}[p,q]$ by replacing each register in R with the corresponding copy in R_2, where $\mathcal{A}[p,q]$ is the sub-automaton of $\mathcal{A}$ that accepts the strings starting from the state p and ending at the state q.
- $t_{(p,q)} := (t_{(p,q),r})_{r \in R}$ and $t_{(p,q),r} = r^{(1)} + r^{(2)}$ where $r^{(1)}$ and $r^{(2)}$ are the copies of r for each $r \in R$.

Note that in the backward propagation of $\mathcal{A}$ with respect to an equality $\mathfrak{z} = $ write$(\mathfrak{x}, it, \mathfrak{y})$, the constraint $r' = it$ is added to the LIA constraint to assert that r' is equal to the index it. Formally, write$^{-1}(\mathcal{L}(\mathcal{A}))$ is a finite collection of $(\mathcal{B}_{(p,q)} \cap \mathcal{A}_0, \mathcal{A}_{R_2/R}[p,q] \cap \mathcal{A}_1, t_{(p,q)})$, where $(p,q) \in Q \times Q$, and $\mathcal{B}_{(p,q)} = (R_1 \cup \{r'\}, Q', \Sigma_\dagger, \delta', I', F')$ such that $Q' = Q \times \{pre, idle, post\}$, $I' = I \times \{pre\}$, $F' = F \times \{post\}$, and δ' comprises:

- $((q_1, pre), a, (q_2, pre), (\vec{v}, 0))$ such that $(q_1, a, q_2, \vec{v}) \in \delta$ and $a \in \Sigma$ (thus $a \neq \dagger$),
- $((q_1, pre), \dagger, (q_2, pre), (\vec{v}, 1))$ such that $(q_1, \dagger, q_2, \vec{v}) \in \delta$,
- $((q_1, pre), \dagger, (p, idle), (\vec{v}, 1))$ such that $(q_1, \dagger, p, \vec{v}) \in \delta$,
- $((p, idle), a, (p, idle), (\vec{0}, 0))$ such that $a \in \Sigma$,
- $((p, idle), \dagger, (q_2, post), (\vec{v}, 0))$ such that $(q, \dagger, q_2, \vec{v}) \in \delta$,
- $((q_1, post), a, (q_2, post), (\vec{v}, 0))$ such that $(q_1, a, q_2, \vec{v}) \in \delta$ and $a \in \Sigma$,
- $((q_1, post), \dagger, (q_2, post), (\vec{v}, 0))$ such that $(q_1, \dagger, q_2, \vec{v}) \in \delta$.

From the construction of $\mathcal{B}_{(p,q)}$, we can observe that the pair (p,q) should satisfy that in $\mathcal{A}$, there is a $\dagger$-transition into p and a $\dagger$-transition out of q. Moreover, q should be reachable from p according to the construction of $\mathcal{A}_{R_2/R}[p,q] \cap \mathcal{A}_1$.

Example 3. Consider the constraint $\mathfrak{v} = \mathsf{write}(\mathfrak{u}, 1, \mathfrak{y}) \wedge \mathfrak{v} \in \dagger(a^+\dagger)^* \wedge \mathsf{strlen}(\mathfrak{v}) \geq 4$. Let $\mathcal{A} = (\{r_1\}, \{q_0, q_1, q_2\}, \Sigma_\dagger, \delta, \{q_0\}, \{q_1\})$ be the CEFA, where the register r_1 is used to record the string length and δ comprises the transitions $q_0 \xrightarrow[(1)]{\dagger} q_1 \xrightarrow[(1)]{a} q_2 \xrightarrow[(1)]{a} q_2 \xrightarrow[(1)]{\dagger} q_1$. Let us consider the pairs (p, q) in $\mathcal{A}$ satisfying that there is a $\dagger$-transition into p and a $\dagger$-transition out of q, moreover, q should be reachable from p. One can easily observe that there is exactly one such pair, that is, (q_1, q_2). Therefore, $\mathsf{write}^{-1}(\mathcal{L}(\mathcal{A}))$ comprises exactly one tuple $(\mathcal{B}_{(q_1, q_2)} \cap \mathcal{A}_0, \mathcal{A}_{R_2/R}[q_1, q_2] \cap \mathcal{A}_1, (r_1^{(1)} + r_1^{(2)}))$ such that $\mathcal{B}_{(q_1, q_2)} = (\{r_1^{(1)}, r'\}, Q', \Sigma_\dagger, \delta', I', F')$ where

- $Q' = \{q_0, q_1, q_2\} \times \{pre, idle, post\}$, $I' = \{(q_0, pre)\}$, $F' = \{(q_1, post)\}$, and
- δ' comprises the following transitions:
  - $((q_1, pre), a, (q_2, pre), (1, 0))$, $((q_2, pre), a, (q_2, pre), (1, 0))$,
  - $((q_0, pre), \dagger, (q_1, pre), (1, 1))$, $((q_2, pre), \dagger, (q_1, pre), (1, 1))$,
  - $((q_0, pre), \dagger, (q_1, idle), (1, 1))$ (since $(q_0, \dagger, q_1, 1) \in \delta$),
  - $((q_1, idle), a', (q_1, idle), (0, 0))$ such that $a' \in \Sigma$,
  - $((q_1, idle), \dagger, (q_1, post), (1, 0))$ (since $(q_2, \dagger, q_1, 1) \in \delta$),
  - $((q_1, post), a, (q_2, post), (1, 0))$ and $((q_2, post), a, (q_2, post), (1, 0))$,
  - $((q_2, post), \dagger, (q_1, post), (1, 0))$.

To illustrate how $\mathcal{B}_{(q_1, q_2)}$ and $\mathcal{A}_{R_2/R}[q_1, q_2]$ work, we can see that $(\dagger aa \dagger a \dagger, 6)$ is accepted by $\mathcal{A}$, moreover, for any $b \in \Sigma$,

- $(\dagger ab \dagger a \dagger, 4, 1)$ is accepted by $\mathcal{B}_{(q_1, q_2)}$, witnessed by

$$(q_0, pre) \xrightarrow[(1,1)]{\dagger} (q_1, idle) \xrightarrow[(0,0)]{a} (q_1, idle) \xrightarrow[(0,0)]{b} (q_1, idle)$$
$$\xrightarrow[(1,0)]{\dagger} (q_1, post) \xrightarrow[(1,0)]{a} (q_2, post) \xrightarrow[(1,0)]{\dagger} (q_1, post),$$

- and $(aa, 2)$ is accepted by $\mathcal{A}_{R_2/R}[q_1, q_2]$, witnessed by $q_1 \xrightarrow[(1)]{a} q_2 \xrightarrow[(1)]{a} q_2$.

Thus, $\mathfrak{u}$ and $\mathfrak{y}$ in $\mathfrak{v} = \mathsf{write}(\mathfrak{u}, 1, \mathfrak{y})$ can be $\dagger ab \dagger a \dagger$ and aa, respectively. □

Pre-image Under subseq. Let $\mathcal{A} = (R, Q, \Sigma_\dagger, \delta, I, F)$ be a CEFA. $\mathsf{subseq}^{-1}(\mathcal{L}(\mathcal{A}))$ is computed as $(\mathcal{B} \cap \mathcal{A}_0, t)$ such that $t := true$ and $\mathcal{B}$ introduces two fresh registers r'_1, r'_2 to count the two numbers of occurrences of $\dagger$ that correspond to the starting position and the length of the subsequence, respectively. Moreover, $\mathcal{B}$ simulates the run of $\mathcal{A}$ on the substring representing the subsequence returned by subseq. Formally, $\mathsf{subseq}^{-1}(\mathcal{L}(\mathcal{A}))$ is computed as $(\mathcal{B} \cap \mathcal{A}_0, true)$, where $\mathcal{B} = (R \cup \{r'_1, r'_2\}, Q \cup \{pre, post\}, \Sigma_\dagger, \delta', \{pre\}, \{post\})$ such that $pre, post$ are two fresh states denoting the fact that $\mathcal{B}$ is reading a symbol before and after the subsequence respectively and δ' comprises the following transitions:

- $(pre, a, pre, (\overrightarrow{0}, 0, 0))$ such that $a \in \Sigma$ (thus $a \neq \dagger$),
- $(pre, \dagger, pre, (\overrightarrow{0}, 1, 0))$,

- $(pre, \dagger, q, (\vec{v}, 1, 0))$ such that $(p, \dagger, q, \vec{v}) \in \delta$ for some $p \in I$,
- $(q, a, q', (\vec{v}, 0, 0))$ such that $(q, a, q', \vec{v}) \in \delta$ and $a \in \Sigma$,
- $(q, \dagger, q', (\vec{v}, 0, 1))$ such that $(q, \dagger, q', \vec{v}) \in \delta$,
- $(q, \dagger, post, (\vec{v}, 0, 1))$ such that $(q, \dagger, q', \vec{v}) \in \delta$ for some $q' \in F$,
- $(post, a, post, (\vec{0}, 0, 0))$ and $(post, \dagger, post, (\vec{0}, 0, 0))$ where $a \in \Sigma$.

Note that in the backward propagation of $\mathcal{A}$ with respect to an equality $\mathfrak{z} = \mathsf{subseq}(\mathfrak{x}, it_1, it_2)$, the constraint $r'_1 = it_1 \wedge r'_2 = it_2$ is added to the LIA constraint to assert that the value of r'_1 and r'_2 are equal to the beginning index and the length of the subsequence respectively.

Example 4. Let $\mathfrak{v} = \mathsf{subseq}(\mathfrak{u}, 2, 1) \wedge \mathfrak{v} \in \dagger(a^+\dagger)^* \wedge \mathsf{strlen}(\mathfrak{v}) \geq 4$ and $\mathcal{A} = (\{r_1\}, \{q_0, q_1, q_2\}, \Sigma_\dagger, \delta, \{q_0\}, \{q_1\})$ be the CEFA, where the register r_1 is used to record the string length and δ comprises the transitions $q_0 \xrightarrow[(1)]{\dagger} q_1 \xrightarrow[(1)]{a} q_2 \xrightarrow[(1)]{a}$ $q_2 \xrightarrow[(1)]{\dagger} q_1$. Then $\mathsf{subseq}^{-1}(\mathcal{L}(\mathcal{A}))$ is $(\mathcal{B} \cap \mathcal{A}_0, true)$ such that

$$\mathcal{B} = (\{r_1^{(1)}, r'_1, r'_2\}, \{q_0, q_1, q_2, pre, post\}, \Sigma_\dagger, \delta', \{pre\}, \{post\})$$

where δ' comprises the following transitions:

- $(pre, a', pre, (0, 0, 0))$ such that $a' \in \Sigma$,
- $(pre, \dagger, pre, (0, 1, 0))$,
- $(pre, \dagger, q_1, (1, 1, 0))$ (since $(q_0, \dagger, q_1, 1) \in \delta$),
- $(q_1, a, q_2, (1, 0, 0))$, $(q_2, a, q_2, (1, 0, 0))$,
- $(q_2, \dagger, q_1, (1, 0, 1))$,
- $(q_2, \dagger, post, (1, 0, 1))$ (since $(q_2, \dagger, q_1, 1) \in \delta$ and q_1 is an accepting state in $\mathcal{A}$),
- $(post, a', post, (0, 0, 0))$ and $(post, \dagger, post, (0, 0, 0))$ where $a' \in \Sigma$.

To illustrate how $\mathcal{B}$ works, we can see that $(\dagger a \dagger aa \dagger, 4, 2, 1)$ is accepted by $\mathcal{B}$, witnessed by

$$pre \xrightarrow[(0,1,0)]{\dagger} pre \xrightarrow[(0,0,0)]{a} pre \xrightarrow[(1,1,0)]{\dagger} q_1 \xrightarrow[(1,0,0)]{a} q_2 \xrightarrow[(1,0,0)]{a} q_2 \xrightarrow[(1,0,1)]{\dagger} post.$$

Pre-image Under elem. Let $\mathcal{A} = (R, Q, \Sigma, \delta, I, F)$ be a CEFA. $\mathsf{elem}^{-1}(\mathcal{L}(\mathcal{A}))$ is constructed similar to $\mathsf{subseq}^{-1}(\mathcal{L}(\mathcal{A}))$. Nevertheless, the construction is slightly different since the output of elem is a string, instead of a sequence. Intuitively, $\mathsf{elem}^{-1}(\mathcal{L}(\mathcal{A}))$ is computed as $(\mathcal{B} \cap \mathcal{A}_0, t)$ where $t := true$, a fresh register r' is introduced to count the number of occurrences of $\dagger$ that corresponds to the position where the element is extracted. Formally, $\mathsf{elem}^{-1}(\mathcal{L}(\mathcal{A}))$ is computed as $(\mathcal{B} \cap \mathcal{A}_0, true)$ such that $\mathcal{B} = (R \cup \{r'\}, Q \cup \{pre, post\}, \Sigma_\dagger, \delta', \{pre\}, \{post\})$, where δ' comprises the following transitions:

- $(pre, a, pre, (\vec{0}, 0))$ such that $a \in \Sigma$ (thus $a \neq \dagger$),
- $(pre, \dagger, pre, (\vec{0}, 1))$,

- $(pre, \dagger, p, (\vec{v}, 1))$ such that $p \in I$,
- $(q, a, q', (\vec{v}, 0))$ such that $(q, a, q', \vec{v}) \in \delta$ and $a \in \Sigma$ (thus $a \neq \dagger$),
- $(q, \dagger, post, (\vec{0}, 0))$ such that $q \in F$,
- $(post, a, post, (\vec{0}, 0))$ and $(post, \dagger, post, (\vec{0}, 0))$ where $a \in \Sigma$.

Note that in the backward propagation of $\mathcal{A}$ with respect to an equality $\mathfrak{z} = \text{elem}(\mathfrak{x}, it)$, the constraint $r' = it$ is added to the LIA constraint to assert that the value of r' is equal to the index it.

Finally, we remark that the operation seqlen($\mathfrak{x}$) can be modeled as a CEFA, similarly to the CEFA for strlen in [19].

6 Implementation and Experiments

We implement a solver OSTRICH^{SEQ} on top of the string solver OSTRICH [20] and the SMT solver Princess [39], using about 5,000 lines of Scala code. The core functionality, preimage computation for dedicated string operations such as write, subseq, elem and seqlen is implemented in about 2,000 lines of code and is integrated directly into the OSTRICH framework. To support the representation of sequences, we built a lightweight library of automata which treat the separator as a special transition. The library is implemented in about 1,000 lines of code.

6.1 Benchmarks

To evaluate the effectiveness of OSTRICH^{SEQ}, we curate two benchmark suites, SEQBASE and SEQEXT, where SEQBASE only uses operations that are directly supported by some existing SMT solvers while SEQEXT uses some string sequence operations that are not directly supported by any existing SMT solvers.

SEQBASE. The SEQBASE benchmark suite comprises SeqStr formulas that contain only the generic sequence operations, that is, sequence operations that can be applied to the elements of any type (not necessarily string), such as sequence length seqlen, sequence concatenation $\cdot$, subsequence $seqt[it_1, it_2]$, sequence read $nth(seqt, it)$ and sequence write $seqt[it \rightarrow strt]$. SEQBASE is designed to facilitate a fair comparison with existing solvers since they do not support the string-specific sequence operations. SEQBASE contains 140 SeqStr constraints that are generated from three templates.

- The first template $\mathfrak{u}_1 \in e_1 \wedge \mathfrak{s}_2 = \mathfrak{s}_1[n_1 \rightarrow \mathfrak{u}_1, n_2 \rightarrow \mathfrak{u}_1] \wedge \mathfrak{u}_2 = \text{nth}(\mathfrak{s}_2, m_1) \cdot \text{nth}(\mathfrak{s}_2, m_2) \wedge \mathfrak{u}_2 \in e_2 \wedge \text{seqlen}(\mathfrak{s}_2) < \text{strlen}(\mathfrak{u}_2)$ is utilized to curate 40 random instances, where $\mathfrak{u}_1$ is a string variable, $\mathfrak{s}_1, \mathfrak{s}_2$ are sequence variables, and e_1, e_2 are randomly generated regular expressions. In the first 20 instances, n_1, n_2, m_1, m_2 are integer variables while in the other 20 instances, they are random integers ranging from 0 to 10.
- The second template $\mathfrak{u}_1 \in e_1 \wedge \mathfrak{s}_2 = \mathfrak{s}_1[n_1 \rightarrow \mathfrak{u}_1, n_2 \rightarrow \mathfrak{u}_2] \wedge \mathfrak{s}_3 = \mathfrak{s}_2[n_3, len_1] \cdot \mathfrak{s}_2[n_4, len_2] \wedge \mathfrak{u}_3 = \text{nth}(\mathfrak{s}_3, m_1) \cdot \text{nth}(\mathfrak{s}_3, m_2) \cdot \text{nth}(\mathfrak{s}_3, m_3) \cdot \text{nth}(\mathfrak{s}_3, m_4) \wedge \mathfrak{u}_3 \in e_2 \wedge \text{seqlen}(\mathfrak{s}_3) < \text{strlen}(\mathfrak{u}_3) + 1$ is utilized to curate 40 random instances,

Table 1. Experimental results on SEQBASE.

	cvc5	Z3	Princess^{ARR}	OSTRICH^{SEQ}
sat	48	14	**52**	**52**
unsat	87	59	77	**88**
solved	135	73	129	**140**
unknown/timeout	5	67	11	**0**
avg. time (s)	3.53	24.36	6.84	**3.23**

where u_1, u_2 are string variables, $\mathfrak{s}_1, \mathfrak{s}_2, \mathfrak{s}_3$ are sequence variables, and e_1, e_2 are randomly generated regular expressions. Similar to the first template, n_i, m_i, len_1, len_2 for $i \in [1,4]$ are integer variables in the first 20 instances but are random integers ranging from 0 to 10 in the other 20 instances.

- The third template $\mathfrak{s}_1 = \mathfrak{s}_0[m_1 \to u_1] \wedge \cdots \wedge \mathfrak{s}_i = \mathfrak{s}_{i-1}[m_i \to u_i] \wedge u_1 = \mathsf{nth}(\mathfrak{s}_1, n_1) \wedge \cdots \wedge u_j = \mathsf{nth}(\mathfrak{s}_j, n_j) \wedge u_1 \in e_1 \wedge \cdots \wedge u_j \in e_j$ is utilized to curate 60 random instances, where i and j are randomly selected from the range 0 to 20, $\mathfrak{s}_0 \cdots \mathfrak{s}_i$ are sequence variables, $u_1 \cdots u_j$ are string variables, $e_1 \cdots e_j$ are randomly generated regular expressions, and $m_1, \cdots m_i, n_1 \cdots n_j$ are randomly generated integers constant ranging from 0 to 5. In this template, write $(\mathfrak{s}[\cdot \to \cdot])$ and read $(\mathsf{nth}(\mathfrak{s}, \cdot))$ operations are performed randomly on a string sequence, and the strings read from the sequence are checked against some regular expressions.

SEQEXT. The SEQEXT benchmark suite comprises 60 SeqStr formulas that use specific string sequence operations, namely, filter$_e$, matchAll$_e$, split$_e$ and join$_u$. Among them, 19 formulas are manually generated for the unit tests of OSTRICH^{SEQ}, and 41 formulas are generated from the real-world JavaScript programs collected from GitHub. Moreover, to compare with SMT solvers that do not support the considered string sequence operations, we rewrite them using the basic string operations whenever possible. (matchAll$_e$ is not rewritten since it cannot be expressed using existing string operations.)

6.2 Experimental Results

We conduct experiments by comparing OSTRICH^{SEQ} with SOTA solvers, including cvc5, Z3, Z3-noodler, OSTRICH and Princess^{ARR} (referring to an array-theory-based solver implemented within Princess). SeCo [33] is excluded due to soundness issues. Additionally, `foldleft` and `map` operations are not used to simulate join, as most constraints return unknown under such usage in Z3. On SEQBASE, we evaluate OSTRICH^{SEQ} along with sequence solvers cvc5, Z3 and Princess^{ARR}. For SEQEXT, we rewrite the constraints using only the basic string operations and compare OSTRICH^{SEQ} with string solvers cvc5, Z3, Z3-noodler and OSTRICH.

Table 2. Experimental results on SEQEXT.

		cvc5	Z3	Z3-noodler	OSTRICH	OSTRICH^{SEQ}
SEQEXT-N	sat	19	4	4	20	**23**
	unsat	21	6	4	18	**25**
	solved	40	10	8	38	**48**
	unknown/timeout	8	38	40	10	**0**
	avg. time (s)	10.83	0.13	**0.05**	15.92	3.53
SEQEXT-M	sat	–	–	–	–	**12**
	unsat	–	–	–	–	**0**
	solved	–	–	–	–	**0**
	unknown/timeout	–	–	–	–	**0**
	avg. time (s)	–	–	–	–	**1.77**

All experiments are run on a 24 × 3.1 GHz-core server with 185 GB RAM, where each solver is started as a single thread, with a 60 s time limit and without the memory limit.

The results on SEQBASE are reported in Table 1. We can see that OSTRICH^{SEQ} outperforms all the other solvers on SEQBASE in terms of both the number of solved instances and the solving time per instance. Specifically, OSTRICH^{SEQ} solves all the 140 instances in SEQBASE, while cvc5, Z3 and Princess^{ARR} only solve 135, 73 and 129 instances, respectively. Moreover, OSTRICH^{SEQ} is more efficient than cvc5, Z3 and Princess^{ARR} (OSTRICH^{SEQ} spends 3.23 seconds in solving each instance from SEQBASE on average, while cvc5, Z3 and Princess^{ARR} spend 3.25, 24.36, and 6.84 seconds, respectively).

The results on SEQEXT are reported in Table 2. Since the SOTA sequence solvers do not support filter$_e$, matchAll$_e$ or split$_e$ directly, the SeqStr constraints are rewritten to string constraints (instead of solving the SeqStr constraints directly) when we compare with them on SEQEXT. Moreover, while we can use str.replace_re_all to encode filter$_e$ and split$_e$, the encoding of matchAll$_e$ requires finite-state transducers which have not been supported by most SOTA string solvers. As a result, we do *not* generate the string constraints for the 12 instances in SEQEXT that contain matchAll$_e$, which are denoted by SEQEXT-M, whereas the rest 48 instances are denoted by SEQEXT-N.

From Table 2, we can see that Z3 and Z3-noodler solve only 10 and 8 out of 48 constraints in SEQEXT-N, respectively, and cvc5 and OSTRICH solve 40 and 38 instances, respectively, indicating that the complexity of the string constraints generated from the SeqStr constraints. On the other hand, OSTRICH^{SEQ} solves all of them, demonstrating its superiority in solving the SeqStr constraints with string sequence operations. For efficiency, OSTRICH^{SEQ} spends 3.53 s per instance on average, significantly less than cvc5 and OSTRICH (10.83 and 15.92 s on average, respectively). For the constraints in SEQEXT-M, OSTRICH^{SEQ} successfully solves all 12 instances with an average time of 1.77 s. As aforementioned, for the constraints in SEQEXT-M, we do not generate string constraints or compare against cvc5, Z3, Z3-noodler and OSTRICH, as they cannot be expressed using only the basic operations of string theory.

7 Related Work

String Constraint Solving. String constraint solving has received considerable attention in the literature. Amadini [5] provides a comprehensive survey of the literature up to 2021. In particular, prior approaches are classified into three main categories: automata-based (relying on finite automata to represent the domain of string variables and to handle string operations, e.g., [3,12,17,22,28,31,37]), word-based (algebraic approaches based on systems of word equations, e.g., [7,11,12,22,25,36,38,45,46,50]), and unfolding-based approaches (explicitly reducing each string into a number of contiguous elements denoting its characters, e.g., [6,24,34,35,41,42]).

From another perspective, there are two lines of work aiming for building practical string constraint solvers. (1) One could support as many operations as possible, but primarily resort to heuristics, offering no completeness/termination guarantees. Many string constraint solvers are implemented in SMT solvers, allowing combination with other theories, most commonly the theory of integers for string lengths. Some (non-exhaustive) examples include cvc4/5 [7,36], Z3 [13,25], Z3-str2/3/4 [11,38,50], S3(P) [45,46], Trau [2] (or its variants Trau+ [4]), Slent [47], etc. More recent ones include Z3str3RE [12] and Z3-Noodler [22] (which is based on stabilization-based algorithm [15,21] for solving word equations with regular constraints). (2) The second approach is to develop solvers for decidable fragments, including Norn [3], SLOTH [31] and OSTRICH [17,20], which are usually based on complete decision procedures (e.g. [4,28,37])

We also mention that there are solvers which emphasize certain aspects of string constraint solving by providing dedicated methods or optimization. These include, for instance, those for more expressive regular expressions [10,18], regex-counting [32], string/integer conversion and flat regular constraints [48], Not-Substring Constraint [1], integer data type [19], etc.

Sequences as an Extension of Strings. Strings and sequences are closely related, but may exhibit in different forms. For instance, a string can be considered as a sequence over a finite alphabet. Jez et al. [33] recently studied sequence theories which are an extension of theories of strings with an infinite alphabet of letters, together with a corresponding alphabet theory (e.g. linear integer arithmetic). They provided decision procedures based on parametric automata/transducers, giving rise to a sequence constraint solver SeCo. Our work is different in that we essentially work on a sequence theory where the element is instantiated by the string type.

Theory of Arrays. There are many studies on solving formulas in the theory of arrays or its extensions, for instance, [16,23,26,27,30,44], which are also related to the sequence theory. Note that in these studies, the elements are considered to be either of a generic type or of integer type. In other words, the theory of arrays where the elements are of the string type has not been defined and investigated therein.

8 Conclusion

In this paper, we have proposed SeqStr, a logic of string sequences, which supports a wealth of string and sequence operations—especially their interactions—commonly in real-word string-manipulation programs. We have provided a decision procedure for the straight-line fragment, which is implemented as a new tool OSTRICH^{SEQ}. The experiments on both hand-crafted and real-world benchmarks demonstrate that OSTRICH^{SEQ} is an effective and promising tool for testing, analysis and verification of string-manipulation programs in practice.

References

1. Abdulla, P.A., et al.: Solving not-substring constraint with flat abstraction. In: Asian Symposium on Programming Languages and Systems (APLAS), pp. 305–320 (2021)
2. Abdulla, P.A., et al.: Flatten and conquer: a framework for efficient analysis of string constraints. In: PLDI, pp. 602–617 (2017)
3. Abdulla, P.A., et al.: String constraints for verification. In: CAV, pp. 150–166 (2014)
4. Abdulla, P.A., Atig, M.F., Diep, B.P., Holík, L., Janku, P.: Chain-free string constraints. In: ATVA, pp. 277–293 (2019)
5. Amadini, R.: A survey on string constraint solving. ACM Comput. Surv. **55**(2), 161–1638 (2023)
6. Amadini, R., Gange, G., Stuckey, P.J.: Propagating LEX, FIND and REPLACE with dashed strings. In: van Hoeve, W.-J. (ed.) CPAIOR 2018. LNCS, vol. 10848, pp. 18–34. Springer, Cham (2018). https://doi.org/10.1007/978-3-319-93031-2_2
7. Barbosa, H., et al.: cvc5: a versatile and industrial-strength SMT solver. In: Tools and Algorithms for the Construction and Analysis of Systems (TACAS), pp. 415–442 (2022)
8. Barrett, C., Fontaine, P., Tinelli, C.: The SMT-LIB Standard: Version 2.7. Technical report, Department of Computer Science, The University of Iowa (2025). www.SMT-LIB.org
9. Barrett, C., Tinelli, C.: Satisfiability Modulo Theories. In: Handbook of Model Checking, pp. 305–343. Springer, Cham (2018). https://doi.org/10.1007/978-3-319-10575-8_11
10. Berzish, M., et al.: Towards more efficient methods for solving regular-expression heavy string constraints. Theor. Comput. Sci. **943**, 50–72 (2023)
11. Berzish, M., Ganesh, V., Zheng, Y.: Z3str3: a string solver with theory-aware heuristics. In: Formal Methods in Computer Aided Design (FMCAD), pp. 55–59 (2017)
12. Berzish, M., et al.: MAn SMT solver for regular expressions and linear arithmetic over string length. In: Computer Aided Verification (CAV), pp. 289–312 (2021)
13. Bjørner, N., Tillmann, N., Voronkov, A.: Path feasibility analysis for string-manipulating programs. In: TACAS, pp. 307–321 (2009)

14. Bjørner, N., Ganesh, V., Michel, R., Veanes, M.: An SMT-LIB format for sequences and regular expressions. In: Proceedings of the 10th International Workshop on Satisfiability Modulo Theories (SMT) (2012)
15. Blahoudek, F., et al.: Word equations in synergy with regular constraints. In: Formal Methods (FM), pp. 403–423 (2023)
16. Bradley, A.R., Manna, Z., Sipma, H.B.: What's decidable about arrays? In: Verification, Model Checking, and Abstract Interpretation (VMCAI), pp. 427–442 (2006)
17. Chen, T., Chen, Y., Hague, M., Lin, A.W., Wu, Z.: What is decidable about string constraints with the replaceall function. PACMPL 2(POPL), 31–329 (2018)
18. Chen, T., et al.: Solving string constraints with regex-dependent functions through transducers with priorities and variables. Proc. ACM Program. Lang. 6(POPL), 1–31 (2022)
19. Chen, T., et al.: A decision procedure for path feasibility of string manipulating programs with integer data type. In: Automated Technology for Verification and Analysis (ATVA), pp. 325–342 (2020)
20. Chen, T., Hague, M., Lin, A.W., Rümmer, P., Wu, Z.: Decision procedures for path feasibility of string-manipulating programs with complex operations. Proc. ACM Program. Lang. 3(POPL)(2019)
21. Chen, Y., Chocholatý, D., Havlena, V., Holík, L., Lengál, O., Síc, J.: Solving string constraints with lengths by stabilization. Proc. ACM Program. Lang. 7(OOPSLA2), 2112–2141 (2023)
22. Chen, Y., et al.: Z3-noodler: an automata-based string solver. In: Tools and Algorithms for the Construction and Analysis of Systems (TACAS), pp. 24–33 (2024)
23. Daca, P., Henzinger, T.A., Kupriyanov, A.: Array folds logic. In: Chaudhuri, S., Farzan, A. (eds.) CAV 2016. LNCS, vol. 9780, pp. 230–248. Springer, Cham (2016). https://doi.org/10.1007/978-3-319-41540-6_13
24. Day, J.D., Ehlers, T., Kulczynski, M., Manea, F., Nowotka, D., Poulsen, D.B.: On solving word equations using SAT. In: Filiot, E., Jungers, R., Potapov, I. (eds.) RP 2019. LNCS, vol. 11674, pp. 93–106. Springer, Cham (2019). https://doi.org/10.1007/978-3-030-30806-3_8
25. de Moura, L., Bjørner, N.: Z3: an efficient SMT solver. In: TACAS, pp. 337–340 (2008)
26. Falke, S., Merz, F., Sinz, C.: Extending the theory of arrays: memset, memcpy, and beyond. In: Verified Software: Theories, Tools, Experiments (VSTTE), pp. 108–128 (2013)
27. Farinier, B., David, R., Bardin, S., Lemerre, M: Arrays made simpler: an efficient, scalable and thorough preprocessing. In: Logic for Programming, Artificial Intelligence and Reasoning (LPAR), volume 57 of EPiC Series in Computing, pp. 363–380 (2018)
28. Ganesh, V., Minnes, M., Solar-Lezama, A., Rinard, M.C.: Word equations with length constraints: What's decidable? In: HVC, pp. 209–226 (2012)
29. Ganzinger, H., Hagen, G., Nieuwenhuis, R., Oliveras, A., Tinelli, C.: DPLL(T): fast decision procedures. In: Alur, R., Peled, D.A. (eds.) CAV 2004. LNCS, vol. 3114, pp. 175–188. Springer, Heidelberg (2004). https://doi.org/10.1007/978-3-540-27813-9_14
30. Habermehl, P., Iosif, R., Vojnar, T.: What else is decidable about integer arrays? In: Foundations of Software Science and Computational Structures (FOSSACS), pp. 474–489 (2008)

31. Holík, L., Janku, P., Lin, A.W., Rümmer, P., Vojnar, T.: String constraints with concatenation and transducers solved efficiently. PACMPL **2**(POPL), 41–432 (2018)
32. Hu, D., Wu, Z.: String constraints with regex-counting and string-length solved more efficiently. In: Dependable Software Engineering. Theories, Tools, and Applications (SETTA), pp. 1–20 (2023)
33. Jez, A., Lin, A. W., Markgraf, O., Rümmer, P.: Decision procedures for sequence theories. In: Computer Aided Verification (CAV), pp. 18–40 (2023)
34. Kiezun, A., Ganesh, V., Artzi, S., Guo, P.J., Hooimeijer, P., Ernst, M.D.: Hampi: a solver for word equations over strings, regular expressions, and context-free grammars. ACM Trans. Softw. Eng. Methodol. **21**(4) (2013)
35. Li, G., Ghosh, I.: PASS: string solving with parameterized array and interval automaton. In: Bertacco, V., Legay, A. (eds.) HVC 2013. LNCS, vol. 8244, pp. 15–31. Springer, Cham (2013). https://doi.org/10.1007/978-3-319-03077-7_2
36. Liang, T., Reynolds, A., Tinelli, C., Barrett, C., Deters, M.: A DPLL(T) theory solver for a theory of strings and regular expressions. In: CAV, pp. 646–662 (2014)
37. Lin, A.W., Barceló, P.: String solving with word equations and transducers: towards a logic for analysing mutation XSS. In: Principles of Programming Languages (POPL), pp. 123–136 (2016)
38. Mora, F., Berzish, M., Kulczynski, M., Nowotka, D., Ganesh, V.: Z3str4: a multi-armed string solver. In: Formal Methods (FM), pp. 389–406 (2021)
39. Rümmer, P.: A constraint sequent calculus for first-order logic with linear integer arithmetic. In: Cervesato, I., Veith, H., Voronkov, A. (eds.) LPAR 2008. LNCS (LNAI), vol. 5330, pp. 274–289. Springer, Heidelberg (2008). https://doi.org/10.1007/978-3-540-89439-1_20
40. Rümmer, P.: Princess - the scala theorem prover (2024). https://philipp.ruemmer.org/princess.shtml. Latest release 08 Nov 2024
41. Saxena, P., Akhawe, D., Hanna, S., Mao, F., McCamant, S., Song, D.: A symbolic execution framework for javascript. In: Security and Privacy (SP), pp. 513–528. IEEE Computer Society, USA (2010)
42. Scott, J.D., Flener, P., Pearson, J., Schulte, C.: Design and implementation of bounded-length sequence variables. In: Salvagnin, D., Lombardi, M. (eds.) CPAIOR 2017. LNCS, vol. 10335, pp. 51–67. Springer, Cham (2017). https://doi.org/10.1007/978-3-319-59776-8_5
43. Sheng, Y., et al.: Reasoning about vectors using an smt theory of sequences. In: Automated Reasoning, pp. 125–143. Springer International Publishing, Cham (2022). https://doi.org/10.1007/978-3-031-10769-6_9
44. Stump, A., Barrett, C.W., Dill, D.L., Levitt, J.R.: A decision procedure for an extensional theory of arrays. In: Logic in Computer Science (LICS), pp. 29–37. IEEE Computer Society (2001)
45. Trinh, M., Chu, D., Jaffar, J.: S3: a symbolic string solver for vulnerability detection in web applications. In: CCS, pp. 1232–1243 (2014)
46. Trinh, M., Chu, D., Jaffar, J.: Progressive reasoning over recursively-defined strings. In: Computer Aided Verification (CAV), pp. 218–240 (2016)
47. Wang, H.-E., Chen, S.-Y., Yu, F., Jiang, J.-H.R.: A symbolic model checking approach to the analysis of string and length constraints. In: ASE, pp. 623–633. ACM (2018)
48. Wu, H., Chen, Y., Wu, Z., Xia, B., Zhan, N.: A decision procedure for string constraints with string/integer conversion and flat regular constraints. Acta Informatica **61**(1), 23–52 (2024)

49. Z3Prover. Sequences | online z3 guide (2025)
50. Zheng, Y., et al.: Z3str2: an efficient solver for strings, regular expressions, and length constraints. Formal Methods Syst. Des. **50**(2–3), 249–288 (2017)

AI and Compiler Optimisation for Performance

ELTC: An End-to-End Large Language Model-Based Tensor Compilation Optimization Framework

WenBo Ma[1], QingZeng Song[1(✉)], Fei Qiao[2], YongJiang Xue[1], and MingZe Sun[1]

[1] Tiangong University, No. 399 Binshui West Road, Xiqing District, Tianjin 300387, China
qingzengsong@163.com
[2] Tsinghua University, No. 1 Tsinghua Yuan, Haidian District, Beijing 100084, China
https://www.tiangong.edu.cn/, https://www.tsinghua.edu.cn

Abstract. Tensor program optimization is a non-convex optimization problem, and efficiently solving it while balancing optimization efficiency and execution performance remains a challenging task. Search-based tensor program compilers have proven effective by constructing large-scale exploration spaces that include potentially high-performance program variants, thus overcoming the performance bottlenecks of traditional program optimization methods. However, these approaches still face significant challenges in search strategies, as existing compilers often require hours or even days to identify the optimal program representation. This paper proposes ELTC, an end-to-end tensor program compilation framework based on large language models (LLMs), designed for efficient optimization of tensor programs in deep neural networks. ELTC formulates the tensor program exploration problem as a generation task for language models. By training a large language model offline, it generates transformation sequences for tensor programs in an end-to-end manner based on their feature representations. While preserving the broad search space, this approach significantly improves optimization efficiency. Moreover, we introduce a language-model-friendly intermediate representation, which encodes key features of tensor programs using structured textual formats. Based on this representation, we construct a tensor program dataset tailored for language models. Experimental results demonstrate that ELTC achieves superior performance in both optimization quality and tuning speed. Compared with the fully converged Ansor-TenSet, ELTC achieves a 34.07× compilation speedup and an average performance improvement of 1.06× under convergence conditions. Furthermore, ELTC outperforms the manually optimized kernel library TensorRT, achieving a 1.3× performance gain.

Keywords: Program Transformation · Compiler · Large Language Models

1 Introduction

With the widespread adoption of deep learning (DL) models in areas such as image processing, language generation, and augmented reality [1], a proliferation of emerging network architectures, increasingly complex model structures, and a growing variety of operators have led to higher demands for computational performance. To improve runtime efficiency, existing deep learning frameworks (e.g., TensorFlow [2], PyTorch [10], MXNet [8]) often rely on manually optimized kernel libraries provided by hardware vendors (e.g., cuDNN [11], oneDNN [12]). However, the development of such kernel libraries is time-consuming and labor-intensive, making it difficult to keep pace with rapidly evolving model architectures and increasingly diverse hardware platforms—gradually becoming a bottleneck to performance improvements. To address this issue, the community has introduced search-based tensor compilers (e.g., TVM [3], Halide [4], Tensor Comprehensions [5], FlexTensor [6], NeoCPU [7]), which automatically explore efficient tensor program optimization strategies. These compilers typically construct a search space over various program transformations—such as parallelization, data layout reordering, and vectorization—and search for the optimal combination of transformations. However, to ensure comprehensive coverage of the search space, current methods often suffer from high-dimensionality and long search times. Although Ansor [15] improves efficiency by designing a two-level search space, its lower level still relies heavily on random sampling, resulting in slow search speeds.

To address the aforementioned challenges, this paper introduces ELTC, an end-to-end tensor program optimization framework based on large language models (LLMs), which reformulates the tensor program optimization process as a language generation task. ELTC guides the search process using an end-to-end LLM, significantly improving optimization efficiency while preserving a broad search space. The framework consists of two core components: a high-level search space construction module and a low-level transformation sequence generation module. The search space construction module automatically generates a structured skeleton of the search space based on predefined rules, thereby delineating the scope of exploration and eliminating the overhead associated with manual template design. Building on this, the transformation sequence generation module leverages the LLM to produce program transformation sequences targeting high-performance implementations within the structured skeleton. These sequences are ultimately mapped to concrete tuning parameters and scheduling strategies, enabling efficient tensor program optimization. We refer to the large language model proposed in this paper as the ELTC model.

Given that both the input and output of the ELTC model are expressed in domain-specific languages (DSLs) and contain a substantial amount of technical terminology, we fine-tuned it based on Code Llama 7B-Instruct [18]. The model was pretrained on a large corpus of compiler intermediate representations and further optimized through reinforcement learning using transformation sequence-specific datasets. Notably, ELTC is trained using offline data, which significantly reduces the time required for online search. The training dataset consists of approximately 410,000 labeled samples, derived from transforming 52 million program performance records in the TenSet [19] dataset. These samples are categorized into three types of corpora based on different training stages of the ELTC model, resulting in a high-quality dataset better suited for LLM-based compilation tasks.We evaluated ELTC against some of the most widely-used inference frameworks, including PyTorch, TensorFlow, and TensorRT [20]. Results show that ELTC achieves a speedup of 2.19× over PyTorch, 2.01× over TensorFlow, and 1.30× over TensorRT on deep learning model inference. Compared with the widely adopted compilation framework Ansor-TenSet, ELTC achieves a 34.07× compilation speedup under comparable performance, and a 1.06× performance gain when both approaches are fully converged.

In summary, this paper makes the following key contributions:

- An end-to-end tensor program compilation framework based on large language models, which formulates the tensor program optimization task as a sequence generation problem. This effectively enhances optimization efficiency.
- A language-model-friendly intermediate representation and construct a large-scale tensor program dataset. Program features are expressed in structured textual form, improving the language model's capability to capture and model program structures.
- A language-model-driven search strategy, where a trained large language model generates program transformation sequences, enabling effective exploration and identification of high-performance tensor programs.

2 Background

2.1 Search-Based Tensor Compilers

Figure 1 illustrates the typical workflow of mainstream deep learning tensor compilers. These compilers take model files packaged by deep learning frameworks as input. Essentially, a deep learning model is a graph-structured data representation written in high-level programming languages. The compiler transforms it into a computation graph representation, upon which a series of high-level graph-level optimizations are performed, followed by operator-level optimization on each subgraph. Due to differences in input/output shapes, data layouts, data types, and target hardware specifications across subgraph program representations, the potential optimization strategies form a vast search space. The tuning system explores this space to identify tensor programs with optimal performance. These high-performance programs are then handed off—based on the target hardware platform—to backends such as LLVM [9], CUDA, or other custom hardware accelerators, and finally deployed as executable binaries.

In previous work, Ansor employed a random sampling-based approach to construct its search space, resulting in a vast and expressive optimization space. While this strategy pushed program performance to a state-of-the-art level, the excessive size of the search space also introduced significant challenges in terms of

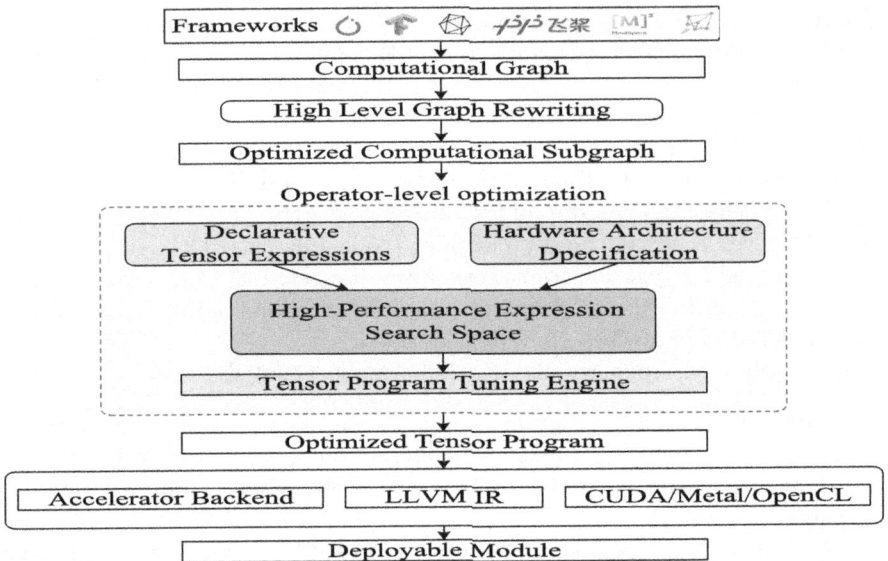

Fig. 1. Workflow of common deep learning compilers. The components highlighted in the red box indicate the operational scope of ELTC. (Color figure online)

long compilation times [22]. In contrast to search frameworks that rely on random sampling strategies, ELTC leverages learned domain-specific knowledge and uses a large language model to generate potential high-performance tensor programs within the search space, thereby significantly improving search efficiency.

2.2 Language Models for Code Generation

In recent years, general-purpose large language models such as GPT-4 [27], Gemini [23], and DeepSeek [21] have achieved remarkable progress across a wide range of natural language processing tasks [24]. Trained on massive text corpora, these models demonstrate outstanding performance on diverse tasks. However, despite their versatility, their large parameter sizes present high barriers to usage, including significant demands for computational resources. As a result, in specific domains, leveraging smaller-scale language models combined with domain-specific datasets has emerged as a more efficient and adaptable strategy. In particular, in the code generation domain, code-focused large language models (Code LLMs) such as StarCoder [25], Codex [26], and CodeLLaMa have shown impressive performance by being efficiently pretrained on specialized code corpora. The CodeLLaMa model is fine-tuned from the general-purpose language model LLaMa2, and under a limited computational budget, it outperforms models of the same architecture that are trained solely on code data [18]. In this work, the ELTC model is required to handle both human-written instructions and code inputs. Therefore, we choose to fine-tune based on the CodeLLaMa-Instruct variant, which enhances the model's comprehension and performance on code transformation tasks.

2.3 TenSet

TenSet introduces a large-scale public dataset tailored for tensor compilers. This dataset encompasses workloads from 120 deep learning networks executed on diverse hardware platforms, summarizing a total of 13,848 computational subgraphs. For each subgraph, up to 4,000 candidate programs are sampled from its corresponding search space, with actual runtime measurements collected on target hardware. Additionally, TenSet improves upon Ansor's online data collection strategy by employing an offline dataset to train a learnable cost model, TenSetMLP, which significantly accelerates the search process—achieving approximately 10× speedup over traditional methods [19].

3 System Overview

ELTC is an automated framework focused on the generation of high-performance tensor programs, with the goal of efficiently producing tensor implementations optimized for specific hardware platforms. The core task of the framework is to optimize the tensor programs based on computation subgraphs that have undergone prior graph-level optimization. The processes of graph optimization and final deployment rely on the existing infrastructure provided by TVM. Figure 2 illustrates the overall workflow of ELTC, which comprises three main components: Search Space Constructor, Large Language Model Training Module, Search Space Explorer.

To support an efficient search process, ELTC constructs a highly expressive search space that preserves diverse program transformation paths through rule-based design, thereby avoiding premature elimination of potentially high-performance implementations. This search space is further converted into a structured intermediate representation, enabling it to be fed as a sequence input to the language model, which enhances the model's understanding of tensor programs.

ELTC leverages the language model as the core component for program generation, learning tensor program transformation strategies from large-scale offline data. The language model takes the structured intermediate representation (IR) at the end of the search space as input. To enhance the model's understanding and training efficiency, ELTC proposes three distinct structured datasets to accommodate the supervised learning and reinforcement learning methods used during training, enabling the model to effectively capture patterns and features in tensor program transformations. After training, the language model generates a series of candidate program transformation sequences. In the program generation process, ELTC transforms the tensor program optimization problem into a language modeling task, leveraging the candidate sequences generated by the language model. The generated candidate programs are then filtered by a performance evaluation model to select the optimal high-performance implementation. This language model-driven search mechanism significantly improves the efficiency and quality of program generation while demonstrating strong generalization capability.

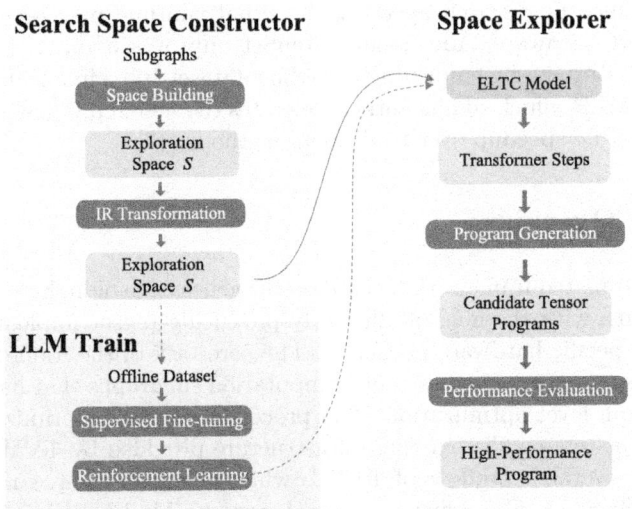

Fig. 2. System overview of the ELTC framework. Solid arrows indicate the online execution path, while dashed arrows represent components preprocessed through offline learning.

4 Search Space Constructor

The core objective of the search space constructor is to generate a search space that is both precise and efficient, ensuring the inclusion of high-performance programs. This section delves into the design of an effective and suitable search space generation strategy, aiming to strike a balance between comprehensiveness and the facilitation of efficient exploration by large language models.

4.1 Space Building

Given ELTC's unique architecture based on an end-to-end language model, generating candidate high-performance programs does not require specifying concrete parameters for each variant. Instead, ELTC focuses on guiding the search process by defining the dependencies among tensor program parameters.

To achieve this, ELTC adopts a rule-based search space construction strategy. This strategy generates tensor programs through flexible rule applications. The specific rules are summarized in Table 1. It should be noted that the transformation rules in Table 1 do not affect the correctness of the tensor program, they only alter its program structure. Each rule defines explicit conditions for use and the applicable components. In this context, p denotes a tensor program, t represents the loop structure table analyzed from p, and g refers to the computation graph derived by abstracting the data dependencies within the tensor program. Rule 1 performs loop tiling and is applied only when the loop exhibits significant data reuse potential. Rule 2 introduces cache blocks for operations like matrix multiplication, which involve frequent data access. Instead of writing results directly to main memory—causing latency due to repeated access—this rule ensures that intermediate results are stored in cache and written back only after all computations are complete. Rule 3 is mutually exclusive with Rule 1 and is applied to loops where no data reuse is detected, thereby skipping loop tiling. Rule 4 inline simple computations into other operations to reduce overhead. For typical subgraphs, the number of tensor programs constituting the search space is limited to no more than 64. This setting meets the minimum requirement for optimizing performance convergence.

Table 1. Derivation Rules for Search Space Generation.

No	Rule Name	Condition	Application
1	Split	IsDataReuse(p,t)	p' = Split(t)
2	Add Cache	AnalyzeMemoryAccessPattern(p,g)	p' = AddCache(g)
3	Skip	!IsDataReuse(p,t)	p' = Skip(t)
4	Compute Inline	DetectInlinable(p,t)	p' = Inline(t)

As an example, the upper part of Fig. 3 shows the mathematical definition of a multiply-accumulate subgraph along with its initial tensor program. By analyzing this program, the corresponding loop structure table and computation dependency graph are generated. This paper starts with the initial tensor program, loop structure table, and computation dependency graph, applies two sets of transformation rules (r_1 and r_2), and obtains the transformed tensor programs (p_1 and p_2). It should be noted that the tensor programs in the figure only illustrate the high-level program structure; specific parameter values are not yet filled in.

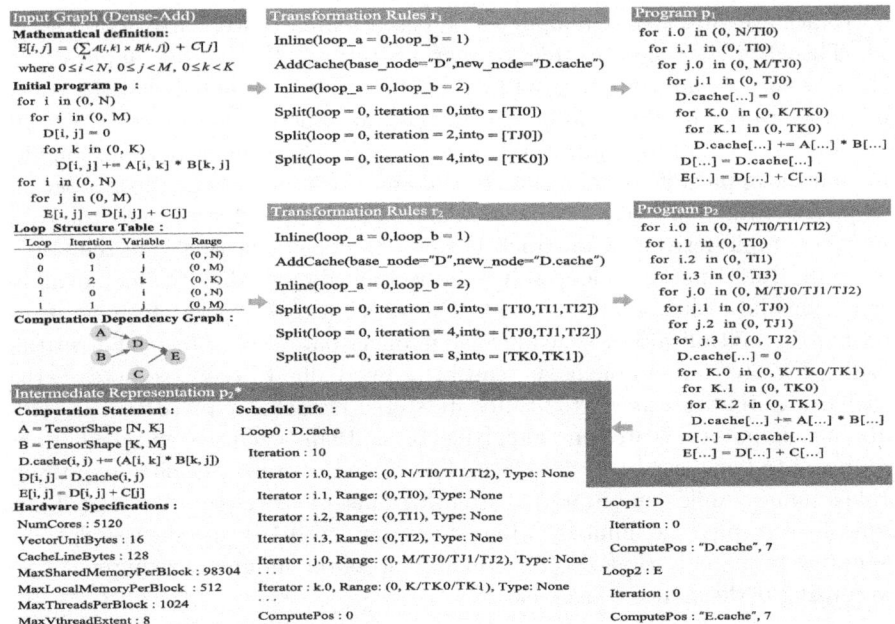

Fig. 3. Example of a multiply-accumulate subgraph search space generated based on rules.

4.2 IR Transformation

Tensor programs within the search space serve as inputs to the language model for generating sequences of transformations that yield high-performance programs. However, the source code of tensor programs often exceeds ten thousand tokens. To mitigate this, we designed an intermediate representation (IR) that simplifies the tensor programs while preserving their complete semantics, thereby reducing input complexity. Additionally, the ELTC model retains key hardware platform information related to the tensor program optimization process during generation.

The lower part of Fig. 3 illustrates tensor program p_2 and its transformed IR form p_2^*. p_2^* will serve as the input to the ELTC language model. This IR contains global computation statement, hardware specifications, and schedule information specific to each IR. In the schedule information, the annotation of computation location effectively reduces token redundancy while preserving critical information. For example, when recording scheduling information for cached loop structures, we only need to indicate its computation location as 7, avoiding redundant representation of loop axes and reducing token length. Additionally, loop axes are annotated with type information, which is initially None (indicating no additional information) in the initial schedule and may later become compiler optimization directives (e.g., unroll, parallel) or hardware binding information (e.g., BlockX, ThreadX) after subsequent processing. During deep learning model tuning, we adopt a unified global hardware information graph, exemplified here with details from the V100 GPU. For clarity, this IR is referred to as ELTC IR throughout this paper. ELTC IR is primarily represented in natural language form rather than programming language, a design choice that improves efficiency and compatibility when interfacing with language models. Furthermore, the offline dataset is also rewritten according to this IR format to ensure consistency in the language model input, which is crucial for effective training.

5 Dataset Preparation and Model Training

5.1 TenSet ELTC Dataset

Datasets are fundamental to deep learning model training, determining the upper bound of achievable model performance. In this work, we improve upon the TenSet dataset to better support training of the ELTC model.

The transformation sequences in the TenSet dataset originally consist of eleven scheduling primitives. Here, primitive CI shares a similar function with the rule4 inlining rule used in generating tensor programs. The cache block rule applied by Rule2 has essentially the same effect as primitive CHW, which is used to create cache blocks. Since the CHW primitive does not affect the execution order of other operation primitives, we reposition it to follow the CI primitive. Additionally, we redefine the functionality of the SP primitive to perform loop axis splitting and introduce a new primitive, FI, for padding parameters on specified loop axes. After these modifications, the TenSet ELTC dataset's transformation sequences include twelve scheduling primitives. To accommodate model training, we split the transformation sequences: the first part is used to generate high-level tensor programs serving as the initial samples of the TenSet ELTC dataset, while the second part serves as the input transformation sequences for training the model. Figure 4 illustrates the detailed rewriting process of the TenSet dataset.

5.2 Progressive Training

Progressive training is a strategy that gradually increases the difficulty of training tasks, enabling the model to progressively learn and adapt to more complex language tasks during training. In this work, we choose to perform progressive training based on Code Llama 7B-Instruction. During the training process, we categorize the TenSet ELTC dataset into three types of tasks:

1. Given a transformed tensor program, predict its runtime on the target platform.
2. Given an original tensor program p_1 and its transformed version p_1^*, predict the sequence of transformations applied from p_1 to p_1^*.
3. Given a tensor program representing only the high-level structure, predict the sequence of transformations required to achieve the shortest runtime.

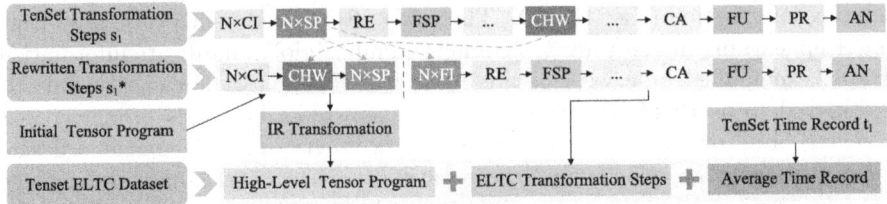

Fig. 4. The generation process from the TenSet dataset to the TenSet ELTC dataset. The blue dashed lines indicate the splitting process of the SP primitive, while the orange dashed lines represent the repositioning of the CHW primitive. (Color figure online)

The training process of the ELTC model consists of three stages: pretraining, fine-tuning, and alignment. In the first stage, we perform pretraining using data from Task 1 and Task 2. Data from Task 3 is reserved for the fine-tuning and alignment stages. The training data is split into two parts with a 7:3 ratio. The first part selects only the fastest transformation steps for fine-tuning, while the second part is used directly for alignment training. The training parameters during fine-tuning are consistent with those in the pretraining stage.

During the alignment stage, reinforcement learning is employed, using TenSet-MLP as the reward model. This cost model evaluates the performance of different tensor programs within the search space. In reinforcement learning training, tensor programs are input into the language model, whose outputs are then fed to the reward model for performance ranking. The training process is adjusted based on the ranking of the language model's outputs.

The model is trained on a single NVIDIA V100 GPU, with a total training time of approximately 300 h. Figure 5 illustrates the overall training workflow of the language model.

6 Search SpaceExplorer

The search space explorer utilizes a large language model (LLM) to explore high-performance tensor programs within the previously constructed search space. The model outputs a simplified transformation sequence for tensor programs.

We need to map the transformation sequences to the sampled tensor programs in the search space. According to statistics, transformation sequences in the TenSet ELTC dataset can contain up to 54 primitives, including numerous computation index modifications. To improve mapping efficiency and reduce computational overhead, we perform all index adjustments after mapping the entire transformation sequence. First, transformation primitives—including their types and parameters—are extracted from the sequence. Then, the intermediate representation of the tensor program is divided into a computation graph and scheduling information, which are transformed according to the primitive types. Finally, redundant loop axes are removed, computation indices corrected, and the transformed ELTC IR is returned.

To effectively evaluate the performance of candidate tensor programs and select the optimal expression, we adopt the deep learning-based cost model proposed by TenSet. Specifically, we employ its best-performing MLP architecture combined with a Ranking Loss training strategy for fine-grained ranking of candidate programs. To extract features from the ELTC IR for performance evaluation, we construct complete loop structures using computation statements as the basic units—a process methodologically similar to converting tensor programs into ELTC IR. After construction, the system conducts static code analysis to extract structured representation vectors for the cost model. Since static features rather than runtime information are used, this evaluation achieves very high efficiency. Experiments show that the cost model can evaluate thousands of candidates within seconds, making the evaluation overhead negligible for typical ELTC tuning scenarios involving around 64 candidates.

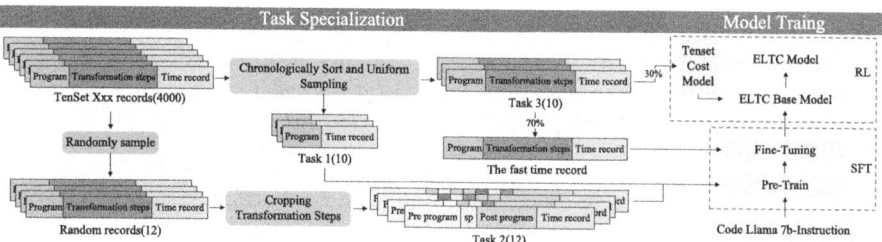

Fig. 5. Data processing and training workflow of the ELTC model. The TenSet ELTC dataset is divided into three task types according to fine-tuning requirements. The first two fine-tuning stages use SFT, while the final fine-tuning stage employs reinforcement learning.

7 Evaluation

7.1 Experimental Settings

To comprehensively evaluate the performance of ELTC, we designed a three-level experimental scheme: convergence verification experiments, subgraph-level performance comparisons, and end-to-end neural network performance assessments. The experiments selected 11 representative deep learning models as workloads, covering various key computation types such as 2D convolution, transposed convolution, 3D convolution, fully connected layers, and matrix multiplication. The hardware platforms used include a 24-core Intel Core i9-13900HX CPU and an NVIDIA Tesla V100 GPU, ensuring coverage of mainstream computing environments. Baseline comparison frameworks comprise PyTorch 2.1, TensorFlow 2.15, TensorRT 8.6, and Ansor 0.9. To improve Ansor's search efficiency and eliminate the variability caused by online training of the cost model, the TenSet offline-trained cost model was integrated into Ansor, ensuring fair conditions in the comparison with ELTC.

7.2 Convergence Analysis of ELTC

We designed a set of experiments to evaluate the convergence performance of ELTC. A total of 1,000 subgraphs covering mainstream deep learning operation types from the TenSet dataset were selected for tuning on both the NVIDIA Tesla V100 GPU and the Intel Core i9-13900HX CPU. Figure 6 presents the convergence curves on both platforms, with the horizontal axis representing the cumulative number of tuned programs (up to 128K, corresponding to a search space of 128 candidate programs per subgraph), and the vertical axis showing normalized latency.

The results indicate that ELTC-GPU achieves preliminary convergence at around 32K entries (performance improvement < 1%), and performance stabilizes at 66K entries (improvement < 0.1%). ELTC-CPU converges faster, reaching the same performance thresholds at 29K and 59K entries, respectively. In contrast, mainstream search frameworks such as Ansor typically require about 1,000 measurements to complete tuning for a single subgraph, demonstrating that ELTC significantly reduces measurement overhead. In subsequent experiments, ELTC-64 is set as the default configuration, with convergence defined as a performance improvement of less than 0.1

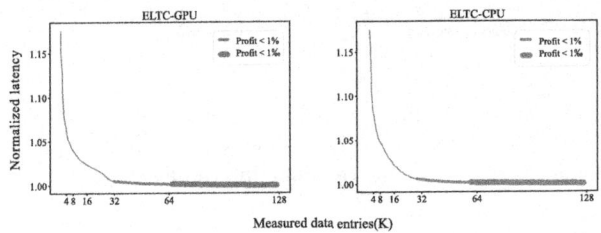

Fig. 6. Convergence curves of ELTC on test data for both CPU and GPU platforms.

7.3 Subgraph Benchmark

For the subgraph-level experiments, we compared ELTC with the search framework Ansor-TenSet on the NVIDIA V100 platform. A total of 515 subgraphs from eleven deep learning networks were selected to evaluate performance. The tuning durations of ELTC under different search space sizes were regarded as the measurement times for the subgraphs. Table 2 summarizes the performance comparisons between ELTC and Ansor-TenSet at various time points, as well as the performance changes within those intervals. The key findings are as follows:

The data highlighted in green shows that ELTC achieves 85.4% of ELTC-256's performance with only a single measurement, demonstrating the effectiveness of ELTC's trained language model in searching for high-performance tensor programs. ELTC-64 and ELTC-128 reach 99.5% and 99.9% of ELTC-256's performance, respectively, with performance gains under 0.1%, consistent with the convergence analysis.

The blue-highlighted data presents the critical performance comparison between ELTC and Ansor-TenSet-256. Within 256 time units, Ansor-TenSet completes approximately 1,000 measurements and reaches full convergence. ELTC-8 has already surpassed Ansor-TenSet-256, achieving 1.018× its performance with room for further improvement; ELTC-64 further improves performance by 1.054×.

The red-highlighted data in the table shows the performance comparison between ELTC and Ansor-TenSet at full convergence. The results indicate that within the same time frame, ELTC achieves a 1.06× speedup over Ansor-TenSet.

7.4 End-to-End Network Benchmark

We designed three sets of experiments for deep learning network workloads:1) Performance comparison of seven frameworks on ten deep learning models using the NVIDIA Tesla V100 GPU platform; 2) Performance optimization comparison of five optimization schemes on eight deep learning models on the Intel CPU platform; 3) Comparison of the tuning process and efficiency differences between ELTC-64 and Ansor-TenSet on both Intel CPU and V100 hardware platforms.

Comparison of GPU Performance Optimization on End-to-End Networks. Fig. 7 presents the end-to-end performance comparison results on the NVIDIA V100 GPU. First, among automatic search frameworks, ELTC-64 achieves speedups ranging from 1.00 to 1.21× over Ansor-TenSet-256 across ten deep learning tasks, with an average improvement of 1.06×. Compared to Ansor-TenSet-64, ELTC-64 attains speedups between 1.16 and 2.05×, averaging 1.31×. Similarly, ELTC-8 shows average speedups of 1.02× and 1.26× over Ansor-TenSet-256 and Ansor-TenSet-64, respectively. This trend further confirms ELTC's performance advantage in tensor program generation.

Table 2. Overall Performance Comparison between ELTC and Ansor-TenSet on Experimental Subgraphs. A higher overall speedup indicates better performance. The "Times" column refers to the tuning duration corresponding to ELTC's specified search space size.

		Ansor			ELTC
	Times	8	64	256	256
ELTC	1	1.462	1.124	0.905	0.854
	8	1.644	1.263	1.018	0.96
	16	1.671	1.284	1.03	0.976
	32	1.697	1.304	1.05	0.991
	64	1.703	1.309	1.054	0.995
	128	1.71	1.314	1.059	0.999
	256	1.712	1.316	1.06	1
Ansor	256	1.615	1.241	1	0.943

Second, comparing ELTC with mainstream hand-optimized kernel libraries reveals that ELTC-64 excels in small-scale networks, outperforming PyTorch, TensorFlow, and TensorRT. Such networks, due to their smaller scale, struggle to fully utilize GPU resources; ELTC effectively exploits latent performance through automatic tuning strategies like improved parallelism and cache reuse.

For medium-scale networks such as ViT-B/32, ELTC's performance is slightly behind TensorRT, which benefits from extensive manual optimization of matrix multiplication kernels tailored to hardware platforms. While this yields superior computational performance, it requires hardware-specific code adjustments. In contrast, ELTC maintains strong generality and scalability across different hardware platforms through a unified automatic search strategy. Even so, ELTC still outperforms PyTorch and TensorFlow with speedups of 1.46× and 1.27×, respectively.

For large-scale models including BERT-base, BERT-large, and LLAMA-7b, ELTC-64 also surpasses PyTorch and TensorFlow, achieving average speedups of 1.5× and 1.16×, respectively, while reaching 86%âĂŞ96% of TensorRT's performance, with an average of 92%. Overall, ELTC demonstrates superior optimization capabilities across the vast majority of workloads. Its automated tuning pipeline significantly improves usability while maintaining high performance, outperforming state-of-the-art search frameworks such as Ansor-TenSet and some manual kernel libraries. Notably, traditional static kernel libraries still hold advantages in deeply optimized common operators, but ELTC shows greater potential in adaptability and extensibility.

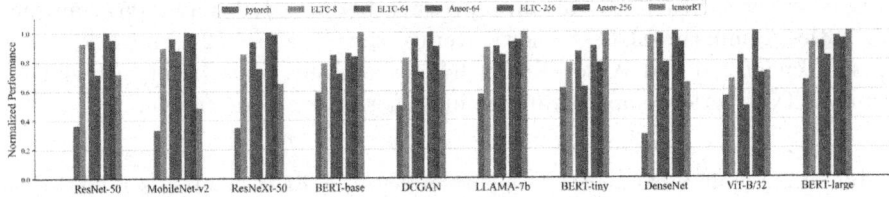

Fig. 7. Performance comparison of ELTC, Ansor-TenSet, and hand-optimized kernel libraries on networks running on the V100 GPU.

CPU Performance Optimization Comparison on End-to-End Network. Due to memory limitations, BERT-large and LLAMA-7b were not tested on the CPU in this experiment. Figure 8 presents the performance comparison results, showing acceleration metrics. Across these eight deep learning networks, compared to Ansor-TenSet, ELTC-64 achieves a performance improvement of 1.2 to 1.44 times within the same time budget, with an average speedup of 1.31. Even under full convergence, ELTC-64 still delivers a 1.02 to 1.1 times performance gain, averaging 1.06. Compared to PyTorch, ELTC-64 improves performance by 1.25 to 5.1 times, with an average speedup of 2.13; relative to TensorFlow, ELTC-64 shows a 1.19 to 2.49 times increase, averaging 1.78.

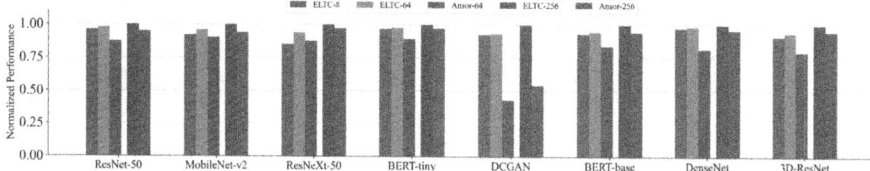

Fig. 8. Performance comparison of ELTC, Ansor-TenSet, and manual kernel libraries on the Intel i9-13900HX CPU across various neural networks.

Comparison of Tuning Effectiveness Between ELTC and Ansor-TenSet. This set of experiments aims to evaluate the performance improvement and time cost of ELTC-64 compared to Ansor-TenSet-256 during the tuning process. Figure 9 illustrates the tuning curves of both methods on CPU and GPU platforms for five representative deep learning models. The x-axis represents the cumulative tuning time (in seconds), while the y-axis shows the execution latency (in milliseconds) of the current best tensor program on the target hardware.

In the GPU experiments (Fig. 9(a)), due to the lengthy tuning time of Ansor-TenSet-256, only its curve within the tuning time range of ELTC-64 is displayed, except for the LLAMA-7b test where the full curve is retained for comparison. The tuning curves indicate that ELTC-64 reaches the lowest latency early in the process. Focusing on the complete curve for the LLAMA-7b network, ELTC-64 achieves full convergence with a tuning speed 4.33 times faster than Ansor-TenSet-256. ELTC-64 reaches the best performance of Ansor-TenSet-256 within 620 s, which is only 33.04% of the time Ansor-TenSet-256 requires. For the other four networks, ELTC-64's tuning times are shortened by 3.62, 4.37, 4.64, and 3.21 times respectively, averaging a 4.03× speedup. When achieving equivalent performance, ELTC's tuning time accelerates by 23.97 to 46.41 times, with an average speedup of 34.07 times.

In the CPU experiments (Fig. 9(b)), ELTC-64 converges even faster, primarily due to the smaller optimized search space on the CPU. Across these five networks, ELTC-64 achieves a 3.03 to 4.57 times speedup under full convergence compared to Ansor-TenSet-256, averaging 4.09 times; under equivalent performance conditions, the speedup ranges from 22.34 to 49.36 times, with an average of 33.8 times.

8 Related Work

In the performance optimization of deep learning tensor programs, current mainstream approaches can be broadly categorized into two types: search-based optimization methods and polyhedral model-based optimization methods.

The first category centers on constructing a search space to explore potential high-performance tensor programs. In search-based tensor compilers, Halide introduced the concept of separating computation from scheduling, using a domain-specific language to define computation and scheduling primitives. TVM

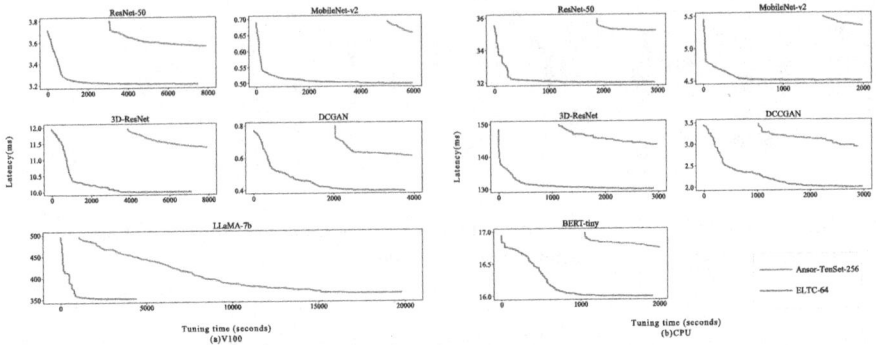

Fig. 9. Comparison of the best program performance (measured by network inference latency) and search time between ELTC and Ansor-TenSet on GPU and CPU. ELTC demonstrates a significant advantage in search time, with the complete tuning curve of Ansor-TenSet shown only for the LLaMA-7b network.

has two versions: AutoTVM, which optimizes tensor programs through hand-crafted template-based search, and Ansor, which improves upon AutoTVM by eliminating the need for manual template design and instead adopts evolutionary algorithms to search for effective tensor programs. Following Ansor, to further reduce compilation time and explore high-performance tensor program representations, the new generation of search-based tensor compilers propose distinctive solutions. TenSet and TLP [17] address Ansor's long search time caused by online training of cost models by adopting offline cost models. Felix [16] maps discrete program features to continuous functions and employs gradient descent to shorten search time.

The second category consists of optimization strategies based on polyhedral theory, which transform the optimization problem of tensor programs into integer linear programming problems. The core idea is to design affine functions to optimize tensor programs. Tiramisu [14] inherits the separation of computation and scheduling, designing a flexible programming model and is a polyhedral compiler specifically tailored for deep learning.

With the increasing number of deep learning compilers, MILR [13] proposed a set of extensible compiler infrastructure measures to address the software fragmentation issue in this field.

9 Discussion

Limitations. Like all offline-trained models, ELTC faces challenges when there is a discrepancy between the target deployment scenarios and the training scenarios, which can affect result accuracy. Achieving optimal performance requires appropriately representative training data. Moreover, ELTC demands hundreds of hours of training before it can optimize deep learning networks, making the time cost prohibitively high when tuning only one or two neural networks. Therefore, ELTC is better suited for large-scale tuning tasks involving batches of neural networks.

Future Work. 1) The ELTC model currently uses 7 billion parameters, making it difficult to run efficiently on resource-constrained hardware platforms and heavily dependent on cross-device tuning and deployment. Thus, exploring model compression and lightweight versions of ELTC is a promising direction. 2) Designing a language model architecture better tailored for tensor compilers is another key avenue. The current Code Llama model focuses on general code optimization and is not specialized for the structural characteristics of tensor programs. Future work could explore dedicated language model architectures specifically for tensor exploration tasks to further enhance code generation quality and performance awareness. 3) Establishing a more diverse and flexible search space is also important. ELTC currently relies on rule-based search space construction, which limits its adaptability to the structural diversity of tensor operators. Given ELTC's significant acceleration in tuning time, adopting more flexible search space construction methods could help discover even more powerful tensor programs.

10 Conclusion

This paper presents ELTC, an end-to-end tensor compiler framework based on a large language model. ELTC consists of two main components: a search space constructor and a tensor program generator, which are connected through a custom intermediate representation. Leveraging the powerful exploration capabilities of large language models in search space traversal, ELTC can generate high-performance tensor programs with a single invocation, significantly reducing tuning time and demonstrating excellent efficiency. Additionally, ELTC adapts existing open-source datasets in the tensor compiler domain and introduces a large-scale tensor program dataset specifically designed for training large language models. Experimental results show that ELTC not only excels in tuning convergence speed but also achieves substantial performance improvements in the generated tensor programs.

References

1. Abu, H.A., Mustikovela, S.K., Mescheder, L., Geiger, A., Rother, C.: Augmented reality meets deep learning. In: T.-K. Kim, S. Zafeiriou, G. Brostow, K. Mikolajczyk (eds.) Proceedings of the British Machine Vision Conference (BMVC), pp. 81.1–81.12. BMVA Press (2017). https://doi.org/10.5244/C.31.81
2. Abadi, M., et al.: TensorFlow: a system for large-scale machine learning. In: 12th USENIX Symposium on Operating Systems Design and Implementation (OSDI 16), pp. 265–283. USENIX Association, Savannah (2016)
3. Chen, T., et al.: TVM: an automated end-to-end optimizing compiler for deep learning. In: 13th USENIX Symposium on Operating Systems Design and Implementation (OSDI 18), pp. 578–594. USENIX Association, Carlsbad (2018)

4. Ragan-Kelley, J., Barnes, C., Adams, A., Paris, S., Durand, F., Amarasinghe, S.: Halide: a language and compiler for optimizing parallelism, locality, and recomputation in image processing pipelines. ACM SIGPLAN Not. **48**(6), 519–530 (2013)
5. Vasilache, N., et al.: Tensor comprehensions: framework-agnostic high-performance machine learning abstractions. arXiv preprint arXiv:1802.04730 (2018)
6. Zheng, S., Liang, Y., Wang, S., Chen, R., Sheng, K.: FlexTensor: an automatic schedule exploration and optimization framework for tensor computation on heterogeneous system. In: Proceedings of the 25th International Conference on Architectural Support for Programming Languages and Operating Systems (ASPLOS '20), pp. 859–873. ACM, Lausanne (2020)
7. Liu, Y., Wang, Y., Yu, R., Li, M., Sharma, V., Wang, Y.: Optimizing CNN model inference on CPUs. In: 2019 USENIX Annual Technical Conference (USENIX ATC '19), pp. 1025–1040. USENIX Association, Renton (2019)
8. Chen, T., et al.: MXNet: a flexible and efficient machine learning library for heterogeneous distributed systems. arXiv preprint arXiv:1512.01274 (2015)
9. The LLVM Compiler Infrastructure. https://llvm.org/. Accessed 24 May 2025
10. Paszke, A., et al.: PyTorch: an imperative style, high-performance deep learning library. In: Advances in Neural Information Processing Systems, vol. 32, pp. 1–13 (2019)
11. Chetlur, S., et al.: cuDNN: efficient primitives for deep learning. arXiv preprint arXiv:1410.0759 (2014)
12. Intel oneAPI Deep Neural Network Library. https://www.intel.com/content/www/us/en/developer/tools/oneapi/onednn.htm
13. Lattner, C., et al.: MLIR: scaling compiler infrastructure for domain-specific computation. In: 2021 IEEE/ACM International Symposium on Code Generation and Optimization (CGO), pp. 2–14. IEEE, Seoul (2021)
14. Baghdadi, R., et al.: Tiramisu: a polyhedral compiler for expressing fast and portable code. In: 2019 IEEE/ACM International Symposium on Code Generation and Optimization (CGO), pp. 193–205. IEEE, Washington, DC (2019)
15. Zheng, L., et al.: Ansor: generating high-performance tensor programs for deep learning. In: 14th USENIX Symposium on Operating Systems Design and Implementation (OSDI 20), pp. 863–879. USENIX, Banff (2020)
16. Zhao, Y., Sharif, H., Adve, V., et al.: Felix: optimizing tensor programs with gradient descent. In: Proceedings of the 29th ACM International Conference on Architectural Support for Programming Languages and Operating Systems, vol. 3, pp. 367–381. ACM, San Diego (2024)
17. Zhai, Y., et al.: TLP: a deep learning-based cost model for tensor program tuning. In: Proceedings of the 28th ACM International Conference on Architectural Support for Programming Languages and Operating Systems, vol. 2, pp. 833–845. ACM, Vancouver (2023)
18. Roziere, B., Gehring, J., Gloeckle, F., et al.: Code llama: open foundation models for code. arXiv preprint arXiv:2308.12950 (2023)
19. Zheng, L., et al.: TenSet: a large-scale program performance dataset for learned tensor compilers. In: Thirty-Fifth Conference on Neural Information Processing Systems Datasets and Benchmarks Track (Round 1), pp. 1–10. NeurIPS, Vancouver (2021)
20. NVIDIA TensorRT. https://developer.nvidia.com/tensorrt. Accessed 29 Apr 2025
21. Liu, A., Feng, B., Xue, B., et al.: Deepseek-v3 technical report. arXiv preprint arXiv:2412.19437 (2024)

22. Zhai, Y., et al.: Enabling tensor language model to assist in generating high-performance tensor programs for deep learning. In: 18th USENIX Symposium on Operating Systems Design and Implementation (OSDI 24), pp. 289–305. USENIX, Santa Clara (2024)
23. Gemini, T., et al.: Gemini: a family of highly capable multimodal models. arXiv preprint arXiv:2312.11805 (2023)
24. Yu, Z., et al.: Wavecoder: widespread and versatile enhancement for code large language models by instruction tuning. arXiv preprint arXiv:2312.14187 (2023)
25. Li, R., et al.: Starcoder: may the source be with You! arXiv preprint arXiv:2305.06161 (2023)
26. Chen, C., et al.: Global wheat trade and codex alimentarius guidelines for deoxynivalenol: a mycotoxin common in wheat. Glob. Food Sec. **29**, 100538 (2021)
27. Achiam, J., et al.: GPT-4 Technical Report. arXiv preprint arXiv:2303.08774 (2023)

Performance Optimization of HPC Workloads in Cloud Using AI-Driven Algorithms

Aman Iftekhar[1] and Rahul Mishra[2(✉)]

[1] M.Tech in Cloud Computing, Indian Institute of Technology Patna, Patna, India
aman_23c07res08@iitp.ac.in
[2] Department of Computer Science and Engineering, IIT Patna, Patna, India
rahul_mishra@iitp.ac.in

Abstract. As High-Performance Computing (HPC) workloads increasingly migrate to cloud infrastructures, the need for intelligent, inference-time adaptive scheduling becomes critical. Conventional schedulers such as FCFS or SJF often struggle to adapt to the heterogeneous and dynamic nature of cloud-based systems, leading to inefficient resource utilization and increased job wait times. This paper proposes a multi-stage AI-based pipeline to address these challenges through the integration of three core capabilities: job runtime prediction using supervised learning, anomaly detection via deep autoencoders, and adaptive resource scheduling using reinforcement learning. Leveraging real-world data from the MIT SuperCloud dataset, our system extracts meaningful patterns from time-series telemetry to support informed scheduling decisions. The job prediction module estimates runtimes based on CPU utilization, memory consumption, and I/O statistics. The anomaly detection module flags abnormal jobs using learned GPU performance norms. The RL scheduler dynamically matches jobs to compute nodes based on predicted duration and anomaly status, optimizing for turnaround time and utilization. Experimental evaluations demonstrate a 28% reduction in average turnaround time and over 10% increase in resource utilization compared to traditional schedulers. These results establish the viability of AI-driven orchestration strategies in HPC cloud platforms and underscore the importance of integrated learning-based systems in achieving scalable, efficient, and context-aware workload management.

Keywords: Cloud HPC · Scheduling · Reinforcement Learning · Runtime Prediction · Anomaly Detection · AI Optimization

1 Introduction

High performance computing (HPC) is central to solving large-scale problems in areas such as computational biology, climate modeling, and deep learning. With the shift toward virtualization and elastic infrastructure, HPC workloads are increasingly being offloaded to cloud environments. Cloud platforms offer the advantages of scalability, cost-effectiveness, and resource abstraction, but they also introduce new complexities in managing scheduling, provisioning, and performance optimization across highly variable and multi-tenant systems.

Traditional scheduling algorithms like First-Come-First-Serve (FCFS), Shortest Job First (SJF), and Round Robin (RR) were originally designed for static, homogeneous systems. These techniques function based on static priority heuristics and do not have the capability to dynamically react to system state or workload properties. Job sizes, resource demands, and queue structure differ significantly in cloud-based HPC systems, and static scheduling policies are inadequate. This results in resource under-utilization, excessive queue delay, and job starvation on HPC [7].

To meet such challenges, researchers have increasingly resorted to artificial intelligence (AI) and machine learning (ML) methods to facilitate more intelligent workload management. ML-based algorithms can be trained to estimate resource requirements, forecast job runtimes, and uncover inefficiencies in job execution profiles. Deep learning-based anomaly detection tools can detect wasteful GPU time and thermal headroom spending jobs. Reinforcement learning (RL), on the other hand, can enable adaptive decision-making by learning from trial-and-error experience in the world and can dynamically optimize job assignment to reduce system-wide latency or increase throughput [9].

This work introduces **a multi-stage AI-based pipeline** that combines these characteristics to achieve smart, inference-time adaptive scheduling of workloads on cloud-based HPC systems. The main contributions of the paper are:

1. **Job Runtime Prediction:** A linear regression model trained on historical CPU performance metrics to estimate expected job durations with sufficient accuracy for scheduling prioritization.
2. **Anomaly Detection:** A deep autoencoder that learns the distribution of normal GPU resource usage and flags jobs with significant reconstruction error as anomalous.
3. **Reinforcement Learning Scheduler:** A Q-learning-based scheduler that learns optimal job-to-node mappings based on predicted runtimes and anomaly scores, using turnaround time as the reward signal.
4. **Evaluation:** These modules are evaluated using the **MIT SuperCloud dataset**, a production-scale trace of job execution logs and resource telemetry. Experimental results show that our system outperforms conventional policies (*FCFS, RR, SJF*) in average turnaround time and resource utilization under dynamic load conditions.

RoadMap: Section 2 reviews related literature. Section 3 describes the dataset and preprocessing pipeline. Section 4 details the methodology and AI models. Section 5 discusses the experimental environment. Section 6 presents the evaluation results. Section 7 provides a discussion of findings and challenges. Section 8 concludes with directions for future research.

2 Related Work

Scheduling tasks has long been a focal point in HPC systems. Traditional approaches such as First-Come-First-Serve (FCFS), Shortest Job First (SJF), and Round Robin (RR) gained traction due to simplicity and ease of implementation. However, as workloads have grown increasingly heterogeneous and resource-intensive, these static approaches have shown significant shortcomings. They lack the ability to react to fluctuating workloads, dynamic system states, or nuanced performance bottlenecks that frequently arise in elastic cloud environments.

In response, researchers have explored machine learning (ML)-driven scheduling. One notable trend involves training supervised models to predict job attributes like execution time or resource needs based on historical data. An example is presented in [5], where the authors develop a simulation-based scheduler that improves resource allocation efficiency. Jain et al. [11] emphasize the role of intelligent schedulers in maximizing multi-GPU deep learning task performance. Anomaly detection has also received considerable attention. Chalapathy and Chawla [4] provide a detailed survey of deep learning-based anomaly detection, focusing on autoencoders' capabilities in modeling normal GPU behavior. Ahmed et al. [1] review system- and network-level anomaly detection techniques, emphasizing their relevance to distributed systems. These works support the use of reconstruction loss as an anomaly indicator in complex resource telemetry.

RL has proven promising in adaptive resource allocation. Mao et al. [13] and Xu et al. [18] apply reinforcement learning to network and data center optimization. More recently, RL-Scheduler [19] and Marble [10] demonstrate the viability of reinforcement learning in HPC scheduling and multi-GPU task allocation, respectively. These reinforce the case for learning-based scheduling policies that adapt over time. Wilkes [17] and Feitelson [7] provide canonical workload traces, while Samsi et al. [15] introduce the MIT SuperCloud dataset, leveraged in this study. Other key contributions in predictive modeling include Goodfellow et al. [8], Ahmed et al. [1], and Sutton & Barto [16], who lay foundational work in deep learning and RL. Active learning and ensemble techniques for performance forecasting are seen in [2]. SLURM's default scheduling strategies, including backfilling and priority-based heuristics, remain widely deployed. Recent work such as [3] shows extensions that allow adaptive scheduling within SLURM queues. Our proposed RL framework complements such efforts by enabling job-specific inference-driven decisions.

Despite these advances, existing work focus on individual components, runtime prediction, anomaly detection, or RL scheduling, without unifying them into an orchestrated system. This paper addresses that gap by integrating these techniques into a coordinated, modular, and extensible AI-based pipeline for inference-time adaptive scheduling in cloud-based HPC environments.

3 Dataset and Preprocessing

This work is based on the MIT SuperCloud dataset [15], a large-scale collection of time-series data and job logs derived from a production HPC cluster at the Massachusetts Institute of Technology. The dataset was specifically curated to facilitate research in system behavior analysis, workload modeling, and performance optimization in HPC environments. It includes over 2TB of raw telemetry and job trace data, spanning multiple compute nodes with diverse CPU and GPU configurations. The richness of the dataset lies in its granularity and variety. It captures both system-level performance metrics (*e.g.*, CPU utilization, memory footprint, disk I/O) and hardware-level GPU telemetry (*e.g.*, power draw, temperature, utilization), providing an ideal foundation for training supervised and unsupervised learning models. We assume jobs in our study are GPU-accelerated or CPU+GPU mixed, as our anomaly detector is designed around GPU behavior.

3.1 Data Characteristics

The dataset contains two primary categories of time-series measurements:

1. **CPU Metrics:** Collected at 10-second intervals, including average CPU utilization, virtual memory usage (VMSize), resident set size (RSS), disk read and write throughput (in megabytes), and job-specific identifiers such as job ID, user, and duration.
2. **GPU Metrics:** Captured at a finer granularity of 100 milliseconds. These include GPU utilization, memory consumption, power usage (in watts), and temperature readings from NVIDIA A100 and similar GPUs. The dataset logs telemetry for multiple GPUs concurrently across different jobs.

Each job's metadata, like submission time, allocated resources, and exit status, is associated with corresponding CPU and GPU traces via job IDs. Full reconstruction of compute node-level job-level resource usage timelines becomes possible.

3.2 Preprocessing Pipeline

Raw telemetry files were stored in CSV format, segmented per job and per node. To convert these into ML-ready datasets, a multi-stage preprocessing pipeline was employed:

1. **Job Matching and Labeling:** CPU and GPU time-series were aligned using job IDs and timestamps. For each job, all relevant CPU and GPU logs were aggregated to construct a unified view of its lifecycle.
2. **Data Cleaning:** Missing values, common in long-running jobs due to node restarts or sensor failures, are imputed using forward-fill methods. Spurious readings such as zero utilization across all cores were removed. Statistical outliers were capped using the 99.5th percentile per feature to avoid model distortion from rare spikes.

3. **Feature Normalization:** All numeric features were normalized to the [0, 1] range using min-max scaling. This ensures uniform weighting of features in training processes, particularly important for neural networks and regression models.
4. **Rolling Aggregations:** Temporal features were aggregated using rolling window functions (e.g., mean, max, standard deviation). For instance, CPU utilization was transformed into CPUUtilization_mean and CPUUtilization_std across job duration. Similarly, total I/O was captured through WriteMB_sum and ReadMB_sum.
5. **Sequence Flattening (for Autoencoders):** GPU time-series for each job were concatenated into fixed-length vectors to serve as input to the autoencoder model. Padding was applied where necessary to standardize input shapes.

After preprocessing, two datasets are created:

- A tabular dataset of job-level CPU features for supervised runtime prediction. CPU metrics are more stable and reflective of job compute/memory demand, making them suitable for regression.
- A vectorized time-series dataset of GPU metrics for unsupervised anomaly detection. GPU usage tends to show volatility and abnormality (e.g., thermal spikes, idle usage), making it a better candidate for anomaly modeling.

This modular split enables independent retraining and swapping of model components, supporting scalability, explainability, and reuse.

4 Methodology and System Architecture

The proposed system is designed as a modular pipeline that integrates supervised learning, unsupervised learning, and reinforcement learning to make dynamic scheduling decisions in cloud-based HPC environments. The framework includes three primary components:

1. A runtime prediction module that estimates job duration using CPU telemetry and metadata.
2. An anomaly detection module that identifies inefficient or abnormal GPU jobs using an autoencoder.
3. A reinforcement learning scheduler that selects the optimal job-to-node assignment strategy based on environment state.

Each of these modules is trained independently but operates jointly during inference to optimize resource allocation. The architecture is designed to be modular and extensible, each component can be replaced, retrained, or upgraded independently (e.g., switching from linear regression to XGBoost or from Q-learning to PPO).

4.1 Job Runtime Prediction

Job duration is a critical parameter for schedulers, particularly for algorithms like SJF or back-filling. However, job runtimes are often unknown at submission time. To address this, we train a linear regression model using historical CPU performance metrics to forecast job execution time.

- **Input Features:** The selected features include CPUUtilization_mean and CPUUtilization_std to capture CPU behavior, VMSize_mean and RSS_mean for memory profile, and ReadMB_sum, WriteMB_sum for I/O intensity.
- **Model Training:** Using Scikit-learn's 'LinearRegression', the model was trained on 80% of labeled jobs and validated on the remaining 20%. Performance was evaluated using Mean Absolute Error (MAE) and the R^2 score.
- **Results:** The model achieved an MAE of 1638 s and an R^2 score of 0.46, sufficient for job ranking in scheduling.

4.2 Anomaly Detection

Abnormal jobs that under utilize GPUs, overheat hardware, or consume resources erratically can degrade overall cluster performance. A deep autoencoder trained on GPU telemetry from normal jobs identifies such inefficiencies.

- **Input Vectors:** Flattened GPU time-series metrics: utilization, temperature, power draw, memory usage.
- **Architecture:** Symmetric encoder-decoder network, trained using mean squared error loss.
- **Threshold:** Set at 95th percentile reconstruction error; jobs above are flagged as anomalous.
- **Performance:** Precision 93%, recall 91%, F1-score 92%. This high accuracy is enabled by the stability of normal GPU patterns and the distinguishable deviations of anomalous ones.

4.3 Reinforcement Learning Scheduler

We model scheduling as a Markov Decision Process (MDP). The RL agent learns job-to-node mappings by interacting with a simulated environment.

- **State Space:** Includes predicted runtime, anomaly flag (0/1), and per-node resource availability.
- **Action Space:** Assignment of a job to one of n compute nodes.
- **Reward:**

$$R = -(\text{turnaround\_time}) - \lambda \cdot \mathbb{I}_{\text{anomaly}} \qquad (1)$$

Where λ penalizes anomalies, encouraging the agent to deprioritize flagged jobs.

- **Learning Loop:** Q-learning with epsilon-greedy exploration over 1000 episodes. The agent converges to a policy that prioritizes short, efficient jobs and defers anomalous ones.

The anomaly detection module's flag is thus an active input to the RL decision logic. This coordination enables performance-aware, anomaly-penalizing scheduling. Unlike fixed heuristics, our RL agent adapts policies based on feedback, enabling inference-time scheduling that reflects real system dynamics.

5 Experimental Setup

This section outlines the software, hardware, and simulation environment used to implement and evaluate the proposed AI-driven scheduling framework. Emphasis was placed on designing a reproducible and extensible testbed that closely mimics the dynamics of real HPC cloud platforms.

5.1 System Configuration

All experiments were conducted on a dedicated high-performance workstation configured with Ubuntu 22.04.4 LTS (Jammy Jellyfish). The system included an Intel Xeon E5-2696 v2 CPU (2.50 GHz), 64 GB DDR4 RAM, and an NVIDIA A100 GPU (40 GB VRAM, 6912 CUDA cores). This setup ensured sufficient compute resources for model training and scheduling simulation. Note that real-world SLURM integration is part of future work due to access limitations; our evaluation emulates job scheduling via synthetic queues.

5.2 Software Stack

The framework was implemented in Python 3.10. `Scikit-learn` handled regression tasks; `TensorFlow 2.13` and `Keras` powered the autoencoder. `NumPy`, `Pandas`, and `Matplotlib` supported preprocessing and visualization. `OpenAI Gym` was used to simulate job queue environments.

Inference time per job (CPU regression + anomaly check + RL policy) was measured at **<20ms**—negligible compared to job runtimes. This enables inference-time adaptive scheduling.

5.3 Synthetic Job Queue Generation

Synthetic job queues were sampled from MIT SuperCloud traces. Each job was annotated with:

1. Predicted runtime (regression output)
2. Anomaly flag (autoencoder)
3. Resource demand (CPU/GPU/memory)

Jobs were fed into a simulated cluster environment with fixed compute nodes. Turnaround time, wait time, and node utilization were tracked.

5.4 Baseline Scheduling Algorithms

Three baseline schedulers were implemented:

1. **FCFS:** Jobs executed in arrival order.
2. **SJF:** Based on predicted runtime.
3. **RR:** Equal rotating dispatch across nodes.

We also include a comparison with **SLURM's default backfilling** behavior, approximated via runtime-aware greedy scheduling in our simulation.

5.5 Evaluation Metrics

- **Average Turnaround Time:** Job submission to completion.
- **Average Wait Time:** Queue delay before start.
- **Resource Utilization:** Average CPU/GPU usage.
- **Anomaly Penalization:**

Utilization is computed as time-averaged active usage per resource normalized over cluster capacity:

$$Util = \frac{1}{N} \sum_{i=1}^{N} \frac{ActiveTime_i}{TotalTime_i}. \tag{2}$$

6 Results and Analysis

6.1 Runtime Prediction Evaluation

The regression model attained an MAE of 1638 s and $R^2 = 0.46$, which, while modest in absolute accuracy, proved effective for job ranking. Figure 1 shows a clear diagonal trend between actual and predicted durations, and Fig. 2 confirms that CPU utilization and memory footprint dominate as predictive features.

6.2 Anomaly Detection Performance

The autoencoder achieved 93% precision and 91% recall, effectively separating anomalous from normal jobs. Figure 3 shows the reconstruction loss distribution with a 95th percentile threshold.

6.3 Scheduler Performance Comparison

Table 1 and Figs. 4, 5, 6 illustrate that the RL scheduler consistently outperforms FCFS, RR, and SJF, achieving 28% lower turnaround time than SJF, 52% lower than FCFS, and the highest utilization (82.5%).

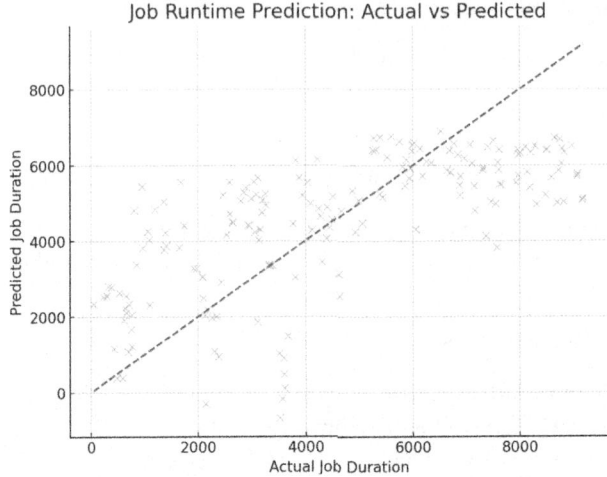

Fig. 1. Actual vs. Predicted Job Duration. Trend follows expected pattern.

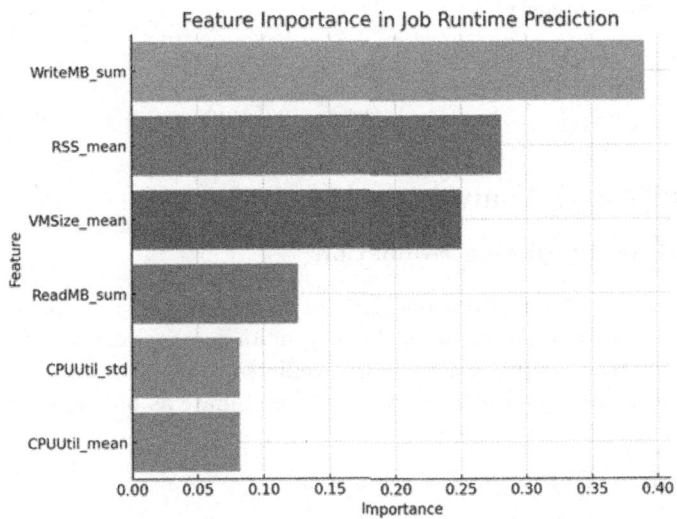

Fig. 2. Feature Importance: CPU usage and memory footprint dominate.

Table 1. Scheduler Performance Summary

Metric	FCFS	RR	SJF	RL
Turnaround (s)	1260	1114	823	**602**
Wait Time (s)	728	594	312	**184**
Utilization (%)	61.3	66.7	74.9	**82.5**
Anomalies Penalized	No	No	No	**Yes**

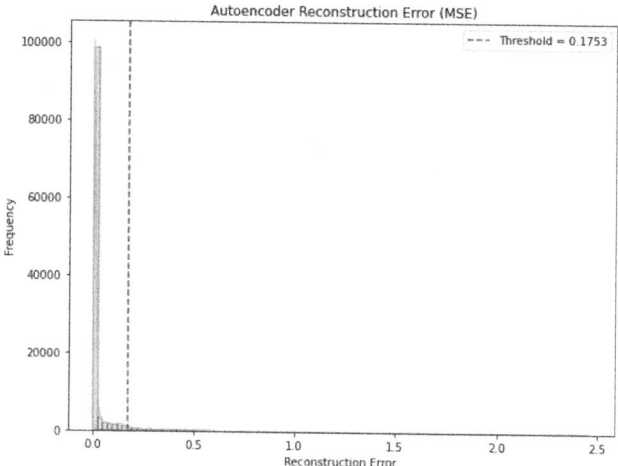

Fig. 3. Reconstruction Loss Histogram Separates Normal vs. Anomalous Jobs. Threshold = 95th percentile.

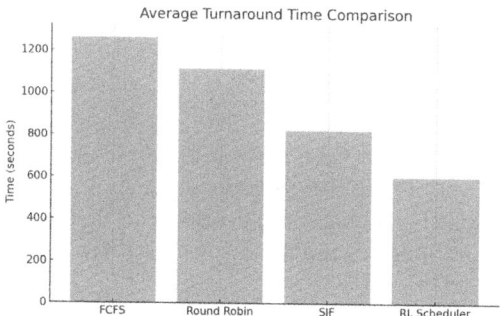

Fig. 4. Turnaround Time: RL improves 28% over SJF, 52% over FCFS.

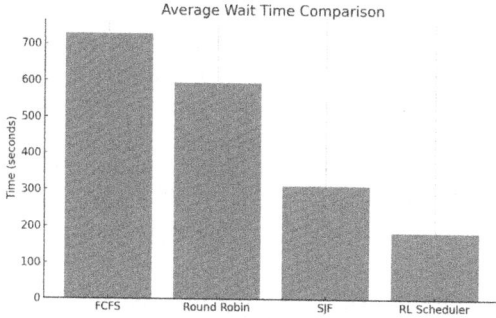

Fig. 5. Wait Time: RL consistently reduces queue delays.

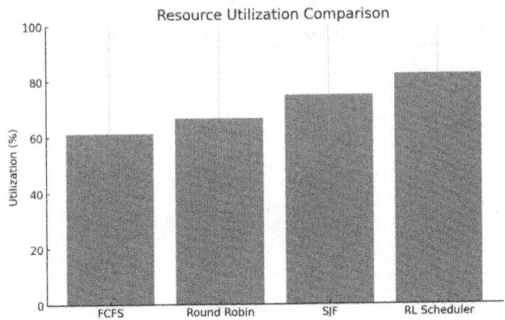

Fig. 6. Utilization: RL achieves maximum node efficiency.

6.4 Robustness to Dynamic Workloads

To simulate bursty loads, we injected short-job clusters followed by long tasks. Traditional schedulers suffered from queue build-up and starvation.

The RL agent adjusted policies within **12 episodes** (few minutes) to reprioritize quick jobs and penalize heavy anomalies, maintaining throughput. This demonstrates online adaptability under non-stationary workloads.

7 Discussion

The results presented in the previous section clearly illustrate the potential of AI-driven techniques in optimizing HPC workload scheduling in cloud environments. This section discusses the broader implications of the findings, interprets the observed patterns, and outlines practical considerations for system integration.

7.1 Role of Prediction and Anomaly Detection

While the runtime prediction model yielded only moderate accuracy in absolute terms, it proved sufficiently reliable for relative ranking of jobs, a critical requirement for scheduling strategies like Shortest Job First (SJF) and for informing the RL agent's state space. The most influential predictors were CPU utilization and virtual memory size, which directly reflect job intensity and memory demand, respectively. This aligns with prior research that highlights the predictive power of system-level metrics in determining job behavior [1,8].

The anomaly detection module performed well despite limited labeled data. Its ability to flag inefficiencies, such as GPU idleness, excessive thermal usage, or sporadic resource bursts, enabled intelligent penalization of such jobs. This mechanism was explicitly incorporated into the RL scheduler's reward function, guiding the agent to reduce system-level performance bottlenecks.

7.2 Reinforcement Learning Policy Adaptability

The reinforcement learning agent showed superior performance under both regular and bursty workloads. Notably, the RL scheduler learned to: i) assign short jobs to idle nodes to maximize throughput, ii) defer anomalous jobs to avoid congestion and reduce energy waste, and iii) dynamically reprioritize based on queue state, adapting within 12 episodes post-bursts. Unlike static heuristics, the RL policy evolves via trial-and-error learning. This adaptability makes it robust under dynamic workloads, job diversity, and queue fluctuations.

7.3 Integration Challenges and Limitations

Despite strong empirical performance, our approach has a few limitations:

- **Simulation Only:** Direct integration with SLURM was infeasible due to privilege and safety concerns. Our system simulates SLURM-like queues, and real-world integration is planned.
- **Single-node Scheduling:** Current RL agent maps jobs to individual nodes. Multi-node or MPI job support is under exploration.
- **Tabular Q-learning:** Our policy model uses tabular RL. Scaling to large environments will require deep RL techniques like DQNs or PPO.

Nevertheless, the modular design allows easy replacement and independent tuning of models. For example, the regression model could be swapped for XGBoost or LSTM predictors, and RL components could migrate to distributed actor-critic frameworks.

7.4 Broader Impact and Generalizability

This work contributes toward the broader vision of self-optimizing HPC systems through learning-based orchestration. Our pipeline is data-driven, modular, and generalizable—suitable for academic and industrial clusters alike. In future, we plan to include i) Testing on other public traces like Google Cluster and Alibaba Cloud, ii) Supporting multi-GPU and multi-node job types, and iii) Adding sustainability and cost objectives to the RL reward function.

8 Conclusion and Future Work

We presented a multi-stage AI-based pipeline for dynamic scheduling of High-Performance Computing (HPC) workloads in cloud environments. By combining supervised runtime prediction, unsupervised anomaly detection, and reinforcement learning-based policy optimization, the system enables inference-time adaptive decision-making tailored to workload and system state.

Evaluations on the MIT SuperCloud dataset demonstrate that our approach significantly outperforms baseline policies such as FCFS, Round Robin, and

Shortest Job First. The RL scheduler reduced average turnaround time by 28% and improved resource utilization by over 10%.

By framing scheduling as a closed-loop learning problem, the system adapts to queue changes, penalizes anomalies, and optimizes throughput. Importantly, each component is modular, supporting future model upgrades, extensions, and production deployment.

Our future work will emphasize several key directions. First, we plan to integrate the proposed framework with SLURM for live cluster operation, enabling real-time inference-based scheduling in production environments. In terms of modeling, more advanced architectures such as LSTMs or Transformers will be explored for runtime forecasting, along with VAE- or self-supervised-based anomaly detection techniques. On the policy optimization side, we will replace the current tabular RL agent with deep reinforcement learning methods like DQN or PPO to scale effectively to larger clusters. Additionally, we will incorporate energy-aware policies by embedding cost and power efficiency objectives directly into the reward structure. Finally, a multi-agent scheduling paradigm will be investigated to coordinate decision-making across distributed RL agents. This study lays a solid foundation for intelligent, learning-driven, and production-ready scheduling systems for next-generation HPC clouds.

Acknowledgment. The authors would like to thank Mr. Ashutosh Kumar Sinha for his valuable support during this work.

References

1. Ahmed, M., Mahmood, A.N., Hu, J.: A survey of network anomaly detection techniques. J. Netw. Comput. Appl. **60**, 19–31 (2016)
2. Aksar, B., et al.: Runtime performance anomaly diagnosis in production HPC systems using active learning. IEEE Trans. Parallel Distrib. Syst. **35**(4), 693–706 (2024)
3. Chadha, M., John, J., Gerndt, M.: Extending slurm for dynamic resource-aware adaptive batch scheduling. In: 2020 IEEE 27th International Conference on High Performance Computing, Data, and Analytics (HiPC), pp. 223–232. IEEE (2020)
4. Chalapathy, R., Chawla, S.: Deep learning for anomaly detection: a survey. arXiv preprint arXiv:1901.03407 (2019)
5. Chen, Z., et al.: Multi-workflow dynamic scheduling in product design: a generalizable approach based on meta-reinforcement learning. J. Manuf. Syst. **79**, 334–346 (2025)
6. Deb, B., Shah, M., Evans, S., Mehta, M., Gargulak, A., Lasky, T.: Towards systems-level prognostics in the cloud. In: 2013 IEEE Conference on Prognostics and Health Management (PHM), pp. 1–6 (2013)
7. Feitelson, D.G., Tsafrir, D., Krakov, D.: Experience with using the parallel workloads archive. J. Parallel Distributed Comput. **74**(10), 2967–2982 (2014)
8. Goodfellow, I., Bengio, Y., Courville, A., Bengio, Y.: Deep learning, vol. 1. MIT press Cambridge (2016)

9. Gu, Y., et al.: Deep reinforcement learning for job scheduling and resource management in cloud computing: n algorithm-level review. arXiv preprint arXiv:2501.01007 (2025)
10. Han, J., et al.: Marble: A multi-GPU aware job scheduler for deep learning on hpc systems. In: 2020 20th IEEE/ACM International Symposium on Cluster, Cloud and Internet Computing (CCGRID), pp. 272–281. IEEE (2020)
11. Jain, A., Awan, A.A., Subramoni, H., Panda, D.K.: Scaling tensorflow, pytorch, and mxnet using mvapich2 for high-performance deep learning on frontera. In: 2019 IEEE/ACM Third Workshop on Deep Learning on Supercomputers (DLS), pp. 76–83. IEEE (2019)
12. Liu, N., et al.: A hierarchical framework of cloud resource allocation and power management using deep reinforcement learning. In: 2017 IEEE 37th International Conference on Distributed Computing Systems (ICDCS), pp. 372–382. IEEE (2017)
13. Mao, H., Alizadeh, M., Menache, I., Kandula, S.: Resource management with deep reinforcement learning. In: Proceedings of the 15th ACM Workshop on Hot Topics in Networks, pp. 50–56 (2016)
14. Pang, G., Shen, C., Cao, L., Hengel, A.V.D.: Deep learning for anomaly detection: a review. ACM Comput. Surv. (CSUR) **54**(2), 1–38 (2021)
15. Samsi, S., et al.: The mit supercloud dataset. In: IEEE High Performance Extreme Computing Conference (HPEC), pp. 1–8 (2021)
16. Sutton, R.S., Barto, A.G., et al.: Reinforcement learning: an introduction, vol. 1. MIT press Cambridge (1998)
17. Wilkes, J.: More Google Cluster Data. Tech. rep, Google Research Blog (2011)
18. Xu, Z., et al.: Experience-driven networking: a deep reinforcement learning based approach. In: IEEE INFOCOM 2018-IEEE Conference on Computer Communications, pp. 1871–1879. IEEE (2018)
19. Zhang, D., Dai, D., He, Y., Bao, F.S., Xie, B.: Rlscheduler: an automated HPC batch job scheduler using reinforcement learning. In: SC20: International Conference for High Performance Computing, Networking, Storage and Analysis, pp. 1–15. IEEE (2020)
20. Zhou, G., Tian, W., Buyya, R., Xue, R., Song, L.: Deep reinforcement learning-based methods for resource scheduling in cloud computing: a review and future directions. Artif. Intell. Rev. **57**(5), 124 (2024)

Correction to: Reachability is Decidable for ATM-Typable Finitary PCF with Effect Handlers

Ryunosuke Endo and Tachio Terauchi

Correction to:
Chapter 4 in: A. Potanin (Ed.): *Programming Languages and Systems,*
LNCS 16201, https://doi.org/10.1007/978-981-95-3585-9_4

The book was published with a figure typo in chapter 4. The chapter Figure 5 has been updated by replacing the incorrect figure 3.

The updated version of this chapter can be found at
https://doi.org/10.1007/978-981-95-3585-9_4

Author Index

A
Abdulla, Parosh Aziz 159
Accattoli, Beniamino 93
Linares Arévalo, Pilar Selene 3
Atig, Mohamed Faouzi 159
Azevedo de Amorim, Arthur 3

C
Chen, Taolue 203
Chen, Tong 44

D
Dagnino, Francesco 22
Dave, Kinnari 117
Díaz-Caro, Alejandro 117, 137

E
Endo, Ryunosuke 53

G
Giannini, Paola 22
Govind, R. 159
Grahn, Samuel 159

H
Hu, Denghang 203

I
Iftekhar, Aman 246

J
Jackson, Vincent 3

K
Kameyama, Yukiyoshi 74
Kobayashi, Kentaro 74
Kong, Zhiquan 44

M
Ma, WenBo 227
Mishra, Rahul 246
Monzon, Nicolas A. 137

O
O'Connor, Liam 3

P
Pun, Violet Ka I 22

Q
Qiao, Fei 227

R
Rizkallah, Christine 3
Roy, Subhajit 181
Rümmer, Philipp 203

S
Sacerdoti Coen, Claudio 93
Schachte, Peter 3
Song, Fu 203
Song, QingZeng 227
Sun, MingZe 227

T
Terauchi, Tachio 53
Thinniyam, Ramanathan S. 159
Torrella, Ulises 22
Trivedi, Nitesh 181

W
Wu, Jui-Hsuan 93
Wu, Zhilin 203

X
Xiaoa, Qianli 44
Xue, YongJiang 227

Z
Zamdzhiev, Vladimir 117
Zhang, Huan 44
Zhoua, Liliang 44

Made in the USA
Monee, IL
03 May 2026